175042

D0303503

£40.00

Global Experience Industries

Jens Christensen

Global Experience Industries

The Business of the Experience Economy

Aarhus University Press |

Global Experience Industries
The Business of the Experience Economy
© Aarhus University Press and the Author
Cover design by Jørgen Sparre
Printed in Denmark by Narayana Press 2009
Isbn 978 87 7934 432 7

Aarhus University Press
Langelandsgade 177
DK-8200 Århus N
www.unipress.dk

White Cross Mills
Hightown, Lancaster, LA1 4XS
www.gazellebookservices.co.uk

PO Box 511
Oakville, CT 06779
www.oxbowbooks.com

This book is published with the financial support
of the Aarhus University Research Foundation

Contents

UCB
175042

Detailed Contents

Tables

Figures

Abbreviations

ABC	American Broadcasting Company
AEO	Association of Event Organisers, Contractors and Venues
AGA	American Gaming Association
AHLA	American Hotel & Lodging Association
AOL	America Online
ATAG	Air Transport Action Group
ATC	Agreement on Textiles and Clothing
AT & T	American Telephone & Telegraph Company
ATW	Air Transport World
BBDO	Barton, Battin, Durstine & Osborn
BET	Black Entertainment Television
BMG	Bertelsmann Music Group
BN	Billion
BRIC	Brazil, Russia, India, China
CBS	Columbia Broadcasting System
CD	Compact Disc
CIA	Central Intelligence Agency
CIC	Convention Industry Council
CLIA	Cruise Line International Association
CNN	Cable News Network
CNTC	China National Tobacco Co.
CRM	Customer Relationship Management
DAB	Digital Audio Broadcasting
DBS	Direct Broadcast Satellite
DCIP	Digital Cinema Implementation Partners
DDB	Doyle, Dane Bernbach
DRM	Digital Radio Mondiale
DSL	Digital Subscriber Line
DTT	Digital Terrestrial Television
DVD	Digital Video Disc
DVR	Digital Video Recorder
EA	Electronic Arts
EMEA	Europe, Middle East, Africa
EMI	The Electric and Musical Industries
ERIA	European Recorded Industry Association
ESA	American Entertainment Software Association

ESPN	Entertainment and Sports Programming Network
ETC	European Travel Commission
EU	The European Union
FBI	Federal Bureau of Investigation
FCC	Federal Communications Commission
FDI	Foreign Direct Investment
FIFA	Féderation Internationale de Football Association
GDP	Gross Domestic Product
GE	General Electrics
GM	General Motors
HD	High Definition
IAB	Internet Advertising Board
IAC	InterActive Corporation
IAEM	International Association of Exhibitions and Events
IATA	International Air Transport Association
ICCL	Cruise Lines International Association
ICTI	International Council of Toy Industries
IDSA	Industrial Designers Society of America
IFEA	International Festivals and Events Association
IFPI	International Federation of Phonographic Industry
IGDA	International Game Developers Association
IOC	International Olympic Committee
IP	Internet Protocol
ISDA	Industrial Design Society of America
ISES	International Special Events Society
ISIC	International Standard Industrial Classification
ITU	International Telecommunication Union
ITV	Independent Television
JPEG	Joint Photographic Experts Group
JWT	James Walter Thomson Group
LAN	Local Area Network
LMC	Liberty Media Corporation
LP	Long Playing
LVMH	Louis Vuitton. Moët Hennesy
M	Million
MCA	The Music Corporation of America
MGM	Metro-Goldwyn-Mayer
MICE	Meetings, Incentives, Conferencing, Exhibitions

MLB	Major League Baseball
MMORPG	Massively Multiplayer Online Role-Playing Game
MPA	The Motion Picture Association
MP3	MPEG-1 (Moving Picture Experts Group) Audio Layer 3
MTV	Music Television
NAFTA	North American Free Trade Agreement
NASA	National Aeronautics and Space Administration
NASCAR	National Association for Stock Car Auto Racing
NBA	National Basketball Association
NBC	National Broadcasting Company
NFL	National Football League
NHL	National Hockey League
NTT	Nippon Telegraph and Telephone
OL	Olympic Games
PBS	Public Broadcasting Service
PDA	Personal Digital Assistant
PPR	Pinault-Printemps-Redoute
PR	Public Relations
P2P	Peer-to-Peer
PWC	PriceWaterhouseCoopers
RCA	Radio Corporation of America
RIAA	The Recording Industry Association of America
RKO	Radio-Keith-Orpheum
RMJM	Robert Matthew Johnson Marshall
ROW	Rest of the World
RTL	Radio Télévision Luxembourg
SAS	Scandinavian Airlines System
SBS	Scandinavian Broadcasting System
SBS	Spanish Broadcasting System
SFR	Société Française Radiotéléphonie
SNCF	Société Nationale des Chemins de Fer Français
TBS	Turner Broadcasting System
TDC	Tele-Denmark Communications
TIA	Travel Industry Association
TNT	Turner Network Television
TUI	Touristik Union International
TV	Television
UEFA	Union of European Football Association

UMG	Universal Music Group
UN	United Nations
UNWTO	World Tourism Organization of the United Nations
UPN	United Paramount Network
VCR	Videocassette Recorder
VIACOM	Video & Audio COMmunications
VNU	Verenigde Nederlandse Uitgeversbedrijven
VOD	Video on demand
VOK	Vereiniging van Oud Kweedingen
WB	Warner Bros.
WE	Western Europe
WEA	Warner Elektro-Atlantic
WHO	World Health Organization
WPP	Wire and Plastic Products Group
WTO	World Trade Organization
WTTC	World Travel and Tourism Council

1. Experience Industries

The Experience Economy

According to Pine and Gilmore, the experience economy is a fourth economic field different from commodities, goods and services.[1] Experiences are an economic value added to a product or identical with the product. When you buy an experience, you pay to spend time enjoying a series of memorable events that a company stages to engage the customer in a personal way. Entertainment is based on such experiences. But entertainment is just one aspect of an experience. Experienced values arise whenever companies engage customers in a personal, memorable way. So, experiences are staged, just as in theaters. Companies offer experiences to customers when they use services as the stage and goods as props to engage an individual. "While commodities are fungible, goods tangible, and services intangible, experiences are memorable".

The value creation of commodities, goods, services, and experiences may be viewed as historical steps of modern capitalism. While the former three values are connected with the functional dimensions that alternately dominated during the 20th century as societies changed from industrial to knowledge societies, the experience dimension has moved into a predominant place since the 1990s.[2] In developed countries people get richer, and having fulfilled all basic materiel needs, they focus increasingly on personal development and self realization. Demand for experience-based products increases, such as tourism and sports as well as film, music and other contents of media and modern interactive technologies. Furthermore, the demand for experience values is extended to include any product and dimension of modern societies, such as design and advertising. Love, sex, belief, family and the meaning of life may be considered universal experience values that have always been vital to human beings. What is new is the fact that capitalism is invading more and more fields of experiences connected with feelings and emotions and the extension of life proportions. It is in this sense we will use the term experience economy, meaning a series of industries that strive to supply the market with experience oriented goods and consumers who spend money on buying experience goods.

There is no internationally recognized definition of the experience economy. Some focus on the so-called 'creative industries', including music, film, television, radio,

---

1   B. Joseph Pine II & James H. Gilmore (1999). *The Experience Economy*. Boston, Mass.: Harvard Business School Press.

2   A similar well known approach as that of Pine & Gilmore is taken by Rolf Jensen in his book (1999). *The Dream Society*. New York: MacGraw-Hill. According to Rolf Jensen, consumers are increasingly guided by emotions such as identity, care, peace, convictions, and togetherness, rather than functional needs.

publishing, games, amusement, architecture, advertising, art and cultural institutions.[3] Even intellectual properties may be included in creative industries.[4] Other definitions include sports and tourism as well.[5] In some cases, sports are excluded.[6]

In this book, the experience economy will include all industries that do business by creating primarily experience-based values on the one hand and, on the other hand, the experience creating dimension of any other industries. It is the intention to picture the business world driven by an expanding demand for experience-based values.

The Experience Industries

Accurate estimates of the global business of experience economy are hard to get at. In general, you have the problem of defining the content and limits of the experience economy and each of its inherent sub-sectors. It is also difficult to define the reach of the individual industries. Cultural like products of the experience economy are not only content, but also dependent on physical devices and materials to carry out and enjoy this content. Do we include the physical products in the experience economy or is it restricted to content only? The position taken here is that you have to include the physical products when the two aspects cannot be separated in a meaningful way. Otherwise physical merchandises are excluded and experience considered a value adding dimension, such as for example is the case with design. No clear line can be drawn, however.[7]

The demarcation of experience industries from other sectors of the economy also includes the problem of the value chain and value system enforced to create physical and intangible products. Every company is adding value to the processing of a final good within a long line of a value creating system. While it is mostly clear that consumer products are included in the definition of the experience economy, it is much harder

3   Creative London: *www.creative.london.uk.org*. Hartley, John (Ed.)(2005). *Creative Industries*. MA, USA: Blackwell Publishing.
4   Howkins, John (2001). *The Creative Economy*. London: Penguin Books. See also: Markusen, Ann, Wassall, Gregory H., deNatale, Douglas, and Cohen, Randy (2008). 'Defining the Creative Economy: Industry and Occupational Approaches'. *Economic Development Quarterly*, vol. 22, 24-45.
5   For example in PricewaterhouseCoopers (2006). *Global Media and Entertainment Outlook 2006-2010*. New York: PriceWaterhouseCoopers.
6   KK-Stiftelsen (2003). *Upplevelsesindustrien* (The Experience Industry)(Sweden).
7   The problem of separating content from its physical device is discussed in: UNESCO (2005). *International Flows of Selected Cultural Goods and Services, 1994-2003*. The problem is more stated than solved, however.

to draw the line backwards in the value system. Many manufacturing and service industries are needed to reach the final product. The criterion chosen is that unlike the proper experience industries the sub-supplying industries of the experience producing companies are mostly considered part of the wider experience economy. Providers of tangible and intangible supporting products are considered related industries of the primary experience sector. Together they form the wider experience economy, including the core experience industries and the multiplying effects of these industries throughout the general economy.

The relationship between content and its physical device carrier is a tricky one. Tourism would be worth nothing without transportation and hospitality; sports have to include sporting equipment; media must include physical books, newspapers, magazines, television and radio sets; films, music and performing arts include their physical formats and stages; whilst games also include their physical formats. Design, including architecture, industrial and graphic design, and fashion, are probably the only subsectors that may be separated in a meaningful way from their physical dimension. If, for example, industrial design included the physical output of designs it would cover virtually all kinds of manufacturing industries, just as fashion would embrace the large textile and clothing industries. Here a divide is made between what are mostly experience based industries and industries where experience is an added value.

The problems of measuring the business of family, religion, sex and drugs are of a different kind. Family is a non-market activity, although it is based on household income and investment in housing, etc. So what is the economic added value of caring, love, household and other family values? This is probably the most difficult value to measure. But you have to include it in the experience economy, if you want to measure all the cultural values of a society. That is the case with religion, too. What is the value of belief? You can measure the activities of religions to a certain degree, but measuring the life value added by way of belief is a hard nut to break. More measurable are sex and drugs, each having markets of their own, although mostly illegal, except for tobacco. And what is included in the term drugs? Does it also include for example alcohol? Alcoholic drinks are left out, however, because they are considered natural parts of the daily products of the beverage industries. Of course, this is arguable, especially when compared to tobacco. Unlike tobacco alcohol is not necessarily addictive, which is admittedly no strong argument, however.

Finally, there is the problem of illegal economic activities in relationship to subsectors of entertainment (films, music, etc.) and sex and drugs, in addition to the informal economic activities not included in the world Gross Domestic Product (GDP). I have chosen to include all these illicit economic activities, because they are a real part of the experience economy, and some of them may eventually be made legitimate.

Sources of the Experience Industries

Academic research on the experience industries is hard to come by. Although you have specialized academic disciplines in virtually all fields such as tourism, sport, media and design in most advanced countries of the world and many aspects are dealt with, little is done in researching their business activities. As a consequence, you often have to rely on market research produced by trade organizations, for example the World Travel and Tourism Council (WTTC), and commercial market research companies, for example PricewaterhouseCoopers (PWC) in media. Having identified the leading companies of various industries, their Internet sites contain much valuable information, including annual reports and historical outlines. In addition to 'official' encyclopedias on social sciences, media, etc., the updated articles of Wikipedia are other useful sources on subjects and firms.[8] Widespread illicit trade in experience goods does not make life easier for an analyst, however. In most cases, trade organizations and world agencies of, for instance, the United Nations, report on the extent and value of such illegal activities, including films, music, sex, and drugs. The informal and non-market economy of family households constitute another analytical problem to be dealt with.

In this publication, a variety of sources dealing with the many industries of the experience economy are structured on the basis of a holistic view of global developments. Accordingly, the analysis of the experience industries is a matter of encircling and stating the trends and facts of rather complex economic activities and putting them in a wider perspective, based on the global megatrends.

---

8   *www.wikipedia.org.* Schement, Jorge Reina (Ed.)(2002). *Encyclopedia of Communication and Information,* vol. 1-3. New York: Macmillan. Johnston, Donald H. (Ed.)(2003). *Encyclopedia of International Media and Communications,* vol. 1-4. San Diego, CA.: Academic Press. Smelser, Neil J. and Baltes, Paul B. (Eds.) (2001). *International Encyclopedia of the Social & Behavioral Sciences,* vol. 1-26. Amsterdam: Elesevier. Khosrowpour, Mehdi (Ed.)(2005). *Encyclopedia of Information Science and Technology,* vol. 1-5. Hershey, PA: Idea Group Reference.

2. Megatrends

Megatrends

Just like other sectors, the experience industries are driven by overall global drivers, including economic, technological, political, social and cultural developments. Developments are of two kinds. One is the cyclical ups and downs that are important to current business and conditions of life. Cycles are short-term changes at surface level, constituting so to speak the top of the iceberg. Underwater, there is a structural level of society but unlike icebergs, the worldwide structures of nations are not the same. From a structural point of view, the world may be divided into two different groups of societies, the developed countries and the developing countries. Developing countries fall into two subgroups, emerging societies in dynamic growth and countries stuck in poverty and stagnation. In real life, structural differences are crucial. You cannot easily move from one kind of structure to another and in particular, there is a gulf between developed and developing countries that is very difficult for the latter to bridge. Being historically developed and capable of continuous upgrading according to changes in the outside world, a developed nation is a system of interlinked subsystems at high levels in all matters of economy, politics, technology, and social and cultural affairs.

As a consequence of these dynamic capabilities, the developed countries are those that drive the drivers of the world, increasingly assisted by the emerging nations, whereas the poor countries are mainly left behind. Firms not nations, however, create values and compete in global markets, however, and since the great industrial breakthrough a hundred years ago, large corporations tend to dominate most developed economies and the international economy. This is even more the case today. Therefore, the real drivers of the world economy are numerous leading companies and business environments in developed countries each doing business in a huge number of industries. Increasingly, this Western-based economy is joined by emerging countries in Asia, Eastern Europe and Latin America. As a consequence, a growing global middle class of some 2 billion people form the dynamic core of a changing world economy. Developing countries are always part of the global economy, however, so things may change and are changing in some parts of the world. Furthermore, the mere existence of 4 billion poor people makes them a source of labor and purchasing power, although small, that is of some importance. Perhaps, their importance is greater than is generally believed, because much economic activity among the poor is part of the illegal or informal economy.

Globalization

The impact of these drivers is increasingly felt all over the world and simultaneously. That is the reason why we refer to globalization as a universal megatrend. By globalization is meant a worldwide growing integration of nations at all levels of society, affecting all dimensions. Not all levels are of equal importance in this globalization process, however. It all starts with the economy. What does that mean?

We are all part of an economic system called capitalism. Capitalism is a very dynamic system that is fueled by continuous growth and expansion. During the past two centuries, capitalism has ousted other systems of society, including those based on self-sufficiency and, recently, communist societies too.[1] Capitalism grows in scope by expanding throughout the world and in scale by turning more and more fields of life into commodities. This is a so-called market system that works by way of industrialization. The market system has two main actors: One the companies that produce goods to be sold on the market, competing to meet the demands of the other part, the consumers. The industrialization process has immensely changed the nature of world societies. A group of developed countries have been transformed from a state of poverty and dictatorship to that of welfare and democracy. At the same time, capitalist industrialization caused developed nations to be increasingly interdependent and integrated in matters of economy. Furthermore, capitalism spread from its Western origin to eventually all developing countries and created for the first time in history a globally interlinked world. Those societies that managed to drive or actively participate in this globalization process improved conditions of life dramatically, whereas those who did not manage to industrialize remained in the gutter. In this way, a hierarchy of societies at different levels of development arose, including leaders at the top (North America, Western Europe, Japan, South Korea, Taiwan, Hong Kong, Singapore, Israel, Australia, and New Zealand), up-comers in the middle (for example China, India, Brazil, Russia) and laggards at the bottom.

In recent years, capitalism has expanded to such a degree that, what used to be called internationalization is now being described as globalization. What is economic globalization? Globalization is a new phase in the history of capitalism. In spite of increasing international economic relations since the Second World War, modern industrial capitalism of the 20th century was basically national in nature. Many restrictions and interventions to support national companies hindered international trade

---

1   Christensen, Jens (2001). 'Globalisering og industrialisering, to århundreders perspektiv' (Two hundred years of globalization and industrialization), *Den Jyske Historiker*, No. 94-95, 142-186.

in the developed world and even more between the developed and developing countries. Furthermore, on the whole one-third of the world was cut off from the market economy by communism. The crisis-ridden decades of the 1970s and even more the 1980s made Western leadership realize that radical changes were needed. Leading companies in North America and Western Europe and eventually Japan initiated a profound business transformation process.

Three radical business changes took place. 1. What used to be highly specialized and layered bureaucratic organizations, including often many secondary activities, were switched into lean companies that outsourced all non-core business activities. Instead of doing many secondary things themselves, management chose to buy such products and services in the marketplace while focusing determinedly on core competence. 2. To add value to core competence and stay competitive, all activities from sub-suppliers via internal value adding to customers were linked in a market driven network organization. This was done to secure not only increased productivity and knowledge content in products but also to build flexible organizations capable of adapting quickly to a rapidly changing world. 3. The reorganization of business reached out globally. The focus on core competence and the emergence of global markets made management apply a global strategy. Sub-supplying and even end-production was placed wherever in the world that cost, market access and other strategic considerations were best fulfilled.

Two consequences resulted from this global reorganization. First, the previous national division of labor was turned into an international division of labor. R & D, manufacturing, distribution, marketing, sales, IT, and other links of the so-called value chain of creating market goods eventually were spread all over the world. Competitive and strategic considerations determined whether activities were done inside the organization or left to be bought in the marketplace. As a consequence, all value adding business activities were increasingly turned into industries of their own providing all the products and services needed to run a company. Everybody concentrated on their core competence, and therefore an expanding number of industries and firms emerged. Direct international investments skyrocketed and grew even more than international trade, indicating that international production had taken over the dynamic role of international trade. The majority of this so-called 'foreign direct investment' (FDI) took place within the three leading economic centers of the world, North America, Western Europe and Japan. An increasing share went to the most dynamic emerging countries such as China, Russia, India and Brazil, the so-called BRIC countries, too. Next in line followed some expanding Latin American (Mexico, Argentina, Chile), East European (Poland, Hungary, Czech), and South East Asian (Thailand, Vietnam, Indonesia, the Philippines) countries. In this way, globalization spread throughout the world like rings of water.

Secondly, a globalization of markets and industries took place. Companies organized globally, they marketed and sold their products globally and consequently, they had to be able to compete on a global scale. Leading companies in all developed nations and all industries were being faced with the need to globalize or die. An international process of selection started. What happened was that in order to survive, the predominant national companies had to upgrade to a global level. Some gave up pretty soon and many merged, while others decided to go for it. Those companies that came out as winners always built on strong national clusters that gave the sources and strength to compete on a global scale.

During the 1990s, a rush to globalize took place in all industries and by the turn of the century, a consolidation process had created a new global business picture. In all industries, future expansion and even survival depended on the ability to become one of a few companies that came to dominate their respective markets. Besides the stop-or-go choice when confronted with global consolidation, you might also choose to move into another link of the value chain that was more adaptable to the individual company's core competence, for example from end-producer to sub-supplier or from a mainstream producer to a company focusing on front-line innovation. Moving around in the value chain and taking advantage of rapid changes in the world corresponded well with a new era of globalization and innovation, leaving much room to innovating entrepreneurs, too.

The accelerating growth of capitalism throughout the world was evident in the way each and every company reorganized and endeavored to adapt to globalization. Globalization did not move on simultaneously and at the same pace in all industries, however. In some sectors such as pharmaceuticals, IT, communications, transportation and business services, globalization came swiftly, while regional consolidation within North America, Europe and Eastern Asia prevailed in other sectors of the economy, for instance construction and cultural industries. Regional consolidation was not the terminal point, but just a stepping-stone towards final globalization. Globalization was the megatrend that drove all kinds of business activities since the 1990s and increasingly in the new millennium.

The radical transformation and globalization of business could not have taken place without additional profound changes in other sectors of the world, including politics, technology and social and cultural affairs. While corporate America and Europe revolutionized their organizations and strategies, the Atlantic political leadership likewise took radical steps to regain economic growth and prosperity. They began to tear down restrictions and introduced open competition and trade, instead. Monopolized sectors of the economy were privatized and direct intervention in business affairs was replaced by a framework of fair competition rules and improved infrastructures. Liberalization was enforced on a global and regional level, too, based on World Trade Organization (WTO) and regional units such as the European Union (EU) and The North American Free Trade Agreement (NAFTA). Still in spite of worldwide and regional agreements and organizations, the nation state remains the cornerstone of world politics. Neither has the United Nations (UN), including its councils or agencies, any authority over national affairs. The EU is the only international organization to have assumed some sovereignty at the expense of its member states.

In social matters, globalization and increased regional liberalization and cooperation have led to improvements in life conditions, not only in developed countries but also in emerging countries. Still, while two-thirds of the developed population may be considered well off and only one-third is below average living conditions, it is the reverse situation in emerging countries, at best, whereas the majority of inhabitants in poor nations live under miserable conditions. Roughly speaking, two thirds of the world 6.5 billion people are poor, while one-third is a well off middle class. The majority of the global middle class lives in the Atlantic community, Eastern Asia and Oceania, but increasingly in emerging countries in Asia, Europe, and Latin America, too.

In statistical numbers, the global dominance of developed countries is declining from a 55 percent GDP share in 1990, via 50 percent in 2005 to 45 percent in 2015, and from a population share of 17 percent in 1990 to 14 percent in 2015 (Table 1). Measured in purchasing power, the gap between developed and developing countries remains unchanged, but it widens between the rich and poor countries. 15 percent of the world population creates 50 percent of global economic values.

World Trade

The globalization of business has led to an increasing international exchange of goods. As a consequence, the export and import share of GDP and world economies is rising and is projected to double from 1990 to 2015.[2] In 2015, half of all traded goods will be crossing international borders. Global trade is to a high degree dominated by developed countries (about two-thirds), although the share of developing countries is rising, mainly based on growth in emerging countries such as China, India, Russia and Brazil.

Most internationally traded commodities are physical industrial goods, such as manufacturing (the largest share), minerals, energy, and agricultural products. Except for transportation and travel, other services such as communications, business and

---

2   Angus Maddison. The World Economy: Historical Statistics. CIA, World Fact Book 2000-2007. US Census Bureau, International Statistics. World Trade Organization (2007). *International Trade Statistics 2007.* Geneva: WTO.

TABLE 1

World Population and GDP Regional % Shares, 1950–2015

	1950		1970		1990		2000		2005		2010		2015	
	%Pop	%GDP	%Pop	%GDP	%Pop	%GDP	%Pop	%GDP	%Pop	%GDP	%Pop	%GDP	%Pop	%GDP
World Pop., bn	2.5		3.7		5.3		6.1		6.5		6.8		7.2	
World GDP, $bn		5		14		27		37		45		56		70
North America	7	36	6	25	5	23	5	24	5	22	5	21	5	21
Western Europe	12	26	10	26	7	22	6	20	6	19	6	18	6	18
Eastern Europe/Russia	10	11	8	12	7	9	6	6	5	6	5	6	4	6
Asia Pacific	55	13	47	24	48	33	48	36	48	39	48	43	47	44
Latin America	7	8	8	8	8	8	9	8	9	8	9	7	9	7
Middle East/Africa	10	6	12	6	14	6	16	6	17	5	18	5	19	5
Total	100	100	100	100	100	100	100	100	100	100	100	100	100	100

Source: Angus Maddison (2003). *The World Economy: Historical Statistics*. Paris: OECD. CIA (2000-2007).
World Fact Book 2000–2007: www.cia.org. US Census Bureau (2007). *International Statistics: www.census.gov*.

cultural services are less internationalized than physical merchandised goods. While services constitute about two-thirds of world GDP, their share of international trade is probably no more than one-third. The experience industries and international trade in experience goods are included in these numbers. Roughly, total economic values created by the experience industries account for 10 percent of global GDP and 5 percent of international trade (see conclusion). The majority of this value creation and trade is based on developed countries, mainly USA, Western Europe and Japan (about three-fourths). Even within experience industries, export rates vary. As a consequence of the US global dominance, most American experience industries have high export rates, whereas for example German and Japanese (except video games) experience industries first and foremost are based on domestic markets.

Technology

Television and radio, telephones and computers have been around for quite some time and are found in virtually all households of developed countries and are widely used in emerging and to some degree poor countries, especially television. Since the mid 1990s, a new set of digital technologies are spreading rapidly, however (Table 2). The Internet, broadband, and mobile phones are changing many aspects of current societies, clearly having an effect on all experience industries.[3] In developed countries, the great majority of households and companies have access to the Internet and soon the majority will communicate by way of broadband, allowing for easy transfer of movies, music and other capacity-heavy content. Mobile phones are everywhere, and in developed countries even children have cell phones. Furthermore, the digitization of any kind of information and communication, including all business processes and all entertainment content production, establishes the basis of an online world.

The accelerating introduction of online and mobile technologies and broadband to secure high capacity communication influence virtually all segments of the experience economy, including tourism, sports, media and entertainment, such as television, radio, newspapers, advertising, music, films, and games. Therefore, new technologies make up a dynamic driving force of the experience economy. Of particular importance is the accelerating spread of broadband access and the ubiquitous mobile phones that

---

3   International Telecommunication Union (2006). *Digital Life. ITU Internet Report 2006*. OECD (2007). *Broadband and ICT Access and Use by Households and Individuals*. Paris: OECD.

TABLE 2

Global Subscribers to Internet, Broadband and Mobile Phones in Millions, 2000-2010

	2000			2005			2010		
	Inter-net	Broad-band	Mobile	Inter-net	Broad-band	Mobile	Inter-net	Broad-band	Mobile
North America	115	10	135	220	50	235	250	85	325
USA	100	9	125	200	45	215	225	75	300
Canada	15	1	10	20	5	20	25	10	25
Western Europe	100	25	200	225	55	390	250	100	425
UK	15	4	30	35	9	65	40	15	70
Germany	20	4	40	45	10	80	55	20	85
France	10	3	25	25	10	50	35	15	60
Italy	15	3	30	25	7	70	35	15	75
Spain	5	1	15	15	5	35	25	10	40
Rest of Western Europe	25	10	60	55	15	90	60	25	95
Eastern Europe	15	0	50	60	10	250	125	20	300
Russia	5	0	25	30	5	125	60	10	150
Rest of Eastern Europe	10	0	25	30	5	125	65	10	150
Asia Pacific	150	5	300	375	85	925	600	250	1475
Japan	50	5	50	85	20	95	90	50	125
China	30	0	100	125	30	400	250	100	600
South Korea	20	0	25	30	10	40	35	25	50
Taiwan	5	0	10	10	5	20	15	10	25
India	5	0	50	50	10	100	100	25	250
Australia	5	0	10	10	5	20	15	10	25
Rest of Asia Pacific	35	0	55	75	5	250	95	30	400
Latin America	15	0	75	75	5	200	125	15	300
Africa	5	0	50	30	5	125	100	10	200
Middle East	5	0	40	15	5	75	50	10	100
World Total	400	40	850	1000	215	2200	1500	500	3125

Source: PWC. Global Entertainment and Media Outlook 2006-2010. Internet World Stat: *www.internetworldstats.com*. International Telecommunications Union (2007). *The Information Society*: *www. itu. int*. Numbers are rounded.

are including people in emerging and even poor countries in global communications networks. In addition to television and computers, access to Internet and mobile phones are about to be part of most households of the world.

The 2000s started the revolutionary transformation from an age applying many additional technologies such as television and computers to an emerging era of virtual relations making information and communications online united through pervasive digitization. By way of the Internet and increasingly the mobile phone, consumers are given direct access to all market supplying industries. This has great repercussions within the business world seeking to adapt to changing demands and secure direct distribution channels to consumers. Furthermore, consumers are becoming more demanding and individual in their demands. They want something special and often to be on their own. Armed with the new digital, mobile and virtual technologies they are able to enforce their will.

Individualization

On the demand-side, consumers are not only becoming more demanding and resourceful. The rapidly changing nature of modern societies has also changed the lives and mentalities of present day people.[4] By way of globalization as well as the increasing focus on knowledge and the revolutionizing breakthrough of new technologies, the individual human being has become the central actor of modern societies. Companies and markets depend on the competences and choices of the working force and consumers on the one hand, whilst on the other hand, people have become individualized in their approach to work and everyday life. By individualization is not simply meant the spread of a free-market individual, although this may be considered one part of the changes taking place. The dynamics of modern societies has created a new and active individual personality. Human beings are valued on the basis of their individual competences and they value themselves on their own capabilities and act accordingly.

During the past few decades, this individualization process has taken hold of people in developed countries. Traditional social structures and links, such as classes and families, have been replaced or reduced in importance by individually created families and groups of friends and professional networks on the one hand and, on the other, a new set of institutionalized structures in business and state that has taken over many outsourced functions of family life. What is left is a resourceful, demanding, and individually acting human being seeking to fulfill himself in a world of many opportuni-

---

4   Ulrich Beck and Elisabeth Beck-Gernsheim (2002). *Individualization*. London: SAGE Publications.

ties that are structured by the framework and dynamics of global and technologically based business. The identity of a contemporary individual is not a given thing. It is a matter of selection and creation, and therefore, it is a life-project of each person. Making use of the many opportunities and products of the experience industries is an important part of the self-driven culture of modern human beings. That makes experience industries expand.

Authenticity

Consumers want experiences, but not just any kind of experience. The more contrived and fast moving the world seems, the more do people demand what is real. Today, they look for authentic experiences. This is the message of Gilmore and Pine's new follow-up book to their successful book on the experience economy.[5] Because people have got used to a staged world in tourist attractions, cafés, media, entertainment and other experience sectors, they upgrade their demands. They want quality and true experiences that conform to their own self-image. No longer will they accept fake experiences. The demand for authenticity is not limited to specific segments of consumers. It is a general trend that includes eventually all consumers. Craving for authenticity may be considered part of a broader trend, too. Social responsibility in business and organizations in dealing with employees, customers, sub-suppliers, authorities, and other stakeholders as well as consciousness of the environment are other examples of a general trend among people and consumers that demand quality and honesty in all aspects of an experience and any product, for that matter. As man is a social animal, authenticity includes also social togetherness with family, friends and colleagues. Accordingly, the demand for authenticity may be seen as the heading for an age of rapid change and affluence when people respond by looking for more profound and lasting values, an ethical and quality-based approach to a continuous search for the meaning of life. This megatrend will require new management responses and offerings and open new business opportunities, too.

---

5   Gilmore, James H. and B. Joseph Pine II (2007). *Authenticity. What Consumers Really Want.* Boston, Mass.: Harvard Business Publishing.

3. Tourism

Tourism

Tourism is a gigantic field of business and social activity. Its global, regional, national and local importance is large and growing, although it differs in size and nature from nation to nation. Tourism may be defined as travel for predominantly recreational or leisure purposes and the industries that provide the services to fulfil these targets.[1] Tourists are people who travel to and stay in places outside their usual environment for not more than one year for leisure, business and other purposes, excluding continuous work. In tourism is included international outbound and inbound tourism and domestic tourism. Domestic and inbound tourism combined may be called internal tourism. National tourism is a combination of domestic and outbound tourism. International tourism consists of inbound and outbound trans-border tourism.

Tourism has impacts on societies in many ways. On the supply-side, you have those industries that directly supply tourists with goods and services and primarily are dependent on servicing tourism, such as travel, accommodation, and attractions. This tourism industry is backed by several sub-suppliers that provide means of transportation, information and communication as well as food and beverages, clothing, housing and the infrastructure needed to make traveling feasible. Business services and in particular governmental authorities are vital parts of tourism, too. These authorities often provide infrastructure and educations, are responsible for protection of the cultural heritage, and in general produce and operate the legal framework concerning nature, urban environments, travel and trade. Like rings in water, the tourist industry and its sup-suppliers and general preconditions spread into most parts of society. Furthermore, governments support national and local tourism for economic reasons, because tourism generates income to many companies and people as well as export revenues. These broader dimensions of related industries make up the so-called multiplying effects of tourism on the general economy. Including the proper tourism industry, they form the wider tourism economy. At supra national level, the World Travel and Tourist Council (WTTC) represent the interests of the tourist industry while the United Nations' World Tourism Organization (UNWTO) focuses on the preservation and diversity of cultural and environmental values around the world.

On the demand side, globalization and the revolutionary developments of transportation and communication have made it easy to travel almost anywhere you want to go, and millions of people have the time, money, education, health and inclination to do so, particularly in developed countries. When traveling, you have to meet

---

1   *www.unwto.org*

the same demands as at home, but in addition tourists want an extra dimension by seeking out new places and experiences, too. During a vacation you eat, drink, sleep, play, shop, travel, phone, have sex, work, jog, are entertained, etc. All these parts of a vacation experience constitute the basis of a comprehensive tourism industry. The tourism industry is trying to attract people and having done so, they aim at meeting their demands. Because all national governments and tourism industries want people to spend their leisure time and money in precisely *their* country, everybody is competing even harder to attract tourists who nowadays have the opportunity to go virtually wherever they want to.

Tourism is an integrated part of global and national business and market developments. In addition, growing wealth and easy access to transportation and information make people travel more often than they used to do. This is not merely an escape from the daily round. Tourists travel to add new experiences to their lives. Traveling has become part of modern lifestyles, which requires the tourism industry to customize their products to demanding and knowledgeable tourists.[2]

To tourists, traveling is one continuous experience from start to end. No single company or branch supplies all the activities of the value chain of tourists. Therefore, the tourist industry is divided into several specialized industries, such as tour operators, travel agencies, airlines, hotels, restaurants, and attractions. Many related industries provide food, technology and other goods needed to run a tourist business, including a reliable infrastructure and other general preconditions to make life easy for tourists and industry.

In this context, we shall concentrate on the tourism industry. The secondary and wider economic results of tourism, called the 'tourist economy' of tourism, will be included only to a minor degree. The line between the primary and secondary economic dimension of tourism is not easily drawn. What is mostly dependent on tourism, whether supplying end-users or other businesses, will be included in the tourism industry.

To begin with, the historic and current size and growth of world tourism will be outlined.

---

2   OECD (2007). *Innovation and Growth in Tourism*. Paris: OECD.

Global Tourism

The International Tourism

Since the Second World War, tourism has grown substantially. Although many take domestic vacations, growth has been strongest in international tourism.[3] The number of international arrivals has increased from 25 million in 1950 to more than 800 million in 2005, corresponding to an annual growth rate of 6.5 percent (Figure 1). And international tourism is projected to keep on growing in the future. Having passed 900 million international travelers in 2007, it is predicted to reach 1.6 billion in 2020.

FIGURE 1

International Tourist Arrivals in Millions, 1950-2005

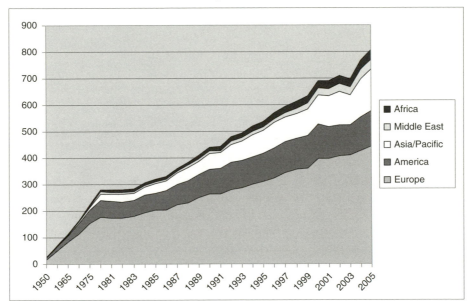

Source: UNWTO. Historical Perspective of World Tourism.

Even though their share has been declining, Western Europe and North America, mainly USA, have dominated international travel up till now. Western Europe and USA were the main tourist-receiving regions with a joint market share of approximately 90 percent in 1950, 75 percent in 1990, 70 percent in 2000 and 65 percent in 2005. And

---

3   World Tourism Organization (UNTWO) (2007). *Historical Perspective of World Tourism. Facts and Figures.* UNWTO (2008). *Tourism 2020 Vision. www.unwto.org.*

they spent a similar share of total international revenues, rising from $2 bn in 1950, $18 bn in 1970, $270 bn in 1990, $482 bn in 2000, $683 bn in 2005, and almost $800 bn in 2007. Western Europe comprised more than three quarters of Western arrivals and revenues. If travels across states had been recorded as international arrivals, the US would have reached the same level as Western Europe and if Western Europe was considered one country, international travel would be reduced to half. Today, half the international arrivals and thereby tourism revenues are in Western Europe. Western decline is just relative, because more and more people travel within or to Western Europe and North America. However, international arrivals and revenues in the rest of the world, in particular Asia and the Pacific, have been growing faster than in Western Europe and North America. While Western Europe comprises half of the international arrivals and revenues, most of the other half is equally divided between North America and Asia Pacific.

Figure 2

The Largest Tourist Incoming and Outgoing Countries in $bn, 2004

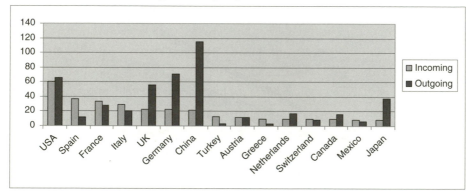

Source: UNWTO. Facts and Figures. Newer data are not available.

At country level, USA has the largest number of incoming and outgoing tourists and tourist spending, followed by Germany, China and Japan (Figure 2). Spain, France and Italy are next in line. In some countries more tourists are coming in than going out, particularly Spain and to some degree France and Italy, and further down the line Turkey and Greece. The reverse is the case in other countries, in particular Germany, UK, China and Japan, while in the USA outgoing and incoming tourists are almost at the same level. Germans and Britons are those who travel most internationally, followed by the Dutch and the Danes. Per capita, they spend more money on traveling than other countries, which results in a travel deficit. The main destination is to the sunshine of Southern Europe. A similar traveling pattern is seen in North America and Asia.

Global Experience Industries

The fifteen nationalities which travel most comprise almost half of all incoming travels and two-thirds of all outgoing travel. Furthermore, 80 percent of all international travel in both 1990 and 2005 took place within the same regions. North Americans travel mainly across the borders of USA and Canada and USA and Mexico, and West Europeans cross borders to other countries in the region. The same is the case in Asia Pacific.

The Global Tourism Economy and Industry

Statistics

While it is not too difficult to measure the amount of international travel, it is more complicated to determine the economic significance of tourism. Tourist demands are met by a number of separate industries dealing with transportation, accommodation, catering, attractions, etc. Because national statistics only measure revenues at total trade level, they do not reveal who buys the goods. To make a national tourist account, it is necessary to extract the relevant parts from several trade or industry statements and methods to do so have been developed, even on an international level, to make a so-called 'satellite account'.[4] Consequently, it is possible to measure the economic significance of tourism on a national and a worldwide level. In practice however, this is no simple task and only few nations have established a national tourism satellite account.

Satellite accounts comprise the value of direct tourism consumption. Indirect impacts of tourism on national and world economies are not included, however: the so-called multiplier effect. Mainly, the tourist satellite account encompasses the supply and demand of goods related to the tourism industry and is therefore, the best estimation of the businesses dealing with tourism. The results of satellite accounts are larger than traditional tourism measures, among other things because they include short-term travel which so far has been excluded from tourism accounts. As a consequence in most official statistics, the economic importance of tourism is underestimated at local, national and global levels.[5]

---

4   OECD (2001). *Measuring the Role of Tourism in OECD Economies.* UNWTO (2000-2007). *The Tourism Satellite Account.* Eurostat (2001). *European Implementation Manual on Tourism Satellite Accounts.*
5   The EU statistics on tourism, for example, are based on travel of minimum 4 overnights: Eurostat (2008). *Panorama on Tourism. http://.eurostatec.europa.eu.* Nor are many local and national tourism activities and effects included in tourism accounts: Smeral, Egon (2006). 'Tourism Satellite Accounts: A Critical Assessment'. *Journal of Travel Research,* vol. 45, 92-98. A review of the worldwide problems of implementing satellite accounts at the national level is: Marion Libreros, Antonio Massieu, and Scott Meis (2006). 'Progress in Tourism Satellite Account Implementation and Development', *Journal of Travel Research,* vol. 45, 83-91. The difficulties in economic measuring of tourism are also connected with the

In spite of these statistical shortcomings, WTTC has commissioned Accenture to make annual global and national accounts of the tourism industry and economy.[6] Although it is called a satellite account, judging from the numbers the results are lower than a full satellite account.[7] The WTTC account may therefore be seen as a conservative estimation of national and global tourism. The account measures the size of the tourism industry that supplies tourist goods and services as well as the size of the broader tourism economy.

Figure 3

The Global Tourism Industry and Economy in $bn, 1970-2015

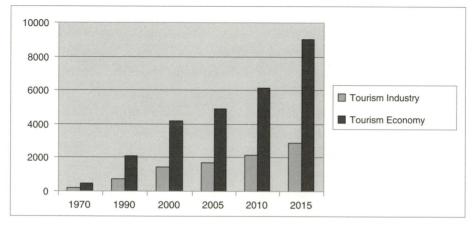

Source: UNTWO. Historical Perspective of World Tourism. WTTC. The 2007 Travel & Tourism Economic Research.

The Tourism Economy and Tourism Industry

Since the 1960s, tourism has grown in step with general economic developments, except somewhat faster, and it is projected to continue growing at the same pace.

Mass tourism, as it is known today, began in the 1960s and continued to expand hereafter. Wealth and technology enabled millions of people to travel at home and abroad by car and airplane. Since the 1960s, the tourism industry accounted for 3 to 4 percent and the broader tourism economy for 10 percent of world GDP, export and employment. Everything indicates that this will continue in the future, and maybe

---

conceptual problem of defining a tourist: McCabe, Scott (2005). 'Who is Tourist? A Critical Review'. *Tourist Studies*, vol. 5, 85-106.

6   World Travel & Tourism Council (2007). *The 2007 Travel & Tourism Economic Research: www.wttc.org.*

7   For example, the Danish tourism satellite account is almost fifty percent higher than the traditional account: VisitDenmark (2006). *Turismen i Danmark 2000-2004* (Danish Tourism): *www.visitdenmark. com.*

Global Experience Industries

even accelerate. In 2005, the world tourism economy totalled about 5000 $bn and the tourism industry about 1700 $bn (Figure 3).

Primarily, the tourism industry includes activities related to travel and stay. Also included, are governmental expenses to cultural institutions, parks and other direct tourism-related activities and, finally, tourist shopping. Personal vacation travel makes up about 80 percent and business travels about 20 percent of all expenses. In addition, the tourism economy includes all indirect private and public expenses and investments which enable tourism to take place (Figure 4).

FIGURE 4

The Tourism Industry and Economy Flows

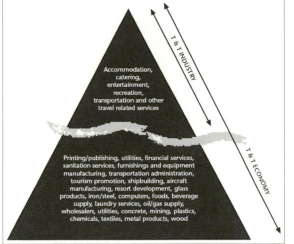

Source: EU (2002). *Structure, Performance and Competitiveness of European Tourist Enterprises*, 6.

Tourists spend more money at home than abroad. However, since the 1970s international tourism spending has increased much more than domestic tourism and the two numbers are approaching each other. While international tourism spending accounted for less than 10 percent of total tourism revenues in 1970, its share increased during the next two decades to 30 percent in 1990 and 40 percent in 2005 (Figure 5). The difference between domestic and international tourism spending varies a lot from country to country, just as developed countries spend much more on tourism compared to developing countries. The North Europeans spend more on international tourism than on domestic tourism, for example, while USA spends five times as much at home than abroad. Although climate and access to sun and beach seem to be the most important factors driving world tourism, the rise of one day and short-term vacations means that shopping, visits to family and friends as well as city tourism, make up an increasing share of total tourism spending.

Figure 5
Global Domestic and International Tourism in $bn, 1970-2015

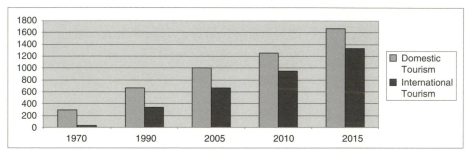

Source: UNTWO. Historical Perspective of World Tourism. WTTC. The 2007 Travel & Tourism Economic Research. Numbers are estimated.

Looking at ways of traveling, cars and airlines dominate completely. In the US, the car is the most important means of transportation for vacations, because here short term vacations prevail. The car is also important in Western Europe as a means of tourism transportation, but the longer vacations in this region means that flying plays a greater role. Ferries, trains and busses are of much less significance.[8]

Figure 6
The Tourism Economy and Industry of the World's Largest Tourist Countries in $bn, 2005

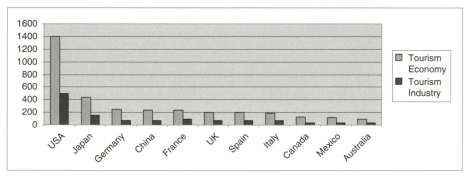

Source: WTTC. The 2007 Travel & Tourism Economic Research.

---

8   Travel Industry Association of America (TIA)(2007). *US Travel Market Overview*: *www.tia.org*. Eurostat. Panorama on Tourism.

Global Experience Industries

The US tourism sector is by far the largest in the world, making up a quarter of total tourism economy and industry (Figure 6). There is quite a gap down to number two, Japan, with an 8 percent global share, followed by China and the five large West European tourist countries, Germany, UK, France, Italy and Spain of 4 to 6 percent. China has just recently joined the top ten and rapidly moved into third place. The ten largest tourist countries account for 70 percent of total world tourism spending. As we shall see later on, the world tourism industry that provides travel services is completely dominated by companies in developed countries.

FIGURE 7
High Income and Low Income Countries' Share of World Tourism in $bn, 2005 and 2015

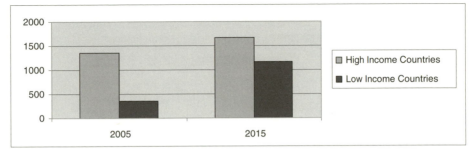

Source: WTTC. The 2007 Travel & Tourism Economic Research.

To a high degree, world tourism deals with travelling in and between developed and high income countries, although emerging countries such as China and Mexico have fueled non-Western tourism (Figure 7). The growing desire of middle classes to travel has increased the economic importance of tourism in developing countries, mainly emerging countries. In relative terms, tourism is growing more rapidly in developing countries than in developed countries. Political stability and good infrastructure are a precondition everywhere for extending tourism.

In numbers, revenues of the global tourism industry have increased from $875 bn in 1990, to $1700 bn in 2005 and a projected $2590 bn in 2015 (Table 3).

Table 3

The Global Tourism Industry in $bn, 1990-2015

	1990	2000	2005	2010	2015
North America	270	485	530	625	750
USA	250	450	490	580	700
Canada	20	35	40	45	50
Western Europe	320	535	605	715	840
Germany	50	80	90	100	115
UK	50	80	90	110	130
France	50	80	90	110	130
Italy	40	75	85	95	110
Spain	50	80	90	110	130
Rest of Western Europe	80	140	160	190	225
Eastern Europe	10	30	40	65	95
Asia Pacific	175	300	355	465	630
Japan	80	140	160	180	225
China	25	40	60	120	200
Australia	20	30	35	45	55
Rest of Asia Pacific	50	90	100	120	150
Latin America	50	80	95	120	150
Middle East and Africa	50	70	75	95	125
Total	875	1.500	1.700	2.085	2.590

Source: UNWTO. Historical Perspective of World Tourism. WTTC. The 2007 Travel & Tourism Economic Research. My predictions are not as optimistic as. WTTC. Numbers are rounded.

From Mass Tourism to Customized Tourism

Rich people have always traveled to distant parts of the world to visit great coastal resorts, see magnificent buildings, experience new cultures, etc.[9] The sons of the nobility and gentry in the 17th and 18th century undertook a Grand Tour of Europe as an educational experience. Health tourism existed even in ancient Rome, but it was

9   Auliana Poon (1993). *Tourism, Technology and Competitive Strategies*, 30-32. Wallingford, UK: C.A.B. International. Smelser and Baltes. International Encyclopedia of the Social & Behavioral Sciences, 'Tourism'. *www.wikepedia.org*: *Tourism/History*.

not until the 18th century that it became important. British spas in Bath and Czech Carlsbad attracted many fashionable travelers during the 19th century. Seaside travel became popular in 19th century Britain, too. As the first country to industrialize Britain invented leisure travel to the French Riviera and Swiss Alps. The UK also pioneered mass tourism.

Thomas Cook was the pioneer of mass tourism. In 1841, he organized the first package tour in history, when he arranged for the rail company to charge one shilling per person for a group of temperance campaigners from Leicester to attend a rally in Loughborough, eleven miles away. Cook was paid a share of the fares. Cook immediately saw the potential of organized holidays and his business expanded as he arranged an increasing number of package tours in Britain and on the European continent, Paris and the Alps being the most popular destinations.

Cook was soon followed by others, with the result that a tourism industry developed in Britain in the second half of the 19th century. Initially the growing middle classes fueled the new industry, but the introduction of the workers' right to take holidays in 1871 established the tradition of the working class holiday before 1900, mainly focusing on seaside resorts. The establishment of a national railway network made it easy to reach seaside towns such as Blackpool and Brighton. Other Western countries such as France, Germany and the USA copied to some degree the British holiday traditions, along the Atlantic, Mediterranean and Baltic coastlines.

From the mid-19th to the mid-20th century, domestic tourism was the norm, with foreign travel being reserved for the rich or culturally curious. The transatlantic ocean liners of the period between the two World Wars were popular ways of traveling for rich people only. The mass immigration from Europe to the United States in the late 19th and early 20th century can hardly qualify as tourism. Cars and small-scale airlines were also introduced as means of travel before World War II. In addition to railway lines, harbors, telegraph and telephone lines, a new infrastructure of roads and some airports widened to some degree the potential of tourism. Before 1950, flights were restricted to leading business men, politicians, and officials, however.

The Age of Mass Tourism

Mass tourism is an offspring of the era of mass production and mass consumption, based on economies of scale.[10] Economies of scale are a certain rational way of organizing

---

10   The relationship between mass tourism and customized tourism or Fordist versus post-Fordist tourism is dealt with by: Rebecca Torres (2002). 'Cancun's Tourism Development from a Fordist Spectrum of Analysis'. *Tourist Studies*, vol. 2, 87-116.

business and any organizational activity for that matter that dominated throughout most of the 20th century. Often this organizational mode is called Fordism or just bureaucracy, indicating on the one hand a radical low cost and standardized way of production and on the other hand a sharp division of labor and authority. The attractive side of this system was that it drew people out of the poverty that ruled everywhere before c.1900 and gave the majority of Western people access to consumer goods that were inaccessible to previous generations, including upgraded housing, clothing, food, health care and education. Everything has a price, and in this case it was a thorough standardization of products and ways of life in general. During the first half of the 20th century, this system expanded slowly. The unleashing of the potentials of Fordism and governmental regulations in the early post-war decades created, however, a welfare society that had never been experienced before.

Relaxed international trade restrictions in the Western world as well as the systematic application of science and technology and governmental intervention to secure over-all welfare, caused rapid changes in many aspects of post-war Western societies. Being born under the modest pre-1950 life conditions, the early post-war generation eagerly grabbed the huge consumption opportunities of affluent societies. That everything was standardized and everybody treated uniformly did not bother this first post-war generation, because to them affluence came as a revelation and was Paradise on Earth. Furthermore, they were not used to international travels and therefore preferred the comfort and security of package tours. Their children, on the other hand, took welfare for granted and during the 1960s and 1970s, they began to protest against the uniform, authoritative and materialistic nature of modern societies. In addition, a continuous economic crisis of the 1970s and 1980s indicated that the era of Fordism had exhausted its potentials and called for radical reforms. But until c.1990, the fundaments of mass production and consumption remained unchanged and dominated the practice of business, governments and consumption behavior.

On this background, modern mass tourism started in the 1950s and broke through during the 1960s and 1970s.[11] The age of mass tourism lies between 1960 and 1990. Package tour operators transported millions of charter tourists from cold Northern Europe to warm Southern Europe. Along the Mediterranean coastline, the pale northerners allowed the sun to tan their skin, giving them a welcome break from a dull everyday and working life. Spain, especially, became a cheap and popular destination, followed by Greece. In the US, people frequented the Atlantic and Pacific coasts, as well as the Caribbean and Hawaii.

---

11   Poon. Tourism, Technology and Competitive Strategies, 32-61.

Mass tourism stemmed from the following factors:

- The post-war economic boom and wealth
- Still longer vacations, particularly in Western Europe
- Growing international trade
- The revolutionary development of air transportation, the building of numerous airports, communication and computer systems, regular and fast domestic and international routes in the US, Western Europe, across the Atlantic and eventually around the world
- The airlines' establishment of computerized reservation systems and cheap group tickets for charter trips
- The general distribution of cars
- The establishment of international hotel chains
- The development of a large package-tour industry, taking care of transportation and accommodation for millions of people.

The main actors of the post-war tourism industry were airlines, hotel chains and package-tour companies. Railways, passenger ships and bus firms, electronic cards and car rent companies as well as restaurants and attractions were secondary parties in the large mass tourism industry. Without modern airlines and car industries, the new basic infrastructure and computer technology and the natural and cultural attractions of destination countries, modern mass tourism would not have existed. Except for the European package tour operators, American companies took the lead in all other fields of the international tourism industry.

Mass Tourism in USA

The United States and Western Europe dominated post-war mass tourism. Mass tourism developed differently in these two regions, however. In the US, hotel chains and airlines were the main actors in developing mass tourism, while the package-tour industry and airlines stood behind Europe's mass tourism. American hotel chains spread around the world in the wake of American businesses and tourists, so that Americans everywhere might feel at home under similar conditions. Franchising made it possible for hotel chains to produce standardized hotel products by reproducing buildings, inventory, feeding, services and management methods, which allowed for economies of scale in purchasing, distribution and booking systems. The fast growth of this franchising principle was an important factor behind the development of American mass tourism.

Unlike the nationally divided Western Europe, the large American continent contained almost every kind of nature and culture, except for the extensive pre-industrial culture of European cities. This made the Americans spend their holidays at home to a much higher degree than the Europeans. Furthermore, a highly developed freeway system, short vacations and tremendous business travelling activities throughout the large continent conduced to the fact that a large domestic American tourism by far overshadowed foreign travel. As a consequence, the car was the preferred transportation means in the United States, whereas European package tours always included a charter flight. American hotels did not arrange package-tours like the European travelling companies did. Instead, motels were built along freeways and city hotels that might be easily reached by car. The package-tour industry therefore never reached the same size as in Europe.

Behind hotel chains and package tour companies, the large American airlines and their booking systems played a decisive role in developing tourism and the tourism industry. Without them mass tourism would never have existed. By way of mergers, American Airlines, United Airlines and Delta Air Lines (merging with Pan Am in 1991) dominated completely American air transportation until the liberalization of the 1990s. Airlines did more than fly. They invested in other links of the travel industry's value chain, including travel agencies, hotels, catering, banking, insurance and car rental. In this way, the American airlines contributed much to the vertical and horizontal integration that marked the American travel and tourism industry. They provided the services for mass tourism, including cheap charter tickets and were an important driver behind the industrial growth. First and foremost, the airlines controlled the large computer-based booking systems that became a nucleus for tourism developments.

Mass Tourism in Western Europe

In Western Europe, mass tourism was based on the rise of a large package tour industry, charter flights, hotel constructions and the development of sunny mass-consuming destinations along the Mediterranean coasts. The package-tour companies organized travel that included transportation, accommodation and extra services such as sightseeing and entertainment. They were sold as a whole package, and by way of mass purchase of charter tickets from airlines or through their own airlines and hotels at destinations, the operators were able to cut prices considerably. Such package tours arranged by tour operators expanded enormously in Western Europe during the 1960s and 1970s and to some degree in the 1980s.

In Western Europe, the tour operators played the same role for tourism as hotel chains in the US. By developing cheap package tours, they staged and drove mass tourism. They offered the same kind of security and safety as the American hotel chains by selecting rooms and assuming full responsibility for delivering the promised vacation. In particular, package tours were sold to North Europeans in Scandinavia, UK, Germany and the Netherlands, who longed for the warmth of sunny Southern Europe. The package tours enabled millions of north Europeans to travel in a way that pre-war generations never had the opportunity to do. The reason why packed tours broke through in Western Europe, unlike the US, is also that the European wage earners had much longer vacations than their American counterparts and therefore were able to take longer vacations.

Charter flights were the precondition for cheap package tours. Charter tickets were linked to certain routes and bought at discount prices long in advance of the summer vacation, allowing for a hundred percent load factor. Charter flights broke through at the same time as jet airlines and mass air transportation in the 1960s. Just like American hotel chains, the tour operators mass produced identical products at low costs and prices, according to the predominant Fordistic way of organizing business activities at that time. Two-thirds of the world charter traffic took place in Western Europe compared to just one-third in the United States. This trend continued and expanded during the 1970s and the 1980s when charter flights constituted one-third of total international air transportation. In Western Europe, Spain was the most popular destination of charter tourism, while the Caribbean and Hawaii occupied that position in the US. A third but smaller wave of tourists crossed the Atlantic.

Even though mass tourism developed differently at the two major markets of the world, both were managed in the same way. Both produced the same services to an undifferentiated group of mass tourists. Economies of scale and standardization were achieved by way of hotel branding in the United States and vacation branding in Western Europe. In the US, the hotel brands were, for example, Holiday Inn and Hilton Hotels, while the leading European tour operators included Nouvelle Frontiers in France, Thomson Holidays in UK, Jahn Reisen in Germany, and Tjaereborg Rejser and Spies Rejser in Denmark. Mass production was achieved by way of large airlines and hotels corporations in the United States and the enormous flight and hotel buying power of package tour operators in Western Europe.

Customized Tourism

Since the 1990s, several factors have radically changed the preconditions of world tourism. The world economy has globalized and liberalized, creating a global division of labor and accelerating economic growth and prosperity. Mass production of consumer goods at lowest possible costs is no longer the driving force of business, although productivity is rising more than ever and enabling radical price cuts. Nowadays, people want customized products that adapt to a dynamic age and individual lifestyles and because of globalization and economic growth consumer alternatives are bigger than ever. To meet these changing demands, companies have to change fundamentally from supply-driven to demand-driven organizations and products must be differentiated according to changing demands.

The transformation of business was accompanied and driven by a globalization of competition and markets that created dramatic economic growth and changing conditions of competition and consumption. To stay in business, companies had to organize on a global scale. Economies of scale did not disappear, they were just woven into a global network like system of interrelated organizations. Inside this network, an increasing number of industries emerged and eventually, each industry came to be dominated by a handful of corporations. The revolutionary breakthrough and accelerating developments of information and communication technologies since the 1990s created the tools needed to make globalization come true. Furthermore, the universal digitalization of business and any other social activity brought to life new kinds of goods, services, communications, and business combinations. Especially, the Internet set a new standard that really gave the customer the upper hand and created a buyer's market.

Hand in hand with the business and technology revolutions that have developed since the late 20th century, radical social and cultural changes have taken place. Increased wealth, higher educational levels, a social dissolution of traditional relations and norms, huge information and communication potentials of the digital age, all this has contributed to bringing about a more individual lifestyle. People want to differentiate according to their personality and will no longer accept to be an anonymous member of a group or the masses. They want more quality in life, too, and each person is eager to decide for himself what is good for him.

As an integrated part of globalized business and individualized markets, the tourism industry was forced to reorganize and adapt their strategies to this changing world. The supply-driven pre-1990 mass tourism had to be customized according to the individual and upgraded demands of new and much more critical and demanding customers.

Modern Tourists

Pre-1990 mass tourists were homogeneous and predictable. They followed the same line along the whole vacation. They felt secure by travelling in numbers, and they took vacations where everything was prepaid and prearranged. Present-day tourists are different. They are spontaneous and unpredictable. They do not follow the same predictable lines either in travel or stay. They purchase different services in different price categories during the same trip. Current tourists want to be different from the crowd. They want to be individual and in control and make decisions for themselves.

Compared to previous generations, present tourists are used to travel and they are better educated and informed about the destinations they visit. Their attitudes are also different from the mass tourists. Unlike previous generations of tourists, they are concerned about the environment and cultures of the host countries they visit and take an interest in the different ways of life. Modern travellers are much more individual, wealthy, knowledgeable, experienced, independent and flexible, and more destination-focused than the mass tourist (Figure 8).

FIGURE 8

Old and New Tourists

Old Tourist	New Tourists
Inexperienced	Experienced
Homogeneous	Hybrid
Predictable	Unpredictable
Destination unimportant	Destination important
Get sunburnt	Active
Escape	Extension of life

Source: Based on Poon. Tourism, Technology and Competitive Strategies, 144.

Modern tourists make demands on all parts of their trip, especially experiences at the place of destination. These different demands imply that the tourist industry must market its products to individual travellers and not to groups or masses. In many ways, the production of tourist services is still based on economies of scale in the background of the supplying organizations, but their products have to be differentiated and multiplied instead of just one mass product, so-called 'dynamic packaging'. Customization of products enables tourist companies to provide flexible travel and other tourist services that meet the demands of modern consumers, including, for example, cruise lines with many different activities and vacations addressing different needs such as wild life, health, culture, shopping, bathing, etc. Fulfilling these new consumer demands require demand driven organizations and management which are able to focus on customers and able to innovate and individualize products. In the globalized and liberalized world of modern technologies, tourists can go almost anywhere and pick whatever companies they want to meet their demands when visiting a certain destination. Many companies have rushed to supply similar products to modern travellers, causing prices to go down, creating new routes, destinations, services and firms. The dynamics of tourism opens for consolidation on a global, regional and national level, but also for many innovative new companies that see new opportunities in the changing patterns of supply and demand.

The changing behavior of tourists can be seen everywhere in developed countries, in North America, Western Europe, East Asia and Oceania, including the rising middle classes of emerging societies. Everywhere tourists want experiences that add quality to their lives. That is also why they travel more often and although they are different and individual, you can identify certain common characteristics. In many ways, every generation seems to act in rather similar ways, and this allows the tourism industry to segment travelers according to age.[12]

Many present-day middle aged people and older people are well off, well educated, live longer and travel more than previous generations, and they also demand high quality travel experiences. These 'junior mates' or 'baby boomers' are the first post-war generation that qualifies for the designation 'new' tourists. They travel often and demand all kinds of cultural and learning activities, now that they no longer have children at home. They focus on life quality, and often organize their trip themselves. The next generation, born in the 1960s and 1970s, often consists of families with children living at home. They demand vacations suitable for both grown-ups and children. The generation of the 1980s and decades to come is so to speak born into a life based on individualism, welfare and new technologies. They want personal experiences and are frequent users of modern interactive and mobile technologies.

Across generations people want more quality from tourism experiences, including culture, nature, togetherness, health and some comfort. The spectrum of demands is wide, however, from the very active and participation vacations at the one end to visits to family and friends and shopping at the other end. People take short trips or long trips to one or more destinations and generally speaking, they want a more holistic experience.

In tourism, the growing number of middle-aged and old people has become increasingly important to the industry. They have got the money and inclination to travel. The age group between 25 and 44 years is still the largest traveling group of tourists in the world, but the age group between 45 and 64 is about to take that position, followed by the older people. Furthermore, the increasing share of older tourists will raise the demand for out-of-season travel. The number of handicapped travelers will

---

12   TIA. '*Travel Insights*', Aug. 2005: *www.tia.org*. EU/Leidner, Rüdiger (2004). *The European Tourism Industry.* Bruxelles: EU: *http://ec.euroe.eu.*

increase, too, for the simple reason that many old people are handicapped. In Western Europe and the United States, probably a quarter of the elders is handicapped.[13]

Whereas the share of middle aged and older tourists is rising, the share of holiday travelers and business travelers for decades has been roughly the same, namely 80 and 20 percent respectively. In relative economic terms, the economic importance of business travelers is much larger, however, because on average each business traveler spends twice as much money as a holiday traveler.

Looking at people's motive for traveling compared to pre-1990, travel patterns remain unchanged to a certain degree. Even though an increasing share of tourists travel to experience culture, sports and other such activities, the majority of West Europeans still travel in the summer time to the coast or warmer climates, at least for longer vacations. Many go for skiing during the winter vacation, too. City tourism is the second important goal for traveling. Out-of-season, tourist preferences are almost equally divided between nature, city and mountains. When including all short term travel, city traveling takes the leading place, however.[14] This is clearly seen in the USA, where statistics on tourist travel and behavior is more detailed than in Europe. In the United States, shopping is the most important reason for traveling, followed by visits to family and friends.[15] Many other and smaller tourism segments include, for instance, backpacking, hiking, biking, rural, adventure, eco, sex, and pilgrimage tourism.

Although tourists to some degree show common behavior according to age and motive, the increasing diversification of travel patterns makes it more and more difficult to categorize the nature of people's vacations. How should we define a vacation, starting off with a cultural city tour and ending up at the beach or playing golf? And what about eco-tourism? Is eco-tourism when you from your hotel watch animals that cannot be reached by car, or when you leave your car to watch them or go for a bicycle tour? Is the growing interest in cultural city tours perhaps just a consequence of rising wealth or have people really become more interested in culture? Generally speaking, vacations to a much greater degree than previously combine a mixture of motives, while many people at the same time organize their own travel, taking advantage of the Internet. Furthermore, in contrast to the the tourism industry, tourists look at their vacation activities as a whole, whereas the tourism industry is divided into several separately specialized industries. No current industry or company comprises all the activities along the travel value chain of tourism. As we shall see, leading tour-

---

13   EU/Leidner. The European Tourism Industry, 18. EU/Leidner, Rüdiger (2007). *The European Tourism Industry in the Enlarged Community.* Bruxelles: EU: *http://ec.euroe.eu.*

14   EU/Leidner. The European Tourism Industry, 15-26.

15   TIA. US Travel Market Overview.

ist corporations are seeking to cover more and more parts of the tourism value chain, however. Present-day tourism is certainly a buyer's market.

Tourists choose their destination before giving thought to the services they want. A destination is a geographical area and has a content that meets the demands of a certain group of tourists. Destinations are the stages where tourists realize their dreams. Whereas tourists at the destination demand services as a whole, the service providers are divided into several separate industries and companies, providing accommodation food and beverage, attractions, entertainment, transportation, etc. The destination seldom involves only one company. The destination encompasses a combination of companies organized around attractions that add extra value to these companies and as a whole attract customers to the area. From the point of view of the customer or tourist, there is rivalry between destinations and not between companies with regard to a certain destination. But once the tourist has arrived at a destination, the local companies compete to attract him. That is why local companies and authorities cooperate in marketing their destination to national and international customers and the arrival of the Internet has truly made that possible.

The tourism industry is not only driven by new customers, new ways of organization and better means of transportation. Increasingly, the new technologies of IT, the Internet and mobile phones have caused changes on the demand side as well as on the supply side. Within tourist companies and between these companies an integrated system of information and communication has been established. By way of the Internet, all tourist products have been made available to consumers, too. They are now visible and comparable, which has created a transparent market. At the same time, the increasing outsourcing and division of labor has made all parties of the tourist industry establish consumer sales channels of their own. By way of the Internet, consumers are now able to book and buy flights directly from airlines, hotel rooms at hotels, rental cars at rental companies and insurance at insurance companies. And if consumers wish, they may also use a travel agency to organize all these activities. Via the Internet, it is possible sometimes to make arrangements with attraction providers also. The different parts of the tourist industry have reacted to the rise of the buyer's market by extending their activities to include links to the whole tourist value chain. For example, airlines and ferries offer whole packages of travel and accommodation for summer and winter holidays. In other cases, operators containing cruise lines, amusement parks or other resorts seek to cover a whole vacation experience. All kinds of tourism services can be provided and obtained by way of the Internet and this has even paved the way for exclusive Internet tourist companies.

In all the current production and distribution of tourist services, information processing has become a clue to value creation in the tourism industry. Airlines, hotels, tour operators, travel agencies and destination companies all extend their activities and sales channels towards customers. In step with the redefinition and blurring of business borders, it is becoming still more important what activities you control in the tourism value chain and this has led to increased competition and remodeling of the tourism industry.

The Tourism Industry

The global tourism industry is big business. It accounts for almost four percent of total world GDP and its wider economic impacts are as high as some 10 percent of world GDP. The tourism industry embraces a number of functionally separate industries, including various forms of transportation (airlines, railways, cars, ferries, buses), accommodation (hotels, holiday homes, camping sites, etc.), food and beverage (restaurants, bars, etc.), attractions (cities, beaches, cultural monuments, museums, amusement parks, events etc.) and finally shopping (malls, fashion shops, etc.). While industries such as airlines, hotels and restaurants are clearly related to tourism and may be analyzed as separate industries, attractions and, even more, shopping are harder to picture precisely. In general, revenues of the individual tourism industries, and therefore total revenue, are based on estimates (Table 4).

TABLE 4

Global Sectors of the Tourism Industry in $bn and % shares, 2005

	$bn	%
Travel	600	35
Accommodation	350	20
Food	250	15
Attractions	500	30
Total Tourism Industry, $bn/ %	1700	100

Source: WTTC. World Tourism Satellite Account. Estimates based on national satellite accounts and revenues presented below.

The Value Chain

The tourism industry includes several sub-sectors. One part of the industry mainly focuses on bringing tourists abroad while other companies deal with incoming tourists from other countries and domestic tourists. In some cases, the same parties include outgoing as well as incoming tourism, for example airlines, and as a consequence of international consolidation the same large corporations serve tourists in many countries. The tourism industry comprises companies and industries related to one or more links of the total tourism value chain (Figure 9).

The core tourism industries are organized in a flow of activities, called the tourism system or tourism value chain. Some produce primary travel and tourism services, including transportation, accommodation, meals, electronic payment cards, insurance, car rental, taxis, and attractions. Airlines, railways, ferries, bus companies, car rental companies, taxi companies, and private cars take care of transportation, mainly airlines on international travels and cars for domestic travels. Accommodation and meals include hotels, holiday dwellings, camping sites, and restaurants.

FIGURE 9

The Tourism Industry Value Chain

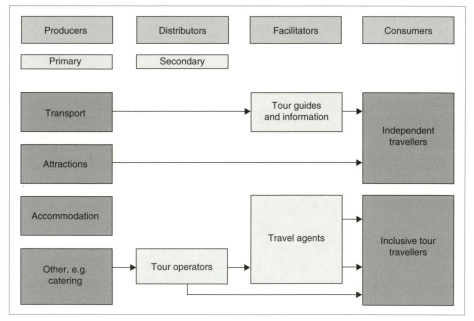

Source: EU/Leidner. The European Tourism Industry, 33.

To reduce the gap between the holistic approach of consumers and the particularity of tourism industries, consolidated companies seek to cover a wider spectrum of the

Global Experience Industries

tourism value chain, while some are almost all-inclusive, such as cruise lines and park resorts. The tourism products are distributed and facilitated by tour operators, travel agents, booking systems providers, incoming agents linking local travel organizers and tourists, tour guides and other travel information. Finally, the consumer or tourist is the customer of one or more of these services, depending on whether he buys inclusive tours or travel on his own. The consumers are the most important link in the value chain. There would be no tourism industry without them and in addition, the turn of power in favor of tourists has transformed a supply-driven industry into a demand-driven industry.

Tourism products are intangible services that exist only when being consumed. That is why distribution channels are of fundamental importance. Travel agencies and tour operators are primary distributors of tourism products, even though airlines, hotels and other tourism providers sell directly to tourists, too. Booking systems have become the predominant distribution channel of travel and leisure products. Some industries and companies provide services at the vacation destination, while others operate from the country of tourist origin. As consolidation expands, most involved companies operate in their home country as well as the country of destination, however. All these links of the tourism value chain are dependent on many sub-suppliers, including transportation means, IT and communication systems, catering, food and beverage industries, shops, marketing and other management services, etc.

Like all other businesses, tourism companies include a back office organization that provides the resources and support needed to run travel and tourist activities. The value chain of a tourism firm includes the following links:

- The company infrastructure: strategic management, planning, financing, accounting, law, authority relations
- Human resources: recruiting, learning, wages, rewarding, negotiations
- R & D: product and organizational development
- Technology: pervasive IT, communications and Internet
- Purchasing: as service providers, tourism companies are very dependent on efficient purchase of a wide variety of sources, for instance catering, accommodation and transportation
- Marketing and sales: product marketing and sales channels are crucial to the existence and competitiveness of tourism companies.

As a consequence of globalization, liberalization, new technologies and demanding consumers, the tourism companies' value chain is being changed. The traditional division of activities between tour operators, travel agencies, airlines, hotels, etc. is blurring. New strategies and business models are being launched as each company remodel their value chain to adapt itself to resourceful buyers that are increasingly able to organize travel and accommodation themselves, as they please.

Airlines, hotels and other transportation and accommodation providers can no longer allow marketing and sales to be left to travel organizers. Adapting their products to changing demands, they have to create direct channels to customers. Therefore, the traditional preserves of tour operators and travel agencies are being invaded by all other sub-sectors of the tourism industry. That includes global reservation systems and new web-based travel agencies, too. Pressure is being put on tour operators and travel agencies in particular and they have to come up with new flexible ways of creating value to customers. Competition on national, regional and global levels is increasing in all parts of the tourism industry, however. Also destinations and their service providers that may be reached via the Internet have to adapt to changing demands of customers, because they are also part of the global competition to attract tourists.

One way of upgrading the competitiveness of companies is to establish direct sales channels to customers. Extending activities to meet more and more of total tourist demands is another strategy taken by all parties. 'Holiday-makers' such as cruise lines and amusement parks and resorts are examples of total vacation services. At destinations, service providers are challenged by the changing consumer demands and a growing global competition to attract tourists. To meet this challenge and develop competitive strategies, companies at destinations have to cooperate with each other and the local authorities.

Tourist Information

From the point of view of the consumer, the tourist process starts with his/her need for information. Traditionally, this information was provided by travel agents, but nowadays increasingly via the Internet.[16] When you have decided on your destination, guide books are another traditional and widespread source of information. The next step is the decision to use individually organized transportation (e.g. car, airplane or railway) or a tour operator and whether you want to book directly or to do so through a travel agent. That includes the choice of accommodation, visiting local attractions, participating in organized activities and finally, the return journey.

The large economic importance of tourism, increasing competition and consumer

---

16   Jun, Hyon Soo, Vogt, Christine A., and MacKay, Kelly J. (2007). 'Relationships between Travel Information and Travel Product Purchase in Pretrip Contexts'. *Journal of Travel Research*, vol. 45, 266-274.

demands have caused tourism companies and tourism organizations to upgrade local and national information throughout most of the world.[17] Public tourist organizations coordinate national or local tourist information for all private and public service providers, linking companies of transportation, accommodation, entertainment, culture, etc. by way of their web sites. Consequently, every person with access to the Internet anywhere in the world might directly search relevant information and book and buy rooms, tickets, etc. according to his wishes. In many ways, each developed country present itself as a whole on the Internet, including detailed information on all parts of its tourism value chain. One Internet site gives you access to all national activities, for example visitbritain, visitfrance, germany-tourism, italiantourism, usatourist, visitjapan and cnta.gov for China. Finally, you have even global tourism information sites, such as virtualtourist and worldtravelguide. Much of this and other kinds of tourism information are being available on mobile phones, too.

The widespread use of web-based national tourism portals and interactive sites has reduced the importance of printed guide books, on the one hand. But on the other hand, the endless information opportunities on the Internet seem to have created greater interest in more knowledge and informative guides on individual destinations. The printed guide is still a widely used source of tourism information that has been around for almost two centuries.

During the 19th century, German Baedeker and British Murray pioneered the classical guide book. Baedeker continued as the well known Blue Guides in the 20th century.[18] After the Second World War, national travel publishing houses emerged in all developed countries, covering many parts of the world in their domestic language, for example Politiken in Denmark.[19] Large international guide book publishers such as Fodor's, Lonely Planet, Michelin and Rough Guides, have marketed guide books that cover most parts of the world.[20] Fodor's and Rough Guides are now part of two global media conglomerates, Bertelsmann and Pearson, respectively, just as other national guide book publishers are normally owned by large media corporations. This is part of the global consolidation process across any source of information and media.

A separate industry of maps is added to the industry of guide books.[21] These maps build on the works of scientifically based national institutions that are responsible for exact and detailed mapping of the individual country and who publish maps of their

---

17 EU/Leidner. The European Tourism Industry, 33-34.
18 *www.blueguides.com. www.wikipedia.org. 'Guide book'.*
19 *www.politikensforlag.dk.*
20 *www.fodors.com. www.lonelyplanet.com. www.roughguides.com*
21 *www.wikipedia.org. 'Map'.*

own, too. Internationally leading map corporations are for example French Michelin.[22] Just like guide books, maps have also been invaded by the Internet. Free maps of any global destination may be found on the Internet (for instance by Google) and this has made the map industry come up with new strategies and business models. Finally, electronic maps have found their way into cars, enabling the driver to guide him to his destination.

Current weather forecasting information is a natural part of all travel preparations as well as during the vacation itself. Tourists are informed by way of the Internet and other media that continuously are updated by international, national, and local weather report stations, based on meteorological organizations through out the world.[23] Skiing resorts even provide webcams to inform tourists of weather and skiing conditions.

Travel

Transportation is the largest sub-sector of the tourism industry. Of all transportation means, private cars are the most widely used way of domestic transportation for American tourists as well as for West European tourists.[24] In most cases, the tourist therefore uses his car instead of transportation companies. The expanding post-war car industry, petrol industry and freeway system have added much to the growing tourism industry. While cars dominate domestic transportation, airlines are the preferred way of international travelling. Less important are railways and ferries, and even more so busses. In economic terms, total global passenger transportation spending in 2005 was at least $2500 billion, of which the United States and Western Europe each shared one-third.[25] Perhaps one-third of all transportation spending may be accounted to tourism.[26] Most spending is attributed to cars, but an increasing share is spent on airlines. Because the car is a common daily transportation means, probably a higher share of spending on air transportation is attributed to tourism than private car transportation.

Although cars and airlines dominate passenger transportation, the large American and European national railway companies, such as Amtrak, Deutsche Bahn, French SNCF and British Arriva are all active suppliers of travel, including cooperative arrangements with other parts of the tourism value chain. For example, SNCF cooper-

---

22   www.michelin.com.
23   www.wikipedia.org. 'Weather forecasting'.
24   Eurostat. Panorama on Tourism, 31. TIA. U S. Travel Market Overview.
25   EU (2006). *Energy and Transport in Figures 2005*. US Census Bureau (2007). Statistical Abstracts. *Transportation: www.census.gov*.
26   EU/Leidner. The European Tourism Industry, 39.

ates with the large international hotel and service chain Accor.[27] Shipping companies, for example Stena Line and Scandlines cooperate with travel organizers and provide organized tours themselves.[28] Worldwide, ferries annually transport more than 1 billion passengers, half the number of airlines.[29] Cruise lines are a specialized kind of shipping company that encompass most parts of a vacation from beginning to end (see below). Compared to all these transportation industries, bus companies constitute a small business. Well known are the American Greyhound busses.

While the car industry is more indirectly a part of the tourism industry, airlines is clearly direct providers of tourism services.

The Airlines Industry

While most domestic tourists travel by car, international travel is dominated by airplanes, depending on the size of the country, too. Modern mass tourism depends on the enormous multitude of cars, airplanes and the industries that produce these transportation and energy means as well as a highly developed infrastructure allowing for fast and flexible movements around the world. The automobile industry and even more, the airplanes industry, is concentrated worldwide in a few global corporations, such as GM, Ford, Volkswagen, Peugeot/Citroën and Toyota and the two leading aircraft manufacturers American Boeing and West European Airbus. Transportation means producers are part of the tourism economy that work to make the tourism industry feasible and may be seen as impacts of the tourism industry, i.e. the tourism economy in a wider sense.

Whereas the global airplanes industry is highly concentrated within the Atlantic business community, the majority of the world's countries have one or more airlines. For historic reasons, one airline dominates in most countries, i.e. the airline that used to monopolize national flights. Alone, USA, Japan and China have more than one large airline. In Western Europe, the core area of international tourism, aviation is still dominated by the previous monopoly companies, led by Lufthansa, British Airways, Air France, SAS, Alitalia and Iberia. Liberalization of the air transportation has only to a certain degree resulted in a consolidation process, mainly because governments have kept ownership of national airlines. Since the late 1990s, however, liberalization, has given rise to new and expanding discount airlines. Ryanair and EasyJet have developed into two of Europe's largest airline companies, followed by other growing discount airlines such as Air

---

27 *www.sncf.com. www.accorhotels.com*
28 *www.stenalines.com. www.scandlines.com.*
29 Drewry (2006). *The European Ferry Industry: www.drewry.co.uk.*

Berlin. The USA aviation industry is also hit by the discount wave, Southwest Airlines being now one of the largest US airlines. The discount attack has threatened to ruin large and traditional airlines in United States and Western Europe. In order to survive, radical reforms have taken place in these airlines, cutting down costs by outsourcing and reorganizing from bureaucratic to flexible and market-oriented organizations.

FIGURE 10

Regional Revenues of the Global Airlines Industry in $bn, 2005

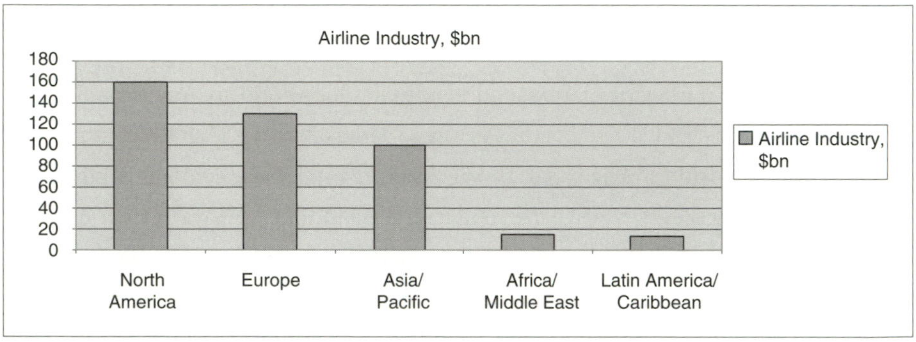

Source: ATW (2006). *World Airline Financial Results 2005: www.atwonline.com*.

The global airline industry is a gigantic business sector, including about nine hundred airline companies.[30] Annually, they transport a continuously growing number of passengers that reached about 2 billion in 2005, served by seventeen hundred airports and a route net counted in millions of kilometers. Until the 1990s, the majority of the global airline traffic took place in or between North America, Western Europe, Japan and Oceania. Within the past decade, the Chinese development has made East Asian aviation expand enormously. The three leading regions of North America, Western Europe and East Asia and Oceania now comprise more than 90 percent of global aviation (Figure 10). Airlines are crucial to international tourism and an important economic sector with global annual revenues of $500 billion. More than half of this income is made by the world's 20 largest airlines, such as Air France, Lufthansa, British Airways, SAS, and Ryanair in Western Europe, American Airlines, United Airlines, Delta Airlines, Northwest Airlines, and Continental Airlines in the US, and Japan Airlines and All Nippon in Japan.[31]

Even though airlines for historic reasons have been divided into many national

---

30 ATAG (2005). *The Economic & Social Benefits of Air Transport: www.atag.org*.
31 ATW. World Airline Financial Results 2005.

companies, they have for decades cooperated on a global scale enabling passengers to fly easily to most parts of the world. As a consequence of standardized tickets and economic sharing organized via IATA (International Air Transport Association), with one ticket you can reach your goal by way of all airlines needed.[32] Because discount airlines only sell tickets point-to-point they are excluded from this service.

Although the consolidation of airlines is moving on only slowly, liberalization and globalization have made airlines join in less binding ways. Three global alliances have emerged to achieve benefits of rationalization and improved customer services: Star Alliance, One World, and Sky Team.[33] The leading members of Star Alliance include United Airlines, US Airways, Air Canada, Lufthansa, SAS, Varig, Singapore Airlines, Thai Airlines and South African Airways. Included in One World are American Airlines, British Airlines, Iberia, Cathay Pacific Airways, Qantas Airways, Aer Lingus, Finnair, LAN and Japan Airlines. The third global alliance, Sky Team, comprises Delta Air, Continental Airlines, Northwest Airlines, Air France and KLM Royal Dutch Airlines, Alitalia, Aeroflot, CSA Czech Airlines, Aeromexico and Korean Air. The route net of each of the three alliances embraces practically the whole world, making them work almost as three large airlines. The majority of all business and holiday travelers fly by way of the members of the three alliances and their individual airlines that offer web-based booking and ticket sales, too. Furthermore, airlines cooperate with most of the other actors in international tourism, including tour operators, travel agencies, insurance companies, electronic card providers, car rental companies, etc.

Reservation Systems

The large American airlines played an active role in developing international tourism. Not only did they transport people, they also used the emerging liberalization of the 1980s to turn their reservation systems into a dynamic driver of many sub-sectors of tourism. The majority of travel agencies were being linked to the leading airlines' reservation systems, and by 1990 in the United States a triopole of American Airlines' SABRE, United Airlines' APOLLO, and WORLDSPAN, merged Trans World Airlines, Delta Air and Northwest Airlines, controlled 90 percent of all American travel agencies.[34]

Threatening to enter Europe, West European airlines quickly responded to the American challenge in reservation systems. First they tightened their hold on national

---

32 *www.iata.org.*
33 *www.staralliance.com. www.oneworld.com. www.skyteam.com.*
34 Christensen, Jens (2000). *IT and Business,* 178-182, 234-236, 370-371. Aarhus; Aarhus University Press. *www.sabre.com/history. www.galileo.com. www.worldspan.com/history.*

travel agencies. British Airways took control of Travicom and thereby most British travel agencies. In Germany, Lufthansa did the same through Start, and SAS through Smart in Scandinavia. Next, the airlines prepared for an approaching liberalization of West European aviation that inevitably would bring the larger American reservation systems into a stronger position, if no countermeasures were taken. In the late 1980s, the leading European airlines initiated the building of two common international reservation systems that on a global scale were able to make a stand against the American systems. Lufthansa, Air France, Iberia and SAS developed AMADEUS, while GALILEO was established by British Airways, Alitalia, Swissair, and KLM in cooperation with American APOLLO of United Airlines, which formed the basis of Galileo. Both systems 'took off' in the early 1990s, just before the liberalization of the European aviation market.

By way of the alliance with United Airlines, the four European airlines behind Galileo bridged the Atlantic, while Sabre was already moving into Western Europe. A similar development took place in Asia. Japan's largest airline company, All Nippon Airways, Hong Kong's Cathay Pacific Airways, and Singapore Airlines, developed their common reservation system ABACUS. By the end of the 1990s, Abacus merged with Sabre. Since the late 1990s, four reservation systems dominated world air transportation: Sabre, Galileo, Worldspan and Amadeus (reduced to three since 2006 when Galileo merged with Worldspan under the name Travelport).

As a consequence of liberalization or deregulation, the four global reservation systems eventually separated from their mother companies and were turned into independent global distribution companies open to any customer, although mother companies kept a preferred position in a transition period. Large databases of these distribution systems contained all vital travel information and became the basis of linking sellers and buyers of travel services and eventually many other kinds of tourism services, including every form of transportation, accommodation, car rental, insurance, travel agencies, etc. At the same time, the booking systems of the individual airlines were reduced to internal warehouses.

Hardly had the four systems conquered the world market of travel information distribution when they were challenged by a new technology, the Internet. The breakthrough of the Internet since the late 1990s paved the way for web-based travel agencies that threatened to reduce the global reservation systems into pure transaction systems. At the same time, these online travel agencies and tour operators were not only customers of the large distribution systems but also their competitors. Sabre, Galileo, Worldspan and Amadeus met the new challenge in two ways. Firstly, they developed improved search and decision support systems to their many customers in the travel business. Secondly, they started or bought strong and expanding online travel agencies to create the vital direct link to consumers.

The competition in consumer distribution channels intensified. All actors moved their activities upwards in the value chain from simple distribution to online services. In the same way, airlines built web-based links to their customers, as did Sabre, Galileo, Worldspan and Amadeus, as well as web-based travel agencies and tour operators. Since the early 2000s, distribution companies, airlines, travel agencies and tour operators, and even hotels and other services providers of the tourism industry, have all established online relations to consumers.

Travel Agencies and Online Distribution

Until recently, travel agencies have been the key intermediary between travel suppliers and consumers. However, the breakthrough of IT and in particular the Internet has allowed travel suppliers and consumers to interact directly, thus threatening the existence of the traditional travel agent.[35] As a consequence, airlines, hotels and other suppliers are on the one hand invading the travel agent market, and on the other hand, consumers increasingly turn to independent travel. To meet the increasing competitive pressure of tourism suppliers and changing consumer behaviour, the travel agencies have responded by a radical move into online distribution and by widening their tourism services to include virtually all aspects of a travel.[36] New online agencies are rapidly replacing the traditional agencies, or traditional agencies are upgrading to online distribution.

The online travel agencies are expanding immensely, first in the US, then in Western Europe, followed by Asia Pacific, Eastern Europe and Latin America. The Atlantic community remains the core of this business sector. In North America, Expedia, Sabre/Travelocity and Travelport/Orbitz quickly conquered a large share of the market. Expedia, Travelocity, Travelport/ebookers and Amadeus/Opodo took the lead in Western Europe. The online intermediaries expanded so rapidly that they began to overtake traditional agencies. By 2005 in the US, Expedia ranked three, behind the industry leaders based on business travel American Express Business Travel and Carlson Wagonlit Travel, and BCD Travel and Travelocity ranking four and five. By 2005, the global online travel market was an estimated $15 billion, probably half of all travel agencies' revenues. Gross' sales were up to five times higher. The largest market

---

35   Cheyne, Jo, Mary Downes, and Stephen Legg (2005). 'Travel Agent vs. Internet: What Influences Travel Consumer Choices'? *Journal of Vacation Marketing*, vol. 12, 41-57. Hyde, Kenneth F. and Rob Lawson (2003). 'The Nature of Independent Travel'. *Journal of Travel Research*, vol. 42, 13-23.

36   Dolnicar, Sara and Christian Laesser (2007). 'Travel Agency Marketing Strategy: Insights from Switzerland'. *Journal of Travel Research*, vol.46, 133-146.

was the US, followed by Western Europe. Online developments in the United States were about two years ahead of Western Europe.

The new online intermediaries have mainly used two business strategies, the merchant model and dynamic packaging. In the merchant model, the intermediary receives an inventory of products and services from suppliers at negotiated rates. The online intermediary then determines the price of the final product and service by including costs and a profit. Dynamic packaging is the term for a user-centerd, cheaper and more flexible way of assembling and booking a personalised holiday through the Web. In other words, the Internet has allowed for a radical retransformation and recombination of all links in the travel value chain.

The breakthrough of online travel agencies and the upgrading of global distribution systems as well as the interrelated ownership and cooperation between the wholesale and retail level of travel intermediaries have led to a consolidation of this industry around a few distribution companies and their included online travel agencies. Within a few years since the turn of the millennium, they have come to dominate global travel distribution and sales.

Sabre

Being the reservation system of American Airlines since the 1960s, Sabre has for decades been the trend-setter for airline reservations and distribution systems.[37] Sabre provides IT solutions to its mother company and other airlines, too. As a consequence of deregulation and liberalization, Sabre Holdings Corporation was formed in the 1990s. With the breakthrough of the Internet, Sabre added Travelocity, an online travel agency, to its distribution system. Past the turn of the millennium, it starts to become increasingly obvious that the Internet opens for radical changes in the travel and tourism industry. The central point is moving upwards to online systems giving consumers direct access to book and buy almost any travel service. Just as the global distribution systems of the 1990s reduced the airlines' reservation systems to mere internal information warehouses, the online travel agencies of the 2000s are about to turn the distribution systems into simple transaction bases. In order to avoid being left behind, Sabre invested heavily in making a strong position in the expanding online business as well as in upgrading its distribution system. Like many other corporations, Sabre was taken over by an investment company at the end of 2006, having no influence on its strategy, however.

In 2005, Sabre had total revenues of $2.5 billion and in 2006, $2.7 billion. 60 per-

---

37   www.sabre.com

cent stemmed from its distribution system, 30 percent from Travelocity and 10 percent from its IT solutions.[38] Following the sluggish years of 2001 to 2004, revenues take off from 2005. The online business expands strongly, and by merging with lastminute.com, Travelocity almost doubles its income and moves into a position as one of the world's leading travel agencies. It provides travel information, booking and sales to holiday and business travelers as well as travel producers. Furthermore, Travelocity extends its business to include almost every kind of travel service to holiday and business travelers.

The distribution system of Sabre Travel Network is upgraded, too. On the one hand, this network works as the wholesale of travel information for Travelocity, the retailer. On the other hand, Sabre Travel Network provides similar information to several airlines, railway companies, cruise ships, car rental companies, hotels, tour operators, travel agencies, insurance companies, etc. By upgrading and extending its services, Sabre Travel Network penetrates further into the value chain of its customers, paving the way for airlines and others to outsource their booking portals. By 2007 in addition to numerous travel producers, more than 50000 thousand travel agencies in plus one hundred countries on all continents use Sabre Travel Network.

TABLE 5

Revenues of Global Travel Agencies and Distribution Companies in $bn, 2007

	Travel agencies	Travel databases	Total
Sabre	1.1	1.6	2.7
Amadeus	1.0	1.7	2.7
Travelport	1.1	1.8	2.9
Worldspan	0.9	-	0.9
Priceline.com	1.1	-	1.1

Source: *www.sabre-holding.com. www.amadeus.com. www.travelport.com. www.worldspan.com. www.priceline.com*. Estimates, excluding IT solutions for airlines.

In 2006, Sabre Travel Network had an estimated 30 percent global market share of travel distribution, leaving the remaining market share to its three competitors Amadeus, Travelport (Galileo) and Worldspan (Table 5). All four companies provide almost the same services. Sabre Travel Network competes by upgrading its products to more comprehensive solutions, in cooperation with Travelocity, too. New competitors have entered the travel distribution market, however, which have made this market more

---

38   Sabre (2007). *Annual Report 2006: www.sabre.com.*

complex and marked by intensive competition. For example, strong search companies such as Google and Yahoo offer combined searching across travel producers, travel agencies and other travel related websites. As countermeasures towards this blurring of industry boundaries, Sabre Travel Network has partnered with Yahoo!, AOL and American Express. Finally, new alternative distribution system providers covering more narrow market segments and with limited functionality competed by way of low prices, for example ITA Software, G2 Switchworks and Farelogix.

Sabre Travel Network also competes with airlines that have developed web-based consumer booking systems and sales channels of their own. Simultaneously, the airlines put pressure on the global distribution systems by requiring reduced prices. A reverse development is seen, too, as some airlines begin outsourcing the operation of their sales channels to Sabre, for example US Airways and Delta.[39] Business men and holiday travelers are not really interested in shopping from one airline website to another.

The direct marketing and sales of travel services take place through Travelocity. Buying lastminute.com is an important part of Travelocity's expansion plan. But it includes much more than that. Several other online travel agencies are bought, including Scandinavian Rejsefeber, and the global car rental firm HolidayAutos.com. Through subsidiary companies and acquisition of other companies and brands outside its main basis in the USA, Travelocity has positioned itself in, for example, Canada, Mexico, UK, Germany, France, Scandinavia, Japan, and Australia.

Travelocity's main competitors are Expedia, Orbitz and ebookers, Priceline, the leading US and world travel agencies, as well as Opodo in Europe.[40] A new group of competitors are emerging based on information consolidators and consumer generated content (see below: Social Travel Networking). To meet these challenges Travelocity will have to upgrade to a higher level of competitiveness based on consumer interaction.

Travelport/Galileo and Worldspan

Just like Sabre was disengaged from American Airlines during the 1990s, the distribution system Galileo was separated from its mother companies United Airlines, British Airways and KLM, as was Worldspan from Delta Air Lines and Northwest Airlines.[41]

---

39   Information Week. 2.2.2006.
40   EU (2006). *ICT and e-Business in the Tourism Industry*. Sector Report No. 8/2006: *www.union-network. org. www.wikipedia.org*. 'Computer reservation systems'.
41   *www.galileo.com. www.travelport.com. www.worldspan.com*.

Galileo was taken over by investor companies, first Cendant and renamed Travelport.[42] Travelport includes the distribution system Galileo, the online travel agencies Orbitz and eBookers as well as the wholesale travel provider Gulliver's Travel Associates. By the end of 2006, the travel and tourism activities of Cendant were spun-off to the investor company Blackstone Group. At the same time, Blackstone acquired Worldspan, owned by Worldspan Technologies. The two companies merged to form a stronger Travelport, becoming thereby the world's largest distribution system in addition to its leading online travel agencies.[43]

Merged Travelport and Worldspan complement each other well. Worldspan is a world leader in IT and web-solutions for travel distributors and intermediaries, covering more than half the world's online transactions of the travel and tourism industry. Most of Worldspan's revenues originate from the USA. In reverse, Travelport, of which Galileo is the largest part, receives most of its revenues from outside the USA. Concerning online travel agencies, Orbitz is strong in the USA and eBookers in Western Europe. The new Travelport has annual revenues of almost $4 billion. Tens of thousands of travel agencies around the world, hundreds of airlines and several car rental companies, cruise ships and railway companies, etc. depend on the travel information and solutions of Travelport.

Amadeus

In the 1990s, Amadeus started as a mutual distribution company owned by four European airlines, Lufthansa, Air France, Iberia and SAS, of which SAS gave up its ownership.[44] Gradually Amadeus expanded into a global distribution company that loosened bonds to its mother airlines. In 2005, Amadeus was taken over by the investor group WAM Acquisition. Although Amadeus expanded world wide, Europe remained its main base and market, serving primarily airlines, just like the other two large distribution systems. In 2005, Amadeus had revenues of $2.5 billion.[45]

Similar to the other two leading distribution systems, Amadeus operates numerous airline reservation and booking systems, and in addition tens of thousands of travel agencies who provide travel information about tour operators, cruise lines, ferry lines, railway companies, car rental companies, hotels, insurance companies, etc. Like the other distribution companies, Amadeus meets the increasing competition from web-based travel intermediaries by upgrading its services and redefining its business model

---

42   *www.cendant.com. www.blackstonegroup.com*
43   *www.cendant.com. www.blackstonegroup.com.*
44   *www.amadeus.com.*
45   Amadeus (2005). *Annual Report 2004-2005.*

to include more and more parts of the customers' value chain. At the same time, several online travel agencies have been acquired, including e-Travel, a leading provider of 'hosted' technology products for business travel, the British online Travel agency, Quest Travel, specializing in overseas travel, French Vivacances, Italian E-viaggi and Scandinavian Travellink. Furthermore, together with nine European airlines, Amadeus set up the online travel agency, Opodo.[46] Through Amadeus e-Travel Management, Amadeus provides travel solutions and information for leading European corporations and governments, too.

As a consequence of this massive offensive and strategic remodelling, Amadeus is able to meet the challenges of the Internet and consolidate its position as one of three leading global travel intermediaries. Furthermore, Amadeus is a global leader in IT and web-solutions to the same group of travel providers and is partnering with ITA, BroadVision and SAP to develop new and more advanced e-commerce solutions to the travel industry. Partnerships with Terra Lycos, the world's third largest general web portal, and the travel portals of Spanish Rumbo and French Vivacances in cooperation with Groupe Galeries Lafayette is meant to strengthen Amadeus' sales channels to consumers. By way of the Internet and changing strategies, Amadeus connectes more closely with travel producers and consumers, providing total solutions and also being part of a global consolidation that blurs traditional boundaries of industries.

Expedia

Since 2005, Expedia is the largest online travel agency of the expanding online market.[47] Expedia, Inc. is the parent company of some of the world's leading travel companies that provide travel products and services for holiday and business travel in the United States and the rest of the world. Until 2005, Expedia is part of the investor group InterActive Corp. (IAC). During the second-half of the 1990s and the early 2000s, IAC launches a comprehensive acquisition process of companies in e-commerce, including online travel agencies such as Expedia.com and Hotels.com. A business unit of online travel agencies is concentrated under Expedia, Inc., including Expedia.com, Hotels.com, Hotwire.com, TripAdvisor, Expedia Corporate Travel and Classic Vacations, among many other US and international companies. Its main market is the United States. In 2005, Expedia had revenues of almost $3 billion. Like other leading online travel agencies, Expedia provides travel information for many airlines, hotels, cruise

---

46   *www.opodo.com*
47   *www.expedia.com.*

lines, car rental companies, etc. and for consumers everywhere. Towards consumers, Expedia uses the 'merchant' business model that allows people to book tickets, rooms, etc. directly on the web, while the 'agency' business model just takes care of transactions for other travel providers. Unlike the other online travel agencies, Expedia has no historic links to the leading airlines.

Expedia competes in a rapidly developing market of increasingly intense competition. Online travel services are a strongly growing market. From a small start in the early 2000s, it is expanding enormously to cover about one-third of the US market in 2005 but just one-tenth of the European market. By 2010 however, online travel booking and sales is projected to be the most common distribution form.

Expedia competes with online as well as offline travel companies and any other travel provider for that matter. The strength of Expedia is its ability to provide services to many suppliers. Expedia feels the increasing competition from the vertically expanding travel providers and distribution companies as well as new competitors such as search machine operators that collect prices and other information from many sites, especially Google and Yahoo.

The global online travel agency companies are concentrated in the US. The US online travel market is also the largest in the world, followed by Western Europe and Eastern Asia, mainly Japan (Table 6).

TABLE 6

The Global Online Travel Agencies Market in $bn and % Shares, 2001-2010

	Revenues $bn	Share of Total Market	Revenues $bn	Share of Total Market	Revenues $bn	Share of Total Market
	2001	2001	2005	2005	2010	2010
USA	10	6	60	26	100	35
Western Europe	3	1	30	10	70	25
Rest of the World	2	1	20	5	40	15

Source: Markussen, Carl H. (2003). *Trends in the US Online Travel Market 2000-2002: www.crt.dk*. Clikz. *The US Online Travel Market*, 10.11.2004: *www.clickz.com*. New Media Review (2006). *The Online Travel Market: www.etcnewmedia.com*. Markussen, Carl H. (2007). *Trends in European Internet Distribution of Travel and Tourism Services: www.crt.dk* 'The Rest of the World' is estimated.

Social Travel Networking

So, online you can access one of the big travel agencies such as Expedia, Travelocity and Orbitz for airfare, hotel and car rental, etc. But innovation and competition do not stop there. A whole new set of travel websites and services have emerged within recent years.[48] One response is to pull data from a variety of sources enabling you to compare airfares, hotel prices, etc.

Kayak.com is such an aggregator of travel information, finding the perfect flight, hotel, cruise, or rental car.[49] Once the choice is made, the consumer is linked to the travel sites to make his purchase at will. Unlike online travel agencies, Kayak is not a store and does not sell anything. It just searches for travel goods across the Web and provides details on hundreds of options without any hidden agenda or biased displays. And the information is free to use. Kayak was started in 2004 by the founders of Orbitz, Travelocity and Expedia, the three worldwide leading online travel agencies, who wanted to create a better and more user-oriented online travel service. Kayak makes money when travelers click on its advertisements and on the results from travel suppliers such as airlines, hotels and rental car companies. This is a revenue model similar to Google and Yahoo. Yahoo and Google have developed aggregate travel services, too, and form tough competitors to Kayak in the rising industry of aggregate travel information that also includes SideStep and Farecast. This industry of consolidated travel information and supplier links is directly challenging the online agencies.

A different source of innovation and competition to online travel agencies springs from the rapid rise of virtual communities on the Internet. Since 2007, some few hundred million users have joined large communities such as YouTube, MySpace and Facebook.[50] The success of these communities quickly caught the interest of leading media and online companies. In 2006, the media conglomerate News Corp. acquired MySpace and Google bought YouTube. In 2007, Microsoft followed suit and invested in Facebook. These three broad community sites function as widely-used communication forums for the new Internet generation. By way of expensive advertisement deals, the leading search engines of Google, Yahoo and Microsoft make sure that they have access to a worldwide audience through three communities.

Soon people with like interests began to divert into specialized sites. Some of these sites deal with traveling. Travelers meet on the Internet to share information on destinations, means of transportation, hotels, etc. in several sites. TripAdvisor is perhaps the largest travel community in the world, attracting more than 30 million monthly visitors.[51] What TripAdvisor does is to provide travel information by creating a web

---

48   *www.etcnewmedia.com*
49   *www.kayak.com.*
50   *www.youtube.com. www.myspace.com. www.facebook.com.*
51   *www.tripadvisor.com.*

service open for travelers, but does not take reservations. It is a free travel guide that offers reviews and information to help plan a vacation.

TripAdvisor is an example of a new and growing trend of consumer generated media and recommendations that are shown to have a big impact on buyer choices. Just as the general communities of YouTube, MySpace and Facebook caught the interest of leading search engine providers and led to mergers, so the challenged group of online agencies has moved quickly to become part of these new developments. Accordingly Expedia has taken over the ownership of TripAdvisor.[52] Travelocity and Orbitz are moving in the same direction, offering a new social networking component with realtime updates and tips from travelers. Professionals also offer reviewing of hotels and restaurants in a particular site.[53] Some sites combine user-generated reviews, meta-search capabilities and social networking (inter alia TripAdvisor, Kayak plus Facebook) for personalized hotel recommendations and booking at best prices, such as VibeAgent.com.

Generally speaking there is on the one hand a trend towards one-stop shop for travel information of almost any kind and on the other hand, this is increasingly based on consumer input and dialog. Service upgrading by offering total travel plans in one itinerary is also seen. It is all a matter of making it easier for the consumer, informing the consumer better, and making the consumer wishes come true. Finally, new sites and online travel agencies including consumer recommendations seek to match different travel personalities with best destinations. Travelers take a test and are classified into one of six travel personalities, ranging from 'ventures' who take extreme risks to 'authentics' who want a relaxing vacation.[54]

Tour Operators

Traditionally, and until the 1990s, the tour operator was a wholesaler that packaged travel products like flight seats and hotel rooms to be sold through the travel agency retailer. The tour operator was the intermediary between airlines, hotels and other producers and the travel agencies that sold the travel products to the consumers.[55] Being of less significance in the US, the tour operator was an important part of the West European tourism industry. As a result the global tour operator industry was concentrated in Western Europe. Radical changes in tourism since the 1990s have

---

52   *www.expedia.com.*
53   *www.professionaltravelguide.com.*
54   *www.besttripchoices.com.*
55   EU/Leidner. The European Tourism Industry, 33-35.

reduced the importance of tour operators, but still in the 2000s they operate one-third of all long European vacations. Since the 1990s, the tour-operating or package-tour industry is continuously being consolidated.[56]

The total European tour-operator market in 2005 amounted to some $80 billion, embracing at least half the world tour-operator market.[57] In Western Europe, there are about 150000 tour operators and travel agencies, probably one-third of world total. Most of the European travel market is consolidated in a few large tour operators that also control most travel agencies. The top 8 tour operators control two-thirds of the market (Figure 11). In 2007, TUI and Thomas Cook merged with First Choice and My Travel respectively, consolidating their position as the world's two leading tour operators.

Figure 11

Europe's Top Eight Tour Operators' Revenues in $bn, 2007

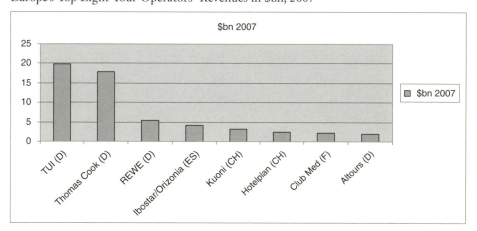

Source: Annual reports.

TUI

In 2005 and 2006, TUI (Touristik Union International) was the world's largest tour operator with travel revenues of $22 billion, two-thirds of total group revenues.[58] The company used to be called Preussag and did not engage in tourism until 1998 when it acquired Hapag-Lloyd's tourism company and started a comprehensive acquisition process of tourism companies while quitting most other fields of business. Under its

56   Research on the tour operating industry is sparse, see for instance: Dale, Christie (2001). 'The UK Tour-Operating Industry: A Competitive Analysis'. *Journal of Vacation Marketing*, vol. 6, 357-367.
57   Kuoni (2006). *Annual Report 2005*, 56-57: *www.kuoni.com*.
58   TUI (2006-2007). *Annual Reports 2005 and 2006: www.tui.com*.

new name TUI since 2002, it continues to consolidate the tour operator business by acquiring airlines, tour operators, travel agencies, hotels, etc. and establishing national subsidiaries in one European country after another. TUI has been expanding beyond Western Europe into Eastern Europe, North America and Asia. By 2006, TUI comprised about 4000 travel agencies, including incoming agencies, numerous national tour operators, a large fleet of airplanes, several brand hotel chains and other hotels and a few cruise lines. The reduced and changing tourism markets in the early 2000s made TUI carry out a radical reorganization process to reduce costs. They introduced the dynamic package business model to meet the demands of the modern tourist that often required individual vacation modules and discount flights.

Since the early 2000s, TUI has established a leading position in the largest tour operator markets of Germany, UK, France, Benelux and Scandinavia. In 2005, TUI was much larger than number two, Thomas Cook, followed by MyTravel, REWE, First Choice and Kuoni. A new wave of mergers took place in 2007 when Thomas Cook merged with MyTravel and TUI with First Choice, both British tour operators.[59] By 2007, TUI and Thomas Cook controlled almost half the European and maybe one-third of the global tour operator market.

FIGURE 12

The TUI Tourism Value Chain

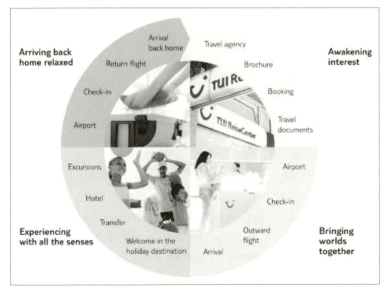

Source: *www.tui-group.com*.

---

59   *www.tui-group.com. www.thomascookgroup.com.*

TUI is a vertically integrated travel company dealing with almost all parts of the tourism value chain (Figure 12). It includes distribution through travel agencies or via its own direct sales channels through the Internet, call centers and travel television. TUI sells package tours and individually booked travel modules and transports travelers to and fro vacation destinations on its own fleet of airplanes with busses connecting airports to property hotels, adapting to peak seasons by way of third party airlines and hotels. Through third-party agreements, TUI provides additional travel services such as car rental and insurance. It is TUI's strategy to continue its global expansion and determinedly gain all benefits of the Internet by more and more direct sales to consumers. TUI's main market is Germany that has the largest number of package tour travelers of all nations, followed by UK, Scandinavia and the rest of Western Europe. By way of its merger with First Choice, TUI has extended its British market considerably.

In 2007, the acquired First Choice was the fourth largest European tour operator with revenues of $5 billion.[60] Like TUI, First Choice comprises most of the tourist value chain, including package tours, individual travels with airplanes, cruise lines, and even camping and biking tours. First Choice has its own airline fleet, hotels, travel agencies and many subsidiaries. Through third parties, First Choice arranges car rental, insurance and other travel activities. The UK is its main market.

Thomas Cook and MyTravel

Thomas Cook originated back in the 19th century when it pioneered mass tourism in the UK.[61] Throughout the 20th century, it remained a leading international tour operator. In the 1990s, Thomas Cook was taken over by a German capital group that started a process of consolidation along with other tour operators. By its merger with MyTravel in 2007, Thomas Cook becomes one of the two worldwide leading tour operators. Most of its total $16 billion sales lie in Western Europe, with Germany and the UK being the two predominant markets. Thomas Cook comprises many firms within most parts of the travel value chain, including tour operators and their subsidiaries, travel agencies, airlines and hotels. The economic crisis of the early 2000s, forced Thomas Cook to carry out a radical reorganization process similar to other large tour operators. Focus is strengthened on its core business by introducing the dynamic packing strategy, by replacing much capital bindings with third-party purchases, and by upgrading the use of the Internet as sales channel. In this way, Thomas Cook is to

---

60   *www.firstchoice.co.uk*
61   Thomas Cook Group (2006-07). *Annual Reports 2006-07: www.thomascookgroup.com.*

a higher degree turned into a distribution company where customers, via its website, can book and buy travel, accommodation, car rental, etc.

With annual revenues in 2007 of $5.5 billion, the acquired travel corporation MyTravel is one-third the size of Thomas Cook.[62] 60 percent of its sales stem from the UK, 25 percent from Scandinavia and 15 percent from North America. By merging with the two large Scandinavian tour operators Spies and Tjaereborg in the 1990s, MyTravel creates also a stronghold in Scandinavia. As a result of deficits in the early 2000s, MyTravel sells most of its airline fleet and reorganizes according to the dynamic packaging strategy and use of third-party providers. MyTravel complements Thomas Cook in its main markets making Thomas Cook a market leader in the UK and some other European countries.

In 2006, merged Thomas Cook and MyTravel have combined annual revenues of $21 billion, Thomas Cook 16 $bn and MyTravel $5 bn. The Thomas Cook Group is no. 1 in the UK, France, Scandinavia and Hungary, and no. 2 in Germany (after TUI and closely followed by REWE), Poland and Austria.

REWE

German REWE is part of a large retail corporation.[63] Since the turn of the 20th century, REWE's tourist division has expanded much and is now the third-largest European tour operator. By way of acquisitions such as the DER Group and the LTU Airline, including Jahn Reisen, it reaches revenues of $5.5 billion in 2007, just 10 percent of the total revenues of its mother group.

Kuoni

Swiss Kuoni has taken almost the same road as REWE, becoming the fourth-largest European tour operator with 2007 revenues of $4 billion.[64] Unlike the other European tour operators, however, Kuoni mainly offers intercontinental tours to Africa, South East Asia and Central America, but it is expanding increasingly in European travel, too. Until the 1990s, Kuoni was primarily a Swiss based company, but then launched an international expansion that made it one of the consolidating companies of the tour operator industry. Kuoni expanded in North America, Asia and Europe, including its neighbouring countries and Scandinavia.

---

62   MyTravel (2006-07). *Annual Reports 2005-06: www.mytravel.com.*
63   *www.rewe-group.com.*
64   *www.kuoni.com.*

Business Travel Agencies

Carlson Wagonlit

Together with American Express and BCD, American Carlson Wagonlit (CWT) constitutes the world's three leading business travel agencies.[65] CWT is part of the larger Carlson Companies. Since the 1960s, and especially during the 1980s and 1990s, Carlson Companies expanded by several acquisitions in more and more parts of the tourism value chain, mainly in business travel. In 1997, when the Carlson Travel Group merged with French Accor's Wagonlit Travel and formed Carlson Wagonlit Travel, it created the first truly global business travel agency with three thousand offices in one-hundred-and-fifty countries. Carlson Companies includes two other travel subsidiaries, Carlson Leisure Travel Services, including many travel agencies, tour operators and cruise lines, as well as Carlson Hotel Worldwide, for example the hotels of Radisson and Friday's. The total travel business revenues of Carlson Companies amounted to $20 billion in 2007.

American Express Business Travel

Since the mid-19th century, American Express has been a leading American company of money transportations and money transfers.[66] During the 20th century, American Express began to organize business travel and to a minor degree holiday travels, including cruise lines. Electronic cards are a third business area which has developed since the 1960s. American Express had total revenues of $27 billion in 2007.

BCD Travel

TQ3 is a business travel agency equally owned from 2004 to 2006 by TUI, the world's largest tour operator, and Navigant International, the second largest US business travel agency.[67] TQ3 had revenues of $10 billion in 2005, doing business in 80 countries. While Navigant kept its share, in 2006 TUI sold its part to Dutch BCD. Simultaneously, BCD changed its strategy from being a business travel organizer to becoming a global travel logistics provider. BCD is the third largest business travel agency (next to American Express and Carlson Wagonlit) with revenues of $12 billion in 2007 and activities in almost one hundred countries. The merger has made BCD market leader in several European countries, including Germany, Benelux and Denmark, and among the top five in USA, UK and Italy.

---

65   www.carlson.com.
66   www.americanexpress.com
67   www.tq3.com www.bcd-nv.com.

Cruise Lines

Cruise vacations have become a popular way of spending a holiday.[68] A cruise is an all-inclusive holiday on board a large ship, including stopovers at different ports of call. All kinds of entertainment and comfort are found on board the ships, including delicious food, good music and dancing, swimming pools, sports facilities, cinemas, gaming, wellness facilities, medical care, etc. all of which are meant to give you good experiences in company with hundreds of people, mostly middle aged and older.

Like most other tourism sectors, cruising developed in the US before it spread to the rest of the world.[69] For decades, Americans have been able to take cruises to the Caribbean, along the North American West coast up to Alaska, to Hawaii, the Far East and Europe. In the 1990s, cruise lines were introduced to Europe, too. Norwegian, German, British, Dutch and Italian shipping companies began investing in cruise ships and started to organize trips for Europeans around the Baltic coasts, along the Norwegian west coast, across the Atlantic and in the Mediterranean, just like the American cruise lines increasingly brought American tourists to Europe. For example, a leading international cruise line harbour has been developed in Copenhagen.[70] Cruise tours re-created some of the glamour that surrounded the Atlantic Ocean liners between the two World Wars. The shipping companies address customers directly through the Internet or via travel agencies that increasingly put cruises on their agenda.

Cruise lines are an American invention, and American tourists and shipping companies have continued to dominate this business into the new millennium. The number of cruise-passengers keeps on growing, having reached 11 million in 2004, of which some 80 percent were Americans.[71] Direct revenues of the industry are $20 billion and the deriving economic effects twice as much, corresponding to one percent of total tourism revenues. More than half the American cruise lines leave from Florida. Continued growth is projected for the cruise line industry that might double its revenues within the next decade.[72] The popularity of cruise tours may be seen from the fact that every sixth American at one time or another has been on a cruise vacation. Most passengers are middle aged and older.[73]

Like any other industry, the international expansion of cruise line tours has resulted in a global consolidation process around a few companies. American Carnival Cruise Lines of the Carnival Corporation and the Royal Caribbean are the world's two largest

---

68   Cruise Lines International Association (ICCL): *www.iccl.org*.
69   ICCL (2005). *The Cruise Industry, 2004: www.iccl.org*.
70   Cruise Copenhagen: *www.cruisecopenhagen.com*
71   ICCL. The Cruise Industry.
72   Seatrade (2007). *Cruise Report 2007: www.seatrade-global.com*.
73   Cruise Line International Association (CLIA) (2006). *CLIA 2006. Cruise Market Profile*.

cruise lines, followed by Star Cruises in Asia Pacific.[74] Most independent cruise lines have been swallowed by the global consolidation process of these three leading cruise lines.

Electronic Cards

Around 1960, American Express and Hilton Hotel Corporation launched the world's first electronic payment cards.[75] It took a decade, before the American banks engaged in electronic cards when Visa and Master Card were introduced.[76] Even today, Visa, Master Card and American Express are the most widely used electronic payment cards. With payment cards, one no longer depends on travels checks. Since the 1960s and 1970s, Americans spread the use of electronic cards throughout the world, much supported by its leading airlines and hotel chains. The Europeans did not adopt electronic cards until the 1980s, but until the 1990s, electronic cards were mainly used by business travellers. In addition to travel use, electronic cards were being gradually used in shopping stores. It was the spread of the computer and communication technologies that opened the road to electronic cards, because electronic systems require the quick transferring of payment information between airlines, hotels, and banks, including authorisation of cards and services in relation to lost and stolen cards, etc.

Currently, Visa and Master Card are internationally the most used electronic payment cards, followed by American Express. They are all separate companies of their own. VISA is a partnership of more than 20,000 financial businesses, 20 million companies and 1 billion users around the world.[77] VISA originated from Bank of America and was turned into an independent company in the 1970s. Globally, VISA had its real breakthrough in the 1990s. In 2007, VISA had revenues of some $20 billion and is used in about 200 countries.

Master Card is the other large international electronic payment card.[78] Like Visa, it derived from the American banking sector, and has about the same global extension as Visa. American Express started in the 19th century as a company for money transfers.[79] Since the 1960s and 1970s, American Express developed its electronic payment business along with its travel activities. Addressing particularly well-off people, American Express is less used than the other two cards.

---

74 *www.carneval.com. www.royalcaribbean.com. www.starcruises.com.* Kworntnik, Robert J. Jr. (2006). 'Carnival Cruise Lines: Burnishing the Brand'. *Cornell Hospitality Quarterly,* vol. 47, 286-300.
75 *www.americanexpress.com.*
76 *www.visa.com. www.mastercard.com.*
77 *www.visa.com.*
78 *www.mastercard.com.*
79 *www.americanexpress.com.*

Few countries include an all-encompassing national card system such as Denmark's Dankort.[80] A Country with a population of 5.5 million people has 3.5 million cards, of which one-third is combined with VISA or another international payment card. The use of electronic cards in Denmark accelerated in the 1990s and today, it is the most common form of direct payment. The Dankort company is owned by the Danish banks.

Car Rental

Car rental developed into a global business, too. A few American and European companies have consolidated the global market. In the US, the world's largest car rental firm, Hertz, has revenues in 2007 of $8 billion and more than 7,000 offices in almost 150 countries with more than 400,000 cars for rent.[81] Number two is Avis with revenues in 2007 of $5 billion and 5,000 offices around the world.[82] While Hertz originated around the time of the First World War, Avis started just after the Second World War. For long periods of time, these two companies were part of General Motors and Ford, before being taken over by investor groups.

In Europe, Auto Europe with 4,000 offices, Europcar with 3,000 offices dominate the West European car rental market.[83] Both have revenues in 2007 of about $2 billion and both have offices around the world too. All car rental firms partner with many airlines, hotels, electronic payment systems, insurance companies, tour operators and travel agencies.

Intensified competition put pressure on all the car rental companies, while the cost of their growing number of cars also increased. The car rental industry is affected by the airline industry, because car rental often begins where planes land. The Internet also has radically affected the car rental business. On the one hand, the Internet is an important sales channel for car rental companies, but on the other hand it gives customers free access to compare prices. Furthermore, car rental companies increasingly become dependent on third parties, primarily web-based travel agencies. A special kind of third party and competition pressure is caused by HolidayAutos, a part of Sabre's Travelocity.[84] HolidayAutos is a car rental firm that does not own any cars but is a commissioner for the traveller. Through HolidayAutos one gets the best and cheapest

---

80   *www.dankort.dk.*
81   *www.hertz.com. www.hoovers.com.*
82   *www.avis.com. www.cendant.com. www.avisbudgetgroup.com*
83   *www.auto.com.* Eurazeo (2008). *Annual Report 2007: www.eurazeo.com.*
84   *www.holidayautos.com*

offer. The consumer rents the car with HolidayAutos, which intermediates with the car rental firm, for example Europcar.

With the Internet, many new discount car rental companies have emerged that make competition even more intensive. Large capital requirements and logistics create high barriers for the potential growth of new companies, however, and the other links of the travel value chain also prefer international car rental firms. World wide the same companies continue to dominate the car rental business and are even consolidating the industry further, while leaving only small market shares for other firms.

Insurance

Globally, the insurance business is huge.[85] Life, accidents, property, fire, health, etc. are all heavy insurance areas in which the insurance industry concentrates its activities. Worldwide consolidation has been on the march since the 1990s, driven by the diversification of major financial companies into adjacent industries. On the one hand, banks diversify into insurance through acquisitions and expansion. On the other hand, the traditional insurance companies strengthen their competitive positions by diversifying into banking. Among the independent insurance companies some continue to specialize in travel insurance, which remains a rather marginal field compared to the core areas of insurance.

Yet, consolidation has not broken completely through. It is growing, however, at national, regional and global levels. The large insurance companies that fuel consolidation are domiciled in the world's three economic centers, the US (for example America International Group), Western Europe (for example Allianz and Zürich) and Japan (for example Nippon Life Insurance Company). While heavy insurance areas are still dominated by national companies, travel insurance is more of an international business moving towards regional and global consolidation.

In the US, World Access is one of the leading travel insurance companies, through its Access America division.[86] World Access with $1.5 billion revenues in 2007 is part of Mondial Assistance Group, which is the result of a merger between a French and a Swiss insurance company.[87] One of the leading international insurance companies, German Allianz, which is also a large shareholder in Mondial, has revenues in 2007 of almost $100 billion.[88] Independent travel insurance companies in the US and in

---

85   ReportSURE (2006). *Insurance Survey 2006: www.reportsure.com.*
86   *www.worldaccess.com. www.accessamerica.com*
87   *www.mondial-assistance.fr.*
88   *www.allianz.com*

Europe still hold significant market shares however, the largest company being Austrian 'Europäische Reiseversicherung' with revenues of $2 billion in 2007.[89] Second largest is Dutch Goudse Verzekering with revenues in 2007 at $1 billion. Europäische and Goudse originated in the early 20th century and expanded after the Second World War in Europe and since the 1990s worldwide. Western Europe remains its core market, however.

Even though insurance companies have established direct sales channels to consumers through the Internet, third parties, often being travel agencies, dominate insurance implementation. Insurance companies partner with several companies within travel, health care, etc.

Hospitality

The hospitality industry consists mainly of hotels and restaurants that provide accommodation and food to tourists. Hospitality is therefore an intimate part of the tourism sector and one of the cornerstones at destinations. Through decades, thousands of hotels and restaurants have worldwide serviced tourists in developed and increasingly emerging and developing countries. Currently, new technologies, globalization and changing consumer behavior are challenging hospitality companies that will have to improve competitiveness by branding, online communications, improved service and products, as well as increased productivity.[90]

Hotels

At destinations, hotels are the most common way of accommodation and hospitality. Less coomon are holiday homes and camping sites, although it differs much from country to country.[91] In Denmark for example, many German and Scandinavian visitors rent holiday homes along the west coast.[92] However in general terms, hotels dominate the global 'hospitality' industry. Since the Second World War, hotels have been a crucial force behind domestic and international American tourism. The American hotel industry quickly consolidated and the large US hotel chains continued their expansion abroad in Western Europe, Asia and Latin America, following in the foot-

---

89   *www.europäische.at*
90   Ottenbacher, Michael C. (2007). 'Innovation Management in the Hospitality Industry: Different Strategies for Achieving Success'. *Journal of Hospitality & Tourism Research*, vol. 31, 431-454. Deloitte (2007). *Hospitality 2010: www.deloitte.com.*
91   EU. Panorama on Tourism, passim.
92   VisitDenmark. Turismen i Danmark 2000-2004 (Tourism in Denmark).

step of American business. In Western Europe and even less in the rest of the world, a similar consolidation of hotels did not take place. Small and family-based hotels still dominate outside the US, except for the international American hotels. It was not until the 1990s and the breakthrough of globalization and expanding international tourism that the European hotel industry began slowly to consolidate. European hotel chains are being established, while the American hotel corporations start a new wave of international expansion that further stimulated European concentration. In order to meet the pressure of increasing competition and demands from modern tourists, small hotels have to cooperate or engage with external capital to carry out needed improvement of facilities. Everywhere access to capital, management and technology are crucial to creating a profitable hotel industry. Roughly, the hotels are of three kinds or segments, luxury, middle-class and economy class.

The InterContinental Hotels Group is the world's largest hotel corporation.[93] InterContinental has almost 4,000 hotels at its disposal with half a million rooms in more than 100 countries. 70 percent of its capacity is in the US, 20 percent in Western Europe and 10 percent in the rest of the world, mainly Eastern Asia, Oceania and Latin America. InterContinental is present in virtually all large cities of the world. The Holiday Inn and Express middle-class hotels make up 80 percent of all its rooms, leaving the remaining share to Continental and Crowne Plaza luxury hotels. Everywhere, franchising is the predominant way of management, while hotel ownership declines. An increasing number of hotel owners let InterContinental or any other large hotel chain manage or franchise their business. In 2007, InterContinental had revenues of $5 billion.

According to InterContinental, the global hotel market has an estimated capacity in 2007 of about 19 million rooms, the number growing three percent annually, of which one-third in the US, one-third in Western Europe, and almost one-third in Asia Pacific and Latin America.[94] The hotel market is geographically concentrated within 12 countries accounting for two-thirds of worldwide hotel room supply, InterContinental having a leadership position in half of these countries. This includes the US, Canada, Mexico, Germany, the UK, France, Italy, Spain, Japan, China, South Korea and Australia. The hotel market is a fragmented market with the four largest companies controlling only 11 percent and the ten largest hotel chains controlling just 20 percent of total room capacity. InterContinental is the largest of these groups with a three percent market share. Hotel chains are by far most common in the US,

93   www.ichotelsgroup.com.
94   InterContinental Hotels Group (2008). Annual Reports 2007: www.ichotelsgroup.com.

Global Experience Industries

controlling two-thirds of the hotel capacity, whereas their share is much smaller in the rest of the world, about one-fourth. The major competitors include other large global hotel companies, smaller hotel companies and independent hotels. Since the 1990s, Intercontinental, Wyndham (formerly Cendant, now InterContinental), Marriott, Choice, Best Western, Starwood, Carlson, Hyatt and Accor make up the global leader group of hotels, gradually increasing their market share. Except for French Accor, all large hotel chains domicile in the US.

The strategy of InterContinental and roughly all leading hotel chains is to build a strong operating system of purchase, sales, technology and other management dimensions focusing on the biggest markets and segments where scale really counts. According to InterContinental, four developments truly strengthen the hotel industry and its continuous consolidation. The general spread of the Internet made travelling more visible and accessible to much more people. With the breakthrough of discount airlines, one could cheaply reach almost any destination. Restrictions to travel are continuously being relaxed all over the world. Finally, the hotel chains are benefiting by the fact that people prefer well-known brands.

Like all other large hotel chains, InterContintental Hotels & Resorts, as is its full name, includes more and more links of the travel and vacation value chain. Inter-Continental gives access to self organized package tours including plane, hotel and car and arranged family or business venues. In addition, InterContinental hotels has been extended to include 'resorts', offering many kinds of relaxation, recreation, sports, shopping and entertainment. The 'resort' idea is simply to make people spend more time and money within the frames of the hotel. Still there is a gap between this kind of resort and the holiday-maker resorts of amusement parks and cruise lines.

Consolidation of the hotel industry is growing in all developed and merging countries of the world. At the top of the industry, an increasing number of hotels franchise with international hotel chains such as InterContintental, primarily in large cities. Below that level, a national consolidation process is bringing existing and new smaller hotels to cooperate on a franchise basis, often led by some investor group. Taking advantage of the Internet and innovative business models such as concept based hotels, new and old smaller hotel chains are always able to attract a share of the market.

Consolidation takes place by way of horizontal and vertical integration. Both dimensions are included in the consolidation processes of large hotel chains. In some cases like Carlson Companies, vertical integration is more prominent, including large parts of the total travel and tourism value chain, such as restaurants, holiday homes, tour operators, travel agencies, cruise lines, etc. Instead of integrating more parts of the consumer oriented travel and tourism industry, you might integrate backwards and add the role of supplier to your consumer activities. That is for example the route taken by French Accor.[95] Accor expands at two vertical levels. It integrates eventually all the tourism services, including accommodation, catering, transportation, entertainment, information, etc., partnering with numerous third parties, including airlines, railway companies, telecommunication companies, car rental companies, banks, electronic card providers. At the same time, Accor serves its suppliers with catering, human resources management, etc., diversifying by taking advantage of its strong management competences.

By 2007, the global hotel industry had estimated revenues of $200 billion, approximately one-third in America, one-third in Europe, and one-third in Asia Pacific.[96]

Restaurants

The world counts millions of restaurants, cafés and bars. Restaurants are more locally based than hotels. Except for a few exclusive places and international chains, they are all part of the local environment. Globalization and individualism have not left restaurants untouched, however. Furthermore, restaurants increasingly seek to differentiate and market their business by way of the Internet and other channels in order to meet a growing competition and pressure on profits. People want more and higher quality than they previously did and many customers can afford it. An increasing number of people look for gastronomic or cultural experiences when they visit a restaurant or café.

Restaurants, cafés and bars are the last link in the food and beverage chain. Generally speaking, they reflect the national culture of food and drinking. Food and beer and sometimes wine, however, were often domestically produced. As a consequence of internationalization and even more globalization, some countries have been able to export their food and drinking culture. World wide people have adopted Italian pizzas and spaghetti and most countries house several McDonalds and Burger King restaurants, meeting an increasing demand for fast-food. You find Irish pubs in most cities of the world, and the French have paved the way for an international wine drinking and dining culture. From France and Italy, the café has spread to the rest of the developed world, sometimes in the form of an international café chain such as American Starbucks.[97]

Within restaurants, cafés and bars, consolidation is progressing by way of chains. The global expansion of McDonalds and Starbucks are two obvious examples. In the

---

95   Accor Hotels (2008). *Annual Report 2007: www.accor.com*.

96   American Hotel & Lodging Association (AHLA): *www.ahla.com*.

97   *www.starbucks.com*.

pub industry, large breweries have taken control, creating vertical backward links. Hotel chains have restaurants of their own, too. Except for international chains, economies of scale are primarily seen in the catering business. Still, small independent restaurants, cafés and bars dominate in developed countries, even in the US.

The United States house about one million restaurants, cafés and bars. Three out of four of these companies are independent units. In 2007, they had total revenues of circa $500 billion.[98] Including sub-suppliers of the food and beverage industry and other industrial providers, the economic effects of restaurants were to be trebled. Total US restaurant revenues have grown tenfold since 1970 and doubled during the past decade. More and more the Americans eat out. Half a century ago, they used only a quarter of their food and drink spending in restaurants. By 2007, this share doubled and meanwhile people became more affluent.

Western Europe embraces about one million restaurants, cafés and bars.[99] In 2007, they had total revenues of about $350 billion. American hotel chains and restaurant chains are spreading continuously throughout Europe, including some European chains. Outsourcing has fuelled the catering business even more.

World wide, the restaurant, café and bar industry market is about $1,500 billion, of which only a minor share may be assigned to tourism.

Cuisine

When travelling one naturally enjoys the cooking traditions and practices of the destination.[100] Everywhere cooking or 'cuisine' is associated with a specific culture. A cuisine is primarily influenced by the ingredients that are available locally and through trade, which also includes beverages, such as wine, liquor, beer, tea and coffee. Enormous improvements in food production, preservation, storage and shipping has given almost everybody access not only to the local cuisine but also to many other cuisines of the world. As a consequence, cuisines everywhere are typically a combination of local traditions and international cuisines. The 'fusion cuisine' is a term for developments in many contemporary restaurants that combine elements of various culinary traditions.

Some cuisines have strongly influenced many other national cuisines even to the extent of a global reach. Such internationally spread cuisines are the Chinese and Indian cuisines, mainly following the international settlement of Chinese and Indians in Southeast Asia and other places of the world. In the Western world, American burgers

---

98   *www.restaurant.org.*
99   *www.eurofound.europa.eu.*
100 *www.wikipedia.org*: 'Cuisine'.

spread with the expansion of the McDonald's fast food chain and then, even elsewhere, mainly to emerging countries. The Italian pizza and pasta dishes have become popular on a global scale, too. When it comes to fine cuisine, all Western cuisines are influenced strongly by French cooking techniques. The growing search for authentic experiences and quality food has stressed the importance of making food from local vegetables and meat. What might be called a 'slow food' movement has emerged as an alternative to the industrial like productions methods of fast food.

The world may be divided into several regional cuisines including many similar or related national and local cuisines. The Asian cuisine may be a term for various cuisines in East, Southeast and South Asia, based on staples such as rice and noodles accompanying dishes of vegetables, meat and fish.[101] Rice is a vital component of many Asian cuisines, and in contrast to the cuisines of Northern Europe and the USA, or the Western cuisine in general, meat or fish are not considered the main ingredients of a dish, but more like most of the Mediterranean cuisines which are based on wheat-derived components such as pasta or cous cous. Asian dishes include various spices and are to a lesser or greater extent well seasoned. Chopsticks are the primary eating utensils, contrary to the fork and knife of Western cuisines. Soup is usually served at the start of a meal, but unlike most Western meals, an Asian meal does not typically end with a dessert. If it does, however, it may be sliced fruit or a sweet soup. The Latin American cuisine, which of course also is diverse, includes maize-based dishes (for instance tortillas), meat, spices, and beverages such as mate and horchata. The Latin American cuisine is a blend of all the many groups of immigrants and commercial influences from Europe, Africa, and North America. The US cuisine is a combination of the nation's rich supply of almost every kind of food and beverage and strong European as well as African and Latin American cooking traditions.

Exploring national and local cuisines reveals how people originally adapted to local natural conditions to make a living and, later on, as industrialization took-off, combined local traditions with other cuisines of the world. Gastronomy is the term for the study of relationship between culture and food.[102]

---

101 *www.wikipedia.org*: 'Asian cuisine', 'European cuisine', 'North American cuisine', 'Latin American cuisine', 'African cuisine'.
102 *www.wikipedia.org*: 'Gastronomy'.

Attractions

The choice of destination is often the first point that is decided when planning a holiday, e.g. one might want to visit a particular country, city or type of countryside.[103] As a rule, some attractions are attributed to the chosen destination, including sea and climate, landscape, city, cultural and historic memorials or amusement parks. In connection with such attractions, one typically finds hotels, holiday houses, camping sites, restaurants and shopping facilities. Summer tourism is mostly connected with beaches, cities and/or cultural monuments, cruising and amusement parks. Winter tourism has produced numerous skiing resorts mainly in North America and Western Europe, including lifts, ski schools, rental of skiing equipment, transportation, hotels, restaurants, etc. Coastal, city and skiing vacations are the kind of tourism that attracts the majority of world tourists. In addition, several niche tourism forms have been cultivated, including adventure in rugged regions or adventurous sports, backpacker tourism, health tourism, etc. So, destinations compete with each other seeking to attract the tourists of the world.[104]

Cultural and Natural Attractions

The world heritage list of UNESCO includes approximately 800 cultural and natural sites around the world.[105] In many ways, cultural tourism is linked to several of these attractions and the tourism services of transportation, hospitality, souvenirs and sightseeing that have been built around them. Such outstanding sites include the Great Barrier Reef and the Blue Mountains of Australia; the historic centre of Vienna, Prague, Budapest, Saint Petersburg and Lima among other places; the Great Wall and Imperial Palaces of China; the Pyramids of Egypt; the Palace and Park of Versailles, the Eiffel Tower, the Banks of the Seine and Mont-Saint-Michel of France; the Acropolis in Athens; the Taj Mahal in India; historic Rome, Florence, Venice, Assisi and Siena of Italy; the Buddhist Monuments in Japan; the Old City of Jerusalem; the Historic Centre of Mexico City and Mexico's pre-hispanic cities; Alhambra, Cordoba, Granada and Toledo in Spain; Stonehenge, Bath and historic London in England; Serengeti

---

103 *www.wttc.org. www.unwto.org.*

104 The matter of tourism destination competitiveness is dealt with in several articles, recently by: Mazanec, Josef A., Wöber, Karl, and Zins, Andreas H. (2007). 'Tourism Destination Competitiveness: From Definition to Explanation?'. *Journal of Travel Research*, vol. 46, 86-95. Govers, Robert, Go, Frank M., and Kumar, Kuldeep (2007). 'Promoting Tourism Destination Image'. *Journal of Travel Research*, vol. 46, 15-23.

105 UNESCO. *Cultural Heritage: www.unesco.org.*

National Park in Tanzania; and Yellowstone National Park, Grand Canyon National Park and the Statue of Liberty in the USA.

The cultural and natural heritage localities of the world have become the hotspots of national and international tourism.[106] Nature and adventure tourism may be included in this segment of tourism, too. Airlines, tour operators, the hospitality industry and the craft, souvenir and cultural sectors make billions of dollars by servicing these attractions. Without the sites of cultural and natural heritage, the craft industry and museums would probably attract much less attention. The revenues of museums, historical sites and the like in the USA amounted to more than $10 billion in 2005.[107] A global estimate might be approximately $50 billion. This is only peanuts compared to the income that transportation and hospitality industries make from organizing travel, accommodation, etc. to cultural and natural attractions. The worldwide crafts industry is found throughout all nations and corners of the world (see also below chapter on Crafts and Hobbies). Based on US and UK figures, the global industry of crafts may be estimated at a $100 billion business.[108]

City Tourism

City tourism has become increasingly important to all the cities and countries of the world.[109] People travel frequently to attractive places, mainly for cultural reasons, but they are also drawn by shopping opportunities. For one-day tourists, shopping is a major reason for travelling, while natural and cultural tourism dominates vacations of longer duration. A European study of city tourism indicates that it is motivated by several factors.[110] Culture is one reason for travelling, including historic and contemporary artefacts, arts and museums. Experiencing lifestyle and creative industries represent additional reasons to visit a city. Finally, city tourism springs from business and shopping trips.

City tourism is the most expanding kind of tourism. Millions of people travel to

---

106 Heritage tourism is dealt with by: Jamal, Tazan and Kim, Hyounggon (2005). 'Bridging the Interdisciplinary Divide: Towards and Integrated Framework for Heritage Tourism Research'. *Tourist Studies*, vol. 5, 55-83. Bonn, Mark A., et al. (2008). 'Heritage/Cultural Attraction Atmospherics: Creating the Right Environment for the Heritage/Cultural Visitor'. *Journal of Travel Research*, vol. 45, 345-354.
107 US Census Bureau (2007). Statistical Abstracts of the United States. *Museums, Historical Sites, and Similar Institutions: www.census.gov.*
108 Crafts Council and Arts Council of England & The Arts Council of Wales (2004). *Making It in the 21st Century. A Socio-Economic Survey of Crafts Activity in England and Wales, 2002-2003: www.craftassoc.com.*
109 Paskaleva-Shapira, Krassimira A. (2007). 'New Paradigms in City Tourism management: Redefining Destination Promotion'. *Journal of Travel Research*, vol. 46, 108-114.
110 European Travel Commission (2005). *City Tourism & Culture. The European Experience.* ETC Research Report: *www.etc-corporate.org.*

the metropolises of the world. Most frequently visited cities are New York, London, Paris and Rome. In second place, follow the cities of Mexico, Tokyo, Beijing, Sydney, Berlin, Barcelona, Hamburg, Madrid, Athens, Vienna, Copenhagen, Stockholm, Milan and Lisbon. New York City is probably the most popular city of all cities of the world. Some 40 million foreign and American tourists visit New York each year. Hotels, restaurants, shopping stores and centres as well as cultural attractions live and die by this enormous flow of people and money into the city.[111] More than 80 pct. of the visitors are American. In total, domestic and international visitors spend some $20 billion each year. Just like other cities, tourists are attracted by the sights of the city, in particular Manhattan and its avenues and districts, including Times Square, Chinatown, Soho, Greenwich Village and Wall Street. Famous are Central Park, the Statue of Liberty, Broadway, the Empire State Building and the Museum of Modern Art. Shopping opportunities are great, too.

Beach and Sun Tourism

Historically, and even today, most tourists travel from the temperate zone to the subtropical and tropical zones of the world. Each year, millions of people from Northern Europe spend their vacation in Southern Europe, just as North Americans seek to the Southern parts of the continent, the Caribbean and Hawaii, and to a lesser extent, people living in similarly temperate conditions elsewhere follow the same route from north to south. Most people travel during the summer months and the seaside and a warmer climate still holds first place when choosing a destination for vacation. For European tour operators, the sun-bound package products of airline seats and hotel rooms remain a vital part of their business, although they have become more adapted to individual travel patterns.[112] Mass tourism may be changing to a more individualized kind of tourism but the core of traditional mass tourism has succeeded since the 1960s and 1970s in adjusting to modern terms, based on huge investments in airlines, hotels, apartments and other tourism services at both the point of departure and arrival.

Tourists expect interesting experiences during their trips, while they also want the sunshine and comfort as well as other pleasantries of an organized trip to hotter destinations. Furthermore, tourist demands can be divided into several categories, moving from pure sun to pure culture or adventure. More and more destinations around the world compete to attract tourists. To meet this competition and to get hold

---

111 New York City: *www.nycvisit.com*
112 EU/Leidner. The European Tourism Industry in the Enlarged Community, 7-25.

of an increasing part of tourism spending, the tourism industry has been expanding their activities across a greater part of the consumer value chain. Airlines address most transportation and accommodation needs. Hotels build resorts for sports, wellness and shopping activities to make guests stay longer within their particular business field. On huge cruiser ships, travellers can stay for weeks to enjoy the sea, the pleasure of fine food, swimming pools, shopping, music, gaming and other kinds of entertainment. This trend to offer a system-like vacation can be seen in the expanding field of pleasure resorts throughout the world.

Winter Tourism

While winter sport is a broader term for several sports such as skiing (alpine, cross-country, jumping, snow-boarding), ice hockey, ice skating, sledding, etc., winter tourism includes mainly skiing and snowboarding. Along with mass summer tourism, winter tourism has expanded into a big business in several countries, first and foremost in West European countries such as Norway, Austria, Switzerland, Italy and France and in USA and Canada. In some countries such as Austria and Norway, winter tourism is even more important than summer tourism.[113] Mainly, winter tourism includes alpine skiing resorts in the Alp and North American countries, whereas cross-country skiing predominates in the Nordic countries. Many Alpine towns and regions depend economically on skiing tourism and have a wide range of skiing resorts with lifts, tracks, ski equipment rental, ski instruction, etc. as well as hotels, restaurants and many other facilities and their suppliers. Often, thousands of employees and hundreds of firms in a region depend on winter tourism. Ski trips are largely provided by the same tour operators, travel agencies and transportation companies that deal with summer tourism, although some companies have specialized in winter tourism.[114] Winter tourism in the Alps and the Nordic countries as well as North America has paved the way for an industry of skiing equipment (see the chapter on Sports). Furthermore, great winter sport events such as Winter OL have blurred the line between tourism and sports, too. Sports tourism, in winter as well as in summer, has turned into a considerable business.[115]

---

113 Dolnicar, Sara and Leisch, Friedrich (2003). 'Winter Tourist Segments in Austria: identifying Stable Vacation Styles using bagged Clustering Techniques'. *Journal of Travel Research*, vol. 41, 281-292. *www. wikipedia.org*: Tourism.

114 Except for seasonal and regional tourism, cross-combinations of tourism have emerged, too, including for instance sport tourism, see Ritchie, Brent W. and Adair, Daryl (Ed.)(2004). *Sport Tourism. Interrelationships, Impacts and Issues*. Tonawanda, New York: Channel View Publications.

115 A number of issues focusing on the relationship between sport and tourism are dealt with in: *Journal of Sport & Tourism*, vol. 11, no. 1, 2006.

Amusement Parks

Amusement parks are typically outdoor venues that provide rides as their primary attraction.[116] An amusement park addresses adults, as well as teenagers and children. Spending consists of admission fees, rides, food, souvenirs, and other related purchases made at the parks. The world spending in amusement parks is growing from $19 billion in 2001 to $22 billion in 2005, with a projected $28 billion in 2010 (Table 7). The US will remain the largest market, including half the world market, while Asia Pacific will be the fastest-growing market. The West European market is also growing.[117]

In the US, more than 300 million people annually attend amusement parks, spending more than ten billion dollars, half in destination parks and half in regional parks. One-third visit large destinations parks and two-thirds the regional parks. While the Disney Worlds and Disneyland dominate destination parks, major regional parks include Six Flags, Anheuser Park, Cedar Fair and Paramount Parks, all backed by large corporate ownerships. The US parks also dominate the Canadian amusement parks.

TABLE 7

The Global Amusement Parks Market in $bn, 2001-2010

	2001	2005	2010
USA	10	11	13
Western Europe	3	4	5
France	1	1	1
UK	1	1	1
Rest of WE	1	2	3
Asia Pacific	5	6	8
Japan	3	3	4
China	1	1	2
Rest of Asia Pacific	1	2	2
ROW	1	1	2
Total	19	22	28

Source: PWC. Global Entertainment and Media Outlook, 535-562.

---

116 PWC. Global Entertainment and Outlook, 534-562.
117 Milman, Ady (2001). 'The Future of the Theme Park and Attraction Industry: A Management Perspective'. *Journal of Travel Research*, vol. 40, 139-147.

Destination parks tend to be open year-round, and people generally plan their trips to them far in advance. As a result, normal weather conditions such as rainy days have relatively little impact on attendance levels at destination parks. By contrast, many of the regional parks are open only during the summer, meaning that the Memorial Day, Fourth of July, and Labor Day periods provide a significant portion of their total attendance. So a rainy Memorial Day or Labor Day has a much greater impact on the regional parks, because potential visitors can modify their plans on short notice.

While destination parks address families, the regional parks have been appealing mostly to teenagers looking for thrilling experiences. Because of declining attendance, regional parks are changing their profile towards family rides and experiences, including more shows, parades, fireworks, coasters, adventure rides, water parks as well as indoor water parks.

The West European amusement park market has grown from $3 billion in 2001 to $4 billion in 2005, with a projected $5 billion in 2010. Attendance in 2005 reached approximately 125 million visitors. France has a major amusement park market and has the most popular parks in the region. Disneyland Paris and Walt Disney Studios Park attract more than 12 million visitors annually, about 10 percent of the regional total. The UK has a number of amusement parks, too. The largest, Blackpool Pleasure Beach, attracts 6 million visitors annually. The German market includes Europa Park, the fourth most-popular park in Europe. Tivoli Gardens in Copenhagen is the third largest park. The ten largest West European parks had 44 million visitors in 2005, about 40 percent of the regional total.

Although amusement parks have a long history in Europe, Europe is a less mature market than the US in that new parks are still opening in many markets. However, the new parks will be relatively small compared to the major parks that opened in recent years, such as Walt Disney Studio Park in Paris and Warner Brothers Movie World in Madrid in 2002. Disney is strongly positioned in Europe. A number of small parks are being planned in Eastern Europe and the Middle East. In Dubai, however, the world's largest tourism, leisure, and entertainment development is being built and expected to be open in 2008. It will include several amusement parks, the largest shopping mall in the world, and a variety of residential and recreational facilities.

A consolidation of the European park industry is taking place, with many of the parks owned by private equity houses rather than group operators. Dubai International Capital, a firm controlled by the Dubai government, bought in 2005 the Tussauds Group, Europe's largest attractions operator. The Tussauds Group owns four parks, Alton Towers, Chessington World of Adventures, and Thorpe Park in the UK, and Heide Park in Germany, as well as a number of other attractions, including Madam Tussauds Wax museum. The US based private equity firm Blackstone Group acquired the Merlin Entertainment Group in 2005. Merlin operates numerous attractions in eight European countries. In 2005, the Blackstone Group purchased the four Legolands, too, in the UK, Denmark, Germany and California. Merlin Entertainments is now the third largest operator of attractions in Europe, surpassed only by Disney and Tussauds. Merlin will turn the four Legolands into destination resorts by adding hotels.

Japan is by far the largest market in the region, spending more than half of the $6 billion total in 2005. China is the second-largest marked with some $1 billion in 2005. Total attendance in 2005 was 234 million visitors. Lower admission levels in merging countries such as China, India and the Philippines yield a relatively lower market than in Western Europe, the US and Japan. New Disneylands are being opened in Hong Kong and China, and more are expected to come. Disneyland Tokyo and Tokyo Disney Sea are the two largest Asian Pacific amusement parks. Except for Disneyland and Ocean Park in Hong Kong, all the major parks are located in Japan and South Korea. Of the other media conglomerates, Universal, Paramount and Warner have, or are, planning parks in Asia Pacific, too, just as in the US and Europe. China and India, in particular, contain a large potential of new parks.

Performing Arts

The Performing arts include all kinds of arts and onstage performance, such as theatre, literature, dance (solo, partner, group, ballet, performance, participation, etc.), music (folk, popular, classic), painting, sculpture and circus.[118] Arts are performed in theatres, concert halls, the open air, or circus tents and arts are created and exhibited in galleries, museums, halls of institutions, companies and open places. Arts may be divided into two groups: One is the group of Western arts that make up an almost shared history since the Renaissance, with national variations. Two, is the group containing pre-industrial based arts of Asia, Africa and Latin America that come in many different kinds. Although the traditional art objects of developing countries are sold to tourists and others throughout the world and provide some income for poor people, this accounts for only a very small portion of global arts revenues. The dynamic majority of the world arts business is based on Western performances in theatres, music halls, etc.

Until the breakthrough of movie pictures and television, arts lived more or less in separated worlds. Theatres performed drama, opera and ballet, based on classical

---

118 Smelsen and Baltes. International Encyclopedia of the Social & Behavioral Sciences, 'Art'. *www.wikipedia.org*: 'Performing Arts', 'Arts'.

or modern literature. In concert halls, symphony orchestras played classical music. Popular music was played in music halls and elsewhere. Visual arts created paintings and exhibited them in galleries, etc. As the electronic media of entertainment proliferated and commercialization increased, all artforms increasingly intertwined. The same story began to appear in all forms, starting perhaps as a book or a movie picture or television film and moving on to the theatre and music hall. Spill-over effects can be seen in performing arts as they are in all other entertainment industries.

The Performing Arts Market

It is hard to get an accurate estimate of the world performing arts industry, but most of the income stems from box revenues and a significant share from private funding, including arts sales on commission and on location.[119]

The problem of counting the revenues of performing arts is shown by an American economic report on the non-profit arts and culture organizations.[120] According to this report, about 100,000 non-profit organizations enjoy and inspire Americans in thousands of towns and cities. They generate billions of dollars in revenues for local businesses that supply them with merchandise and services, as well as pay taxes, employ millions of people, and are a cornerstone of tourism. In the US, they created revenues of $166 billion in 2005, up from $134 billion in 2000 and $75 billion in 1990, of which 40 percent came from organizations and 60 percent from event-related spending by their audiences, equivalent to several million jobs. These numbers include the wider economic impact of non-profit arts performance organizations, however. Direct revenues and income are much smaller, perhaps $10 billion.

Box office revenues in profit arts performing companies were also an estimated $10 billion in 2005, including estimated private funding of $5 billion. It makes a total of $25 billion for the US in 2005 and $15 billion for profit companies. Total West European arts performance revenues are probably of the same size as the US numbers, as are the revenues of the rest of the world. Including non-profit arts performance organizations, it results in a world total of $75 billion in 2005, with a projected $90bn in 2010 (Table 8).

The English-language profit performing arts are centred on New York's Broadway and London's West End. Succeeding plays and musicals are the revenue drivers of these two centres, and they are often staged in other parts of the world, too. Large audiences are also found in opera houses and theatres. From 2000 to 2005, Broadway

---

119 Howkins. The Creative Economy, 102-103.
120 Americans for the arts (2006). *Arts & Economic Prosperity III. The Economic Impact of Non-Profit Arts Organizations: www.artusa.org.*

shows had an annual audience of 11 to 12 million people in New York and a similar audience on road shows, American opera houses 5 to 6 million and non-profit professional theatres and symphony orchestras each about 30 million.

TABLE 8

The Global Performing Arts Market in $bn, 2001-2010

	2001	2005	2010
USA	20	25	30
Western Europe	20	25	30
Japan	5	6	7
Rest of the Developed World	5	6	7
Developing Countries	10	13	16
Total	60	75	90

Source: Howkins. The Creative Economy, 102-103. US Census (2007). Statistical Abstracts/Performing Arts: *www.census.gov*. Americans for the Arts. Arts & Economic Prosperity III. The Economic Impact of Non-Profit Arts Organizations.

Events

Celebration is as old as humanity.[121] We commemorate birth, life and death; discovery, victory, and remembrance; history, new beginnings, and patriotism; food, shelter, and family; where we come from, who we are, and what we believe; careers, achievements, and milestones; music, sports, military prowess, children, love, hopes, community, beauty, talent and peace on earth. The need to celebrate seems inherent in everything we do.

In the course of time these celebrations have changed. From informal affairs to spectacular productions requiring new sets of skills, experience, creativity, tools, financing, planning and leadership, celebration has often evolved into a business and an industry with professional standards and expectations, academic programs and educational certifications, and with new demands and challenges every day. The events industry has become a worldwide affair, including international organizations for professionals and companies, too.[122] Globally, it is estimated to include some one million regularly re-occurring events (including community festivals, parades, fairs, air shows, sporting

---

121 International Festivals and Events Association (IFEA): *www.ifea.com*.
122 International Special Events Society (ISES): *www.ises.org*. IFEA: *www.ifea.com*.

events, carnivals, car shows, art shows, flower shows, corporate events, balloon rallies and more), with an estimated economic impact in the hundreds of billions of dollars and combined attendances that touch virtually every life on the planet. Each person has his events through his life. Each family has its events to celebrate birth, confirmation, exams, weddings, anniversaries, vacations, etc. Each company and organization has its events: meetings, exhibitions, parties, team building, anniversaries, special occasions, annual meeting, etc. Each industry has its events: conferences, trade show, exhibitions, annual meeting. Each local community has its events: festivals, music performance, sports events, elections, etc. Each nation has its events: national championships, elections, royal birthdays, festivals, etc. International events are celebrated, too: World Cup, OL, etc.

Business, culture and sports events therefore are fields of increasing economic and cultural importance – for citizens, business, local communities and nations. Events are of many kinds and sizes, from great international sports, cultural or political events at one end of the spectrum to family events at the other end. Large events are attractive because they create employment and economic revenues for businesses and state and offer people experiences of great quality and excitement. In addition, international events serve to upgrade nations' and cities' facilities which qualify for new events and increased tourism, too. Winning in international competition to become the organizer of great events is based on long-term planning, hard and professional work. That includes such international events as the FIFA World Cup, the Olympic Games and the America's Cup. Other recurring events include the London Marathon, New York Marathon and Berlin Marathon, the Cannes Film Festival and Vienna New Years Eve Concert.

Although sport events, concerts, music and film festivals and other cultural events are an important part of events per se, there is much more to events than that. Most events actually take place in the business world, such as exhibitions, trade shows, the launch of new products, conventions, meetings, career and job centers, company parties, receptions and other business occasions. Business events are arranged for the same reasons as they are in private and entertainment contexts, except that they are done for commercial reasons. Great experiences will always be remembered. They tighten bonds between friends, customers, employees and business relations. 'Be in touch', may be the slogan.

In business events, all kinds of media are used on the one hand, but on the other hand it is the face-to-face communication, which has become part of companies' marketing activities, that has given rise to many new firms and has encouraged existing marketing companies also to diversify into the business of events. The events industry is large and diverse. Within exhibitions in the UK alone, the industry contributed almost

$20 billion to the UK economy in 2005.[123] Events must be organized and marketed. Staging an event is a major logistical and organizational undertaking based on creative thinking and business knowledge. Business events have become so important that event management is being taught at universities throughout the world, including the US, UK, Germany, France and Australia. Events companies target many groups: business leaders, employees, people in certain industries, and for different purposes, often team building.

Events are a many-sided business, dealing with special occasions:

- Festivals and special events: have grown into a massive industry worldwide, generating billions of dollars for companies, centers, states and countries. Festivals and special events bring people together to celebrate, to remember, to support and to identify as a community or nation.[124]
- Special interest tourism: is one of the fastest growing segments within the tourism industry. A more mature traveling public is increasingly seeking experiences which satisfy a whole spectrum of interests. Accordingly, there is a need for new tourism products, services and experiences that cater to these markets. Special interest tourism incorporates various sectors such as regional, urban community, environmental, cruise, heritage, cultural, sex and educational tourism.
- Business and management conventions: The MICE sector is one of the fastest growing and most lucrative areas of the tourism industry worldwide.
- Behind the scenes at special events: covers the essentials of designing and executing a successful theme party or special event, from presenting a menu of theme ideas to creating a color scheme to designing and building stage sets.
- Professional event coordination: includes the full event planning process and provides tools and strategies to effectively procure, organize, implement, and monitor all the products, services, and service providers that will bring an event to life: Event design, Project management techniques, Site selection and development, Infrastructure services, Entertainment possibilities, Food and beverage options, Safety and security, Inviting attendees.
- Event marketing: from sales and advertising to public relations and community involvement.
- Event sponsorship: guidelines for attracting, signing, and keeping sponsorship

---

123 Association of Event Organisers, Contractors and Venues (AEO): *www.aeo.org*.
124 Special Events Magazine: *www.specialevents.com*. ISES: *www.ises.org*.

for any event, including festivals, conventions, expositions, sporting events, arts and entertainment spectaculars, charity events, and much more.

-   Event risk Management and safety: with any event comes risk, from rowdy guests at a festival or convention to a life-threatening riot at a sports event.

The US Meetings Industry

According to the US Convention Industry Council (CIC), the impact of the meetings, conventions, exhibitions, and incentive travel industry in the United States in 2004 as a whole generated $122 billion in total spending.[125] This is more than the 'pharmaceutical and medicine manufacturing industry' and only slightly less than the 'nursing and residential care facilities' industry. The industry's spending and tax revenue cross through every sector of the local economy, from restaurants and transportation to retail stores and other services, while supporting 1.7 million jobs in the US it generated $21 billion in direct taxes. It generates more than 36 percent of the hotel industry's estimated $109 billion in operating revenue, and its attendees account for nearly 17 percent of the air transportation industry's operating income. Associated sponsored events accounted for two-thirds, or $82 billion of the direct spending industry total. Corporate sponsored events, including incentive travel, accounted for the remaining one-third, or $40 billion. The largest share of the convention and exhibition dollar (35 percent) is spent in hotels and other facilities. The rest is widely distributed throughout local economies. After air transportation (24 percent), the biggest categories of attendee, exhibitor, and sponsor spending were: restaurant and outside catering food & beverage outlets (14 percent) and business services (12 percent).

The exhibitions and events industry brings sellers and buyers together.[126] It displays products and services. It educates participants and creates networking among them. Exhibitions drive economic impact at: convention centers, hotels, restaurants, transportation, shops and entertainment venues at leading American cities, Las Vegas, Chicago, New York, Toronto, Atlanta, Orlando, Boston, Washington D.C., Dallas, San Diego. In 2004, more than 13,000 exhibitions took place in the US, split into industry sectors:

-   Medical and Healthcare 23.4 %
-   Business services 14.4 %,
-   Communications and IT 12.7 %

---

125   The Convention Industry Council (CIC): *www.conventionindustry.org*.
126   International Association of Exhibitions and Events (IAEM): *www.iaem.org*.

- Government, public and not-for-profit services 11.9 %
- Sports, travel, entertainment, art and consumer services 9.2 %
- Raw materials and science 8.1 %
- Consumer goods and retail trade 5.8 %
- Industry/Heavy machinery and finished business products 4.4 %
- Transportation 3.9 %
- Building, construction, home & repair 2.4 %.

The US $122 billion spending in the meetings and incentives industry in 2004 was an estimated one-third share of the world total of $366 billion that year. Total events industry amounted to an estimated $559 billion, leaving almost $200 billion to other events. The events industry has an annual growth rate of ten percent, making a total of $615 billion in 2005 and a projected $900 billion in 2010.

The events industry on the one hand is an important part of business travels and tourism. For example, hotels and airlines are highly engaged in business events. On the other hand, the events industry has moved into other sectors, including companies dealing with advertising and business information. The world's leading organizer of trade and consumer events is probably Reed Exhibitions, a division of Elsevier Reed, one of the globally leading providers of professional and business information.[127] Reed Exhibitions organizes hundreds of events worldwide, serving some fifty key industries (Aerospace, defense and marine; Arts and entertainment; Building, property and interior design; Electronics end electric engineering; Energy, oil and gas; Engineering, manufacturing and processing; Food service and hospitality; IT and communications; Jewellery; Marketing, business services and training; Retail; Safety and security; Sports, leisure and health; Travel). Other internationally leading special events companies include: The Special Event Company that produces corporate, pharmaceutical, media and academic events in North America, Western Europe and China.[128] Extraordinary Events plan and produce entertainment and other events.[129] MGM Mirage Events annually plan and produce hundreds of mega-events.[130] VOK Dams Gruppe specializes in corporate events, trade shows, corporate communication and incentive programs.[131] Steve Kemble Event Design, cover events from celebrating the accomplishments of NFL football players to organizing presidential parties and reality TV.[132]

---

127 Reed Exhibitions: *www.reedexpo.com.* Reed Elsevier: *www.reed-elsevier.com.*
128 *www.specialevent.co.uk.*
129 *www.extraordinary-events.com.*
130 *www.mgmmirageevents.com.*
131 *www.vok.nl.*
132 *www.stevekemble.com.*

Tourism Shopping

Shopping is a vital part of tourism and tourist spending. Tourism shopping is estimated to account for one-quarter of all tourism revenues. All types of tourism are, in one way or another, a form of consumption. Shopping is itself subject of tourism, too.[133] The main purpose of some tourist activities is simply to shop. Doing leisure shopping is not a simple economic activity to meet your functional demands. It is a social activity and cultural event that satisfies your desire for experiences. This may be seen in the light of shopping in general as a means of creating your identity, benefiting from increasing leisure time and living conditions. Shopping is fun and as a consumer, one may even be addicted to shopping, almost just like any kind of drugs and drinking.

Shopping is one of the most common motives for leisure travel in the world. For example this is the case in the US and UK. Leisure consumption is part of the general shopping patterns and types of shoppers that market analysts and retailing follow closely. Tourist shoppers can properly be categorized as active shoppers, price shoppers, leisure shoppers or even social shoppers, going to the mall to show somebody around or meet somebody.

Shopping is different from buying. While buying refers to obtaining a specific item from a seller, shopping also includes servicing and social needs. For example, you might be looking for innovative ideas and products and the leisure experience is more important than the buying act. In general, recreational shoppers often do not know what they want to buy and do not mind distance of travel. They will also tend to make more spontaneous buys, shop more often, spend more time shopping per trip, shop with others, and continue shopping after making a purchase. Socializing is an important part of leisure shopping, shopping with friends and family, especially teenagers and elderly. Recreational shoppers are more inclined to enjoy the complete process of retail consumption, including pleasant and playful surroundings and presentations. As a result, shopping malls are being designed to attract leisure shoppers as a place where they can go and enjoy various activities besides shopping. Shopping is also related to leisure visits to heritage destinations, for example at historic sites, or even sunbathing. In recent years, shopping centers and malls are increasingly seeking to attract leisure shoppers, organizing and designing shopping areas and surroundings accordingly.

Besides consumer experiences at shopping venues, Internet shopping is becoming popular as a recreational activity, too, although still much less important than physical shopping in retail stores. Many feel e-commerce is safer, you can search a wide selection of products, and you can avoid crowds, if you do not like to socialize too much.

---

133 Dallan, J. Timothy (2005). *Tourism Shopping, Retailing, and Leisure.*

Shopping as an added attraction to the destination being visited probably accounts for the majority of tourist shopping. Shopping as the primary reason for taking a trip is an important factor for millions of travelers each year, too. Indeed, the tourism industry offers many specialized international shopping tours in Europe, North America and Asia, for example Christmas shopping in London or Paris, escorted shopping tours in Florence to famous fashion shops, and shopping tours to Mexico for fine crafts and jewelry. The driving forces behind shopping include the selection of merchandise, destination, and price advantages. Themed shopping is an important part of tourism in many places, including festivals and other spectacular events that mix culture, food and maybe ethnicity. Hong Kong is one of the world's attractive shopping cities, similar to New York and London. Large malls and shopping centers function as magnates of tourism shopping. In connection with multi-millions attractions such as New York's Museum of Modern Art and Disneyland, shopping is part of the experience, too. Finally, price reductions or simply lower prices in another country motivate many people to travel for shopping, for example from the US to Mexico.

Combining attraction and shopping is the most popular form of tourism shopping. When you travel to other cities, heritage destinations, sunny beaches, ski resorts, or for gambling in Las Vegas there is always an additional shopping element. And the destinations and resorts make sure that shopping potentials are supplied. Between destinations and shopping there is a synergy. Even people who do not normally like to shop (primarily men) participate more in shopping activities while on vacation. On vacations everybody has the time to shop, whereas most people are often too busy at home to shop for fun.

Shopping travels are also motivated by the quest for authenticity, when visiting heritage destinations, crafts destinations, etc. In the end, authenticity is a matter of the meanings that the tourist assigns to their merchandise. Novelty seeking in tourism shopping is another motive for traveling. Some nationalities are very keen shoppers, for example the Japanese, who typically spend more money on each trip than Europeans and Americans, among other things because brands and prestige are important elements to the Japanese, including the custom of gift-giving.

The things that tourists buy may often be categorized as products of fashion, including clothing and shoes, jewelry, leather, watches, cosmetics, fine art, crafts, etc. that may take the form of souvenirs to remind you of the place visited. Shopping venues are placed at destinations, including city centers, heritage sites, beach towns, as well as travel points such as airports. At large airports, for example, virtually all the well-known brands of fashion run duty free shops, just as the international ferry lines do.

Management initiatives are required to attract people. This includes shopping policies, marketing, design of, for example, city quarters to make enjoyable shopping environments, and interior design, as well as infrastructure and regulations. Given the enormous demand for shopping by tourists, many destinations are preparing shopping promotional campaigns and developing shopping policies. Often tourism companies and organizations join hands with town and city shopping centers and trade organizations to promote their destination as an attractive shopping place.

4. Sports

Sports

Sports may be defined as physical and mental activities on an individual or team basis that often involves competition between two or more people.[1] As any other social activity, sports are organized and regulated. Without rules, sports would turn into violence. A wide range of sports exist. According to UNESCO, the worldwide number of sports makes a total of at least 8,000.[2] Some sports are widely practiced, such as football and soccer, while others form small niches, including dance and mountain bicycling. Sports come in many forms such as athletics, combat sports, cycling, football, gymnastics, handball, hockey, horse racing, motor racing, racket sports, skiing, swimming, and target sports. Furthermore, these sport categories split into several specialized sports. For example, almost fifty different athletic events took place at the 2004 OL in Athens.[3] The Olympic Games illustrate another divide within sports. The OL are for the professional elite only, while amateurs and other interested people remain spectators. Having just a few thousand athletes competing in the sporting arenas, hundred of thousands watched the games and half the world population had access to the television coverage. On the one hand, you have professional athletes that form part of an increasingly commercialized sports world. On the other hand, sports are a widespread leisure activity on an amateur or spectator basis. Perhaps half the world population performs some kind of regular sport activity. Sport as a widespread leisure and professional activity is a product of modern industrialized societies. To equip athletes and joggers, a large industry has emerged, too.

Participant sports have become an increasing source of income to the sports industry as more and more people practice some kind of sport activity and increasingly want to be dressed in proper sporting equipment. Furthermore, a sporting life style has taken hold of the world, adding even more to the potentials of the sports equipment industry. Globalization, new technologies, increasing wealth, individualized lifestyles and the global spread of Western ways of living have not only all added to the present rapid growth of the sports industry, but have also increasingly blurred the distinction between sport, recreation, leisure, entertainment and business.

As an integrated part of social life, however, sports have probably existed as long as mankind. What has changed is the nature of sports. In this context, we shall concentrate on sport as business. Sport has a long history.

---

1   Smelsen and Baltes. International Encyclopedia of the Social & Behavioral Sciences, 'Sport'. *www. wikipedia.org*: 'Sport'.
2   *www.sportencyclodia.com*.
3   *www.olympic.org*.

The History of Sport

In pre-industrial ages, sport emerged from the religious and combat rituals of hunting and farming societies.[4] The worship of great hunters, soldiers and leaders was common throughout the ancient world. In most parts of the world, people organized feasts and games to celebrate the achievements of heroes or to symbolize for example the struggle of light against darkness. Organized games occurred regularly in ancient Greece to honor Zeus, and by praising the wealthy males in wrestling and running games, it affirmed simultaneously the social structure of society. Sports became such a prominent part of their culture that the Greeks created the Olympic Games. In Ancient Rome, sport-like activities prepared young men for warfare, and warfare spectacles such as gladiator fights and chariot races took place in massive arenas to distract the ever-increasing masses. Ancient China, Egypt, Aztec and other high cultures of the past developed and practiced similar symbolic sports adapted to each of their particular culture, including athletics, combats, strengths, racing, ball games and target games.

As the Roman Empire dissolved, local games and tournaments spread throughout medieval Western Europe. The Catholic Church adapted rituals that included symbolic games to represent for instance the struggle between good and evil. As the Church provided seasonal holidays, too, ball games and other playful activities flourished amongst the great majority of peasants. No written rules existed in those days, and each game evolved differently from one place to another according to local customs. Gradually, these games lost their religious origins and became enjoyable pastimes of their own. Many modern ball games such as handball and football date from the play of medieval peasants. The sport of the aristocracy developed quite differently. Since they had won their high standing through warfare, the aristocracy arranged war games known as tournaments, affirming at the same time the supremacy of the male upper-classes.

In the emerging West European capitalist societies of the 17th and 18th centuries, popular sports thrived as never before, particularly in England as it rose to be the economic, political, social and cultural leader of the world. Ball games, wrestling, boxing, rowing, fencing, horse racing, cricket and golf became popular sports amongst the upper, middle and lower classes. At the same time, the emphasis was beginning to shift from religious and military purposes to just interesting ways to pass free time among people in general. A final break with the religious and military roots of sport-

---

4   Mechikoff, Robert A. (2006). *A History and Philosophy of Sport and Physical Education from the Ancient Civilization to the Modern World*, 4th Edition. New York: McGraw-Hill. Modern Developments are outlined in McComb, David (2004). *Sports in World History*. Abingdon, UK: Routledge. Dyreson, Mark (2003). 'Globalizing the Nation-Making Process: Modern Sport in World History'. *International Journal of the History of Sport*, No. 1, 91-106. Missiroli, Antonio (2002). 'European Football Cultures and Their Integration: The 'Short' Twentieth Century'. *Sport in Society*, 5:1, 1-20.

ing games, however, did not occur until the second half of the 19th century, when sport activities evolved into standardized and internationally recognized sports. The expanding bourgeoisie of industrializing England initiated this 'sportification' process, but soon the working and middle classes joined the new sport movement and created the foundation of modern sports. By 1900, most types of sport had been established.

From England modern sports spread to the USA, Continental Europe and other developed countries of the world. To a certain degree, developing countries and colonies of Latin America, Asia and Africa adopted organized sports since the early 20th century, too. National leagues of football, soccer, rugby, handball, basketball, etc. became the focus of elite and spectator sports and in leading countries such as the UK and USA, they turned into professional and commercial sports. The first Olympic Games in modern times in 1896 underlined the breakthrough of organized sports on a secular basis, to be continued every fourth year. Soccer WM and EM followed suit as did international events of other sports.

During the first half of the 20th century, organized professional and in particular amateur sports spread around the world as did an increasing number of specialized sports. Sports became a massive movement that expanded for several reasons. Industrialization made secular societies prevail at the expense of religious and traditional societies. By the transformation of traditional social structures into modern classes and the breakthrough of competitive market economies, new ways of social organization and cultural identification arose. In addition, nationalism developed as a strong means of identification across social divides. Finally, the all prevailing mass way of organizing economic, political, social and cultural activities created mass markets and mass audiences for an emerging sports business. These trends took radical and changing forms during the second half of the 20th century.

The American-led postwar golden age of the developed countries and its stimulating effects on the developing world created a new beginning for modern sports. The economy internationalized and welfare spread in national economies of the West. In addition to books, magazines, newspapers and radio, new technologies, especially television, paved the way for increasingly commercialized sports. National teams, leagues and clubs as well as international federations joined hands with public and private broadcasting corporations. The general spread of television created a mass audience for sports that also attracted corporate advertising and sponsorship. Mainly this included football, baseball, basketball and hockey in the USA, soccer in Western Europe and internationally, world tennis tournaments, soccer world cups and OL. The weakened economic conditions of the 1970s and 1980s as well as the lingering divide between the East and West damped the commercialization of sports, although by 1990 national professional leagues of football, soccer and a few other sports had been around for quite some time in North America and the major nations of Western Europe. Football in the USA and soccer in Europe were by far the most important games and business. The FIFA World Cup, the UEFA European Championship and other international club soccer tournaments stimulated commercialization and strengthened the rise of a small group of internationally leading clubs. The 1990s breakthrough of globalization, electronic technologies and the end of the Cold War paved the way for a global sport-based industry that made sports more commercialized than ever before.

The Business of Sports

Corporate sport lends itself to commercialization for three principal reasons.[5] First, corporate sport has mass spectator appeal and companies support sports that attract popular interest. Second, because of this appeal the sport has the ability to generate substantial income, based on gate receipts, television and Internet rights, sponsorships, merchandise and licensing rights. Third, because of substantial sources of revenue, the sport can apply highly skilled and experienced professional managers and marketers, who further capitalize upon the commercial opportunities sport offers. Just as companies use sponsorship and adverts to create or increase global brands and media buy sporting rights to attract subscribers and viewers, national leagues and clubs may develop global brands and merchandise sales as a consequence of TV transmissions.

In all respects, soccer is the world's most popular sport. FIFA has more than 200 members and is by far the biggest sport association in the world. Member nations are distributed over six confederations and regions. In most nations, soccer is the most popular sport. Worldwide a quarter of a billion people are regular soccer players, about 4 percent of the world population. Of all players, some 22 million are professionals, including a small minority of women. Of all professional soccer players three-quarters play in Europe or South America. Most broadcasted European sport programs are soccer games. The top sponsored sports in Europe are soccer and OL, with tennis and Formula One in secondary places at a much lower level. Soccer however is not the most popular sport in North America and Australia where a rugby-kind of football is number one. Not surprisingly, soccer and football are the sports that attract the spectators – led in numbers worldwide by American football, and next British, German, Italian, Spanish and Dutch soccer and Australian football. Of course American baseball, basketball and hockey attract a large number of spectators.

---

5   H. Westerbeek and A. Smith (2003). *Sport Business in the Global Marketplace*. New York: Palgrave Macmillan. Slack, Trevor (Ed.)(2004). *The Commercialisation of Sport*. Abingdon, UK: Routledge.

The globalization or Westernization, or perhaps even Americanization, of sports mirrors the general development of business. The basis of growth for the sport industry is the developed nations, in particular the United States and Western Europe. Corporate sport in the USA has been able to sell its services to many international markets, including the NFL expansion in Europe and the NBA in Asia, and also includes many European players in the domestic US leagues. The US business is far more successful in expanding their services than companies of any other nationality. The internationalization of sport services reflects the general trend of globalized services. This is based on worldwide reorganized companies, including core knowledge focus, outsouring, increasing wealth and leisure time, the technology revolution in communications, media, transportation, medicine, materials etc. The technology trend in particular will play a major role in transforming the world, including the provision of services and the penetration of sport. Sport has become an expanding industry affected by globalization, specialization and technology.

Sport services may be split into two categories, including products that directly involve the sporting contest (facility dependent sport services) and products that merely contribute to the sporting contest (sporting goods and sport consulting services). Furthermore, a distinction may be made between corporate-related products (spectator services, sponsorship services, TV and Internet rights and license rights) and participant services.

Media are of particular importance to the commercialization of sport.[6] It provides our main connection to sport, but also impacts greatly our culture in many ways, including nationality, class, race, gender, age and disability. As major networks are forced to pay high sums for the rights to broadcast sport, they naturally want to maximize their investments. The result has been a trend towards pay-per-view, although this trend has developed only slowly, partly because of political actions taken to defend amateur and national interests, partly because of consumer support of national and local sport and culture. The media is not all-powerful. Nevertheless, media corporations find new ways of packaging sport events with other lucrative products such as merchandise and computer games. Through strong media relations or ownership, sport organizations can dramatically increase the value of their products and brands and in turn affect their sponsorship, licensing and broadcast rights.

Organizing an international sporting event has become such a huge undertaking

---

6   The crucial interrelationship between professional sports and media are dealt with in several books and
     articles, including Gratton, Chris and Solberg, Harry Arne (2007). *The Economics of Sports Broadcasting*.
     New York: Routledge. Bernstein, Alina (2002). 'Meeting the Industry: An Interview with Alex Gilady'.
     Sport in Society, 5:3, 115-138.

that major sport enterprises are forced to look for substantial multinational sponsorship to secure the financial success of the event. Global sporting events delivered to a global audience and supported by global corporations are based on a triangle cooperation of the sport, the sponsor and the media. Not surprisingly, the growth of sport follows the growth of sponsorship that follows the growth of the media industry as a global business. Sport sponsorship has increased its value enormously since the 1980s and 1990s. The link between large corporations and sport is logical. The national and international coverage of sporting events allows the sponsor to be associated with the event and in the process raise his profile and communicate to relevant markets. Soccer is a highly used means of sponsorship as the most watched of all sports. If a company wants to be globally exposed and associated with an exciting sport, Formula One offers plenty of opportunities traveling around the world. Accordingly, sponsorship is part of corporate marketing.

Technology such as the computer, the Internet and mobile phones has become an integral part of modern life and economies. With the rapid spread of broadband, interactive media are within the reach of most people in high income nations. The interactive media make up an opportunity for leagues and clubs to interact with fans and the public in general. Furthermore, they may extend their electronic services to include television, DVD's, computer games, betting, club visits, chat rooms, second life opportunities and other ways of linking supporters to clubs in particular. The Internet, the computer and mobile phones allow clubs to build communities of their own that eventually may challenge the media industry. Virtually all clubs in Western soccer and football leagues have created such interactive sites. Leading British, German, Spanish, Italian and American clubs such as Manchester United, Bayern Munich, Real Madrid and Washington Redskins are the most frequently visited portals. The global media corporations have responded to the challenge of interactive media by investing in sporting clubs and preparing for interactive product developments.

Global Sport and Culture

Sports contain an alternative to the complexity of modern life: the playing field and the rules are simple and unchanged, and the televised sporting events are broadcasted in a way that allows you to be emotionally involved in a collective experience. Culture is a powerful sport business variable.[7] At the individual and small group level, sport

---

7   Westerbeek and Smith. Sport Business in the Global Marketplace, 172-196.

may develop a sense of belonging. At the national level it may produce a sense of national identification.[8]

Therefore, sport in matters of the values that drive spectators and fans is highly emotional. In business terms it means that sport consumers tend to be non-rational in purchasing behavior. In other words, their decision to buy is strongly mediated by their love for the sport, their passion for a club or their admiration for an athlete. When emotional attachment is combined with the relative importance of sport in a particular society, the sport marketer can achieve a competitive advantage. The flipside of the coin is the risk of a significant loss, when the inherent marketing power of a sport product is exploited with little understanding of emotional and cultural interplay, such as, for example, is the case in the continuing struggle of soccer in the USA and Australia to become a nationally popular and accepted sport. The multicultural characteristics of the USA and Australia combined with a certain and strong British origin require a careful management and recognition of the cultural values of different nationalities and ethnic groups, including clubs, to ensure a successful development of soccer.

When sport organizations distribute products in more than one country, the way the organization brands itself becomes increasingly important. The challenge of truly international brands is to stand for something that appeals to 'all' people, while in-corporating opportunities to extend the brand for cultural niche markets. McDonalds stands for hamburgers all over the world (or fast food standardized in quality), but the ingredients are adjusted to local customs. FIFA stands for soccer all over the world, but the development, style and organization of the game are adjusted to local needs. At national and local level, leagues and clubs have branded themselves. Some of the soccer club brands are as strong as, if not stronger than, the FIFA brand. Clubs such as Manchester United, AC Milan and FC Barcelona have fan clubs all over the world and their respective merchandise can be bought from stores in many nations and on the Internet. It even includes sport stars that make up businesses of their own. This is the greatest threat to sport governing bodies such as FIFA and the IOC.

The commercial independence of wealthy clubs and athletes is likely to erode the power of the umbrella brand to form smaller, yet very powerful, sub-brands in their own right. This is strongly exemplified by the G14 or G24 alliance of Europe's strongest soccer clubs. If they so choose, the G14 could form their own competition by way of a European Super League, without the involvement of governing bodies

---

8   European and American football are considered important components in the development of national identities, see for instance: Goig, Ramón Llopis (2008). 'Identity, Nation-State and Football in Spain. The Evolution of Nationalist Feelings in Spanish football', *Soccer & Society*, No. 1, 56-63. Falk, Gerhard (2005). *Football and American Identity*. New York: The Haworth Press.

such as UEFA or FIFA. In case of a super league, this would change Europe's football landscape dramatically into perhaps three levels of super, regional and domestic leagues.

As hyper-developed corporate sport entities, US professional leagues may be the blueprint examples for future international governing bodies or competitions such as a European Super League. They control competition, stimulate development and legislate in relation to the rules, regulations and format of the game. Clubs are increasingly owned by investors, making it hard for governing bodies to tell them what they can and cannot do. There are great benefits in using established brands as a means to sell new products into new markets. Global entertainment conglomerates are successfully using the established brand power of sports organizations to increase the profitability of their sales, and increasingly they are building their own sport properties (teams and events) from scratch for the purpose of harnessing the inherent branding power of sport.

The Global Sports Market

Since the 1990s, the commercialization of sports has been growing. Significant investments have been made in the construction of new arenas and re-development of existing facilities. The price and salary of professional players have skyrocketed, too. Just like Hollywood, superstars are being created and by way of expanding television and other media, sports have become the pivotal center of entertainment, advertising and marketing. Sports are big business and around the sporting activities and actors, a wide web of manufacturing and service industries supply players, managers and other sporting club staff with an increasing number of products and services. Some of these industries serve the consumer markets, too, especially producers of sporting goods.

The sports market may be seen from three perspectives. From a narrow point of view, the sports market consists of corporate sports revenues. In a wider sense, the sports market includes also those industries that supply sports equipment, facilities and management services. The first perspective corresponds to the sporting industry that organizes and performs the events, while the second perspective is equivalent to the sports industry. A third and even broader perspective might include all the remaining industries that benefit from sporting activities, incl. transportation, accommodation, restaurants, shops, the food and beverage industries, the building industry, IT and the like. This may be called the sports economy, including all the value creating activities and impacts of sport.

While it is difficult to specify the size and composition of the sports industry and sports economy in a wider sense (see below), it is possible to outline the structure of the sports market and the sporting industry as such. The sports market from a narrow perspective consists of gate revenues for live sporting events; rights fees paid by broadcast and cable television networks and television stations to cover these events; merchandising which includes the sale of products with team player logos; sponsorships which include naming rights and payments to have a product associated with a team or league; and the Internet, mobile, and other rights packages to sports events.

FIGURE 13

The Global Sports Market in $bn, 2001-2010

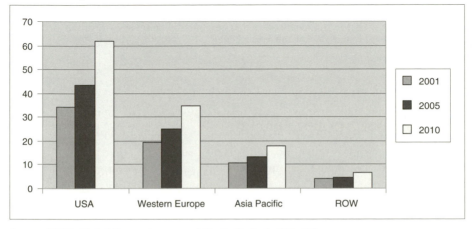

Source: PWC. Global Entertainment and Media Outlook, 595, 605.

Spending on the overall global sports market expanded from $68 billion in 2001 to $86 billion in 2005 and an estimated $121 billion in 2010.[9] The USA includes half the world market and is underlining its dominating position in the sporting industry as well as in other industries of the experience economy (Figure 13). From the slow increase of the early 21th century, the sporting industry is projected to accelerate its growth towards 2010. In second place, the West European sports market is concentrated in the five large countries: Germany, UK, France, Italy and Spain, covering 90 percent of the regional marked and led by Germany and the UK. In Asia Pacific, Japan is the largest market, followed by China, South Korea, Australia and India. The sports markets of Latin America, Africa and the Middle East are relatively small in a global perspective.

---

9   PWC. Global Entertainment and Media Outlook, 594.

Figure 14

The Global Sports Market in Regions and Revenue Sources in $bn, 2005

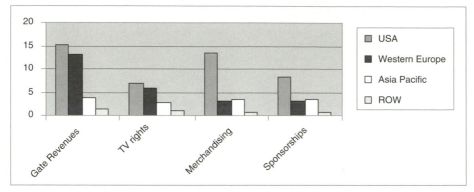

Source: PWC. Global Entertainment and Media Outlook, 597, 605, 610, 614, 617.

The sporting industry is based on four large income sources: gate revenues, TV rights, merchandising and sponsorships (Figure 14). Gate revenues make an important source of income in all parts of the world, particularly in Western Europe. In the United States, merchandising is much more important than in any other region. To some degree, this is the case for sponsorship, too. Revenues from TV rights are of relatively less importance to the US and Western Europe, but are relatively more important to the rest of the world. In conclusion, the US sports market is more developed in merchandising and sponsorship than the rest of the world, whereas Western Europe is more dependent on gate revenues, while in Asia Pacific and ROW, revenues are almost equally divided between the four income sources. Merchandising and sponsorships will continue to benefit from expanding economic conditions, from the emergence of new revenues generated by the Internet and mobile phones, and from the companies' interest in developing relationships with their customers. The FIFA World Cup in Germany 2006 and South Africa in 2010, along with the Winter Olympics in Italy 2006, the Beijing Summer Olympics in 2008 and the Winter Olympics in Canada in 2010 boosted and will boost markets and particularly expand the TV rights fees.

USA

The United States is by far the largest and most commercialized of all sports markets.[10] It is based on the two interrelated pillars of leagues and clubs on the one hand and

---

10   PWC. Global Entertainment and Media Outlook, 596-603.

TV-networks and media corporations on the other. Leagues and clubs create revenues from gate sales, TV rights, online and wireless rights, sponsorships, advertising and merchandising. Media corporations get access to a most-wanted content and to advertising revenues, while sponsors and advertisers reach large markets through TV. Although TV rights fees make up an important source of income to leagues and clubs, the major sports revenues increasingly stem from gates, merchandising and sponsorship. TV is by far the most important media, however, because it attracts sponsors and advertisers, too. Online and wireless income from the Internet, satellite radio and mobile phones has been increasing rapidly since 2005, but from a low starting point.

FIGURE 15

The US TV Rights Fees Market in $bn, 2001-2010

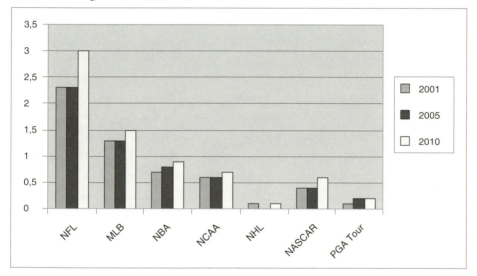

Source: PWC. Global Entertainment and Media Outlook, 594-618.

Four large networks control the American TV sports market: NBC, CBS, ABC (ESPN) and Fox. They are all part of huge media and industrial conglomerates, namely General Electric (NBC), Summer Redstone (CBS), Walt Disney (ABC/ESPN) and News Corporation (Fox). Except for part of the golf broadcasting rights (The Golf Channel), these four corporations have bought all rights to broadcast sports from the four large national leagues and international sports events on the US market. The new five year contracts of 2006-2007 add growth to a slow TV rights market. The divide of TV rights fees between the various leagues and sports underlines the dominant position of football (Figure 15).

In 2003, NFL created its own network to promote the league and provide loyal fans with daily coverage.[11] The network reached 40 million homes by 2005, one-third of all homes, and continues to grow in its number of subscribers. Several teams have created their own networks, too. This is also the case in baseball, including for example The Boston Red Sox and New York Yankees, while others share networks, such as Cubs, White Sox and Bulls in Chicago. Furthermore, leagues and clubs use the Internet and videos to reach their fans and a broader audience. For instance, NFL made a $400 million license agreement with the computer games software developer Electronic Arts. Through clubs and networks, international branding and sales are increasing, too. The players get more than half of the total club revenues. In recent years, many leading clubs have invested large sums in building new arenas and larger and improved facilities have created more gate revenues and sponsorships. The lucrative sale of naming rights has become an important revenue source, too. In addition, several clubs have been taken over by rich investors that recognize the branding opportunities of sports. Because of the deep interest of the sports fans in the sports they follow, sports sponsorship and TV rights give advertisers and media corporations a closer relationship with consumers than through traditional advertising. Pressed by league and club networks and the breakthrough of the Internet and mobile phones, too, the media corporations show growing interest in buying league clubs to control the vital sports content, although this remains to be seen in a wider sense.

The increasing income from merchandising is very much based on fans that buy shirts, scarves, memorabilia, etc. A strong fan culture is found around all league clubs, in particular within football, similar to soccer fans in Europe, for example. Most large corporations invest considerable sums in sport sponsorships, including IBM, Coca-Cola, Budweiser, etc. in order to expose themselves through high profiled sports events.

Commercial American sports are completely dominated by the four large leagues, including NFL (32 football clubs) (Table 9), MLB (30 baseball clubs), NBA (30 basketball clubs) and NHL (30 hockey clubs).[12] NFL, MLB and NBA, in that order, are worldwide the most profitable sports leagues. In 2005, the largest and most popular American League, NFL, reached total revenues of some $6 billion. Attended by more than one hundred million people, the four leagues total revenue was $20 billion in 2005.[13]

---

11   www.nfl.com.
12   www.wikipedia.org. 'Major Professional Sports Leagues'. www.nfl.com. www.mlb.com. www.nba.com. www. nhl.com.
13   www.forbes.com.

TABLE 9

NFL Clubs' Revenues in $m, 2005

Washington Redskins	303	Kansas City Chiefs	186
New England Patriots	250	New York Giants	182
Dallas Cowboys	235	New York Jets	179
Houston Texans	222	St. Louis Rams	179
Philadelphia Eagles	218	Detroit Lions	178
Denver Broncos	207	Buffalo Bills	176
Cleveland Browns	206	Cincinnati Bengals	175
Tampa Bay Buccaneers	203	Jacksonville Jaguars	173
Baltimore Ravens	201	Oakland Raiders	171
Chicago Bears	201	San Francisco 49ers	171
Carolina Panthers	199	San Diego Chargers	170
Miami Dolphins	194	Atlanta Falcons	170
Green Bay Packers	194	Indianapolis Colts	167
Seattle Seahawks	189	Minnesota Vikings	167
Tennessee Titans	189	New Orleans Saints	160
Pittsburgh Steelers	187	Arizona Cardinals	158
Total			6160

Source: *www.forbes.com*. *NFL Team Valuations*. Special Report 31.08.2006.

Western Europe

The West European sports market is dominated by the five largest countries: Germany, UK, France, Italy and Spain. Led by Germany and the UK, these five countries cover almost 90 percent of the market. Germany and the UK alone generate half of West European sports spending, with $7 and $6.6 billion in 2005, respectively (Figure 16).

Following the expanding TV rights market of the latter part of the 1990s and the slow down of the early 2000s, the TV distribution market revitalized since 2005 and is projected to continue its growth towards 2010. Similar to the USA, corporations in Western Europe are using sport to develop closer relationships with consumers and are thereby fuelling sponsorship and merchandising spending. Gate revenues continue to grow, but growth is dampened by high entrance rates.

Figure 16

The West European Sports Market in $bn, 2001-2010

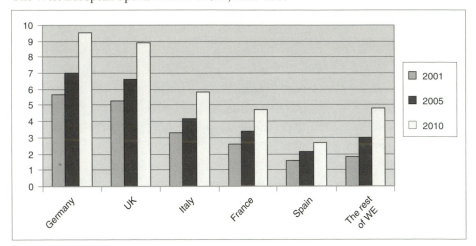

Source: PwC. Global Entertainment and Media outlook, 605.

The improving economic conditions and increasing TV subscription spending since 2005 has made cable and satellite networks bid up fees, boosted by the 2006 FIFA World Cup in Germany and the emerging markets of the Internet and mobile phones, too (Figure 17). Large deals were concluded between leading network providers and the national soccer leagues that play the same crucial role to the West European sporting market as the NFL, MLB, NBA and NHL do in the USA. The broadcast rights in Western Europe are concentrated in the hands of a few national network corporations, including Unity Media and Deutsche Telekom in Germany, BSkyB in the UK, Sky Italia in Italy, Canal Plus in France and La Sexta and Audiovisual Sport in Spain and Talpa in the Netherlands. The World and European Cups, Champions League and national leagues drive the sports market. Clubs make lucrative sponsorship agreements with large corporations, too, such as the several hundred million dollar contracts between Manchester United and Nike; Real Madrid with Siemens, Adidas, Audi and Pepsi; and Bayern Munich with Deutsche Telekom, Audi and Coca-Cola. Merchandising revenues are increasing, too.

The West European sports market is less commercialized than the American market, however. Gate revenues make up half its sports market and continue to grow as a consequence of renewed and enlarged arenas and relative low prizes, although British gate rates have accelerated to a degree that threatens to exclude the working classes, the traditional core of British soccer fans.

FIGURE 17

Revenue Sources of the West European Sports Market in $bn, 2001-2010

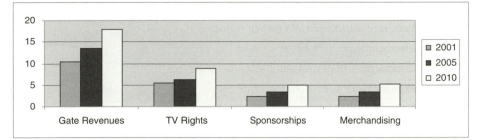

Source: PWC. Global Entertainment and Media outlook, 605.

Football in Western Europe

Except for North America and Oceania, football (meaning soccer) is the most popular sport in the world.[14] West European national leagues dominate global soccer, led by the UK's Premier League, Germany's Bundesliga, Spanish Primera Liga, Italian Serie A and the French Ligue 1. Western Europe is the primary focus of soccer in matters of sport and money, and the vast majority of the world's top players play in a club in one of the five big leagues. Over the years, a handful of clubs continue to lead the national leagues and Champions League. This can be clearly seen from the top 20 list of European clubs for the past decade since the mid-1990s (Table 10). British and Italian clubs top the list, including British Arsenal, Chelsea, Liverpool, Manchester United, Newcastle United and Tottenham Hotspur and Italian Inter, Juventus, Lazio, AC Milan and AS Roma. Only Spanish FC Barcelona and Real Madrid and German Munich have managed to join this UK-Italy dominance. Between this leading pack of clubs and the less frequently appearing clubs there is a gap that has been rather permanent. It is difficult to get to the top, but once you get there you apply your organizational resources to stay put. That seems to be the lesson.

---

14   Deloitte. *Football Money League, 2007.*

TABLE 10

Football Clubs' Appearance in a Top 20 Revenue List, 1996-2006

10 Appearances	Arsenal, FC Barcelona, Bayern Munich, Inter, Juventus, Lazio, Liverpool, Real Madrid, Manchester United, AC Milan, AS Roma, Newcastle United, Tottenham Hotspur
9 Appearances	Chelsea
7 Appearances	Rangers
6 Appearances	Leeds United, Borussia Dortmund, Parma, Rangers
5 Appearances	Celtic
4 Appearances	Olympique Lyonnais, Schalke 04
3 Appearances	Aston Villa, Valencia
2 Appearances	Manchestrer City, Olympique Marseille, Paris St. Germain
1 Appearance	Ajax, Atletico Madrid, Benfica, Everton, Fiorentina, Flamengo, Sunderland

Source: Deloitte. *Football Money League*, 2006-2007.

A recent top 20 list will underline the permanent dominance of the same clubs, followed by a second group of clubs that seem to remain followers in secondary position (Table 11). Consequently, they appear seldom in the lucrative Champions League. The most expanding clubs in recent years are the Spanish Top 2, Real Madrid and FC Barcelona, British Chelsea, Italian Inter, French Lyon, German Schalke 04 and Portuguese Benfica. In all European leagues, a few top clubs are taking the lead in financial and sporting matters, including for example Benfica, FC Porto and Sporting in Portugal, and PSV Eindhoven and Ajax Amsterdam in Holland. They come in third position in the European club rankings. Below that, you find a fourth and fifth and even lower ranking levels of clubs.

The Top 20 club revenues amount to half the total revenues of the five big leagues and some quarter of all European leagues' revenues (Figure 18). The British Premier League top the list of European leagues with a 2005/06 total revenue of almost half the total of the big five leagues. From Britain's $4 billion there is a long way to, for example, the $0.2 billion revenue of the Danish League. The European soccer leagues earn more than double the American NFL revenues of $6 billion, but they also include up to ten times as many clubs. Including other parts of the world, Latin America, Eastern Europe, Russia, Japan and Australia, global estimates for professional football and soccer club revenues may add up to $25 billion. Player salaries take about half the total revenues. The gap is wide, however, from the salaries of top players like Ronaldinho of FC Barcelona and Rooney of Manchester United to the ordinary league club players.

TABLE 11

The Top 20 Clubs' Revenues in $m, 2000/01 and 2005/06

	2000/01	2005/06
Real Madrid	184	388
FC Barcelona	146	345
Juventus	230	334
Manchester United	289	323
AC Milan	218	317
Chelsea	157	294
Inter	148	275
Bayern Munich	230	272
Arsenal	142	256
Liverpool	182	234
Lyon	92	170
AS Roma	164	169
Newcastle United	121	165
Schalke 04	73	163
Tottenham Hotspur	106	143
Hamburg	80	135
Manchester City	72	119
Rangers	93	118
West Ham	100	116
Benfica	60	113

Source: Deloitte. Football Money League, 2006-2007.

What the money league reports show is that football or soccer remains a growth sport, especially at the highest level. There is a continued high public and commercial interest in the sport. The catalyst for the remarkable long-term growth was the broadcasting rights revolution of the 1990s. The value of the top class broadcasting rights continues to rise. Since the 1990s, clubs have focused on enhancing their revenues in areas of their control. That includes renewed arenas to increase gate revenues, customized ticketing and a growing focus on merchandising and sponsorships. Clubs have also been able to dampen the skyrocketing player salaries and even to reduce them. Some clubs make more money on TV rights, merchandising and sponsorships than others, namely top clubs such as Real Madrid, Manchester United and Bayern Munich. Recruiting world class players is part of these clubs' strategy to generate more money from other income sources than gates and, to some degree, TV rights. Real Madrid and Manchester United, for instance, have high valued sponsorship contracts with Siemens and Adidas, respectively, including several other and smaller sponsorship agreements.

FIGURE 18

Revenues of European Top 20 Football Clubs, Top Five Leagues and All European
Leagues in $bn, 1996-2006

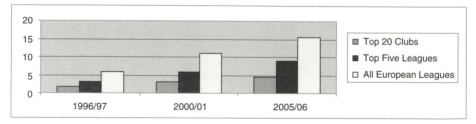

Source: Deloitte. Football Money League, 2006-2007.

National leagues and clubs depend in different ways on the four sources of revenues,
i.e. gates, TV rights, sponsorships and merchandising. Italy and France rely strongly
on TV rights fees, Spain and Germany rely more on the three other sources, while
British revenues are more equally split between all four sources of income. Not only for
the five big leagues and their clubs, but for all other West European leagues and clubs,
there has been a commercial revolution turning clubs into big business. Furthermore
as noted, professional football has become the focus of the whole business world as a
promising way of profiling and marketing companies and goods.

Real Madrid

Since the turn of the millennium, Real Madrid has more than doubled its revenue to
reach $388 million in 2005/06, becoming the world's highest earning football club.[15]
While other clubs typically increased their income by way of TV rights and renewed
stadiums, Real Madrid expanded primarily through increased commercial income. A
change of strategy since 2000 made Real Madrid take advantage of its popularity and
sporting success.

Real Madrid wants to develop a product that people from around the world can
identify with, and ultimately buy. Real Madrid aims at commercializing its content
and as the primary content of the club is its players, the new strategy is based on a
collection of world class players and football stars that has been acquired since 2000,
such as Figo, Zidane, Ronaldo and Beckham and, later on, Van Nistelrooy and Raûl.

Perhaps the most visible effects of acquiring world-class players are the soaring
sales of shirts and associated merchandise. Merchandising and licensing contributes

15   Deloitte. Football Money League 2006.

almost half the club's commercial revenues, the remainder being derived from sponsorship and advertising. Real's merchandising and licensing strategy is built on an outsourcing model. The club forms partnerships with commercial organizations that acquire the right to use the club's name and associated logos, and sell the products in return for paying Real Madrid a fixed fee and proportion of the sales. Both parties benefit and Real Madrid is not burdened with investment and stores.

In terms of sponsorship, the Real brand is hugely popular in Spain and around the world. The Real brand is an effective marketing tool for corporations to bring global visibility and consumer credibility. Sponsorships are not simply a matter of offering advertising opportunities to companies. Like other leading football clubs, the sponsorships are partnerships, benefiting both parties. Sponsorships are divided into tiers. On the top tier, Real Madrid has two main sponsor partners, Adidas and Siemens Mobile. The deal with Siemens Mobile, alone, is worth almost \$20 million each season. Below these two top-sponsors, is a group of four international sponsors, including Pepsi, Audi, Telefonica and Mahou. A third tier contains several national sponsors.

Real Madrid has millions of fans in Spain and increasingly throughout the world. From the globalized fan crowds flow expanding merchandising revenues. While the majority of merchandising revenues in 2000 came from the domestic market, five years later almost half originated from international markets, including pre-season tours around the world. Few clubs have as many fans as Real Madrid. Only Manchester United, claiming to involve 75 million fans, may surpass Real Madrid in numbers of fans.

The Global Sporting Goods Industry

One industry is directly related to sports. A large industry provides the sport equipment needed to enable modern sporting activities, in professional competitive sports as well as in amateur and personal sport activities.[16] Corporations such as Nike and Adidas provide the football boots, athletic shoes and apparel needed for summer sports.

---

16   Scholars rarely study the business of the sporting goods industry. A first overview is presented by Sage, George H. (2004). 'The Sporting Goods Industry: From Struggling Entrepreneurs to National Businesses to Transnational Corporations', in Slack. The Commercialisation of Sport, 29-51.Except for market research companies, one therefore has to rely on websites of the leading corporations, including their often informative annual reports.

Specialized companies produce balls, clubs, skis and other tools for sporting activities in winter and summer. Often these specialized companies have been acquired by larger firms as part of an ongoing consolidation process. While Nike and Adidas, and to some degree Puma, are consolidating the businesses of team sports and walk-out equipment, Amer has taken the lead in winter sports equipment. Nike is the leading North American firm and Adidas is the European leader. These companies are expanding across the Atlantic and worldwide, too. Of an estimated global sporting goods industry sales at $75 billion, almost half is consolidated in the four companies mentioned. Sales, products, strategies and relations are changing rapidly in the equipment industry, as globalization and markets are increasingly being changed by the spread of a sporty lifestyle, blurring the traditional divide between the sports equipment industry and the clothing fashion industry.

Nike

US-based Nike is one of the two leading worldwide sellers of sports footwear, apparel, equipment and accessory products.[17] Named after the Greek winged goddess of victory, Nike started out in the 1960s as a provider of athletic footwear. During the 1970s and 1980s, sports apparel was added to its product portfolio, and Nike began to expand in Europe, Asia and Latin America. A radical transformation took place since the 1990s. The liberalization and globalization processes of the 1990s made Nike develop a true global strategy and organization. Production was outsourced to low-cost countries in Latin America and Asia. Since the early 2000s, virtually all footwear and apparel are produced outside the United States, while equipment products are produced both in the United States and abroad. As a consequence, Nike's principal business activity is the design, development and worldwide marketing of its products. Regional logistic centers were built around the world to distribute the products from the factories to Nike-owned retail stores, independent distributors and license in over 160 countries. At the same time, Nike merged with several companies to cover all main sports markets for men, women and children.

Nike's core product is athletic footwear. It is designed primarily for specific athletic use, although a large part of the products are worn for casual or leisure purposes. Running, soccer, sport-inspired urban shoes and children's shoes are some of the top-selling products. Nike also market shoes for tennis, golf, basketball, baseball, hiking, skateboarding, bicycle racing and virtually any other athletic and recreational uses.

---

17   *www.nike.com.*

Nike apparel and accessories are designed to complement its athletic footwear products and are sold through the same marketing and distribution channels.

Furthermore, a line of performance equipment is sold under the Nike brand name, including golf clubs and balls, sport balls, eyewear, electronic devices, bats, gloves and other equipment designed for sports activities. That includes the Nike Bauer Hockey subsidiary which produces and distributes ice skates, skate blades, protective gear, hockey sticks and a full selection of products for street and roller hockey. Finally, Nike has increasingly moved into a line of casual footwear, apparel and accessories to take advantage of a widespread sporty lifestyle. Nike's diversification into performance and lifestyle equipment is partly based on existing resources, partly based on mergers with other companies such as Converse, Cole Haan, Hurley and Bauer.

Because Nike is producing consumer goods, demand for its products is highly dependent on fashion trends and the changing popularity of sports activities and design. Nike must therefore respond to trends and shifts in consumer preferences by adjusting its mix of product offerings, by developing new products, and by influencing sports preferences through aggressive marketing. Increasingly, Nike focuses on research and development and technological innovation in the design of footwear, apparel, and athletic equipment in its efforts to produce products that enhance performance and maximize comfort. In addition to Nike's own staff of specialists in such areas as biomechanics, physiology, engineering, and industrial design, Nike also consult external experts in matters of design, materials and concepts, including athletes, coaches, equipment managers, orthopedists, and podiatrists. Performance and reliability of shoes, apparel, and equipment, new product development, prize, product identity through marketing and promotion, and customer support and service are important aspects of competition in the athletic footwear, apparel and equipment industry. Nike contracts with prominent and influential athletes, coaches, teams, colleges and sports leagues to promote its brands, and actively sponsor sporting events. Worldwide, the athletic footwear, apparel and equipment industry is highly competitive. Nike competes internationally with an increasing number of athletic and leisure companies in sports footwear, apparel and equipment, including Adidas.

From a flat level of about $9 billion in the late 1990s and early 2000s, Nike's revenues started to increase strongly from 2004, reaching $15 billion in 2005-2006 and more than 18 $bn in 2007/08 (Figure 19).

FIGURE 19

Nike's Revenues in $bn, 1997/98-2007/08

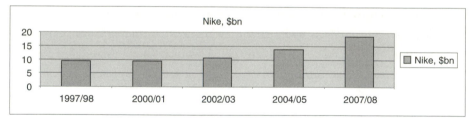

Source: Nike. *Annual Reports: www.nike.com.*

Nike's main markets are the United States and Western Europe that account for three-quarters of all sales, followed by Asia Pacific and Latin America (Figure 20). With success, Nike has focused on increasing its markets worldwide. Nike's strategy is focusing more and more on the sporty, designed, but also relaxed lifestyle of young and adult people. Its products are connected with the music and easy styles of urban life. By way of its interactive site, Nike makes room for communities of runners and other active groups. This corresponds to its strategy of addressing the global athletes and sporty people that want to extend their experiences and improve their quality of life. For years, footwear has made up 60 percent of Nike's sales, while some 30 percent comes from apparel and 7 percent from equipment. Nike remains a footwear and secondly an apparel company.

FIGURE 20

Nike's Regional Markets in $bn, 2000/01-2007/08

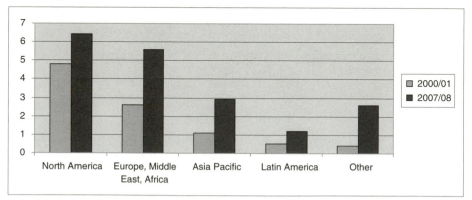

Source: Nike. Annual Reports.

Adidas

Based in Germany, Adidas is the other leading footwear, apparel and equipment company.[18] Adidas' postwar history starts in the 1950s as mainly a soccer boots producer. During the 1960s and 1970s, Adidas established itself as the leading German provider of soccer and athletics footwear and apparel and began its international expansion in the 1980s in Western Europe. Adidas contracted several sponsorships with leading German and international teams and athletes. Like Nike, Adidas started a turn around of strategy and organization in the 1990s. Production was outsourced to low cost countries, mainly in Asia, and Adidas shifted its focus from production and sales to innovation and marketing, including a worldwide supply chain organization. Passing into the new millennium, heavy investments were made in reorganization, R & D, worldwide logistics, its retail stores and retail partners, seeking to create a global organization and market.

Adidas looked for expansion by diversifying into other sport products, too. By acquiring Taylor-Made, Adidas moved into the increasingly popular golf sport. Adidas also diversified into quite different sports such as outdoor products when French Salomon was taken over in 1997. This diversification process was given up in 2005, however, when Salomon was sold to Amer. Instead, Adidas decided to strengthen its core business of footwear and apparel and as a consequence, American Reebok was acquired in 2006. The world number two merged with world third challenging the position of number one, Nike. By acquiring Reebok, Adidas created a true global platform in the sports industry with strong market positions in America, Europe and emerging Asia Pacific. The acquisition of Reebok also enabled Adidas to establish a multi-brand strategy and attack different markets. While Adidas is known for its strong emphasis on team sports, particularly soccer, Reebok celebrates individuality and appeals to consumers that combine sport and lifestyle, including strong positions with women and American sports. As a consequence of the Adidas expansion within the past decade, the Adidas Group trebled its revenues to reach nearly $13 billion in 2007 (Figure 21). Reebok stands for some 20 percent of total sales and Taylor Made for less than 10 percent.

---

18   *www.adidas-group.com.*

FIGURE 21

The Adidas Group's Revenues in $bn, 1997-2007

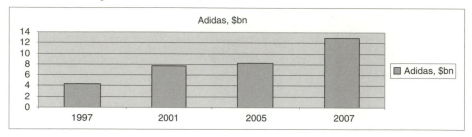

Source: Adidas. *Annual Reports: www.adidas-group.com.*

By way of the Reebok merger, Adidas strengthened considerably its market share worldwide and particularly in North America, making it a true global business and organization. The two brands were continued, based on Adidas' strong position in Western Europe and Reebok's in the United States (Figure 22).

FIGURE 22

Adidas' Regional Markets in $bn, 2001 and 2007

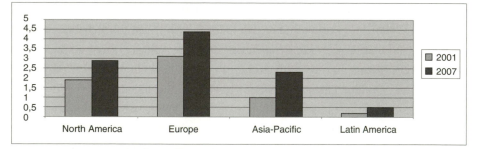

Source: Adidas Group. Annual Reports.

In segments, footwear and apparel in 2005 and 2006 accounted for some 45 and 40 per cent, respectively, with a small increase for footwear and decrease for apparel, Reebok's core business. The golf equipment share increased from 13 per cent in 2005 to 16 per cent in 2006 (Figure 23).

Global Experience Industries

FIGURE 23

Adidas' Product Segments in %, 2001 and 2007

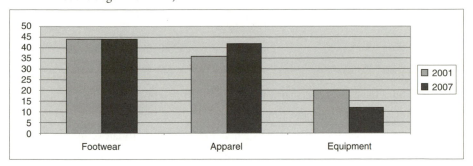

Source: Adidas Group. Annual Reports.

Just like Nike, Adidas sells its products all around the world and is a leading sponsor at FIFA World Cups, UEFA Cups, OL and other major international sports events. Furthermore, Adidas and Reebok are main sponsors in American Football (Payton Manning), basketball (Kevin Garnett) and European soccer leagues, teams and players, runners (Haile Gebrselassie) as well as golf players (Sergio Garcia), to mention just some of its many sponsorships.

By 2006, 15 percent of sales were made through its own retail stores and 85 percent through retail partners. To be successful in the sports industry you have to be close to the consumer, however. Therefore Adidas upgrades collaboration with its retail partners at every point-of-sales to increase their profitability, whether by shop-in-shop such as JJB in the UK and Dick's Sporting Goods in the USA, or partnership agreements like those with INTERSPORT in Europe. The goal is to increase Adidas' impact at retail. Furthermore, through its global supply chain Adidas has turned into a demand-driven and consumer focused business that swiftly markets products according to consumer demands.

Branding and performance are the keys to keep on expanding worldwide.[19] Adidas' strategy is to 'lead the sporting goods industry built on a passion for sports and sporting lifestyle'... and 'to achieve leadership positions in all the categories and markets in which we compete'.[20] Adidas is a consumer-driven company that is 'continuously developing and commercializing industry-leading technologies and designs. Innovation plays a significant role in differentiating our product offering from competitors'. Based on the Group's technological innovations and partnerships with famous designers such

19   *www.adidas.com.*
20   *www.adidas.com.*

as Stella McCartney, Yohji Yamamoto and Porsche Design, Adidas continues to adapt to consumer demands. Like Nike, Adidas is increasingly focusing on a combination of professional sports and the growing sports lifestyle in footwear and apparel.

Puma

Just like Adidas in postwar Germany, Puma expanded as a provider of soccer boots and athletic track shoes.[21] During the 1960s, 1970s and 1980s, Puma transcended Germany and sponsored famous football players such as Pelé, Eusebio, Johan Cruyff and Diego Maradona that played in Puma boots at World Cups. Many leading athletic jumpers and runners in Western Europe and even the USA wore Puma shoes, too. Eventually, apparel and other sports shoes were added to its product portfolio, including tennis in the 1980s and sponsorships of famous tennis players such as Martina Navratilova and Boris Becker. Leading sponsorships included the German Bundesliga team Werder Bremen, too.

FIGURE 24

Puma's Revenues in $bn, 1993-2006

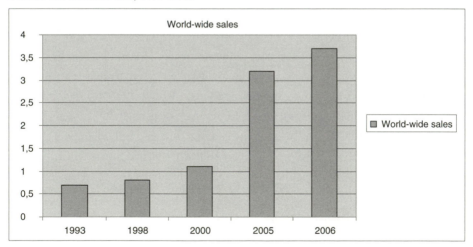

Source: Puma. *Annual Reports: www.puma.com.*

In order to create a leading global and market oriented firm, Puma started in the 1990s a long-term radical reorganization process that is still going on. By focusing on marketing, innovation and product development, the company is seeking to position the Puma brand while outsourcing production to low cost countries. New technolo-

21   *www.puma.com.*

gies are included in boots and shoes, too, and since the late 1990s Puma determinedly merges sport and fashion in cooperation with leading designers. At the same time, Puma continues to expand its markets in Western Europe, the USA and Latin America. Since the turn of the century, Puma has been focusing even more on marketing and branding, innovation and designing to expand its business worldwide. At all international sports events and national leagues, Puma is one of the leading sponsors, including sponsorships of teams and sports stars of the 1990s such as German footballer Lothar Mathaus, athletes Heike Drechsler, Linford Cristie, Merlene Ottey, Serena Williams, replaced by new sports stars in the 2000s, and the soccer teams of Werder Bremen and Atletico Madrid as well as North American football and basketball teams. Golf, cricket and motor racing shoes and apparel have been added to its products and market focus, too.

As a result of its continuous expansion, Puma's turnover increased from some $1 billion in 2000 to almost $4 billion in 2006 (Figure 24). Puma expanded in all three major markets of the world, mostly in Europe and United States (Figure 25). Its new lifestyle approach was successful in North America and Western Europe, where Puma gained ground. Eastern Europe, The Middle East/Africa and Latin America each had a 5 percent share of Puma's revenues. In Asia Pacific, Puma lost ground in relative terms, however, probably as a consequence of aggressive Nike and Adidas offensives. Like Adidas and Nike, Japan is its leading Asian market, followed by a rapidly growing Chinese market.

FIGURE 25

Puma's Regional Markets in $bn, 1998-2006

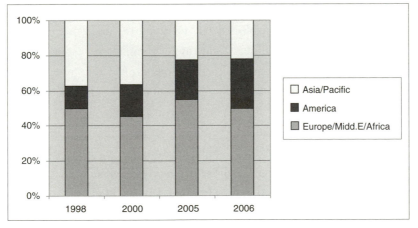

Source: Puma. Annual Reports

In product segments, relative changes over the years have been insignificant. Puma remains a footwear and apparel provider (some 50 percent footwear share and 40 percent apparel share) with some sales in golf and other accessories. Soccer is still its main business field.

In 2006, Puma launched phase IV of its long-term business plan of global reach and of 'becoming the most desirable sport lifestyle company'. Through its long-term endeavors, Puma has been clearly positioned as number three in the sporting goods industry on a lasting basis, after Nike and Adidas. Puma's growing focus on urban sport lifestyle has not been left unnoticed by the business world. As a consequence of the blurring of sports and fashion markets, the French fashion corporation PPR in 2007 presented a take-over offer that was accepted by Puma.

Amer Sports

Finnish based Amer Sports is a world leading provider of sports equipment, particularly winter sports.[22] The story of Amer is in many ways similar to Nokia, the mobile phone gigant, although in minor proportions. Until c. 1990, Amer was a diversified industrial company involved in a range of businesses, sport being just one of them. During the 1990s, the group divested its non-core activities in order to focus on sporting goods. Several companies were acquired, including US Wilson (golf, racket and team sports equipment), Austrian Atomic (winter sports equipment), Finnish Suunto (outdoor and diving instruments), US DeMarini (baseball and softball bats). Since the turn of the millennium, Amer determinedly followed the strategic lines of the other leading companies of the sports industry. It speeded up its reorganization into a market-oriented corporation based on a global supply chain, focusing strongly on global growth in core products and expansion by way of acquisitions. By acquiring US Precor and FPI in 2002 and 2004, a new fitness equipment division was established. Its American base was further strengthened by taking over US Athletic Training Company (pitching machines for baseball and softball) and US Volant (ski equipment). In 2005, Amer made a true strategic move by its merger with French Salomon, the leading European provider of outdoor equipment in bicycling, Alpine skiing, mountain sports, and hiking (apparel, footwear, bags and packs).[23] Buying Salomon from Adidas was also a clear sign of the strategic divide between summer sports and urban life styles on the one hand lead by Nike, Adidas and Puma, and on the other hand the winter and country sports of Amer. The acquisition of Salomon almost doubled Amer's revenues to reach $2.5 billion in 2007 (Figure 26).

---

22 *www.amersports.com.*
23 One of the rare and slightly outdated studies on sporting goods companies is: Desbordes, Michael (2001). 'Innovation Management in the Sports Industry: Lessons from the Salomon Case', *European Sport Management Quarterly*, 1:2, 124-149.

FIGURE 26

Amer Sports' Revenues in $bn, 1998-2007

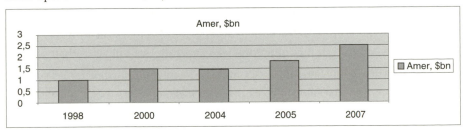

Source: Amer Sports. *Annual Reports: www.amersports.com.*

Geographically, Amer Sports is based on North America and Western Europe (Figure 27). Through many American acquisitions, Amer has established a strong position in US tennis, teamsports, fitness and, to a minor degree, in winter sports and golf. Salomon has given Amer a strengthened position in Europe, particularly in winter and outdoor sports. The major Asia/Pacific markets are Japan and Australia.

FIGURE 27

Amer Sports' Regional Markets in $bn, 1998-2006

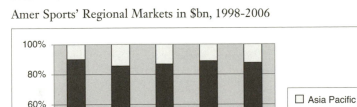

Source: Amer Sports, Annual Reports.

In product segments, Amer is strong in tennis, alpine ski equipment (excl. boots), tennis rackets and balls, in both cases c. a quarter of the world market, and American teamsport, especially football, and to some extent outdoor equipment. In other products (cross country, golf, instruments, fitness and cycling) its world market share is less than ten percent. Since the acquisition of Salomon, Amer's divisions are being organized around its leading brands (Figure 28). Salomon is a world leader in winter sports (alpine, cross-country and snowboarding) and well-established in outdoor sports (climbing, hiking, adventure racing and trail running). Atomic is the world leading manufacturer of alpine skis and produces cross-country skis and snowboards, too. Suunto is the leading manufacturer of instruments for a variety of sports (diving, training, skiing, hiking, sailing and golf). Wilson is the world's leading manufacturer of ball sports products (tennis, squash, badminton, American Football, baseball, basketball, softball and golf). Precor is a full-line supplier of fitness equipment. By acquiring Wilson and Precor, Amer moves into fields of sport that also include Adidas, Nike and Puma. In cycling, Mavic is a leading manufacturer of components and wheels for road cycling, mountain biking and track racing.

FIGURE 28

Amer Sports Brand Segments in $bn, 2006

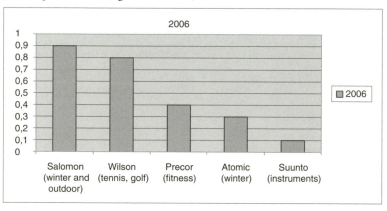

Source: Amer Sports. Annual Report 2006.

Amer Sports sells its product through different types of retail shops: store chains (Wal-Mart and Target in the US), sports shops (Intersport and Decathlon) and specialized sports shops (for example in skiing, tennis and golf). The increasing consolidation of retail puts pressure on Amer to deliver international brand products with a strong consumer appeal. At the same time, solid knowledge of the individual sports and markets is required. A sports shop focusing on expertise is considered the best sales channel for Amer's increasingly high-tech products. In one and the same shop, Amer's wide selection of products enables customers to buy for instance a complete set of running shoes, apparel and wrist computer with heart beat monitor. The core of Amer's partnership model is to offer retailers the opportunity of good profits. Amer is an expert at its sports. Expert knowledge within tennis, winter sport, golf, fitness and sport instruments is placed around the USA and Europe at the centers of the individual brands.

The Wider Sports Industry

The sporting industry that includes the income of sports clubs is just one part of a wider sports industry. Many industries, as providers of equipment, advertising, media, distribution, transportation, management services, betting, etc., profit from the sporting activities. Sport clubs and players have to be managed and paid. Companies invest in advertising at the sporting arenas, players and websites. Equipment for players and merchandise for fans must be manufactured and distributed by retail stores such as Wal-Mart and Intersport. Stadium facilities have to be invested, built and managed and the spectators transported and catered for. By way of the media industry, games are transmitted and reported to a wider public. The difference between the sporting industry and the sports industry in a wider sense is clearly seen from the US figures. In narrow terms, the US sports market amonted to only $44 billion in 2005, while total sports industry revenues are estimated at $213 billion (Table 12).

So sports leagues, clubs, arenas and events have a tremendous impact on many other industries that provide products and services for the sporting industry. Some companies specialize in serving the sporting industry, while others only partly relate to this sector. In general, most of these industries serve other sectors, too, including advertising, gambling, travel, management services, medical aid and facility construction. Precise statistical information is therefore hard to come by. Compared to a total world sports expenditure in 2005 of less than $100 billion dollars, the total economic effects of sports may be an estimated $500 billion, of which 75 percent is based in the Atlantic community.

TABLE 12

The Wider US Sports Industry in $bn, 2005

$bn, 2005			
Advertising	27,4	Medical spending	12,6
Spectator spending	26,2	Media broadcast rights	7
Sporting goods	25,6	Sponsorships	6,4
Operating expenses	23	Facility construction	2,5
Licensed goods	19,5	Multimedia	2,1
Gambling	18,9	Endorsements	0,9
Travel	16,1	Internet	0,2
Management services	15,3	Other	10,3
Total			213

Source: Street & Smith's SportsBusiness Journal. March 25, 2007. Vol. 9, 45.

5. Publishing

Newspapers

Except for television, newspapers are the most widely spread mass media.[1] Daily, at least one national and several local newspapers are published throughout the some 200 nations of the world. More than one billion people read a newspaper every day, equivalent to every fifth or sixth persons on Earth. Based on newspaper sales and advertising, the global newspaper industry made $180 billion in 2005 (Table 13). This is a conservative estimation that might amount to at least $200 billion if revenues of online editions and weekly editions are included. In addition, most newspapers issue free papers, too. In a wider perspective, newspapers depend on several other related industries to produce their content, manufacture and distribute their products and manage their businesses, including providers of print paper, printing machines and IT systems. Total revenues of the newspaper sector may amount to $500 billion.

The Global Newspaper Market

Until three or four decades ago, virtually every household in the developed world bought a newspaper.[2] This market penetration has since been halved and in the early 21th century, only every second household buys a copy of a newspaper. By way of the breakthrough of radio in the 1920s and 1930s, TV in the 1950s and 1960s, digital printing technologies in the 1980s and 1990s, and the Internet and mobile phones since the turn of the millennium, a wide diversity of other media has eventually reduced newspapers' once dominating position. In recent years, the Internet has become the most direct challenge to printed newspapers, but also an opportunity for new distribution channels and possible expansion.[3] All newspapers have a website. Newspaper policies differ on access to the website content. Some are free whereas subscription fees are required for other online newspapers, including achived articles or access to special content.

Partly, newspapers established websites as a defensive strategy to attract readers and advertisers that were abandoning print. However, helped by their long-established news brands and infrastructure, newspapers have become the leading online sites for news and advertising. The number of newspaper web sites visitors equals almost that of print readers. So although printed newspapers continue to lose market share, newspapers have reached new audiences through the Internet. People want to access online news,

1   World Association of Newspapers (WAN): *www.wan-press.org*.
2   Johnston. Encyclopedia of International Media and Communications: 'Newspaper'. Smelser and Batles. International Encyclopedia of the Social & Behavioral Sciences, 'Newspaper'.
3   PWC. Global Entertainment and Media Outlook, 448-487.

just as they want to access online music. Eventually, newspaper companies are learning how to make money from the new potentials of the Internet, just as the recorded music industry. One lesson is that you can make money from Internet readers and advertisers, without cannibalizing the printed version. Secondly, new online readers may be channeled into the printed version, too, as they create a growing interest in news. Finally, the rapid spread of free daily newspapers based on advertising revenues is another way of meeting the challenge of the media revolution and wetting the appetite for in-depth news coverage in paid newspapers. The move to free newspapers may not seem so radical after all, because advertising already makes up the lion's share of total revenues. In spite of competing media channels, the newspaper market continues to grow, however.

TABLE 13

The Global Newspaper Market in $bn, 2001-2010

	2001	2005	2010
USA	55	60	70
Canada	3	3	3
Western Europe	58	57	63
UK	14	14	15
Germany	13	11	12
Italy	6	6	7
Spain	4	5	6
France	4	4	4
Rest of Western Europe	17	17	19
Eastern Europe	3	4	6
Middle East and Africa	2	2	3
Asia/Pacific	43	47	56
Japan	23	21	22
China	5	7	11
Australia	3	4	5
South Korea	4	4	4
India	2	2	4
Taiwan	2	2	2
Rest of Asia/Pacific	4	7	8
Latin America	5	5	7
Total	168	179	208

Source: PWC. Global Entertainment and Media Outlook, 449, 460, 472, 480

Global Experience Industries

Including sales and advertising, the world market for newspaper has been expanding 3 percent annually for years and can be projected to do so in the near future, too. North America and Western Europe each covers one-third of the newspaper world market. Asia and Pacific make up a quarter of the global market, while the remaining share is divided between Latin America, Eastern Europe, Africa and the Middle East. As in any other section of the experience economy, the US is also by far the largest single market, followed by Japan, UK and Germany. 60 per cent of the world marke for newspapers is based in these four leading economies. The newspaper market is first of all a national market and a local market. Only a few newspapers reach beyond national borders, such as the New York Times, International Herald Tribune, Financial Times, Frankfurter Allgemeine Zeitung, and Le Monde. While the newspaper market is slowing down in developed countries, it is boosting in the developing world. China takes the lead, followed by India and some East European and Latin American countries, mainly Russia, Poland and Brazil.

TABLE 14

Global Newspaper Advertising and Circulation Spending in $bn, 2001-2010

	2001		2005		2010	
	Adver-tising	Circu-lation	Adver-tising	Circu-lation	Adver-tising	Circu-lation
North America	44	11	52	12	61	12
Western Europe	35	23	34	23	38	25
Japan	11	12	10	12	10	12
China	3	2	4	3	5	6
Rest of Asia/Pacific	8	8	9	9	14	10
ROW	5	4	7	4	11	5
Total	106	60	115	63	139	69

Source: PWC. Global Entertainment and Media Outlook, 451, 466-469, 472, 477, 482-483, 485, 487.

Worldwide, advertising is the most important income for newspapers. This is particularly the case in the USA and Canada (Table 14), but also in Western Europe. In both regions, the advertising share of newspaper revenues is projected to increase further by 2010 to 85 and 60 percent, respectively. In Japan, the traditional half and half sharing of advertising and circulation revenues continues. This is the case in China and the rest of Asia/Pacific, too. Elsewhere, advertising spending is increasingly becoming the major newspaper income. One reason for the stagnation in newspaper advertising in developed countries outside of North America may be the slow response to the Internet and other challenging media in these parts of the world. Furthermore, as online advertising is not included in the numbers, total advertising is probably somewhat higher and is likely to accelerate in the future, too. According to US numbers, spending on newspaper online advertising was $2 billion in 2005, with a projected $6 billion in 2010. The total US online advertising market, including search engines, publishers and other media, was about $10 billion in 2005 and projected to double in the next five years.[4] Thus, newspapers are gaining ground in the online advertising market. In other developed countries, online advertising is somewhat delayed compared to USA, but it has been accelerating since 2005. The West European online market is probably half the size of the US market.[5] In total, the world online market may be estimated at twice the size of the US market.

In developed countries the long-term decline of unit circulation of newspaper print editions continues (Table 15). The opening of the populous and economically expanding Asian markets, in particular China and India, has boosted circulation in these parts of the world, however. As a consequence, total global circulation is increasing. More than half the world circulation of half a billion copies is being distributed in Asia/Pacific. The number of readers may be estimated to three times the number of circulation copies, i.e. almost 1.5 billion of a world total population of 6.5 billion. The share of newspaper readers is largest in developed countries, amounting to half the population, more elderly people and fewer young people. In developing countries, only one in ten people read a daily newspaper. Accordingly, in developing countries there is much room for circulation and advertising growth.

Western business consolidation, changes in the retail marketplace and unfavorable shifts in demographics has had a negative impact on advertising. As a consequence of retailer concentration and the low share of young newspaper readers, newspapers have become less attractive as an advertising media to reach consumers. Newspapers are strong in the 45+ group, on the other hand. Not withstanding these adverse developments, newspapers remain an important way for retailers to reach consumers. Actually, newspapers reach almost half the adult population. No other single outlet reaches as many people in a single market. Furthermore, retailers have discovered the enormous buying power of the 45+ age group. Retail advertising made up nearly half of all newspaper advertising in 2005. Classified advertising is the other large income source, including mainly recruitment, automotive and real estate. It is very profitable, but highly cyclical and vulnerable to competition from the Internet.

---

4   Jupiter Media Corporation: *www.jupitermedia.com*.
5   MarketingVOX: *www.marketingvox.com*.

TABLE 15

Global Newspaper Circulation in millions, 2001-2010

	2001	2005	2010
USA	55	53	49
Canada	5	5	5
Western Europe	84	78	75
Germany	24	22	20
UK	19	17	15
France	8	8	7
Italy	6	6	6
Rest of Western Europe	27	25	27
Asia/Pacific	253	291	325
Japan	72	70	69
China	68	92	107
India	60	76	94
Rest of Asia/Pacific	53	53	55
ROW	33	32	33
Total	430	459	487

Source: PWC. Global Entertainment and Media Outlook, 454, 466, 474, 481, 485.

Since 2004-2005, newspapers have shown signs of recovering after years of decline. In Western Europe, increased distribution of free dailies have attracted many young people and given advertisers access to a group that has been difficult to reach through paid newspapers. Publishers of paid newspapers are also experimenting with new formats and new features to attract the young audience, including news distribution to mobile phones. A division of content may be developing between more in-depth articles in the daily print version and continuous updating of news in the online newspaper.

Types of Newspapers

Until a few decades ago, newspapers were primarily the massive mouthpiece of different social classes.[6] The social transformation of developed societies and the breakthrough

---

6   Smelser and Batles. International Encyclopedia of the Social & Behavioral Sciences, 'Newspaper'. *www. wikipedia.org*: 'Newspaper'.

of new communication technologies such as TV and the Internet have made the newspaper companies rethink their strategy. People can get information from many sources and today they are better educated than a generation ago. To attract readers, newspapers must upgrade their content to suit the changing demands of an individualized audience of the 21th century. Contemporary newspapers come in five forms, roughly speaking.

Most newspapers are local and serve the local community by covering all fields of politics, business, social and cultural matters. National newspapers are mainly of four kinds. One is the tabloid newspaper that tends to focus on brief information, sensational stories, celebrities, sports and entertainment. Such newspapers include The Daily News in the USA, The Sun in the UK and Bild in Germany. Tabloid newspapers often attract a large readership. 'Tabloid' also refers to a smaller newspaper format that has also become popular among the second group of national newspapers. Newspapers such as New York Times, The Times in London, Frankfurter Allgemeine Zeitung and Le Monde address a different group of readers, mainly national or international decision makers. Therefore, the content is based more on analytical articles of some length. Although political and economical subjects dominate these newspapers, they also inform on social and cultural matters. A third newspaper category may be found inbetween the tabloid and analytical newspapers. Large national newspapers around the world present daily a wide selection of news on political, economic, social, environmental and cultural matters. Most of these newspapers reflect the general political divide in developed nations between a center-right or a center-left approach. Such newspapers include USA Today, the Daily Telegraph and the Guardian in the UK, German Tagesspiegel and French Le Figaro and Liberation. Finally, you find specialized newspapers that address sport and finance. They include The Economist, Financial Times and Wall Street Journal that address the financial elite. The Italian passion for sports has resulted in three daily sport newspapers, La Gazzetta dello Sport, Tuttosport and Corriere dello Sport. L'Équipe is a French counterpart. Japan has a few specialized sports newspapers, too. Sports Illustrated and Sporting News are American magazines.

Although newspapers are different in content and target group, they have all been obliged to upgrade in order to keep their readers. There seems to be two ways to do so. First, by addressing a wider spectrum of people's life in work, family and leisure, they try to create more permanent links to their readers. Newspapers addressing decision makers and more well-off people also present articles or whole themes on certain subjects of lifestyle and attract advertising that relate to, for example, fashion, housing, cars, tourism, etc. Large national newspapers take the same road when they deal with similar subjects, including books, films, operas, theater performances, concerts, radio and TV. In tabloid newspapers, betting and competitions are a popular means of making people buy the daily paper. A second method to strengthen relations with readers is to use the Internet to create more information value to subscribers. Subscribers are given free access to the online version, including other information services and activities initiated by the company. Such extra services may include interactive tools and access to other parts of the large media conglomerates that control most leading newspapers of the world. Consequently, in most advanced nations a few newspaper corporations account for the majority of newspaper circulation.

The Global Newspaper Industry

Virtually in all developed nations, the newspaper industry is dominated by a few lead- ing media corporations.[7] The US newspaper industry includes the following leading media corporations: The New York Times Company that also includes International Herald Tribune and Boston Globe; The MediaNews Group (newspapers in California, Colorado, etc.); multimedia corporations such as News Corp. (The New York Post, Fox Television, etc.); The Tribune Company (Los Angeles Times and other state-papers, television stations, etc.); the Hearst Corporation (state-papers, magazines, and televi- sion stations); Gannett (USA Today, etc.); McClatchy, the largest US chain of daily newspapers (including acquired Knight Ridder, state-papers in California, Pennsylva- nia, Florida, etc.); The Sun-Times Media Group (Chicago based newspaper group).[8]

Leading newspaper and media corporations in the UK are News Corporation (The Sun, the largest daily newspaper, The Times, a.o.) that owns several Australian newspapers, too; Trinity Mirror (Daily Mirror a.o.); Daily Mail & General Trust (Daily Mail).[9] The leading German news and media corporation is Axel Springer (Bild, Die Welt), while most German newspapers are medium sized independent papers such as Frankfurter Allgemeine Zeitung and Süddeutsche Zeitung or German versions of foreign newspapers.[10] France has several large national newspapers, such as the inde- pendent Le Figaro and Le Monde. Hachette Filipacchi Média or rather Lagardère that owns La Parisienne and L'Équipe is the only large French media corporation, but is mainly strong in magazines.[11] RCS Media Group in Italy and Spain (Corriere

---

7   *www.wan-press.org*. WAN (2007). *World Press Trends. The WPT 2007 Report*. The concentration process took off since the 1980s and 1990s, see Muehlfeld, Katrin and Sahib, Padma Rao (2007). 'Completion or Abandonment of Mergers and Acquisitions: Evidence from the Newspaper Industry, 1981-2000'. *Journal of Media Economics*, 20:2, 107-137. Schement. Encyclopedia of Communication and Information: 'Newspaper Industry'.

8   *www.wikipedia.org*: 'History of American newspapers'.

9   *www.wikipedia.org*: 'History of British Newspapers'. A detailed treatment of the UK print industry is pre- sented by: Keeble, Richard (Ed.) (2005). *Print Journalism. A Critical Introduction*. Abingdon, UK: Routledge.

10 Axel Springer: *www.axelspringer.de*. Frankfurter Allgemeine Zeitung: *www.faz.net*. Süddeutsche Zeitung: *www.sueddeutsche.de*.

11 Le Figaro: *www.lefigaro.fr*. Le Monde: *www.lemonde.fr*. Lagardère: *www.lagardere.fr*.

della Sera, El Mundo),[12] Bonnier in Sweden (Dagens Nyheter),[13] Schibsted in Norway (Aftenposten),[14] and Jyllands-Posten/Politiken in Denmark, are other leading media corporations that own large national newspapers.[15] The Japanese newspaper industry is much concentrated on the basis of a few national companies.[16] Worldwide, the newspaper industries of the USA, the UK, the Scandinavian countries, Japan and Australia (Murdoch) are the most consolidated. Increasingly, the newspaper industry is being integrated with others through media conglomerates (see chapter on Television).

Although some corporations stick mainly to newspapers, such as Gannett, all these media corporations have diversified from the ownership of numerous newspapers into other and more profitable media, including television and the Internet. Next, radical changes in the newspaper industry is about to happen: Fragmentation of news consumption, fragmentation of advertising, converging media, and the digital pressure on the core print product all line up for radical changes in the business models of the newspaper industry.[17] Probably, that includes a combination of online and interactive distribution of news and information on the one hand, and on the other hand, an upgraded content that digs deeper into local, national and global problems of politics, economics, social affairs and culture.[18]

Magazines

The Global Magazines Market

The magazine publishing market consists of spending by advertisers in consumer and business magazines, plus spending by readers who purchase magazines either in subscription or in single copy form.[19]

North America and Western Europe are by far the most dominant market regions,

---

12   RCS media Group: *www.rcsmediagroup.it*.
13   The Bonnier Group: *www.bonnier.com*.
14   Schibsted: *www.schibsted.no*.
15   Jyllands-Posten: *www.jp.dk*. Politiken: *www.politiken.dk*.
16   The Japan Newspaper Publishers & Editors Association: *www.pressnet.or.jp*. *www.wikipedia.org*. 'Japanese newspapers'.
17   Schoder, Detlef et al. (2006). 'Mass Customization in the Newspaper Industry: Consumers' Attitudes toward Individualized Media Innovations'. *International Journal on Media Management*, 8:1, 9-18. Fetscherin, Marc and Krohmayer, Gerhard (2004). 'Business Models for Content Delivery: An Empirical Analysis of the Newspaper and Magazine Industry'. *International Journal on Media Management*, 6:1, 4-11.
18   An overview of the challenges of the new technologies is given in: *www.wan-press.org*. WAN (2007). *World Digital Media Trends*.
19   PWC. Global Entertainment and Media Outlook 2006-2010, 414-446.

followed by Asia Pacific (Table 16). The other regions are only small markets. Much more than newspapers, magazines are primarily published and bought in developed countries.

The six largest industrial countries account for three-quarters of the world market. Unlike newspapers, magazines are not projected to grow much more in developing countries than in developed countries. Magazines are a wealth product, the 15 to 44 year-old population being the principal target group. The growth of this group in developing countries and increasing wealth has a favorable impact on magazine spending, while a decline in developed countries has an adverse impact. Rising income and changing consumer behavior will neutralize this trend, however, and will result in growth in all global markets.

TABLE 16

The Global Magazine Market in $bn, 2001-2010

	2001	2005	2010
USA	34	36	43
Canada	1	1	1
Western Europe	37	38	43
France	8	9	10
UK	7	7	9
Germany	6	6	6
Italy	5	5	6
Rest of WE	10	11	12
Eastern Europe	2	3	5
Asia/Pacific	15	17	21
Japan	10	10	11
China	1	2	4
Australia	1	2	2
Rest of Asia/Pacific	3	4	5
ROW	3	4	5
Total	93	99	118

Source: PWC. Global Entertainment and Media Outlook, 414-446.

There are roughly two kinds of magazines.[20] One kind is the consumer magazine that contains entertaining and instructive information for various groups of women, men, teens and children, including topics such as art, food, hobby, animals, music, religion, science, sports, computers and video games. A second kind of magazine brings professional and business information to certain target groups. Each group of magazine is published weekly or monthly. Business magazines differ from scientific journals that address the scientific communities at less regular intervals. In the USA, more is spent on consumer magazines than on business magazines. Spending is probably more evenly divided between the two kinds of magazines in Western Europe and elsewhere.

In North America the majority of magazine income depends on advertising, particularly in the case of business magazines, while circulation and advertising spending is equally important in Western Europe, and circulation sales are the largest revenue source in the rest of the world. The majority of magazines in the Atlantic community are sold by subscription, whereas retail sales are the dominant trade form elsewhere.

Market growth in developed countries is mainly based on the issue of an increasing number of new magazines that seek to catch the changing trends of lifestyle. Growth in this part of the world is also a consequence of consolidation that allows for greater investments in marketing and product customization. Elsewhere, growth follows from an increasing middle class in emerging economies.

The Global Magazines Industry

Thousands of magazines are published weekly, every fortnight or monthly.[21] Some are sold in millions, some in just a few thousand copies. Most popular in the USA is AARP Magazine that addresses the 50+ group.[22] Classical Reader's Digest has still a million copies sale.[23] Just like AARP, the most popular American magazines deal with family, women, homes and gardens subjects (Better Homes and Gardens, Good Housekeeping, Family Circle, Woman's Daily and Ladies' Home Journal) or they are of the more informative type such as National Geographic and TV Guide.[24] A few business magazines are very popular, too. Time Magazine is top scorer with 4 million copies sold each week, while Business Week sells in 3 million copies.[25] Similar to newspapers, the largest magazines and several minor ones are owned by a handful of large media companies,

20   Johnston. Encyclopedia of International Media and Communications: 'Magazines'.
21   Schement. Encyclopedia of Communication and Information: 'Magazine Industry'.
22   *www.aarpmagazine.org*.
23   *www.rd.com*.
24   *www.wikipedia.org*: 'American magazines'.
25   *www.time.com. www.businessweek.com*.

such as Time Warner, Meredith, Reader's Digest and Hearst Corporation.[26] These conglomerates that spread across most media own a majority of the circulated magazines, including the circa one hundred magazines selling more than one million copies.

The American media conglomerates are active in Europe and the rest of the world, too, including Reader's Digest, Time Warner and others.[27] Apart from the American media corporations, large European-based media companies have emerged, such as Springer, Bertelsmann's Gruner+Jahr and Spiegel in Germany, Redwood Publishing, Haymarket Publishing and the Economist Group in UK, Hachette in France and Bonnier Publications in Scandinavia.[28] The large Japanese magazine market, covering 10 percent of world market is concentrated in the same way as the Atlantic community.

Some American media conglomerates have been able to spread their magazines worldwide, including consumer magazines such as Reader's Digest and Donald Duck and Time and News Week business magazines. Most consolidation of the magazine market is first and foremost going on at a national level, however. Still, language and culture make up barriers for international expansion. However, national champions are increasingly trying to expand abroad, for instance in Scandinavia, where Swedish Bonnier and Danish Egmont and Aller are expanding internationally in Northern and Eastern Europe.[29] They address homes, family life, leisure activities, fashion, celebrities and cartoons in the consumer market mainly. Everywhere, new magazines are published, trying to profit from changing trends and lifestyles and an increasing individualization of readers, focusing on golf, wellness, travel, etc. As magazine readers tend to have higher income and more education than average, this is reflected in a growing number of magazine readers in emerging economies.

Books

The Global Book Publishing Market

The book publishing market consists of retail spending by consumers on consumer books; schools and government agencies on educational textbooks; and retail spending on professional books.[30]

---

26   www.rd.com. www.warner.com. www.hearst.com.

27   www.rd.com. www.warner.com.

28   www.springer.com. www.grunerjahr.com. www.redwoodgroup.net. www.haymarketgroup.co.uk. www.economist. com. www.hachette.com. www.bonnierpublications.com.

29   www.egmont-magasiner.dk. www.aller.dk.

30   PWC. Global Entertainment and Media Outlook, 490.

The book publishing market is generally driven by economic growth and increasing digital search capabilities and electronic formats. The electronic book market will grow rapidly from a small base. While electronic books might cut into the textbook and professional book markets, it is not likely to reduce the consumer book market in the projected period.

TABLE 17

The Global Book Publishing Market in $bn, 2001-2010

	2001		2005		2010	
	Print	E-Books	Print	E-Books	Print	E-Books
North America	33	0	37	1	41	3
USA	31	0	35	1	39	3
Canada	2	0	2	0	2	0
Western Europe	41	0	43	0	47	1
Germany	11	-	11	-	11	-
UK	7	-	7	-	8	-
Spain	6	-	7	-	7	-
France	6	-	6	-	6	-
Italy	4	-	5	-	6	-
Rest of WE	8	-	8	-	9	-
Eastern Europe	3	0	4	0	4	0
Middle East/Africa	2	0	2	0	2	0
Asia/Pacific	22	0	22	0	26	3
Japan	9	-	9	-	9	-
China	5	-	7	-	8	-
South Korea	3	-	2	-	2	-
Australia	1	-	1	-	2	-
India	1	-	1	-	1	-
Taiwan	1	-	1	-	1	-
Rest of Asia/Pacific	1	-	2	-	4	-
Latin America	4	0	4	0	5	0
Total	103	0	112	1	124	7

Source: PWC. Global Entertainment and Media Outlook, 490-531.

The world book publishing market is highly dominated by the developed countries (Table 17). Alone, the USA, the five large West European nations, and Japan cover 75 pecent of the world market. Among developing countries, only China makes up a considerable and rapidly growing single market. In developed countries, the book publishing market is growing just a little. Total spending rose from $103 billion in 2001 to $112 billion in 2005, with a projected $131 billion in 2010.

The book consumer market is by far the largest market of the three book publishing markets that also include books for educational and professional use (Table 18). Bestsellers contribute much to total sales, such as The DaVinci Code in 2005 and Harry Potter in 2007. The electronic consumer book market is beginning to generate momentum. However, the lack of a popular eReader similar to the iPod in the music industry has handicapped the market. New and improved eReader technologies are on their way and are likely to hit the market before the end of the projected period. Growth in e-book sales will to some degree dampen print book sales. The ongoing or planned digitization of Western libraries might boost the e-books market even further.

TABLE 18

The Global Consumer, Educational and Professional Book Publishing Markets in $bn, 2001-2010

	2001			2005			2010		
	Cons.	Educ.	Prof.	Cons.	Educ.	Prof.	Cons.	Educ.	Prof.
USA	17,2	8,5	5,1	19,8	10,1	5,8	21,5	12,1	5,2
Western Europe	23,4	12,4	5,5	25,7	12,2	5,3	29	12,9	4,9
Japan	5	2,5	1,6	4,9	2,6	1,5	5,8	2,8	1,4
China	1,9	2,7	0,8	2,4	3,4	0,9	3,5	4,3	1,1
ROW	8	5,7	3,1	8,8	6,2	2,5	9,7	6,9	2,8
Total	55,5	31,8	16,1	61,6	34,5	16	69,5	39	15,4

Source: PWC. Global Entertainment and Media Outlook, 490-531.

Educational books include textbooks for elementary schools, high schools, and colleges. In developed countries, the demographic decline in school and college populations will dampen growth, whereas the text book market in developing countries will increase because of reverse demographic trends in these parts of the world. Increased governmental spending adds to growth in school books.

The professional book market serves the scientific, technical, medical, legal and financiel industries. As professional books are generally used for reference purposes, they are suitable for electronic formats and publishers have invested in e-products and tools to customize material. Professionals are therefore migrating from print versions to e-formats, causing a decrease in sales of print editions.

The Global Book Publishing Industry

The book publishing industry is going through a period of profound change.[31] This has been brought about by globalization and the digital revolution. Consolidation is one impact of recent developments, too, as well as a move to digital distribution in some book publishing industries. The publishing industries of consumer, educational and professional information address different segments in the marketplace.

Consumer Books

The market for consumer books is by far the largest book sector. It had a global market of $62 billion in 2005, some 30 percent in the USA, some 40 percent in Western Europe and about 25 percent in the rest of the world, including nearly 10 percent in Japan and almost 5 percent in China. In the USA, half of the consumer books market is adult fiction and a quarter is juvenile fiction (Figure 29). The rest is primarily divided between mass-market paperbacks, book clubs, mail order and religious literature.

FIGURE 29

The US Book Publishing Industry's Revenues in $bn, 2005

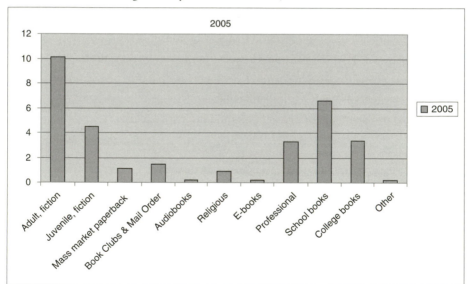

Source: American Association of Publishers: *www.publishers.org*.

---

31   Schement. Encyclopedia of Communication and Information: 'Publishing Industry'. British and US developments are dealt with in Thomson, John B. (2005). *Books in the Digital Age: the Transformation of Academic and Higher Education Publishing in Britain and the United States*. Oxford: Polite Press.

With revenues in 2005, the leading international publishers of consumer books include:[32]

– Pearson:	$1.6 bn
– Scholastic:	1.6 -
– HarperCollins:	1.0 -
– Holtzbrinck:	0.8 -
– Hachette Livre:	2.2 -
– De Agostini:	2.1 -

Language is an important part of the consumer books industry. The English language supports internationalization of consumer books in the English-speaking world, but many books are translated to numerous languages throughout the world, mainly bestsellers. Still, the consumer books industry is primarily nationally based, while international consolidation is just emerging. Virtually all developed nations are dominated by a few large publishers.

Educational Books

Global educational books had a market of $35 billion in 2005 – 30 percent in the USA, 35 percent in Western Europe, 10 percent in Japan, 10 percent in China and 15 percent in the rest of the world. That includes textbooks and other educational material for elementary schools, high schools and colleges. With revenues in 2005, the leading international providers of education books and information are:[33]

– Pearson:	$5.2 bn
– McGraw-Hill:	2.7 -
– Thomson:	2.2 -
– Houghton Mifflin:	1.0 -
– Holtzbrinck:	0.9 -
– Scholastic:	0.5 -
– Wolters Kluwer:	0.4 -
– John Wiley & Son:	0.2 -

---

32 *www.pearson.com. www.harpercollins.com. www.holtzbrinck.com. www.scholastic.com. www.hachette.com. www. deagostini.it.*

33 *www.thomson.com. www.hmco.com. www.walterskluwer.com. www.mcgraw-hill.com. www.wiley.com.*

Pearson

In addition to its leading position in consumer books, Pearson is also the leading learning company worldwide.[34] Pearson Education covers all ages from kindergarten to university and professionals. Pearson Education is found in 110 countries. From its base in the USA, Pearson is expanding in the UK and other English-speaking markets as well as other language markets, such as Spanish. Education is based on national languages, and therefore Pearson is first and foremost an American publisher and, only secondly, an international publisher. Furthermore, Pearson is providing a great deal of educational material online and, in addition, its testing products are expanding.

Pearson Education is the result of several mergers. Its education division started just after World War II. In 1968, textbook publisher Longman was acquired and in 1970 fiction and non-fiction publisher Penguin Books. Pearson Education's expansion continued through the 1980s, including Addison-Wesley that merged with Longman to become Addison-Wesley Longman. The Penguin Group for consumer books acquired Putman Berkley in 1996. The same year, HarperCollins Educational Publishers was bought, merging with Addison-Wesley Longman. In 1998, Pearson acquired the Viacom Simon & Schuster businesses, including Prentice Hall, while Allyn & Bacon and Macmillan Publishing USA were included in the same year in the new Pearson Education division. While reorganizing into divisions, including Education, the Financial Times and the Penguin Group, since the late 1990s Pearson has focused its business increasingly around its core competences while divesting its non-core businesses. Since then, Pearson expanded into educational technology for online learning, enabling school and home to be connected, and into testing and publishing for students with special needs. Pearson Education also includes a wide variety of testing and measurement material.

Professional Books

Professional books had a worldwide market of $16 billion in 2005. It is closely related to the business information market of $78 billion worldwide (see below). The professional books market is divided into three major markets, including 35 percent in the USA, 33 percent in Western Europe, 10 percent in Japan, 5 percent in China and approximately 15 percent in the rest of the world.

While publishers addressing the consumer market often seek to cover many kinds of fiction and non-fiction subjects, the publishers of professional information have to

---

34   *www.pearsoned.com.*

become specialists in their fields to be competitive. Publishers of professional information do not just concentrate on certain market segments, however. Increasingly, they try to cover a whole sector that needs professional information. They want to be system providers of professional information in their field of business. Therefore, information is specialized into several subcategories, such as law and health care. Leading publishers of professional books include Reed Elsevier, Thomson, Pearson, McGraw-Hill, Springer and Wolters Kluwer.[35] Except Reed Elsevier that focuses on professional and business information, all other companies have a broader basis in the book publishing markets, and Thomson, Wolters Kluwer and McGraw-Hill in the business information market, too.

Business Information

The Global Business Information Market

The business information market encompasses the direct purchases of information by businesses and does not include information provided through advertiser-supported media such as business magazines or business TV channels, or through ad-supported Websites, nor does it include information available through professional books, newspapers, or other general-distribution media outlets.[36] The data also excludes information supplied free of charge, because such data neither produce a spending stream nor include information purchased by consumers.

Business information may be classified into financial, marketing, and industry information categories. Financial information relates to securities, economic, and credit data. Marketing information is used for selling products or services and for monitoring sales and includes survey research, mailing lists, and demographic databases. Industry information includes data and content focused on specific industry categories, such as technology, telecommunications, energy, manufacturing, law, real estate, accounting, and healthcare.

Access to business information is sold through subscriptions, through electronic site licenses, or on a pay-as-you-go basis according to the amount of information

---

35 *www.reed-elsevier.com. www.thomson.com. www.pearson.com. www.mcgrawhill.com. www.springer.com. www. wolterskluwer.com.*

36 PWC. Global Entertainment and Media Outlook, 400-412. It is not obvious that business information should be included in the experience economy. On the other hand, it springs from companies that deal with media such as books and magazines, too. The divide between consumer-based and business-based experience and information may lead to a more clear separation of the two industries in the future.

acquired or the amount of time spent using the service. Print formats are generally sold on a price-per-unit basis, although they are also available on a subscription basis.

Business information is an industry increasingly characterized by multinational suppliers selling to multinational buyers. It is a global market, and the issues that affect the market apply to each region.

Spending on business information has grown from $71 billion in 2001 to $78 billion in 2005, with a projected $101 billion in 2010 (Table 19). The market is dominated by the USA and Western Europe, which together constitute more than 80 percent of worldwide spending on business information. Japan is in third place.

The improved economic environment will help the business information market, which tends to follow the overall economic and investment cycle. Global competition will stimulate demand for industry information, both to maintain domestic market share and to penetrate expanding markets such as China and India. Technologies that provide real-time transactions data are fueling marketing information, as is the availability of lower-cost online market research. Rising investment and increased mergers and acquisitions activity will fuel demand for financial information.

After some flat years in the early 2000s, the global market for business information has been increasing 5 percent annually since 2004 and is projected to reach $101 billion in 2010. Financial information, the largest of the three categories of business information, will increase from $33 billion in 2005 to $42 billion in 2010. Marketing information will rise from $22 billion in 2005 to $29 billion in 2010. Industry information will rise from $23 billion in 2005 to $30 billion in 2010.

In all three categories, the US market constitutes half of the world market. Western Europe, led by the UK and Germany, covers some quarter of total world market. Japan is the largest business information market in Asia and worldwide, at the same level as France and Canada. From a low level, the Chinese information business market is the most expansive market in the world, reaching the same size as South Korea in 2010, in global seventh and eighth place. Business information in the rest of the world is relatively small. Business information is mainly an industry based in developed countries and first of all in the US and the large West European countries whose businesses run the global business information industry, as they run the global business world in general, i.e. their customers.

TABLE 19

The Global Business Information Market in $bn, 2001-2010

	2001				2005				2010			
	Financial	Marketing	Industry	Total	Financial	Marketing	Industry	Total	Financial	Marketing	Industry	Total
North America	18	14	11	43	19	16	13	47	23	21	18	56
USA	16	13	10	39	17	15	12	43	21	20	16	56
Canada	2	1	1	4	2	1	1	4	2	1	2	5
Western Europe	9	4	6	19	10	4	6	20	12	6	8	26
UK				6				7				9
Germany				6				6				8
France				3				3				4
Rest of WE				3				4				5
Eastern Europe				2				2				2
Middle East/Africa				1				1				1
Asia Pacific	3	1	2	6	3	1	2	7	5	2	3	9
Japan				3				3				3
South Korea				2				2				2
China				1				1				2
Rest of AP				1				1				1
Latin America				1				1				2
Total	31	20	20	71	33	22	23	78	42	29	30	101

Source: PWC. Global Entertainment and Media Outlook, 403-408.

Industry Information

In addition to generally improved economic conditions, a key driver of the demand for industry information is growing competition. International organizations are promoting open markets and increased competition. Foreign ownership restrictions have also been relaxed in several countries, allowing international companies to play a greater role in domestic economies. Deregulation in a number of countries is also stimulating domestic competition. In the telecommunications industry, for example, most countries now require competition to local services, which has attracted new providers. In addition to specific deregulatory initiatives, the expanding telecommunications infrastructure has reduced barriers to entry and enabled small companies to compete.

With access to the Internet and affordable broadband, small companies now have resources that were previously available only to large players.

A vertical chain of information may be seen, for instance, in healthcare that stretches from consumer non-fiction books and magazines via textbooks, professional and business information to scientific information. Providers of professional and scientific health information are consolidating their market world wide. The leading consolidators include Dutch Reed Elsevier, American Thomson, McGraw-Hill, Blackwell, Springer Science, and Wolters Kluwer that provide professional information for customers such as doctors, hospitals, universities, libraries, biotechnical and pharmaceutical specialists. Leaders of professional health care information also dominate the market of professional legal information. The professional legal information market, providing information to law firms, law schools, government agencies, corporations, accounts and the like, has been highly consolidated since the 1990s. Three companies have taken the lead, namely Reed Elsevier, Thomson and McGraw-Hill, each dividing the $10 billion world market into parts of almost equal size.

In entertainment and media, the development of new audience measurement systems that provide demographic breakouts and more-detailed usage data will drive the information market. Data are continuously collected for recorded music, books, and Internet visits. Similar data are being developed for out-of-door advertising. The emergence of new distribution channels in entertainment and media is generating demand for products that measure these new channels.

As competition heats up, the need for information increases because companies must work harder to retain their market share and fend off competition. At the same time, expanding markets such as China and India are attracting interest among the international companies looking to penetrate these economies. Demand for industry-specific information on these two countries is fueling the industry information market. Similarly for Latin America, as that region stabilizes and as incomes rise, international companies are looking to enter these markets.

Industry information is not limited to countries experiencing economic growth. Expanding industries attract investment and fuel demand for information as part of the decision-making process in evaluating investments. With most economies now growing, there are more expanding industries and greater demand for industry information than in the early 2000s, when the economy was weaker.

Industry information is expected to be the fastest growing category during the next few years, boosted by the demand for information on expanding geographic markets, by the demand for information on growing domestic markets within each region and by new ways of accessing information that make the information more valuable. The US will be the fastest growing region. Interest in participating in expanding Asia Pacific markets combined with intense domestic competition is fueling spending in the USA (Table 19).

The global industry business information market amounted to $23 billion in 2005. In the industry for information provision to a wide spectrum of manufacturing and service industries, a few companies have taken the lead. With revenues of 2005, they include the following:[37]

– Thomson:	$3.6 bn
– McGraw-Hill:	3.3 -
– Reed Elsevier:	2.7 -
– Holtzbrinck:	1.2 -
– Springer:	1.0 -
– Informa:	0.4 -
– VNU/The Nielsen Company:	0.4 -

The leading group of publishers in industry information corresponds with the companies that have taken the lead in professional books, primarily Reed Elsevier, McGraw-Hill and Thomson.

Reed Elsevier

Reed Elsevier is a Dutch based group in business information and communication.[38] It provides information and communication products that enable customers to develop competitive advantage. By way of several acquisitions since the 1980s, Reed Elsevier has become a leading international business publisher and information provider, mainly based in North America and Europe. Business information is provided through a range of channels, such as magazines, online media, directories, marketing services and exhibitions. By 2007, online-based revenues were almost equal to print revenues.[39] Its main market segments are information and service solutions for legal professionals, professionals in science and health, and professionals doing educational tests and resources. In 2007, Reed Elsevier had total revenues of $10 bn, almost equally divided between its four main markets and divisions.

37   *www.reed-elsevier.com. www.cinven.com. www.mcgraw-hill.com. www.informa.com. www.holtzbrinck.com. www.vnunet.com. www.nielsen.com.*

38   *www.reed-elsevier.com.*

39   Reed Elsevier (2007). *Annual Report 2006: www.reed-elsevier.com.*

Marketing Information

Marketing information is used by companies to sell products or develop marketing campaigns. It consists principally of survey research but also includes such information as mailing lists, telephone databases, demographic databases, information from scanners, loyalty cards, response cards from product purchases, and registrations of products.

Online research represents a growing component. Internet panels and online survey research are less expensive than telephone surveys, and online focus groups are substantially less expensive that traditional focus groups. Lower costs are boosting spending on online survey research.

By means of scanning technologies, actual transactions data are becoming available in a growing number of industries. Moreover, as these data are collected electronically, they are available virtually in real time, making them even more useful. Grocery stores, pharmacies, and other retailers collect information on sales and tie those sales to customers through loyalty card programs. The availability of real-time data for actual transactions enables marketers to adjust strategies, develop promotions, and more effectively target their advertising.

Marketing information is also tied to economy. Marketing efforts are more effective when consumers have discretionary income and are eager to buy. Marketers earn a higher return on their investment in marketing information during those periods. Since 2004, improved economic conditions have contributed to the increase in marketing information. Spending on marketing information is expected to continue to grow in the next few years.

The USA dominates global spending on marketing information, a position that reflects the importance of advertising, promotion, and other marketing in driving sales in the US In 2005, the US constituted two-thirds of the total world marketing information market. By contrast, the US accounts for approximately half the global total for industry and financial information. The US is the fastest growing market, too. Asia Pacific is also expected to grow fast, followed by Latin America. The global marketing business information market in 2005 amounted to $22 billion (Table 19).

A leading global provider of consumer and marketing information is *AC Nielsen*, part of the VNU Group (The Nielsen Company since 2007).[40] Knowledge of consumer behavior is relevant to all industries that address end consumers. AC Nielsen is a marketing information leader in media and consumer packaged goods, but also strong in financial services, automotive, travel, IT, telecommunications and pharmaceutical industries. Retail and media measurement is its core business. In 2005, AC

---

40   *www.acnielsen.com.*

Nielsen had revenues of $4.6 billion. A company specialized in market analyses of the pharmaceutical industry, IMS Health, had revenues of $1.8 billion in 2005.[41]

Financial Information

The improved economic climate from 2004 to 2008 also facilitated financial transactions that boosted demand for credit and financial information. Securities values rose, mergers and acquisitions (M&A) activity involving both corporate and private equity buyers increased, and investment spending grew. In addition to M&A activity, business investment has been expanding, both in domestic markets and internationally. Increased investment by foreign companies in Asia Pacific and Latin America, for example, contributed to the overall increase in investment. Rising investment leads to increased borrowing, which in turn leads to increased demand for credit information by potential lenders.

The US is the fastest growing market. Consumer credit is an expanding sector in the US, and the active residential real estate market fueled growth in consumer credit information. Regulations requiring greater transparency in corporate financial reporting are adding to the demand for financial information. Additionally, risk assessment is becoming a more important component of corporate decision making, which further contributes to demand for financial information.

Moderation in economic growth in all regions will ultimately lead to a slowdown in investment and in M&A activity, which in turn will result in slower economic growth and moderation in demand for financial information. With US interest rates rising, these trends are expected to be most pronounced in the Western Hemisphere and make North and South America the slowest growing regions. Western Europe and Asia Pacific are expected to fare better. Western Europe is experiencing a run-up, and Asia will benefit from increased foreign investment, continued growth in China and India and a turnaround in Japan and South Korea (Table 20).

With revenues of 2005, the industry that provides information for the financial sector is dominated by:[42]

- Reuters: $4.5 bn
- Bloomberg: 3.0 –
- Thomson: 1.9 –

41   www.imshealth.com.
42   www.thomson.com. www.wolterskluwer.com. www.pearson.com. www.reuters.com. www.blomberg.com. www.dnb. com. www.factset.com.

– Dow Jones & Company:	1.7 -
– Dun & Bradstreet:	1.4 -
– Pearson:	1.2 -
– Wolters Kluwer:	0.7 -
– FACTSET:	0.3 -

The financial information industry is increasingly being consolidated. Recently Thomson acquired Reuters (2007), while News Corporation bought Dow Jones (2007), including its Wall Street Journal.[43] With Bloomberg, these three corporations now dominate the global financial information business.

Thomson

Thomson is an internationally leading information provider for business people and professionals in several industries, science and education.[44] Primarily by way of the Internet, Thomson delivers workflow solutions to lawyers, brokers, tax advisors, doctors, teachers, etc. In 2006, 80 percent of its $7 billion revenues stemmed from online solutions and only 20 percent from print.[45] Legal, and next financial, constitute its largest market segments. More than 80 percent of revenue is based on North America. In late 2007, Thomson prepared an acquisition of the leading British financial information provider Reuters, adding another $5 billion to its revenues.

Besides its information solutions for business and professionals in various industries, Thomson provides learning and training material for academic managers and instructors, other managers in the academic world, including managers of book stores, libraries, as well as learning products for college, professionals and high school students. Corporate training programs are addressed to corporate managers and managers of government agencies. Corporate learning addresses most business sectors and individual career development in, for instance, automotive, finance, healthcare as well as the various links of the value chain (Business, Economics, HR, IT, etc.).

43   *www.thomson.com. www.news.corp.com.*
44   *www.thomson.com.*
45   Thomson (2007). *Annual Report 2006: www.thomson.com.*

Advertising

Advertising is a huge global industry that addresses every other economic sector and industry.[46] By advertising is meant communication through a medium whereby an advertising company seeks to promote the demand for a client's products or services, but also to promote political parties, politicians, interest groups, etc. Every medium is used for these messages, including newspapers, magazines, television, radio, movies, the Internet and billboards. Advertisements may also be seen on the sides of a grocery cart, on the walls of an airport walkway, on the sides of buses, on clothing, anywhere it is easily accessed or seen by an audience. Communication through media makes advertising a vital part of the media and entertainment industry. All separate sub-sectors of this industry depend heavily on advert incomes.

The Global Advertising Market

Fueled by economic growth and international events such as the Olympic Games in 2004 and 2008, world advertising spending has been increasing since 2004 at a strong pace from $325 billion in 2001 to $385 billion in 2005, with a projected $521 billion in 2010 (Table 20). The US advertising industry and spending comprises almost half the world revenues and spending. Japan is second, followed by the advertsing spending of the UK, Germany, and France.[47]

Internet advertising is skyrocketing and spending has increased fivefold within this decade, coinciding with the surge in the number of households accessing the Internet through a broadband connection. Broadband also facilitates full-motion video ads. Out-of-home will be the second fastest growing advertising medium. As consumers are less able to avoid out-of-home ads than other advertising, it makes out-of-home an attractive medium for advertisers. Digital technologies will also allow for the creation of visually striking displays that increase the effectiveness of out-of-home. Television will expand well, too, boosted by advertising on new channels supported by expanding digital platforms, lifted by OL 2008 and FIFA 2006 and 2010, too. Television remains

---

[46]   Schement. International Encyclopedia of Social & Behavioral Sciences: 'Advertising'. *www.wikipedia.org*: 'Advertising'. Various aspects of the advertising industry are dealt with by: Gudis, Catherine (2004). *Buyways. Billboards, Automobiles, and the American Landscape*. UK: Routledge (Outdoor advertising). Sinclair, john (2007). 'Globalisation and Regionalisation of the Advertising Industry in the Asia-Pacific'. *Asian Studies Review*, Vol. 31, Issue 3, 283-300. Goldfarb, Avi (2004). 'Concentration in Advertising-Supported Online Markets: An Empirical Approach'. *Economics of Innovation and New Technology*, Vol. 13, Issue 6, 581-594. Advidsson, Adam (2003). *Marketing Modernity. Italian Advertising from Fascism to Postmodernity*. UK: Routledge.

[47]   PWC. Global Entertainment and Media Outlook. The numbers of TNS Media Intelligence are 10 percent lower than those of PWC: *www.tns.mi.com*.

Table 20

The Global Advertising Markets in $bn, 2001-2010

	2001						2005						2010					
	USA	Canada	EMEA	Asia Pacific	Latin America	Total	USA	Canada	EMEA	Asia Pacific	Latin America	Total	USA	Canada	EMEA	Asia Pacific	Latin America	Total
Television	52	2	32	25	5	116	67	3	38	31	7	145	89	3	54	45	11	202
Radio	18	1	5	3	1	28	20	1	7	3	1	32	25	1	9	5	2	41
Out-of-home	5	0	6	4	0	16	6	0	8	5	0	20	9	0	11	7	0	28
Internet	7	0	2	1	0	10	16	0	6	4	0	22	26	1	15	10	1	52
Magazines	22	1	20	6	1	49	23	1	20	6	1	52	29	1	25	8	1	65
Newspapers	44	2	37	20	3	106	49	2	38	22	4	115	59	2	44	30	5	140
Total	149	6	101	60	9	325	177	7	116	72	13	365	230	9	158	104	21	521

Source: PWC. Global Entertainment and Media Outlook, 20, 33, 38, 44, 50, 55.

the largest advertising medium. Newspapers, magazines and radio will grow more moderately and lose share of total advertising spending through 2010.

Table 21

Top 25 Ad Spots in the USA in $m, 2005

Corporations	$m	Industries	$m
DaimlerCrysler	528	Automotive	3863
General Motors Corp. Dlr.	456	Restaurants	1329
Ford Motor Co. Dlr.	425	Telecommunications	990
Toyota Motor Corp. Dlr.	364	Car & Truck Dealers	925
General Motors Corp.	341	Furniture Stores	727
Honda Motor	339	Insurance & Real Estate	675
Nissan Motor	312	Financial	543
Ford Motor Co.	242	Government & Organizations	483
Yum Brands	213	Schools, Colleges & Camps	451
Toyota Corp	163	Leisure Time Activities & Events	434
Federated Dept. Stores	179	Food & Food Products	415
Toyota Motor Corp. Loc. Dlr.	163	Travel, Hotels & Resorts	413
Verizon Communications	163	Legal Services	358
General Mills	155	Motion Pictures	324
Procter & Gamble	153	Department Stores	309
General Motors Corp Loc Dlr	149	Food Stores & Supermarkets	276
McDonalds	140	Media & Advertising	212
Hyundai Corp	137	Medicines & Remedies	209
AT & T	126	Discount Department Stores	203
Time Warner	125	Toiletries & Cosmetics	191
Berkshire Hathaway	114	Home Centers & Hardware Stores	169
Walt Disney Co.	114	Clothing Stores	166
Comcast Corp.	110	Audio & Video Equipment	117
Ford Motor Co. Loc. Dlr.	101	Home Electronics & Video Stores	115
Political Adv.	99	Soft Drinks, Candy & Snacks	114
Total	5411		14011

Source: Television Bureau of Advertising: *www.tvb.org*.

Increasing global consumer spending has led to an increase in global advertising revenues.[48] In order to capitalize on new media technologies, new methods of advertising

---

48   ReportSURE. Industry Survey. Global Media & Entertainment, 20-21.

are constantly appearing, and the Internet is now a major advertising medium. Advertising is usually in line with a country's economic performance. The USA spend most on advertising, as a percentage of GDP, approximately 1.4 percent, while the advertising expenditure of Japan, the UK, Germany, France, Italy and developed countries in general varies between 0.6-0.9 percent of GDP. Among emerging countries, Russia has seen the most substantial increase in ad expenditure of GDP from 0.43 percent in 2001 to 0.85 percent in 2005. China's share of GDP is also rising from 0.43 percent in 2001 to 0.59 percent in 2005.

The automobile industry is by far the largest customer of the advertising industry, followed by other consumer industries such as food, furniture, media, entertainment, pharmaceuticals, personal care, clothing, accommodation, travel, and furthermore, telecommunications, insurance and financial (Table 21).

Television remains the most influential advertising media with high image scores (Table 22).

TABLE 22

Image of Most Influential Advertising Media in the USA in %, 2005

TV	82
Newspapers	7
Radio	5
Internet	4
Magazines	4

Source: *www.tvb.org.*

The Global Advertising Industry

Advertising and advertising companies originated in the US in the late 19th century with the breakthrough of big business and branded goods.[49] From a small basis in the early 20th century, advertising accelerated with the arrival of radio between the two World Wars. Television turned advertising into big business after the Second World War, based on advertising spending by the three leading networks ABC, NBC and CBS. The advertising industry kept on expanding until the late 1980s when it was struck by an economic crisis that went on to the mid 1990s. Advertising seemed less efficient than it used to be, because consumers had become less receptive to constant

---

49   *www.answers.com.*

advertising promotions, more price conscious and less loyal to brands. At the same time, technological developments and new communication channels opened new roads to customers, including cable-TV and alternative networks. Computer based market research enabled industries to collect detailed information on their customers and including direct-marketing, in-store sales and price discounts, this led to increased marketing budgets at the expense of advertising. Next, the Internet introduced a new communications and advertising revolution since the turn of the millennium.

Fueled by simultaneous globalization and outsourcing, the radical communications and advertising transformations since the 1990s made advertising companies change to meet quite new demands from their customers in big business. In the beginning, small and medium sized advertising companies were quick to adapt to these new demands. On the other hand, large advertising spenders demanded total solutions to their marketing campaigns which made leading advertising companies turn around their business strategy and organization. During the second half of the 1990s, they regained their momentum and started to expand even more on an international scale. Because American advertising companies expanded abroad with their large industrial customers since the 1950s, the leading US advertising companies came to dominate the global advertising industry, including an increasing share of customers' sales and marketing value chain. As consolidation accelerates, the advertising industry is being polarized between a leading group of very large companies and many small firms, whereas middle-sized companies tend to disappear.

Advertisement turnover in the US increased from a low level in 1900 to $3 to $4 billion in the 1930s and 1940s. It trebled during the 1950s to $12 billion, and from 1960 to 1970 increased to $20 billion. It increased sixfold to $130 billion in 1990 and during the 1990s it almost doubled to $236 billion in 2000.[50] The US comprises about forty percent of the world total. If the other parts of communication services are included – those being dealt with by the large advertising companies, such as market research, PR, and specialized communications, the world total would be three times larger, namely $1.2 trillion, of which specialized communications include almost $800 billion.[51]

Even though the US and a significant share of the global advertising industry has been consolidated by a few big companies, the US and all other developed countries include an underwood of numerous small and medium sized advertising companies that

---

50 US Bureau of the Census (1975). *Historical Statistic of the United States: Colonial Times to 1970.* Part 2, 855-857. Washington D.C.: US Department of Commerce. The US Census Bureau (2007). The 2007 Statistical Abstract of the Unites States/Advertising: *www.censuns.gov*.

51 WPP (2006). *Annual Report 2005*, 71: *www.wpp.com*.

live by way of local, niche and innovative markets. The US has about 40,000 advertising firms and four out of five employees work in companies with less than ten employees.

As a consequence of recent global business and technology developments, the previously separated industries of advertising, marketing and communications are being integrated. Advertising is much affected by increasing political and consumer control of content, too. Furthermore, technological developments make advertising move increasingly from traditional media such as newspapers and television to computers, Internet, iPod and mobile phones.

The relationship between advertising firms and customers has also changed. The advertising company has become a mirror of customer demands. The advertising agency is more than a venue of creative ideas to be turned into television commercials. Marketers want the advertising firms to be their strategic partners. Consequently the two parties are looking for new ways of value creation, including payment according to the value created.

In the early 2000s, the leading US and worldwide advertising companies are WPP, Interpublic and Omnicom, followed by Publicis, Havas and MDC. All have expanded through acquisitions since the 1990s. In addition, many advertising agencies of significant size worked in specialized markets, such as, for example, Lamar in outdoor advertising, although the consolidated companies also marketed such services.[52]

WPP

The world's largest advertising company WPP (Wire and Plastic Products Group) is of recent origin.[53] Starting in the UK in the mid-1980s, WPP has acquired a large number of advertising and other communication companies from around the world, including, for example, J. Walter Thompson Group (1987), Ogilvy (1989), Asatsu Japan (1998), Young & Rubicam (2000), AGB and Nielsen Media Research (2004), and perhaps the largest of all acquisitions Grey Global Group (2005). And WPP continues to merge with companies that are able to strengthen its position within its varirous business areas and fulfill its goals of becoming the predominant communications company in all regions of the world. Unlike WPP, many of its acquired companies have a long history.

In 2007, WPP had revenues of about $12 billion.[54] Based on billings, its turnover is five to six times that size. WPP covers all fields of advertising, PR and marketing

52   *www.lamar.com.*
53   *www.wpp.com.*
54   WPP (2008). *Annual Reports 2007: www.wpp.com.*

through all media, including the Internet. Almost half of its income stems from advertising and media investment management, one-fourth from branding and specialized communications, and the rest from information consulting and PR. By region, 39 percent comes from the US, 14 percent from the UK, 26 percent from Continental Europe and 21 percent from the rest of the world. The various fields covered by WPP are based on its many acquired companies. Within WPP, Ogilvy & Mather, JWT, Young & Rubicam and Grey are the large subsidiaries, including some three-quarters of total WPP revenues.

WPP serves companies of all kinds and sizes, but primarily large corporations throughout the world. As a full-service agency, WPP is a strategic partner that deals with all sides of advertising, marketing and marketing planning. The strategic partner approach of WPP, as well as the consolidation of the advertising and communications industries, reflects the consolidation and outsourcing of its customers. In media investment for example, you have to be big to match Murdoch in News Corporation. Globally, the automobile industry is the largest customer of the advertising industry, including 25 percent of total spending, followed by personal care with 20 percent, media, pharmaceuticals and foods with each 10 percent. American companies dominate world advertising and the world's ten largest advertisers are all American corporations. The most expansive market is that of China, and Asia in general. Customers are focusing strongly on costs on the one hand, and, on the other, on core competence, leading to outsourcing of the marketing function. This brings new opportunities to WPP that is involved in handling such outsourcing projects within the automobile and other industries.

Another trend that increases the business potentials of WPP is media fragmentation. Increasing prices of television commercials, decreasing audiences in step with changing consumer habits, new media technologies and pressure on traditional media, all this make corporations address WPP for consulting in media investment.

WPP is competing with the other large full-service agencies on global markets and many national agencies on national markets. Expanding Google and Yahoo are moving into the business areas of WPP, too.

Omnicom

Omnicom is the world's second largest advertising and communications group.[55] By way of several mergers, Omnicom has expanded since the mid-1980s to become a global company, including all aspects of business market communication, such as advertising,

---

55   *www.omnicomgroup.com.*

media service, specialized communications and CRM. Among its many acquisitions are included three of the world's ten largest advertising brands BBDO, DDB and TBWA. Many of Omnicom's acquired companies have a long history.

Omnicom had revenues of $12 billion in 2007, of which about 55 percent came from the USA, 20 percent from Continental Europe, some 10 percent from the UK and 15 percent from the rest of the world.[56] Almost half of its income stemmed from advertising, one third from CRM and the rest from PR and specialized communications. Just like the other large advertising and communications companies, the world's largest corporations account for half its income.

Interpublic

Interpublic is the world's third-largest advertising and communications company.[57] Similar to the other leading advertising agencies, Interpublic has grown into its current position by way of several mergers. While Interpublic originated in 1961, many of its merged advertising agencies have a long history. Similar to its leading competitors, Interpublic has expanded from advertising into market communication and other fields of communication to become a full-service agency in order to match its many global customers that generate a large share of its revenues. Advertising and marketing is its largest market segment, and about half of income stems from the US and one-fourth from Europe.

Publicis

French Publicis is the world's fourth-largest advertising and communications company.[58] Since its start in 1920, Publicis developed along with the development of media, first newspapers and radio, then television, and recently the Internet, mobile phones and other new technologies and channels of distribution. By way of acquisitions, Publicis started its international expansion in the 1970s in Europe and in the US in the 1980s. Since the 1990s, Publicis became a global company with strong positions in all major regions, outside France especially the English speaking world and in particular the United States. This was clearly demonstrated by the acquisition of the large advertising company Saatchi & Saatchi in 2000. Acquisitions continued into the new millennium, including for example the media consulting company ZenithOptimedia

56   Omnicom (2008). *Annual Report 2007: www.omnicomgroup.com*.
57   *www.interpublic.com*. Interpublic (2008). *Annual Report 2007: www.interpublic.com*.
58   *www.publicis.com*.

in 2001, Bcom3 in 2002, and a strategic cooperation agreement with Japan's leading advertising and communications company Dentsu. This made Publicis a true global company. Its many acquisitions meant to include all areas of the advertising and communications world. In 2007 Publicis had revenues of $7 billion, of which 40 percent were in Western Europe and 40 percent were in North America.

Dentsu

Dentsu is Japan's largest advertising and communications company.[59] With a long history, Dentsu only developed into its current position during the post-war decades, reaching annual revenues of $2 billion in 2007.[60] Unlike the other leading advertising agencies, Dentsu is predominantly Japanese, gaining more than 90 percent of its revenues from its domestic market, which is the second largest in the world, after the US. Dentsu covers one-quarter of the Japanese market, divided between all advertising and communication segments and media.

Internet

The Internet is a worldwide public system of interconnected networks that transmit data by packet switching using the standard Internet Protocol.[61] Since its breakthrough in the middle of the 1990s, the Internet has expanded into a huge network that consists of millions of smaller networks, including business, government, academic, social and other kinds of networks carrying out information services within the World Wide Web. In 2007, far beyond 1 billion people used the Internet and the number of users keep on rising. The Internet is not only an information channel. Its widespread application has made it an economic tool of virtuallt every kind of business. Companies, agencies and consumers exchange money by way of the Internet and furthermore, business and governmental activities are increasingly being carried out through the Internet. Its radical impact on business is clearly seen in the experience industries that are highly dependent on communication.

---

59   *www.dentsu.com*.
60   *www.dentsu.com*: Dentsu (2008). *Annual Report 2007*.
61   *www.wikipedia.org*: 'Internet'.

The Global Internet Market

The Internet market consists of two spending and revenue sources, advertising and access.[62] The Internet advertising and access spending market includes fees paid by consumers to Internet service providers (ISPs) and spending by online advertisers on display, classified, and paid search advertising. Global spending on the Internet market has increased rapidly from $66 billion in 2001 to $145 billion in 2005, and is projected to be $266 billion in 2010 (Table 23). Asia Pacific is the fastest growing region, fuelled by the enormous growth in China.

The rapid spread of the Internet, broadband and mobile phones is creating a new digital infrastructure that radically is transforming the media and entertainment world. In itself, the Internet is becoming a large market. Increased broadband access is the principal driver in each region, surpassing dial-up spending in all regions, except Latin America. Dial-up spending will continue to grow in Asia Pacific and Latin America but will decline in the other regions as dial-up subscribers upgrade to broadband. Increased competition is driving down broadband prices in all regions and is fuelling growth. Triple-play service bundles that combine broadband Internet access with telephone service and television distribution are making broadband increasingly attractive. Increased telecommunications investment is enlarging the landline market and contributing to overall Internet household growth, including dial-up growth in Asia Pacific, Latin America, and Eastern Europe. Internet advertising is growing rapidly, stimulated by an expanding broadband subscriber base and ad formats geared to broadband, including keyword search and full-motion video.

USA

The US online advertising and access spending has grown from $24 billion in 2001 to $40 billion in 2005, and is projected to be $60 billion in 2010. Advertising will be the fastest growing category, almost quadrupling from $7 billion in 2001 to a projected 26 billion in 2010, while access spending will double in the same period from 17 to 35 billion. Broadband access will increase rapidly from spending $7 billion in 2001 to a projected 31 billion in 2010, whereas dial-up spending will decline from $10 billion in 2001 to a projected $4 billion in 2010. From almost nothing, Internet household penetration increased rapidly during the 1990s and continued to spread, including almost 80 percent by 2010. The most important increase, however, took place in

---

62   PWC. Global Entertainment and Media Outlook, 308.

TABLE 23

Global Internet Access and Advertising Spending in $bn, 2001-2010

	2001					2005					2010				
	USA	Canada	Western Europe	Asia Pacific	ROW	USA	Canada	Western Europe	Asia Pacific	ROW	USA	Canada	Western Europe	Asia Pacific	ROW
Access Spending	17	1	17	16	4	28	2	36	45	12	35	2	52	100	25
Dial-Up	10	1	14	11	4	8	0	10	12	8	4	0	4	14	13
Broadband	7	0	3	5	0	19	1	26	33	4	31	2	48	87	12
Advertising	7	0	1	0	1	13	0	5	4	1	26	1	14	10	2
Total	24	1	19	17	5	40	2	41	48	14	60	3	66	110	27

Source: PWC. Global Entertainment and Media Outlook, 308-367.

broadband penetration that grew from 10 percent in 2001, to 35 percent in 2005, and a projected 62 percent in 2010.

Starting in 1995, US Internet advertising grew slowly until it skyrocketed in the 1990s and peaked at $8 billion in 2000.[63] Following a decline in the early 2000s, Internet advertising took-off from 2004 and has been accelerating continuously since then. Virtually from the start in the 1990s, online advertising has been concentrated with the ten leading ad-selling companies, which accounted for almost three-quarter of total revenues in 2005. Companies ranked elleventh to fiftieth accounted for the remainder quarter. Search remains the largest revenue format, accounting for 43 percent of total revenues in 2005, up from only 4 percent in 2001. Displays are second, accounting for 34 percent, including display ads, rich media, sponsorships, and slotting fees, down from 71 percent in 2001 (mainly banners and sponsorships). Classified revenue accounted for 17 percent in 2005, almost similar to its 16 percent in 2001. Referrals and e-mail ads account for the remainder 6 percent, almost the same as its 5 percent share in 2001.

In the US, Internet advertising has grown dramatically since the early 2000s (Table 24). Spending more than doubled since 2001 to $13 billion in 2005 and once more to $26 billion in 2010. Growth in broadband subscribership has been a key driver of online advertising. Broadband subscribers spend more time online than dial-up subscribers do. They visit more Web sites and they buy more products online. Each of these characteristics is attractive to advertisers. Online commerce is especially important because advertisers like to reach people when they are shopping. Online shopping is one of the fastest growing components of the US economy. Consumers spent $86 billion purchasing goods online in 2005 (excluding travel, accommodation, and event tickets), more than twice the total of 2001 and up more than 20 percent from 2004. As consumers shift more of their purchases from traditional retail outlets to Web sites, advertisers will shift more of their spending from traditional media outlets to the Internet.

---

63   PWC. *IAB Internet Advertising Revenue Report, 2001, 2003, 2005: www.iab.net.*

TABLE 24

The US Internet Advertising Market in $bn, 2001-2010

	2001	2005	2010
Online Keyword Search	0	5	11
Newspaper Web Site	0	2	6
Online Classified	0	2	5
Banner ads, video ads, etc.	7	4	4
Total	7	13	26

Source: PWC. Global Entertainment and Media Outlook, 314-315. PWC, IAB Internet Advertising Revenue Report, 2001, 2003, 2005.

Internet advertising accounted for about 5 percent of the total US ad spending in 2005, a total estimated at $267 billion, which included Direct Mail $57 billion, Newspapers $48 billion, Broadcast TV $35 billion, Radio $22 billion, Cable TV $19 billion, Consumer Magazines $13 billion, Internet $12.5 billion, Business Magazines $8 billion, Outdoor $6 billion, etc. Internet advertising is growing more rapidly than all other advertising media and its share of total US advertising spending and revenues is projected to increase from 5 percent in 2005 to 11 percent in 2010.

Consumer advertisers continue to represent the largest category of Internet spending, accounting for 51 percent of 2005 revenues, up from 49 percent in 2004 (covering Retail, Automotive, Leisure, Entertainment, Package Goods, in that order). Computing advertisers represented the second largest category of spending at 13 percent, down from 18 percent in 2004. Financial Services advertisers represented the third-largest category of spending at 12 percent, down from 17 percent in 2004. Telecom companies accounted for 7 percent in 2005, up from 4 percent in 2004. Impression (including sponsorships) and performance based pricing constitute almost 90 percent of total revenues.

Sponsored keyword search, wherein advertisers pay for a prominent listing in search results, has been a key driver of the market. It is the largest component of Internet advertising, rising rapidly from $0.3 billion in 2001, to $5billion in 2005 and a projected $11 billion in 2010. Keyword advertising enables advertisers to target people who are likely buyers of a product. Classified advertising on the Internet is also growing rapidly. Spending grew from almost nothing in 2001 to $2.3 billion in 2005. While independent classified sites compete with print classified advertising in newspapers, newspaper Web sites also attract classified advertising, along with banner ads, full-motion video and other ad formats. Newspaper Web sites are among the most popular sites online and generated $2 billion in advertising, up from $1.5 billion 2004 and almost nothing in 2001. Newspaper Web sites will increase to a projected $6 billion in 2010, accounting for approximately a quarter of the total Internet advertising by 2010. Broadband also facilitates full-motion video ads that were not feasible when most subscribers accessed the Internet through a dial-up connection. People are accustomed to experiencing full-motion video and sound on television commercials, and similar commercials on the Internet have been well received. As broadband penetration grows, the use of video ads will grow as well.

Perhaps the key driver of online advertising is participation by major media advertisers. The Internet was once the province of dot-com advertisers, computer companies, and telecommunications companies. Since the early 2000s, however, growth has been fuelled by increased spending on the part of advertisers that are also heavy users of traditional media. Online advertising by auto companies, for example, rose by approximately 60 percent in 2005.

The Internet has shifted from a niche medium used on an experimental basis to a mass medium that commands a central role in an advertising campaign. The Internet advertising has been larger than 'out-of-home' for several years. It passed consumer magazine advertising in 2006. It will probably exceed radio advertising by 2009 and by 2010, only television and printed newspaper advertising will be larger.

Competition between cable system operators and telephone companies is occurring on multiple fronts. The two have been competing on the broadband Internet access market since the late 1990s and during the past few years, competition in the telephone service market has become heated. It is now common for both sets of providers to offer broadband Internet in a single package with local and long-distance telephone service. The net effect of increasing competition and infrastructure investment is that average prices are falling and average speeds are rising, making broadband a more appealing option for dial-up subscribers. While lower prices and faster speeds are making broadband more attractive, the underlying driver of the broadband market is the desire to access high-speed applications. Among the most popular broadband applications are music, video games, and movies. As the appeal of these applications expands, so will demand for broadband access.

Canada has one of the most advanced Internet markets in the world. Nearly three-quarters of all households are online, and more than half access through a broadband connection. Online household penetration has been rising from half of all households in 2001 to three-quarters in 2005, and will reach almost 90 percent in 2010, by then virtually all through broadband.

In Latin America, dial-up will remain the dominant access technology, but a broadband market is beginning to materialize.

Western Europe

Internet penetration is also high in Western Europe, reaching about 90 percent. Broadband access is high and increasing rapidly, too, causing Internet spending to double from $17 billion in 2001 to $36 billion in 2005 and continue to increase to a projected $52 billion in 2010. Internet advertising spending grew even more from a low level in 2001 to reach $5 billion in 2005 and $14 billion in 2010 (Table 24).

Germany and UK are the largest Internet markets in Western Europe, followed by France. In Eastern Europe, Russia is catching rapidly up to be the fourth largest European Internet market already in 2005 and projected third in 2010. Virtually all of German and Russian markets consist of access spending, while the UK and France have significant Internet advertising markets. All West European countries have well-developed Internet markets in access spending, but are only slowly expanding their Internet advertising markets. Broadband penetration is high and above average in Scandinavia, the Netherlands, Germany, UK and Switzerland. Broadband penetration in Eastern Europe, including Russia and Turkey, is still relatively low.

As the Internet becomes a shopping environment in Western Europe, advertisers want to have a presence so as to influence purchases. Full-motion video is an expanding advertising format that is now feasible because the majority of households access the Internet through broadband connection. Full-motion video with sound allows TV-type ads to be shown on the Internet. Video-and-sound ads provide a more compelling impact than a passive banner ad does and are more likely to be noticed and viewed. The Internet is also an appropriate medium for classified advertising as the search capabilities inherent in Internet browsing match the way in which consumers use print classifieds. In the UK, for example, classified Internet ads are growing rapidly, constituting 19 percent of total Internet advertising in 2005 and are beginning to cut into the print classified market. The Internet is also being increasingly used by many advertisers as an integral component of their overall marketing approach. Virtually all major advertisers have an Internet strategy and look to the Internet to reach people who are becoming more difficult to reach through traditional media. Because of audience fragmentation, no single outlet reaches the same number of people today as it did just a few years ago. Consequently, advertisers have to advertise on many more outlets and must use the Internet to reach people, particularly young men, who spend less time with traditional media. Very little online advertising spending is found in Eastern Europe, the Middle East and Africa.

Asia Pacific

Asia Pacific is the largest and fastest growing region for Internet advertising and access spending. The market more than doubled from $17 billion in 2001 to $48 billion in 2005 and will double once more to projected $110 billion in 2010 (Table 24). Japan started out as the largest market around the turn of the millennium with $8 billion in 2001, rising to $12 billion in 2005 and a projected $17 billion in 2010. South Korea was second in 2001 with $4 billion, rising to $7 billion in 2005 and a projected $9 billion in 2010. Both Japan and South Korea will reach maturity with a broadband penetration of 90 percent in 2010, South Korea already having reached almost that level in 2005. From a low level of $3 billion spending in 2001, China expanded explosively to $24 billion in 2005, and a projected $74 billion in 2010, reaching a broadband penetration of 10 percent in 2005 and 32 percent in 2010. Australia, Hong Kong, Singapore and Taiwan will also reach maturity broadband levels in 2010.

In a number of countries in the region, low levels of landline penetration limit the Internet market. To alleviate such shortfalls, carriers have invested substantial sums in improving the underlying infrastructure. However, due to the difficulties in rolling out landline networks and their higher costs relative to a wireless connection, countries with low Internet penetration are increasingly exploring newer wireless technologies to stimulate Internet penetration and create double digit growth in Internet households. In developed countries in the region, such as Japan, South Korea and Australia, most households already had access to the Internet in 2005 and will reach maturity at a level of 90 percent in 2010. Japan and South Korea in particular have a well-established fiber-optic backbone and are both upgrading their infrastructure to make broadband services even more attractive.

Internet advertising's share of total advertising in Asia Pacific grew from 2 percent in 2001 to 5 percent in 2005, and a projected 10 percent in 2010. This is almost similar to Western Europe.

The Global Internet Industry

Leading corporations of the Internet include telecommunication companies that operate the infrastructure and profit on the one hand from users spending on media content, and, on the other hand, from large search companies such as Google and Yahoo! that catch information from the Internet's millions of websites.[64] Behind telecommunication companies, network system providers such as Alcatel-Lucent, Ericsson, Siemens,

---

64   *www.google.com. www.yahoo.com.*

Nortel, NEC, Samsung, Motorola, and Nokia create the digital infrastructure that allow for content and content distributors to proliferate revenues.[65] Telecommunication service providers such as AT&T, NTT, Deutsche Telekom, France Telecom, and Vodafone are the drivers of global consolidation and the core companies of the operation of digital technologies, including the Internet, broadband and mobile phones.[66] They are all multibillion dollar corporations. In addition to these giants, national and smaller international telecommunication companies dominate the Internet and general telecom market in most minor countries, for example Telia in Sweden and TDC in Denmark.[67] Although the industrial divide between telecommunication and the Internet is blurring, telecommunication companies are considered general communication technology and service providers rather than proper businesses of the Internet.

Number one Google and number two Yahoo! dominate the world market of Internet searching. They are both multi-billion dollar companies. From their original search basis, the two companies are diversifying into an increasing number of information and entertainment fields. In addition, they are important engines of Internet advertising.

Google

"Google is a global technology leader focused on improving the ways people connect with information. Our innovations in web search and advertising have made our web site a top internet destination and our brand one of the most recognized in the world. We maintain the largest, most comprehensive index of web sites and other content, and we make this information freely available to anyone with an internet connection. Out automated search technology helps people obtain nearly instant access to relevant information from our vast online index ... We generate revenue primarily by delivering relevant, cost-effective online advertising".[68]

Google was incorporated in California in 1998.[69] From a small start, Google expanded to become a very profitable multibillion dollar business with revenues of more than $16 billion in 2007, up from $ half a billion in 2002. Google is available in more than one hundred languages.

Based on its strong backbone of thousands of servers around the world and its

65   www.alcatel-lucent.com. www.ericsson.com. www.nortel.com. www.nec.com. www.samsumg.com. www.motorola.com. www.nokia.com.

66   www.att.com. www.ntt.com. www.telekom.de. www.francetelecom.com. www.vodafone.com.

67   www.telia.se. www.tdc.dk.

68   Google (2008). Annual Report 2007, 1.

69   www.google.com.

original search technology, Google has grown rapidly with the breakthrough of the Internet in the early 2000s to include half the world market by the end of 2007, leaving one-fourth to number two, Yahoo![70] In addition to providing easy access to billions of web pages, Google has integrated special features into its web search to help people find exactly what they are looking for on the web, including for example advanced search functionality that enables users to construct more complex queries, web page translation, tools such as a spelling checker, a calculator, a dictionary and currency and measurement converters, search by numbers such as product codes, telephone area codes, patent numbers and vehicle ID numbers, movie, music and weather information as well as news, finance, map, image, book and groups search. Google provides tools for communication, collaboration and communities, too, such as documents and spreadsheets creation, viewing and editing, calendar, e-mail service, and tools for blogging. Google Desktop lets people perform a full-text search on the contents on their own computer.

Google's portfolio of applications is continuously growing. In 2006, the company launched Google Video, allowing users not only to search and view freely available videos but also music users and media publishers to publish their content. Google Earth lets users see and explore the world from their desktop. Google Maps helps people navigate map information. Google Mobile lets users search and view both pages created specifically for wireless devices and the entire Google index.

To develop its many applications, Google has acquired several smart start-up companies, such as Pyro Labs in 2001 (the creator of Blogger), Upstartle in 2006 (the online word processor behind Google Docs & Spreadsheets), YouTube in 2006 (the online video site) and in 2007 DoubleClick (Internet ad serving services). Google has entered into partnerships with leading organizations and companies such as NASA (large-scale computing projects), Sun (technology sharing), Time Warner AOL (enhance each other's video search services) and News Corp.'s Fox Interactive media (providing search and advertising on the popular social networking site MySpace).

Most of Google's revenue is derived from advertising programs. Google AdWords allows web advertisers to display advertisements through Google's search results and network. Google AdSense website owners can display adverts on their own site and earn money every time ads are clicked. Several facilities are developed to support advertisers for targeting their goals and achieve return on investment. Google is spreading its advertising activities to reach all online media, including computers, mobile phones, television, radio, books, newspapers and magazines. By way of new

---

70   *www.google.com*. *www.wikipedia.org*: 'Google'.

media and applications, Google is increasingly moving into a wide spectrum of media and IT industries, creating new competitors (for example broadcasters, advertising companies, and IT corporations such as Microsoft). In conclusion, Google has become a formidable competitor to companies in most experience industries.

Yahoo!

Just like Google, a couple of Californian students started Yahoo! as a garage company in 1994 that eventually evolved into a leading global brand.[71] By 2007, Yahoo! is the world's second largest global online network of integrated services. While Google is stressing information access and use as its primary mission, Yahoo! is focusing more broadly on creating tools for connecting "people to their passions, communities and the world's knowledge". "Yahoo! is also committed to empowering its users and employees through programs, products, and services that inspire people to make a positive impact on their communities". Therefore, Yahoo! has developed an increasing number of services for people interested in autos, finance, games, movies, real estate, radio, sports, travel, news, weather, mail, etc. The number and reach of these services have accelerated since the turn of the millennium.

While all these services are free to users, Yahoo! generates its revenues from advertisements, similar to Google, providing a range of tools and marketing solutions designed to enable businesses to reach their users. In the same way as Google, Yahoo! focuses on expanding its audience of users and deepening their engagement with the company. Like Google, Yahoo! is also extending its activities to include third party entities that have integrated Yahoo!'s search and display advertising offerings into their websites, such as the US Spanish-language television network Telemundo and the IT company Hewlett Packard. In 2006, Yahoo! had revenues of more than $7 billion, up from $1 billion in 2002.

In the early 2008, Microsoft made a bid to purchase Yahoo. Online advertising and online-based services have expanded and are dominated by Google to such a degree that Microsoft decided to act before being left out in the cold by the predominant Google.

---

[71]   *www.yahoo.com*. Yahoo! (2008). *Annual Report 2007*. *www.wikipedia.org*: 'Yahoo!'.

Virtual Communities

User/consumer generated content and media refers to various kinds of publicly available media content that are produced by end-users.[72] Since 2005, user and consumer generated content and media have sprung up as a reflection of new interactive digital technologies on the Internet. It is a two-way media of the second Web generation, a participatory web, that enables and encourages people to publish, share, and comment on their own content. Consumer-generated content has spread to such a degree that it will have great impact on all experience industries. Users interact by way of chat, messaging, e-mail, video, voice chat, file sharing, Podcasts, wikis, blogging, discussion groups, etc. Through social networks and social network services people share interests and activities on the Internet, forming so-called virtual communities. Social networking services normally contain directories of friends, common interest groups, recommending systems, etc. These networking services spread throughout a huge selection of social networking sites. Rapidly, large communities have emerged in a few worldwide sites, such as MySpace (c. 300 million users), YouTube (video sharing web site, including several hundred million videos), Facebook (c. 75 million users), Friendster (25-30 million users, mainly Asia).

You cannot make friends with everybody, however, and you can only cultivate your interest and passion with kindred spirits and people of your kind. Consequently, the huge popularity and number of members in communities such as MySpace and Facebook make people diversify into smaller and more specific social networks. Increasing commercialization of large communities may have pushed in that direction, too. Furthermore, the wide-spread use of the interactive Internet by professionals as well as non-professionals has also paved the way for such niche-like social networks. Specialized social networks include professional networks for eventually all kinds of industries and professions (health care personnel, managers, scientists, etc.) as well as social connections of friends, football fans, art lovers, political and religious groups, numerous hobbies, etc. You might even find a social network for beautiful and rich people. Unlike Metcalfe's law that the value of a network is increasing exponentially with the number of users, the value of social networks seems to be the other way round. You benefit socially and professionally from people you know, like, and with whom you share mutual values and interests. The business world has understood and grabbed the idea, too. Specialized social network services are proliferating as leading companies of all experience industries hasten to offer social networks to their users and customers,

---

72 *www.wikipedia.org*: 'User-generated content', 'Social network service', 'Virtual community'. OECD (2007). *Working Party on the Information Economy. Participatory Web: User-created Content*. Paris: OECD.

such as publishers of newspapers, magazines, and books and other kinds of media and providers of entertainment.

Social networks do not charge money for membership. Instead, they sell online advertising. Sites are also seeking to make money by creating online marketplaces or by selling professional information and social connections to businesses (e.g. LinkedIn). These networks often act as tools for customer relationship for companies selling products and services. In fact, business networking on social networks has grown very popular.

Naturally, the concentration of hundreds of millions of people in one site and its continuous growth has caught the attention of leading Internet and media companies. As a consequence, in 2006 Google acquired YouTube and News Corp. MySpace, and in 2007 Microsoft invested in Facebook. All other large Internet providers and media corporations added consumer-generated content applications to their portfolio or products, too.

Perhaps the largest of all user-generated content websites is Wikipedia.[73] Wikipedia is a user-generated content encyclopedia started in 2001. By 2007, there were more than 250 language editions. The English version is by far the largest one, including more than 2 million articles, mainly produced by US citizens. Wikipedia is based on open-source software and running on dedicated clusters of Linux servers in Florida. While only registered users may create a new article, almost every article may be edited anonymously or with a user account and changes are made available immediately. Unlike peer-reviewed encyclopedias such as Encyclopedia Britannica, Wikipedia relies on the efforts of its community members, called Wikipedians, to remove vandalism, identify violation of neutrality and errors in its articles. The Wikipedia articles are generally considered to be correct and as valuable as peer-reviewed articles in encyclopedias, or maybe even more correct as they are controlled by everybody, including professionals in all fields. Wikipedia is also part of the open source and free software and content movement that is revolutionizing the experience industries and the information and communications industries in particular.

---

73   *www.wikipedia.org*: 'Wikipedia'.

6. Audiovisuals

Television

Each day, television reaches virtually all households in developed countries, an increasing share of emerging countries such as China and is growing in developing countries, too.[1] Television is viewers' primary news source and first choice for local weather, traffic and sports. Television is by far the most reputed advertising media. In conclusion, television is the most widely used mass communications media.

Television (TV) is a telecommunication system for broadcasting and receiving moving pictures and sound over a distance. The term 'television' also refers to a television set, programming or television transmission. In developed countries, the television set has been a common household device since the 1960s and 1970s. Since the 1980s and 1990s, TV sets have spread rapidly in emerging countries (such as China, India, Eastern Europe), whereas poverty dampens the spread of TV sets in developing countries. Almost every fourth person on earth is able to watch television at more than 1.2 billion TV households. Income is based on subscriptions and/or advertising and license fees. Programs reach the receivers from an increasing number of distribution channels which have being developed in recent times. The USA has taken the lead in TV developments.

In the early days of television, i.e. until around 1970, practically all television was broadcasted by radio signal that could be received by everybody. National monopoly networks and broadcast stations ruled throughout the world. In the USA, three broadcasting companies dominated TV, namely ABC, CBS and NBC.[2] Already in the early 1960s, 90 percent of all some 50 millions American households had a black-and-white TV set, which was replaced by a color TV set during the 1970s. By way of wired cable, cable TV began to spread in the USA during the 1970s. The adoption of cable TV accelerated in the 1980s to reach more than half of all the c. 90 million TV households by 1990. By 2005, two-third of the c. 110 million TV households subscribe to cable TV. The spread of satellite television since 1970s helped to push forward the adoption of cable TV. Since the early 2000s, the penetration rate of cable TV seems to have peaked and is slowly declining. This is caused by the breakthrough of digitized media. Slightly delayed, a similar development took place in other developed countries.

Contrary to terrestrial television and cable television, satellite television is television delivered by communications satellites. The first civilian and commercial communication satellites were launched into orbit in the 1960s from the USA, Western Europe

---

1   Johnston. Encyclopedia of International Media and Communications: 'Television Broadcasting'.
2   *Television Bureau of Advertising. www.tvb.org.*

and the USSR, allowing satellite television signals to be delivered to ground stations. The first domestic satellites to carry TV were launched in North America, the USSR and Western Europe in the 1970s. Except for international events such as OL and FIFA World Cup, satellite television was little distributed until the 1990s. Since then, satellite television has been adopted by millions of cable subscribers in the USA and the rest of the world. Another source of TV was the spread of video in the 1980s and 1990, replaced by DVD since the turn of the century.

The breakthrough of the Internet and in particular broadband since the turn of the millennium has paved the way for digital TV, too. By 2010, analog TV will be history and in the USA and most developed countries of the world, only digital TV will exist.

Since the 1980s, developed countries in North America, Western Europe and Asia Pacific moved from national monopoly networks and broadcast stations to a multi-channel system, embracing about 90 percent of all households in 2005.[3] During the 1990s, multichannels moved into emerging countries in Eastern Europe, Asia Pacific and Latin America, too, covering about one-third of all households in Asia Pacific and somewhat less in Latin America. In this way, the television landscape changed radically within two decades, and with digitization on the move it is proliferating even more.

Television includes two groups of companies. One group is distributing television programming to viewers through various distribution channels, including cable operators, direct broadcast satellites, digital and analog terrestrial television. Another group provides the programming and networks to feed the distributed channels.

The total world television market has almost doubled from a quarter to almost half a trillion dollars from 2005 to 2010, of which the US constitutes 40 percent, Western Europe 25-30 percent, Japan 10 percent and declining, China 5 percent and increasing, and the rest of the world is increasing its share to reach almost 20 percent, based on growth in emerging countries and the rapid population growth of developing countries (Table 25).

Television Distribution

The television distribution market consists of revenues generated by distributors of television programming to viewers.[4] In includes spending by consumers on subscription

3   PWC. Global Entertainment and Media Outlook, passim.
4   PWC. Global Entertainment and Media Outlook, 162-218. General economic aspects of television is dealt with in Doyle, Gillian (Ed.)(2006). *The Economics of the Mass Media*. Northampton, Mass.: Edward Elgar Pub.

Table 25

The Global Television Market in $bn, 2001-2010

	2001						2005						2010					
	USA	WE	Japan	China	ROW	World	USA	WE	Japan	China	ROW	World	USA	WE	Japan	China	ROW	World
Broadcast	36	45	19	2	16	118	43	49	19	5	26	142	53	59	24	10	39	185
Advertising	15	28	15	2	14		18	30	15	5	23		23	39	19	10	36	
License Fees	-	17	4	0	2		-	19	4	0	3		-	20	5	0	3	
TV Stations/Adv.	21	-	-	-	-		25	-	-	-	-		30	-	-	-	-	
Cable	72	22	4	2	22	122	87	32	5	5	31	160	148	56	13	10	57	284
Advertising	12	4	1	0	2		19	5	1	1	3		29	9	3	2	6	
License Fees	13	-	-	-	-		22	-	-	-	-		33	-	-	-	-	
Basic Subscript.	33	12	3	2	19		45	17	4	4	28		58	25	8	8	49	
Premium Subscript.	8	5	-	-	1		11	9	-	-	0		14	17	-	-	1	
Pay-per-view+VOD	2	1	0	0	0		4	1	0	0	0		7	5	2	-	1	
Local Advertising	4	-	-	-	-		5	-	-	-	-		7	-	-	-	-	
Total	108	67	23	4	38	240	130	81	24	10	57	302	172	115	37	20	96	469

Source: PWC. Global Entertainment and Media Outlook, 116-218. WE=Western Europe.

to basic and premium channels accessed from cable operators, satellite providers, or Internet protocol television services (IPTV), as well as on video-on-demand (VOD). In the USA, Canada and Europe, Africa and the Middle East (EMEA) it also includes pay-per-view. Advertising on local TV stations and local cable systems is also included in the USA.

TABLE 26

The Global TV Distribution Market in $bn, 2001-2010

	2001	2005	2010
North America	71	93	118
USA	68	90	113
Canada	3	3	5
Western Europe	18	27	44
UK	5	7	10
Germany	3	4	5
Italy	1	2	5
France	3	4	6
Rest of WE	6	10	18
Eastern Europe	3	6	13
Asia Pacific	11	19	36
Japan	3	4	8
China	2	4	8
South Korea	2	4	4
Australia	1	1	2
Taiwan	1	1	2
Rest of Asia Pacific	2	5	12
Latin America	7	7	12
Africa and Middle East	1	1	2
Total	110	154	230

Source: PWC. Global Entertainment and Media Outlook, 162-218.

The global television distribution market has grown from $110 billion in 2001 to $154 billion in 2005, with a projected $230 billion in 2010 (Table 26). The USA is by far the largest market, including two-thirds of the world market in 2001 and 2005 and some half the world market in 2010. Western Europe led by its four large countries is second, and Asia Pacific led by Japan is third.

Subscription TV households will drive spending in Asia Pacific, Latin America and EMEA, while saturated markets will moderate growth in USA and Canada. The introduction of IPTV will contribute to subscriber growth. The migration of subscribers to higher-priced digital servers with more channels will boost spending in all regions and expand the potential market for VOD services. Increased revenue per user from enhanced services such as VOD, pay-per-view and premium services will ensure growth in most regions.

USA

The TV distribution market in the USA will rise from $68 billion in 2001 to $90 billion in 2005 and $117 billion in 2010.[5] End-user spending, including both subscription and non-subscription spending by consumers, will grow at a projected 6 percent annual rate, rising from $43 billion in 2001, $60 billion in 2005 to $80 billion in 2010, some 80 percent on basic subscriptions and 15-20 percent on premium subscriptions. Pay-per-view and VOD, the fastest growing category, each only covers a few percent. Advertising has increased from $25 billion in 2001 to $30 billion in 2005, and is projected to reach $37 billion in 2010, covering c.one-third of total revenues.

Cable system operators and direct broadcast satellite providers have been competing for TV subscribers for a number of years, and telephone companies are prepared to make a major incursion into the market during the next few years. The coming competition between cable operators and telephone companies in TV distribution is an outgrowth of competition in the broadband and telephone markets. Cable operators have been successful in attracting telephone subscribers from telephone companies because of their ability to bundle telephone and broadband with television in a triple-play offering. Since telephone companies in 2004 in each state were granted permission by the FCC to offer long-distance service in their local regions, thereby enabling them to offer local/long-distance packages, Verizon and AT&T (South Bell) have being constructing fiber-optic services by using very-high-speed digital subscriber lines to enter the home by using the Internet protocol (IP) technology. By 2010, telephone companies are expected to have 10 million TV subscribers.

Telephone companies are entering the TV distribution market in large part to protect their principal revenue streams: telephone service and broadband Internet access. Cable operators have been successful in attracting telephone subscribers from telephone companies through their bundle service offerings, and telephone companies

---

5   PWC. Global Entertainment and Media Outlook, 164-173.

are looking to prevent those losses from accelerating. Consequently, the revenue they generate from television will represent only a portion of the return on their investment.

Cable operators are responding to new competition from telephone companies with their own initiatives. The only area where cable does not have a presence is in wireless, and cable operators are addressing that shortcoming through partnerships with wireless carriers. Cable operators are also using VOD as a marketing tool.

The battle for TV subscribers in the US is occurring in an environment that is already virtually saturated. Nearly 90 percent of US households subscribed to a multichannel service in 2005. Consequently, gains achieved by telephone companies will come largely at the expense of existing providers.

Historically, the principal driver of revenue growth in the TV distribution market has been subscriber growth. With the market now saturated and becoming more competitive with the entrance of the telephone companies, digital broadcast satellite providers are looking at a marked slowdown in growth, and cable operators are facing a decline. Consequently, in order to generate revenue growth, the focus has shifted to retaining subscribers and boosting revenue per user. Therefore, cable operators are offering more channels for a few more dollars and are migrating from analog to digital. Digital broadcast satellite providers will benefit from continuing subscriber growth, as will even more telephone companies. Premium subscription is projected to grow, even though it is facing greater competition from enhanced pay-per-view and VOD offerings as well as from more channels in the basic service. VOD is becoming a major vehicle to boost revenue per user for cable operators and telephone companies, because online pay-per-view enables viewers to access a program at any time.

The Canadian television distribution market is much similar to the US market. While a much smaller and technologically less developed region, Latin America, is beginning to adopt new technologies of broadband allowing for new growth in the television market.

Western Europe

The TV distribution market in Western Europe will continue to grow at a ten percent annual rate from $18 billion in 2001, $27 billion in 2005, to a projected $44 billion in 2010.[6] Eastern Europe is growing even faster from $3 billion in 2001 to $6 billion in 2005 and a projected $13 billion in 2010. The Middle East and Africa will grow at a slower pace from $1 billion in 2001 and $2005 to $2 billion in 2010. From a low

---

6   PWC. Global Entertainment and Media Outlook, 174-195.

Global Experience Industries

level in 2005, VOD will reach $3 billion in Western Europe in 2010. UK is the largest market in the region, growing from $5 billion in 2001 to $7 billion in 2005 and $10 billion in 2010. Russia is expanding even stronger from $2 billion in 2001 to $5 billion in 2005 and $10 billion in 2010. Of almost equal size, Germany, France, Italy and Spain are third, fourth, fifth and sixth, Italy and Spain accelerating from a lower level.

The TV distribution market is becoming increasingly competitive with the entrance of telephone companies. Telephone companies are using their DSL infrastructures to transmit television programming into the home. In some countries where cable does not have a significant presence, telephone companies see a potential market with little terrestrial competition, and are making inroads. In 2005, Italy, France and Spain were among the lowest in terms of cable penetration in Western Europe and had the three largest IPTV markets in the region. From a low level in 2004-2005, the IPTV market is projected to accelerate in particularly Italy and Spain, with France in third place. Of the projected 10 million IPTV households in Western Europe by 2010, 8 million will be in those three countries. Telephone companies have launched or will soon launch IPTV in countries with significant cable presence in order to neutralize triple-play packages from cable system operators that consist of television, high-speed Internet access, and telephone service. By 2010, major telephone companies in virtually all countries in Western Europe, and even Eastern Europe and the Middle East and North and South Africa, will have introduced IPTV.

The UK has the most extensive free DTT service in Freeview, which reached the 6-million-user mark in 2005. Freesat, a free service, entered the market in 2006, giving all viewers in UK access to free multichannel television. By the end of 2006, virtually all viewers in the UK have access to free multichannel television. Accordingly, future subscriber growth will be limited. In France, Italy and Spain DTT launches of free digital channels are spreading rapidly since 2005. Germany has the largest number of free subscribers, most of whom access programs via satellite. Free DTT in Germany was introduced in 2003 and has already begun to cut into cable subscribership. From its peak in 2004-2005, cable operators are beginning to loose subscribers that migrate to DTT.

In Eastern Europe, however, where cable penetration is low and IPTV will not be expanding as rapidly as in Western Europe, cable household penetration will continue to rise from 17 percent in 2001 to 23 percent in 2005 and 31 percent in 2010, because of fewer free alternatives than in Western Europe. Telephone companies in Eastern Europe are not nearly as aggressive in introducing IPTV services as they are in Western Europe, in large part because broadband subscribership is much lower.

The subscription satellite market will fare better than cable because satellite providers offer more channels and an array of premium services, although not VOD. The

UK is the dominant European satellite market, with 8 million subscribers in 2005, growing from 6 million in 2001. However, faced with competition by other distribution services, including proliferation of free services, future growth will be limited. Italy's satellite market is growing strongly (from 2 million in 2001 to 4 million in 2005 and 7 million in 2010), reflecting the fact that there is no viable cable service in the country and IPTV is still small. Similarly in France and Spain (from 3-5-6 million and 2-3-3 million, respectively), cable does not have much of a presence and satellite continues to grow rapidly. There were 14 million satellite households in Germany in 2005, most of them (13 million) get their programming for free, although they must pay for premium services if they choose to subscribe (approximately three-quarter of a million households subscribed to a pay service in 2005). Even so, the presence of competition from free services and from a growing IPTV market will cut into satellite household growth. The satellite household penetration in Western Europe has increased from 12 percent in 2001, to 16 percent in 2005 and a projected 20 percent in 2010. As with cable, satellite growth in Eastern Europe will be faster than in Western Europe, and increase from 3 percent in 2001, to 6 percent in 2005 and a projected 10 percent in 2010. Satellite penetration in the Middle East and Africa is not great but has grown from 2 percent in 2001 to a projected 6 percent in 2010.

Premium providers, facing competition from free services, are benefiting from the digitization of cable which provides more channels; from IPTV rollouts, which will also enhance capacity; and from continued growth in digital satellite. Premium services are spending more aggressively on programming in order to attract subscribers.

In the UK, premium TV is well established, with BSkyB continuing to attract subscribers despite the proliferation of free services. In 2006, BSkyB launched HDTV in conjunction with Sony. BSkyB also acquired the Internet service provider Easynet to enable it to offer its own triple-play option. The company's digital video recorder service, Sky+, is also proving to be popular, attracting 1 million subscribers.

In Germany, Premiere acquired exclusive rights to all 64 matches of the 2006 FIFA World Cup, which were broadcast in HDTV. Premiere is also expanding its sports programming in general and launched a package of foreign-language channels and new HDTV channels in late 2005. Rights to live broadcasts of Bundesliga matches, previously held by Premium, were acquired by cable operator Unity Media in early 2006. Premium spending in Western Europe has grown at double-digit rates during the past five years, a trend that is expected to continue through 2010, increasing from $5 billion in 2001 to $9 billion in 2005 and a projected $17 billion in 2010. By far, the UK has the largest premium market in Western Europe, growing from $3 in 2001, $5 in 2005 and a projected $7 billion in 2010. It is the only country where subscribers spend more on premium than on basic services, the result of the popular array of services offered by BSkyB. The slower growth in the UK than the rest of Western Europe since 2005 is a reflection of the maturity of the market compared to other countries.

Asia Pacific

In Asia Pacific, overall spending is rising from $11 billion in 2001, to $19 billion in 2005, to a projected $36 billion in 2010.[7] Japan is the largest market, at $3 billion in 2001, $4 billion in 2005 and a projected $8 billion in 2010, followed by China (from $2, to $4, to $8 billion), India ($1, $2 and $5 billion) and South Korea in fourth place ($2, $4, $4 billion), Taiwan and Australia in fifth and sixth place ($2 billion by 2010). China and India are the most expanding markets, fuelled by satellite launches in India and conversion from analog to digital in China, including satellite services. In Japan, the government is planning to use fiber-optic cable to distribute television in areas where digital is not now available, and give more households access to more channels. In South Korea, digital cable was introduced in 2005. Competition between cable operators and telephone companies is intense.

As a result of these and other initiatives, new channels and a greater variety of content will become available on subscription television, which will stimulate subscription TV household growth. China and India will account for 85 percent of the projected increase and constitute a similar percent of total subscription TV households in the region by 2010. China's number of TV subscription households has increased from 90 million in 2001, to 114 million in 2005, to a projected 182 million in 2010. India will grow from 40 million in 2001, to 64 million in 2005 and a projected 104 million in 2010, out of total households for Asia Pacific at 155 million in 2001, 220 million in 2005, and 347 million in 2010. Japan is third (7, 10, 18 million) and South Korea fourth (6, 15, 16 million).

IPTV rollouts will enhance the subscription market. Telephone companies are offering digital television services to compete with cable. Low subscription-penetration rates in a number of countries and high broadband-subscriber rates create opportunities for telephone carriers and Internet service providers to expand into television. The infrastructure is largely in place, and an added service helps providers reduce churn while increasing average revenue per subscriber. Hong Kong and Japan have the most advanced IPTV markets of the region, accounting for 80 percent of IPTV subscribers in the region. From a low level, China will become the largest IPTV market in 2010,

---

7   PWC. Global Entertainment and Media Outlook, 196-206.

and including Japan and Hong Kong constitute 85 percent of total 12 million IPTV households in 2010.

The cable universe is large and expanding, from 149 million households in 2001, to 207 million in 2005 and a projected 269 million in 2010, rising from a penetration rate of 26 percent in 2001, to 32 percent in 2005 and and a projected 37 percent in 2010. China and India will account for 80 percent of the increase in cable households and a similar share of total households.

Principally because of launches in China and India, the satellite market will expand rapidly, rising to 67 million households by 2010, China and India accounting for 80 percent of total.

Piracy continues to limit the TV distribution market, however. Losses to piracy total billions of dollars, maybe of an equal or larger size than revenues from legal subscription. Governments in the region are increasing their efforts to reduce piracy, with some success in several countries. Recent experience suggests that digital signals are more difficult to steal which might slow the growth of piracy.

Television Networks

The television network consists of advertising spending on broadcast and cable networks, plus other sources of revenues that vary by region.[8] In North America, the television network market includes license fees paid by cable systems and satellite providers to basic and premium cable networks. In Europe, Africa, The Middle East and Asia Pacific, it includes public TV license fees. Multichannel advertising refers to advertising on networks that are accessed by viewers via cable (analog or digital), satellite, digital terrestrial television (DTT), or other means, but that are not otherwise available without these services. Terrestrial advertising refers to advertising by free- to-air broadcast networks, even if viewers may receive such networks through a cable, satellite, or DTT service.

---

8   PWC. Global Entertainment and Media Outlook, 116-159.

TABLE 27

The Global TV Broadcast and Cable Networks Markets in $bn, 2001-2010

	2001	2005	2010
North America	43	63	89
USA	40	59	84
Canada	3	4	5
Western Europe	45	49	59
Germany	11	10	11
UK	10	11	13
France	5	6	7
Italy	7	8	10
Rest of WE	12	14	18
Eastern Europe	4	7	12
Asia Pacific	30	36	51
Japan	20	21	24
China	2	5	10
South Korea	2	3	4
Australia	2	3	4
Taiwan	2	2	3
Rest of Asia Pacific	2	2	6
Latin America	5	7	11
Africa and Middle East	1	2	3
Total	127	164	227

Source: PWC. Global Entertainment and Media Outlook, 116-159.

The global television network market will almost double during the first decade of the 2000s, from $127 billion in 2001, $164 billion in 2005, to a projected $227 billion in 2010 (Table 27). Throughout the whole decade, the USA and Western Europe each covers one-third of the world television network market; in Western Europe mainly based on its four largest countries. The majority of the remaining world market is found in Asia Pacific, Japan covering half of this market, but with a rapidly increasing Chinese market. Latin America is expanding fast, too.

Multichannel advertising will be the fastest growing sector in each region, pushed by rapid growth in digital households and advertising on new channels that the digital platforms support. New analog channels, digital broadcasting, and HDTV will also make free-to-air channels more appealing, while new distribution outlets, including distribution to mobile devices, will expand viewing and boost advertising. Public license fees, which represent a slow-growing component of the market, will hold down overall expansion outside America (Table 28).

TABLE 28

Global Network Revenues in $bn, 2001-2010

	2001			2005			2010		
	Broadcast Adv.	Cable Adv.	License Fees	Broadcast Adv.	Cable Adv.	License Fees	Broadcast Adv.	Cable Adv.	License Fees
USA	15	12	13	18	19	22	23	29	33
Canada	2	0	1	2	1	1	2	1	1
Western Europe	28	4	17	25	5	19	30	9	20
Japan	15	1	4	14	1	4	16	3	5
China	2	0	0	4	1	0	8	2	0
Rest of Asia Pacific	6	1	1	9	2	2	12	3	2
Latin America	4	0	0	6	0	0	10	1	0
Eastern Europe	3	0	1	6	0	1	11	1	1
Africa and Middle East	1	0	0	2	0	0	3	0	0
Total	76	18	37	86	29	49	115	49	62

Source: PWC. Global Entertainment and Media Outlook, 116-159.

USA

There are two basic types of television in the United States: broadcast, or 'over-the-air' television, which is available to anyone with a TV in the broadcasting area, and cable television, which requires a subscription to receive.[9] The USA has a decentralized, market-oriented television system. Unlike most other countries, the US has no national broadcasting stations. Instead, local media markets have their own TV stations, which may be affiliated to a TV network. To ensure local presence in TV broadcasting, federal law restricts the amount of network programming in local stations. Until the 1980s, local stations supplemented network programming with a good deal of their own produced shows. Today, however, many stations produce only local news shows.

---

9   www.wikipedia.org: 'Television in the United States'.

They fill the rest of their schedule with syndicated shows or material sold to individual stations in the local market. Generally speaking, television in the USA is organized around networks with local affiliates.

US television is dominated by three or four major commercial television networks, including NBC and CBS, which both began as radio networks in the 1920s, and ABC, founded in 1953. These three networks own and run hundreds of local affiliates in virtually every US state and city. Major-network affiliates run very similar schedules. Typically, they begin weekdays with an early-morning locally produced news show, followed by a network morning show, such as ABC's Today, which mixes news, weather, interviews and music. Syndicated programming, especially talk shows fill the late morning, followed often by local news at noon. Soap operas dominate the early afternoon, while syndicated talk shows such as The Oprah Winfrey Show appear in the late afternoon. Local news returns in the early evening, followed by the national network's news program. More syndication occupies the next hour before the networks take over the prime time, the most-watched three hours of television. Family-oriented comedy programs or reality TV like dancing with the stars dominates in the early part of prime time, while later in the evening dramas like Crime Scene Investigation and Grey's Anatomy are in the air. At 10 or 11 p.m., another local news program is on, usually followed by late-night interview shows, such as Late Show with David Letterman. Past midnight, TV stations fill the time with syndicated programming or long advertisements, so-called infomercials. Saturday mornings are usually aimed at children with network programming, while Sunday mornings include public service programming to fulfill the stations' legal obligations to provide such programs. Sports and infomercials appear on weekend afternoons, followed by the same type of prime-time shows as on weekdays. Big sports events from the national leagues or international events such as the Olympic Games are also shown, as the big three networks usually acquire the necessary rights to show these events that gather large TV audiences.

In 1987, the Fox Network owned by Murdoch's News Corporation, launched a challenge to the big three networks. Thanks largely to the success of shows like The Simpsons and American Idol, as well as the network's acquisition of rights to show NFL games, Fox has established itself as a major player in broadcast TV. In the late 1990s, three new networks, the WB, UPN and PAX, joined the scene. WB and UPN merged in 2006 into the CW (a joint venture of CBS and Time Warner). PAX, now known as 'ION Television' has fallen behind in audience attraction.

Behind the four large English US networks, NBC, CBS, ABC and Fox, Univision, a network of Spanish language stations, is the fifth largest TV network. The three big networks also address the Spanish speaking Americans, for example through NBC's sister network Telemundo. US television includes a few other popular over-the-air Spanish networks, too.

Non-commercial television plays a much smaller role in the US than in most other countries. They are to a minor degree public funded, but must rely on corporate sponsorships and viewer contributions, too. American public television stations present educational, cultural, and public affairs shows that are not considered profitable by the commercial stations. Non-commercial stations are usually connected to the national Public Broadcast Service.

Besides these national networks, the US television landscape includes several speciality and digital networks over-the-air, dealing with sports, music, business, religion, and shopping. Most speciality and digital networks are cable and satellite networks, however.

Cable and satellite networks come in genres that cover almost every kind of leisure and lifestyle. Cable and satellite networks reach the largest American audience. Some networks and channels are oriented towards: art and entertainment, family, children and teen, gender, ethnicity and specific sexual orientation (men, women, African American, Asian American, Hispanic/Latino, gay and lesbian), learning, lifestyle, movies, music videos, news, weather and information, religion, shopping, sports, adult, etc. Most American cable and satellite networks are controlled by the large national networks and a group of large cable corporations, i.e. the media conglomerates have taken control of virtually all important parts of US television.

In the USA, advertising will continue to be the dominant revenue source, cable network advertising overtaking broadcast network advertising, but moving towards equilibrium. License fees are growing rapidly for cable networks, basic networks as well as premium networks. As broadcast networks are available in virtually all TV households and cable networks in virtually all subscription households, the potential for further gains is limited. This is partially offset by the increasing channels received through digital channels. Basic network license fees will continue to grow, however, in particular with DBS and telephone companies, of which the latter is projected to emerge as significant players.

Successful television programs, generally those with a hundred or more episodes, have always had an afterlife in syndication beyond their run. With the expiration of the financial interest/syndication rules that prevented the broadcast networks from owning the shows they air and from participating in syndication of those shows, the networks have become more proactive in investing in their programming and in enhancing the aftermarket revenue streams from those shows. Cable networks that develop original programs are also participating in the syndication market and in other aftermarket revenue streams. During the past few years, TV programs on DVD have proved to be lucrative revenue sources for broadcast and cable programmers.

DVRs (digital video recorders), HDTV (high definition television) and digital broadcasting are expanding technologies that could affect the TV advertising market.[10] From a low base in 2001, both DVRs and HDTV are spreading rapidly in American households from 9 and 4 million in 2005 to reach 35 and 25 million in 2010, respectively. Technologies are being developed to create ads specifically for DVR playback. DVR penetration is not expected to grow as fast as that of the VCR previously.

Basicly, Canada follows the lines of the US television network market and is dominated by the large US networks. Latin America remains a small network market, but the spreading of multichannels creates some growth.

Western Europe

In Europe, the proliferation of digital platforms and the launch of new channels will drive television advertising.[11] Eastern Europe is the fastest-growing part of the region. Western Europe accounts for 85 percent of the European market that has expanded from $45 billion in 2001 to $49 billion in 2005 and a projected $59 billion in 2010. The UK and Germany are the two largest markets in the region. Italy ranks third, and France fourth. The Middle East and Africa are just small markets.

The transition from analog to digital is accelerating in Western Europe, creating an increasing number of subscribers and channels in its wake. That includes digital terrestrial television and digital satellite television, including for instance widespread DTT in France by 2005 (Canal Plus), DTT in Spain (Canal Plus and La Sexta), Mediaset and Sky in Italy, DTT in Germany (Viacom, NBC, Sony's AXN, Premiere), Talpa and UPC in the Netherlands and STV in Sweden. UK has the most advanced digital market in Europe, with two-thirds of households subscribing to a digital service in 2006, including BSkyB (satellite, News Corp.), Freeview (DTT free service) and ITV (satellite service for ITV and BBC). From a low level in 2000, the number of West European digital households has been increasing rapidly to extend to a projected 100+ in 2010. TV distribution to mobile phones was also introduced in 2005. Subscribers with third-generation high-speed wireless phones in the UK, Germany, Italy, Spain, and eventually all Western Europe, can view video clips from TV programs on their mobile phones. New digital platforms will expand channel capacity and increase the

---

10   PWC. Global Entertainment and Media Outlook, 121-125.
11   PWC. Global Entertainment and Media Outlook, 126-140.

advertising inventory available on television. Advertising is peaking in OL years, just as in the USA.

Most of the new channels entering the market will be available on multichannel platforms, and these platforms are expected to boost multichannel advertising (advertising on channels not accessible via ordinary television antennas). The UK is the leading country in multichannel advertising, on account of its large digital universe. The terrestrial market is mature and expected to grow more slowly than multichannel advertising, but because of its much larger base it will account for almost three-quarters of the total increase in advertising towards 2010.

HDTV started very slowly during the period 2000-2005, but is expanding rapidly since then to reach a projected 15 million by 2010, compared to 25 million in the USA.

Unlike the USA, public fees are levied on TV households to support public television channels. While all broadcasting is based on advertising revenues and half of cable TV in the USA, advertising is covering an increasing share of West European TV revenues and the majority of TV revenues in Eastern Europe, the Middle East and Africa. In 2005 advertising covered 60 percent of all TV revenues and in 2010 is projected to cover almost 70 percent, leaving the rest to public TV fees. In 2005, 85 percent of all advertising income in Western Europe came from terrestrial advertising and the rest from multichannel advertising. In 2010 multichannel advertising will have increased its share from 15 to 25 percent.

Asia Pacific

The Asian TV network market has grown from \$30 billion in 2001 to \$36 billion in 2005, with a projected \$51 billion in 2010.[12] Japan covered more than half of the total market share in 2005 and is projected to cover almost half the market share in 2010. China is the second-largest market and growing rapidly from a quarter of Japan's size in 2005 to almost half its size in 2010. From a low level, populous India, Indonesia, The Philippines, Malaysia and Thailand will expand faster than average.

The launch of new channels will attract advertising and boost the overall market growth, including Time Warner and CNN. The developed countries of the region will transit from analog to digital TV, by terrestrial, satellite and/or Internet, before 2010 (Japan, South Korea and Australia; in Australia with ABC, FOXTEL, SBS, Nine Network, Turner and Sky Channel as the major content providers). The television network infrastructure has been upgraded massively in China, boosted by the Beijing

---

12   PWC. Global Entertainment and Media Outlook, 141-150.

Summer Olympics in 2008, including digital TV and HDTV. Multichannel advertising will show the largest growth, as most of the new channels will be available only on multichannel outlets. Additionally, as new services are rolled out, the multichannel universe will expand, providing a potentially larger audience for programs on multichannel platforms. The number of multichannel households is projected to more than double from 150 million in 2001 to 325 million in 2010. Multichannel advertising is projected to double its share of total TV advertising from 11 to 19 percent from 2005 to 2010. Terrestrial advertising (the rest) is also projected to accelerate, as a consequence of an increase in numbers of terrestrial channels. TV household penetration is almost total in developed countries and in emerging countries, too (China, Malaysia, Philippines, and Thailand). Public TV license fees are practically unknown outside Japan and Taiwan.

The Media Industry

Providers of programming and distribution are much consolidated on a national and international scale.[13] In distribution, consolidation is mainly national, whereas some US companies have created strong global markets in programming. West European and Japanese networks are mostly nationally based. One Japanese company, Sony, has developed into a global corporation of programming and content production in movies and music. Together with Philips and Samsung, Sony is the leading global producer of television equipment, too. German Bertelsmann is strong in most media. French/American Vivendi is the only European based media corporation dealing with network and distribution. The leading US television corporations are: News Corporation's Fox, Walt Disney's ABC, General Electric's NBC, CBS, Viacom, Time Warner, Vivendi, DirecTV, Comcast, Cablevision, and Liberty Media. Many of these European and American companies have turned into media conglomerates embracing several different content producing fields that cover most of what is sent through television. In distribution, the leading American companies also include the telecommunications companies.

---

13   Schement. Encyclopedia of Communication and Information: 'Globalization of Media Industries'. Academic research on media business developments is rare. Some aspects are dealt with in Picard, Robert G. (Ed.)(2002). *Media Firms: Structures, Operations, and Performance*. Mahwah, N.J.: Erlbaum.

CBS Corporation

Columbia Broadcasting System, CBS, is part of CBS Corporation and one of America's largest television and radio networks.[14] CBS traces its origin to the 1920s and the start of national American networks. Between the two world wars, CBS built a national network of radio stations throughout most US states, broadcasting news, sports competitions, drama and shows. Television broadcasting started in the late 1930s, but the real breakthrough of a nationwide television system came after the Second World War. Based on its own large studios and on newly introduced color television, CBS started producing programming during the 1950s: such as series, shows, drama, documentary, news, and sports events, including its continental network of radio stations. News (Walter Cronkite), sports events (NFL), series, documentary (60 Minutes), and shows continued (Dallas, Mash) to dominate broadcasting during the 1960s, 1970s, 1980s, 1990s, and into the 21th century. Since the 1970s, CBS added cable television to its broadcasting services.

As early as the 1930s, CBS started an ever growing diversification into other media, including CBS Records (1938), CBS Musical Instruments Division, New York Yankees baseball club, and book and magazine publishing (the 1960s and 1970s). Increasing economic problems during the 1980s made CBS start a divesting process. In 1985, CBS divested itself of the Music Instruments division, and in 1988 CBS Records was sold to Sony. Activities in the video game market were given up, too. The temporary Viacom and CBS merger in 2000 introduced the widest diversification strategy, including almost every kind of media. The split between Viacom and CBS in 2005 made CBS return to its core business of television and radio, including its profitable billboards advertising entity and the rapidly rising digital media group.

In 1995-97, Westinghouse Electric Corporation merged with CBS and changed its name to CBS Corporation as probably the world's largest combined television, radio and out-of-home media-company. In 1998, CBS made its first broadcast in HDTV. In 2000, Viacom and CBS merged to become Viacom Inc. It included MTV Networks, Showtime Networks, Paramount Pictures, Paramount Television Group, Paramount Stations Group, Blockbuster, Paramount Parks, Simon & Schuster, CBS Sports, CBS News, CBS Television. With Viacom, movie pictures, music videos, video outlet, out-of-home advertising, amusement parks and publishing were added to CBS' radio and television networking and distribution. Spanish broadcasting to the Spanish-speaking people of the US was started in 2000, as was the first reality series 'Survivor'. In the early new millennium, new popular series emerged such as 'The

---

14   CBS Corporation (2002-08). *Annual Reports 2001-07: www.cbscorporation.com.*

Suppli
Order
Quant
Unit ic
Instr

Auth
Tit?

Vol e
For
Sh
Si
F
Sequence
Loan Type
Quantity 1

Bold and the Beautiful' and 'The Young and the Restless'. The increasing use of the Internet made CBS establish CBS Digital Media in 2005 to oversee all new media operations, starting a determined expansion into the digital media in news, sports events, games, etc. In 2005-2006, Viacom was split into two companies, Viacom Inc. and CBS Corporation. While Viacom concentrated on satellite and cable television networks through MTV (Music Television) and BET (Black Entertainment Television), and production and distribution of movie pictures (Paramount), CBS focused on television and radio production and out-of-home advertising and publishing (divesting its amusement parks, too).

After the split, the CBS Corporation is a mass media company with operations in many fields of media and entertainment, including broadcast television, local television, television production and syndication, cable television, radio, advertising and out-of-home media, in-store media networks, digital media and consumer products. In 2006, a new broadcast television network was launched as a joint venture between Warner Bros. Entertainment and CBS Corporation, called the CW.

CBS delivers television, radio and publishing content that appeals to audiences across virtually every segment of the population, including shows like Crime Scene, 60 Minutes, and the Late Show with David Letterman as well as important sports events. CBS is an industry leader in the production and distribution of syndicated programming, including long-running successes such as Jeopardy, The Oprah Winfrey Show, and Dr. Phil. CBS owns, operates and programs radio stations in nearly every format, including the use of the Internet. Publisher Simon & Schuster have issued many bestsellers. CBS has a large television library, including a growing collection of high-definition content and many popular television programs and radio content and movies. Many advertisers reach their consumers via CBS programming.

CBS plans to continue to develop content that can be applied to existing and emerging platforms, including television, radio, the Internet, broadband technologies, wireless communications, on-demand programming and interactivity. These new platforms are expected to provide new ways for the various businesses of CBS to distribute the wealth of content produced by its many operations, and they expect to create new revenue streams from advertising, subscriptions and licensing.

In 2007, CBS had total revenues of $14 billion of which some 10 percent was generated outside the US. CBS' activities may be separated in four segments: television, radio, outdoor and publishing (CBS' theme parks were divested in 2006).

Television

The television segment consists of CBS Television (comprised of the CBS Network, the company's 40 owned broadcast television stations, CBS Paramount Network Television and CBS Television Distribution, the company's television production and syndication operations); Showtime Networks (the company's premium subscription television program services); and CSTC (College Sports Television, a cable and online digital media for college athletics). The CW broadcast network joint venture with Warner Bros. Entertainment was launched in 2006. The company's owned and operated television stations reach almost half of all US households. Television makes up two-thirds of total revenues.

Through CBS Entertainment, CBS News and CBS Sports, news, sports and entertainment programming, and feature films are distributed to more than 200 domestic affiliates throughout the US The CBS Entertainment is responsible for providing entertainment programming to the CBS Network. The CBS Network primarily derives revenues from the sales of advertising time for its network broadcasts.

Through the CBS Interactive, the Internet sites associated with CBS Entertainment, CBS News and CBS Sports are combined to provide key platforms for promotion, as well as a way to expose the brands of these divisions to the broadband Internet audience. It is also creating new revenues through advertising, online consumer products such as fantasy sports leagues, video-on-demand, and interactive television, as well as primetime and other programming on the network. The company's news and program content is also available through various media owned by the company as well as third parties, including certain of its primetime and classic television programs that have been available on Google Video Store from 2006, an open video marketplace on the Internet enabling consumers to buy and rent a wide range of video content. Also in 2006, four of the company's top-rated primetime series became available on Comcast's On Demand video-on-demand service. In 2006, the company's reality series Survivor became available for download on CBS.com for free. CBS has also arranged to distribute the content of certain video news segments and program clips for Verizon Wireless mobile phones and other mobile phone subscribers, broadband video and text news programming to the AOL News channel, and streaming of certain games of basketball on demand and online video player.

The television broadcast environment is highly competitive. The principal methods of competition in broadcast television are the development and acquisition of popular programming and the development of audience interest through programming and promotion, in order to sell advertising at profitable rates. CBS competes for audience, advertising revenues and programming with other broadcast networks such as ABC, FOX, NBC and WB, independent television stations, cable program services as well as other media, including DVDs, print and the Internet. In addition, CBS competes with the other broadcast networks to secure affiliations with independently owned television stations in markets across the country, which are necessary to ensure the effective distribution of network programming to a nationwide audience.

Television stations compete for programming, on-air talent, audiences and advertising revenues with other stations and cable networks in their respective coverage areas. As a producer and distributor of programming, CBS competes with studios, television production groups, and independent producers and syndicators such as Disney, Sony, NBC Universal, Warner Bros. and Fox to sell programming both domestically and overseas. The company also competes to obtain creative talent and story properties which are essential to the success of all the company's entertainment businesses.

Showtime Network primarily competes with other providers of premium subscription television program services in the US: Home Box Office, Inc. and Starz Entertainment Group, L.L.C. Competition among premium subscription television program services in the US is primarily dependent on the acquisition and packaging of an adequate number of recently released theatrical motion pictures; the production, acquisition and packaging of original series, original motion pictures and other original programs; and the offering of prices, marketing and advertising support and other incentives to cable operators, DTH satellite operators and other distributors.

Radio

CBS radio owns and operates 164 radio stations in 31 US states through CBS Radio. CBS Radio is one of the largest operators of radio stations in the US, operating in all large markets. It is the strategy to operate radio stations in the largest markets, acquire radio stations in the most attractive growth markets and take advantage of the company's ability to sell advertising across multiple markets and formats. CBS is favored by offering radio, television and outdoor advertising platforms in large markets.

The radio seeks to maintain diversity among its radio stations, serving diverse target demographics through a broad range of programming formats, such as rock, oldies, all-news, talk, adult contemporary, sports/talk and country, and CBS has established leading franchises in news, sports and personality programming. This diversity allows advertisers to reach a targeted demographic group or broad groups of consumers within and across markets. The diversity also reduces CBS' dependence on any single station. Radio's general programming strategies include employing popular on-air talent, syndicating shows of some of these talents nationally and acquiring the rights to broadcast sports franchises and news content for its radio stations. The majority of radio revenues are generated from the sale of local, regional and national advertising. The major categories of radio advertisers include: automotive, retail, healthcare, telecommunications, fast food, beverage, movies, entertainment and services.

The company's radio stations directly compete with other radio stations within their respective markets, for audience, advertising revenues, and programming. The radio stations include those owned by other group owners such as ABC Radio, Clear Channel Communications, Cox Radio, Emmis Communications, Entercom and Radio One. The company's radio stations also compete with other media, such as broadcast, cable and satellite television, radio, newspapers, magazines, the Internet and direct mail.

The radio industry is also subject to competition from two satellite-delivered audio programming services, Sirius Satellite Radio and XM Satellite Radio, each providing over 100 channels of pay digital audio services. The company's radio stations face increasing competition from audio programming delivered via the Internet and from consumer products such as portable digital radio players. These new technologies create new ways for individuals to listen to music and other content of their choosing while avoiding traditional commercial advertisements. An increasingly broad adoption by consumers of portable digital audio players might affect the ability of the company's radio stations to attract listeners and advertisers.

The radio broadcast industry has begun the process of converting from analog to digital broadcasts. Hundreds of radio stations are already broadcasting digitally. The company has joined the other broadcast radio groups to form the HD Digital Alliance Association which is committed to accelerate the conversion of over 2,000 additional AM and FM stations to digital radio technology over the next several years. The Digital Alliance plans to market digital radio technology to receiver manufacturers, electronic retailers and automobile manufactures. Digital transmissions are believed to improve sound quality and facilitate the convergence of radio to other digital media as well as its positive impact on the company's competitiveness. Radio constitutes 15 percent of the company's consolidated revenues in 2005.

Outdoor

CBS Outdoor sells advertising on outdoor media, including billboards, transit shelters, buses, rail systems, mall kiosks, masts and stadium signage. Outdoor had 15 percent of revenues in 2006. CBS runs outdoor advertising operations in more than 100 markets in North America, including all 50 of the largest metropolitan markets in the US, 19-20 of the largest metropolitan markets in Canada, and 44 of the 45 largest metropolitan markets in Mexico. Additionally, Outdoor has the exclusive rights to manage advertising space on approximately 87 percent of the total bus fleet in the UK and has a variety of outdoor advertising displays in the Netherlands, France, Italy, Ireland, Spain and China.

The major categories of out-of-home advertisers include: entertainment, media, automotive, beverage, financial, real estate, retail, healthcare, telecommunications, restaurants, health and beauty aids, hotels and professional services. Out-of-home media industry advertising expenditures by retailers and the entertainment industry fluctuate, which has an effect on Outdoor's revenues.

Outdoor generally operates in the billboard, transit and street furniture advertising markets, mainly including two types of billboard advertising displays, bulletins and posters. New technologies for outdoor advertising displays, such as changeable message displays and digital billboards using light-emitting diode technology, continue to evolve. Transit advertising includes advertising on or in transit systems, including interiors and exteriors of buses, trains, trams and at rail stations, based on negotiated payment to public authorities and private transit operators, for example New York City Metropolitan Transportation Authority and the Atlanta bus and rail system. Street furniture displays, the most common of which are bus shelters, reach both vehicular and pedestrian audiences, based on negotiated contracts for some years.

The outdoor advertising industry is fragmented, consisting of several large companies involved in outdoor advertising such as Clear Channel Outdoor Holdings Inc., JC Decaux S.A., and Lamar Advertising Company as well as hundreds of smaller and local companies operating a limited number of display faces in a single or few local markets. The company also competes with other media, including broadcast and cable television, radio, print media, the Internet and direct mail marketers, within their respective markets. In addition, it competes with a wide variety of out-of-home media, including advertising in shopping centers, airports, movie theaters, supermarkets and taxis. CBS considers Outdoor a leading provider of advertising services in each of its primary markets.

Publishing

CBS Publishing includes Simon & Schuster, which publishes and distributes consumer books under imprints such as Simon & Shuster, Pocket Books, Scribner and Free Press. CBS Paramount Parks was divested in 2006. CBS Publishing constitutes just four percent of corporate revenues.

The consumer publishing business is highly competitive and has been affected over the years by consolidation trends. Significant mergers have occurred among the leading consumer publishers. Warehouse clubs and book superstores remain significant factors in the industry contributing to the general trend toward consolidation in the retail channel. There have also been a number of mergers completed in the distribution channel. The company must compete with other larger publishers such as Random House, Penguin Group and Harper Collins for the rights to the works of authors. Competition is particularly strong for well-known authors and public personalities.

Viacom

Viacom is an American media conglomerate and leading global entertainment content company with worldwide interests in cable and satellite television networks (MTV Networks and BET Networks), and movie production and distribution (the Paramount Pictures and DreamWorks movie studios), crossing television, motion pictures and digital media platforms.[15] Viacom serves a growing population of kids, tweens, teens and adults. Sumner Redstone is the chairman and through National Amusements, the parent of Viacom, majority shareholder. National Amusements operates more than 1500 movie screens in the US, the UK, Latin America and Russia under its Showcase Cinemas a.o. Having merged in 2000, Viacom and CBS were once more split into two companies in 2006. Viacom had revenues of $13 billion in 2007.[16]

Viacom began as CBS Films, the television syndication division of CBS that was renamed VIACOM (Video & Audio COMmunications) in 1971, and in 1973 it was spun off amid new FCC rules forbidding television networks from owning syndication companies (the rules were later repealed). Viacom was highly profitable during the 1970s and 1980s distributing old classics to syndication. During the 1980s and 1990s, Viacom made several media acquisitions of radio and television stations, including in 1985 Warner-Amex Satellite Entertainment (renamed MTV Networks) that owned MTV (a music, pop culture and reality shows cable television network) and Nickelodeon (a cable TV network for children and pre-teens). In 1986, Viacom was bought by movie theater owner National Amusements, owned by Sumner Redstone.

During the early 1990s, Redstone expanded Viacom by several acquisitions, including Paramount Communications (parent of Paramount Pictures) and Blockbuster Video chain. The Blockbuster acquisition gave access to large television holdings, including old ABC and NBC productions. After these acquisitions, Viacom owned many movie and television production and syndication units, which were slowly integrated into Paramount. In 2000, Viacom made its biggest acquisition by buying its former parent, CBS Corporation. In the next few years, Viacom added a few other acquisitions to its portfolio. In 2005, however, Viacom decided because of stagnation and internal man-

---

15   *www.viacom.com.*
16   Viacom (2002-08). *Annual Report 2001-07: www.viacom.com.*

agement disputes to split the company in two, named Viacom and CBS Corporation. Viacom includes MTV Networks, BET (Black Entertainment Television), an American cable network for Afro-Americans, Paramount's movie studio, and Paramount Pictures' home entertainment operations, considered the high-growth businesses of the former Viacom. The other part of Viacom, CBS Corporation, is still controlled by Redstone.

In 2006, Viacom bought DreamWorks Pictures (founded by Steven Spielberg a.o.), one of the major American film studios which develops, produces and distributes films, video games, and television programming. DreamWorks' revenues 2006 were $2.8 billion and in 2006, Viacom also acquired video game developers Xfire and Harmonix. By summer 2007, Viacom launched internationally a free service for viewing material on their computer, Joost, and MTV and Paramount Pictures, for example, provided programming and movies to this free service. Viacom's main divisions are: Film Production and Distribution (Paramount Pictures, DreamWorks, Nickelodeon Movies, MTV a.o.), Television Networks (BET, Nickelodeon Music a.o.), Television Production and Television Distribution (DreamWorks Television), Video Gaming (Xfire, Harmonix).

Viacom seeks to reach its audiences through television, motion pictures and digital platforms in any way they consume content. Operations are managed through two reportable operating segments: 1. Media Networks (formerly Cable Networks), which includes MTV Networks and BET Networks. 2. Filmed Entertainment (formerly Entertainment), which includes Paramount Pictures Corporation and Famous Music.

In *Media Networks*, MTV Networks reaches almost 500 million households worldwide via its multiplatform properties, which include the cable television program services MTV (Music Television, etc., and digital properties such as MTV.com, etc.). At the end of 2006, MTV networks operated 135 television networks and 171 websites and broadband service around the world. BET Networks is the leading US provider of entertainment, music, news and public affairs television programming that target African-American audiences. The primary BET channel reaches more than 83 million households, and can be seen in the US, Canada and the Caribbean. The global media networks brands are focused on connecting with key demographics attractive to advertisers across multiple distribution platforms. MTV is also a major producer of mobile video content for major carriers and mobile virtual network operators in the US and internationally. Furthermore, MTV made some of its content readily available for download to own through deals with AOL, Amazon, Apple and Microsoft's Xbox 360.

In *Filmed Entertainment*, Paramount has been one of the leading producers and distributors of feature films since 1912 and has a library consisting of approximately 3,500 motion pictures and programs. The group produces and distributes motion pictures under such well-known brands as Paramount Pictures, DreamWorks, Paramount Vantage, Paramount Classics, MTV Films and Nickelodeon Movies. It distributes motion pictures and other entertainment content on DVD, video-on-demand, cable services and other platforms in the US and internationally. Famous Music produces and distributes music to a diversified range of global media, including television programs, motion pictures and digital outlets. Its catalog spans seven decades and ranges from classics to hits from contemporary artists. In 2006, DreamWorks was acquired, a leading producer of live-action motion pictures and television programming.

Its Media Networks segment derives revenues principally from advertising sales ($4 billion), affiliate fees ($2 billion) and ancillary sales ($1 billion), which include sales of home entertainment products and the licensing of consumer products. Revenues from the Filmed Entertainment are generated primarily from feature film exhibition, including motion pictures in theatrical release ($1 billion), home entertainment product ($2 billion), and distribution to pay and basic cable television ($1 billion). Revenues from the Media Networks segment accounted for 63 percent in 2006 (70 in 2005), and revenues from the Filmed Entertainment segment accounted for 38 percent in 2006 (31 in 2005). 24 percent of total revenues in 2006 (22 in 2005) were generated from international operations, mainly Europe. Of total international revenues $2.8 billion in 2006, 63 percent was generated in Europe.

In 2006, Viacom started upgrading its digital interactive activities. Two acquisitions were made in 2006. First, the Xfire was acquired, a freeware instant messaging service that also serves as a game server browser and includes features for video game players. It was followed by computer game developer Harmonix Music Systems, known for its line of music video games. Other acquisitions in 2006 included Quizilla, a user generated online quiz website, and Atom Entertainment that works with creative independent content developers to find and publish the very best casual games, short films, video and so on to meet the new consumer demand for fun, short, accessible and unusual digital entertainment. These acquisitions added interactive digital content to MTV. In late 2007, Viacom and Microsoft announced a long term deal and strategic alliance to collaborate on content distribution, advertising, event promotions and gaming. Microsoft licenses content from Viacom's cable network and motion picture businesses and provide the ad server for Viacom's US websites as well as have the exclusive right to sell display advertising on Viacom's US websites. Microsoft buys advertising on Viacom broadcast and online networks and the companies work together on promotions and sponsorships for MTV Networks and BET Networks award shows. Furthermore, Viacom works with Microsoft on opportunities to become a preferred publishing partner across Microsoft's casual gaming platforms.

Viacom competes with many different entities and media in various markets world wide. Primary competitors in the cable and entertainment businesses include Time Warner, News Corp., The Walt Disney Company, NBC Universal, The E.W. Scripps Company and Discovery Holding Company. In motion pictures, Viacom competes with other major studios, such as Disney, Fox, Sony Pictures, Universal and Warner Bros, and independent film producers in the production and distribution of motion pictures, DVDs and videocassettes. Paramount Pictures' competitive position primarily depends on the quality of the product produced, their distribution and marketing success and public response. Viacom also competes to obtain creative talent and story properties which are essential to its success. In music publishing, Famous Music competes principally with the music publishing companies owned by other major entertainment companies, such as EMI Music Publishing, The Universal Music Group, Sony Music Publishing, BMG Music Publishing and Warner Chappell Music. Famous Music's competitive position primarily depends on its ability to license the works it owns or controls, its ability to continue to acquire important musical works desired by licensees and its ability to maximize its collection of royalty income generated by its works worldwide. In 2007, Famous Music was sold to Sony/ATV Music Publishing. Its music publishing division was divested in order to focus on its core picture and video competencies in television, film, internet and game content.

Laws affecting intellectual property are of significant importance to Viacom, as it is to all content producers.

Viacom's competitive strength is based on one of the largest collections of cable programming assets in the world. Its leading program services reach more than 165 territories through more than 120 worldwide cable networks presented in over 25 different languages, and reach over 440 million subscriber households worldwide. In the US, its leading networks program reaches approximately 150 million television viewers. Many of its brands, such as MTV, Nickelodeon and VH1 are known worldwide. MTV is one of the world's most valuable brands, and Nickelodeon is one of the world's most widely distributed children's television brands, available in over 300 million television households. MTV Networks and BET appeal to a wide range of targeted niche audiences, which also represent demographics sought after by advertisers. In the US, MTV and BET delivered the most multichannel viewers in the 12 to 34 year old group. Nickelodeon accounts for more than half of all viewing by children ages 2 to 11 of advertising-supported children's television programming in the US. Viacom has a significant and growing international presence in Western Europe, Eastern Europe and Russia, Brazil and Japan. Viacom has created global hits in television programming, events and movies and has a strong platform in cable programming and websites.

Walt Disney

Walt Disney developed his famous cartoon characters such as Mickey Mouse and Donald Duck between the two World Wars.[17] These and other well-known characters including Snow White and the Seven Dwarfs were soon used in animated films, too, from the Disney Studios in Hollywood. In the 1950s, Disney moved into amusement parks, creating Disneyland, a family entertainment resort. He also expanded into live feature films in the 1950s, while continuing production of animated films. In the same decade, Disney Studios started production of TV films. All films were distributed through the new subsidiary Buena Vista Distribution. Since the 1960s, the Disney animation/motion picture studios and amusement parks have developed into a multi-billion dollar television, motion picture, vacation destination and media corporation, including other facilities such as hotels, record labels, and television networks.

In 2006-07, the Walt Disney Company had total revenues of $35 billion. Of Disney's $35 billion total revenues in 2006-07, the US and Canada markets accounted for 77 percent, Europe for 17 percent, Asia Pacific for 5 percent and Latin America for 1 percent.

The current Disney corporation operates in four segments.[18]

- Studio Entertainment: $7 bn. This segment produces and acquires live-action and animated motion pictures (Walt Disney Pictures, Pixar, Touchstone Pictures, Miramax Film), direct-to-video programming and distribution of home entertainment, musical recordings (Walt Disney Records, a.o.), and live stage plays (Disney Theatrical Productions and Disney Live Family). The success of Studio Entertainment is heavily dependent on public taste and preferences as well as fluctuating results due to timing and performance of releases. The segment businesses compete with all forms of entertainment that produce and/or distribute theatrical and television films. The company also competes to obtain creative and performing talents, story properties, adviser support, broadcast rights and market share that are essential to success.

- Media Network: $15 bn. This includes the company's presence in television, cable, radio and the internet. The media Networks segment is comprised of a Domestic (US) broadcast television network (The ABC Television Network); Television production and distribution operations (ABC Studios, Buena Vista

---

17   *http://corporate.disney.go.com.*
18   Walt Disney Company (2002-07). *Annual Report 2000/01-2006/07: http://disney.go.com.*

Production, Disney Television, a.o.); Domestic television stations (affiliates of the ABC Television Network); Cable and satellite networks (ESPN in sports, Disney Channel for children, ABC Family for young adults, Radio Disney, a.o.); Domestic broadcast radio networks and stations; and Internet and mobile operations (develop, publish and distribute content for online and wireless services intended to appeal to broad consumer interest in sports, news, family and entertainment, including streaming of popular series and video games). Most revenues derive from the sale to advertisers of time in network programs for commercial announcements.

Disney's media networks compete for viewers and advertising time primarily with other television networks, independent television stations and other video and audio media, such as cable and satellite television programming services, DVDs, video games and the internet. The company's media networks also compete for the acquisition of sports and other programming which is a very competitive market, including for instance NFL, NBA, NASCAR and MLB. The company's websites and products compete with other websites and products in their respective categories, including among others, kids, family, entertainment, sports and news.

- Parks and resorts: $11 bn. The company owns and operates parks and resorts (Disneyworld and Disneyland) in Florida and California and other places in the US, in Paris, Hong Kong and Tokyo and is preparing new theme parks. Disney Cruise Line is also part of the company possessions, selling vacation packages. The segment generates revenues from the sale of admission to parks and sales of rooms, food, beverage, merchandising and vacation packages. The company's parks and resorts compete with other forms of entertainment, lodging, tourism and recreational activities. Parks and resort businesses are influenced by the seasonal nature of vacation travel and local entertainment excursions, peaking during the summer months.

- Consumer Products: $2 bn. This segment includes production and online distribution of Disney's brand merchandise, including clothes, toys, home décor, health, beauty, food and electronics based on existing and new Disney characters and other intellectual property. It also includes children's books and magazines published in multiple countries and languages. Furthermore, Disney Interactive Studios creates, develops and distributes multi-platform video games worldwide, primarily based on the company's creative content, such as Pirates of the Caribbean and Meet the Robinsons. The interactive entity is increasing its investment in games through the acquisition of studios and increased product development. The company competes in its character merchandising and other licensing, publishing, interactive and retail activities with other licensors, publishers and retailers of character, brand and celebrity names.

ABC

The American Broadcasting Company, ABC, is one of the old and leading American networks.[19] Today it is owned by Walt Disney Company. ABC was founded during the World War II. Between the two world wars, CBS and RCA's two programming services of NBC 'Red' and NBC 'Blue' dominated American broadcasting. To reduce the dominance of these two corporations, the FCC required the sale by RCA of one of its chains. RCA chose to sell NBC Blue that carried most of the company's news and cultural programs, while NBC Red was the larger radio network, carrying the leading entertainment and music programs and included many affiliates that were heard nationwide. CBS Blue was bought by Edward Noble, owner of a candy and drugstore chain. Noble formed a company for the deal, the American Broadcast Company.

ABC soon gained ground by a number of popular daily serials and its counter-programming. In 1948, ABC moved into television and by 1953, it was bought by United Paramount Theatres and secured the capital needed to create a full-time television service. Among the shows in the 1950s that brought in record audiences was Disneyland, but still ABC was relegated to secondary status in many markets until the late 1960s, and in some cases well into the 1980s. During the 1960s, ABC grew in popularity and formed an in-house production unit, ABC Films. During the 1970s, ABC developed its programming in sports, movies, comedies and shows. In the 1980s, ABC began satellite delivery via AT&T's Telstar. In 1984, ABC bought a majority stake of ESPN networks and franchises, the Entertainment and Sports Programming Network, an American cable television network dedicated to broadcasting sports related programming. By mid-1980s, ABC seemed to have lost the momentum that once propelled it in the 1970s. ABC's earnings and ratings declined and it was ripe for a takeover. Surprisingly, the buyer was a much smaller media company, Capital Cities Communications. In 1996, The Walt Disney Company acquired Capital Cities/ABC, however. ABC's recovery did not start until the turn into the new millennium, based on such popular dramas as Desperate Housewives and Grey's Anatomy. In 2007,

---

19   *www.abc.com*. Walt Disney Company. Annual Report 2006-07.

Global Experience Industries

ABC Radio Network merged with Citadel Broadcasting Corporation to form a new company called Citadel Communications. Today, ABC can be seen in virtually all American households. It has 10 TV stations and more than 200 affiliated stations. In 1999, CBS took over Worldvision Enterprises, ABC's television program and home video distributor, including most of its library.

ABC is part of the Disney ABC Television Group that includes the Walt Disney Company's worldwide entertainment and news television properties, including ABC Television Network, Cable Networks, Production & Syndication and Radio.[20] The Disney ABC Television Group had revenues of $13.2 billion in 2005 and $14.6 billion in 2006.[21]

NBC Universal

NBC is one of the pioneers of American radio and television networks, originating in the 1920s.[22] In 1986, NBC was acquired by General Electric. In 2004, NBC and Vivendi Universal Entertainment merged to form NBC Universal as a merger of NBC and Universal Studios (GE 80 percent, Vivendi 20 percent ownership).[23] Its principal businesses are the furnishing of US network television services to 230 affiliated stations, production of television programs, the production and distribution of motion pictures, operation of 30 television broadcasting stations, operation of cable/satellite networks around the world, operation of amusement parks, and investment and programming activities in multimedia and the Internet. The NBC Universal Television Group produces and provides entertainment programming to the domestic and international markets. NBC develops content in all areas of mass communication, including news, weather reports, sport, comedy series, talk shows, movies, etc. NBC segments include television production and distribution (including video), digital media (interactive on TV, computer, mobile), film (Universal Studios), parks and resorts. NBC's network reaches almost all US households and it is also seen throughout Latin America (through its Spanish-language Telemundo network), Canada and the Caribbean via cable and satellite. In 2007, NBC Universal had revenues of $16 billion.[24]

---

20   www.disneyabc.tv.com
21   http://corporate.disney.go.com.
22   www.nbc.com. www.ge.com.
23   www.nbcuni.com.
24   www.ge.com.

News Corporation

News Corporation is one of the most vertically integrated media companies in the world, involved in the production and distribution of newspapers, magazines, books, films and television (see respective chapters on the other media).[25]

News Corporation was formerly incorporated in Australia, but reincorporated in the USA in 2004. In 1952, Rupert Murdoch inherited News Limited from his father, based mainly on Australian Adelaide News. Murdoch started to build his media empire in the 1970s and 1980s, by acquiring several Australian, UK and US newspapers. In 1980, News Limited was turned into the holding company News Corporation. In the early 1980s, Murdoch bought the movie studio 20th Century Fox. In the mid-1980s, Murdoch acquired the Metromedia Group of TV stations, starting to build the fourth large US broadcast network, based on the Fox Broadcasting Company of 1986. This Fox network can now reach virtually all US households. Simultaneously, Murdoch built his British TV empire based on BSkyB that has dominated British pay-TV since 1990. Throughout the 1990s, News Corp. continued to expand in all media sectors, including newspapers, network, cable and satellite television, books and magazine publishing, movies and music, mainly in the USA, but to a high degree also in UK, Australia and Italy.

Of its $29 billion revenues in 2007, 22 percent came from television, 11 percent from cable networking programming, 10 percent from direct broadcast satellite television, 4 percent from Magazines and inserts, 17 percent form Newspapers, 6 percent from Book publishing, and other 5 percent.[26] All in all, almost half of its income was made on television. Its television revenues (over-the-air) were based on Fox Broadcasting Company, MyNetwork TV and the many Fox TV Stations throughout the USA and Star in Asia. Cable networking programming included FOX News Channel and Fox Cable Network (sports, etc.) in the USA and the Premiere Media Group in Australia. Direct broadcast satellite television was based on Sky in Italy and UK and part of the DirecTV Group in the USA (until late 2007) and Tata Sky in Asia. About $10 billion was made in American television.

News Corporation has made numerous recent strategic moves including the reorganization of its US operations and various strategic mergers and acquisitions. Going forward, the company aims at having a stronger and smarter internet presence and to this end, 2005 saw the acquisition of Intermix Media in the US, the owners of the social networking website MySpace.com, the fifth most visited website in the

---

25   *www.newscorp.com.*
26   News Corporation (2002-08). *Annual Reports 2001-07: www.newscorp.com.*

country. Other strategic moves are: the acquisition of the controlling interest in QPL, the acquisition of the outstanding 18 percent interest in Fox Entertainment Group, and the company restructured the regional sports network partnership with Cablevision resulting in full ownership of Fox Sports Network Ohio and Fox Sports Network Florida.

The News Corp.'s diverse portfolio throughout multiple entertainment and media segments is a key to its global competitiveness. However, the company recognizes the need to increase market share outside the US. In 2005, the company took full ownership of SKY Italia by acquiring Telecom Italia's 20 percent stake and in an attempt to get a foothold in the Russian market it put in a bid for Ren TV. News Corporation is exploring opportunities in the wireless media market in China, too, which has the largest mobile phone market in the world.

Time Warner

Time Warner is a leading US media and entertainment company, whose businesses include interactive services (AOL), cable systems (The Warner Cable), filmed entertainment (Warner Bros. Entertainment, New Line Cinema), television networks (Turner Broadcasting, Home Box Office) and magazine publishing (Time).[27] In 2007, Time Warner had total revenues of $46 billion. 80 percent of its revenues stemmed from the US, 6 percent from UK, 3 percent from Germany, 4 percent from France, Canada and Japan and 6 percent from the rest of the world. Time Warner primarily remains an American based company. Half of Time Warner's income comes from subscriptions, and the other half from advertising and content.

Time Warner classifies its operations into the following five segments and revenues in 2007:

- AOL: $8 bn
- Cable: $12 bn
- Filmed Entertainment: $11 bn
- Networks: $10 bn
- Publishing: $5 bn.

Time Warner has been using a merger and acquisition strategy to expand in all areas of its business and increase market share in the entertainment and media industry.

---

27   Time Warner (2006-08). *Annual Report 2005-07: www.timerwarner.com.*

Furthermore, it has made a strategic alliance with Google, launched a joint broadcast network between Warner Bros. and CBS and acquired Adelphia Communication Corporation from Comcast. Economic problems and lack of competitiveness have made Time Warner change its strategy and increase focus on its individual business areas.

Time Warner's digital services, AOL (formerly America Online, Inc.), operates a leading network of web brands and the largest Internet access subscription service in the US. AOL is organized around four business units: Access, Audience, Digital Services and International. Historically, AOL's primary product offering has been an online subscription service that includes dial-up Internet access for a monthly fee. This product used to generate the majority of AOL's revenues. Over the past several years, the AOL Access business unit has experienced significant declines in US subscribers and these declines are expected to continue. These decreases are due primarily to the continued migration to high-speed services and lower-cost dial-up services. To meet this challenge, AOL has entered into a number of agreements with high-speed access providers. It includes a strategic alliance with Google, including among other things a modified version of Google's search technology that enabled AOL to sell search advertising directly to advertisers on AOL-owned properties as well as promotional opportunities for AOL content on Google's network and enabling Google and AOL instant messaging users to communicate with each other. In 2006, AOL took more radical measures to meet its rapidly declining subscriber base. It began a transition from a primarily subscription-based business to an advertising-supported global web services business. As a result, as long as an individual has a means to connect to the Internet, that person is able to access and use most of the AOL services for free.

AOL's Audience business unit generates advertising revenues from the sale of banner advertising across its many web properties. AOL's Digital Services business unit works to develop next-generation digital services, including a variety of wireless, voice and other premium services and applications that appeal to AOL Internet users. AOL's International business unit, which primarily includes Europe, has an Internet access business based on paid services and sales of advertising.

Time Warner's cable business, Time Warner Cable Inc. (TWC) and its subsidiaries, is the second largest cable operator in the US, managing about 13 million basic cable subscribers by the end of 2006. TWC principally offers three products: video, high-speed data and digital phone. Video is TWC's largest product in terms of revenues. The matured and industry-wide competition has made TWC upgrade its offerings to advanced digital services such as HDTV, digital video and video-on-demand. High-speed data services have been one of TWC's fastest growing products in recent years and they are a key driver of business results. Digital phone is a new product that offers customers a convenient package of video, high-speed data and voice services.

Time Warner's Filmed Entertainment businesses include Warner Bros. Entertainment Inc. and New Line Cinema Corporation. The division produces and distributes theatrical motion pictures, television shows and other programming, distribution of home video products and license rights to the company's feature films, television programming and characters. Warner Bros. is one of the world's leading suppliers of television programming, distributing programming throughout most parts of the globe. Warner Bros. Interactive Entertainment licenses and produces interactive games for a variety of platforms based on Warner Bros.' and DC Comics' properties (for instance Hanna-Barbara and Looney Tunes, Superman, Batman, Wonder Woman and The Sandman) as well as original game properties. New Line is the world's oldest independent film company. Its primary source of revenues is the creation and distribution of theatrical motion pictures.

Warner Bros. continues to develop its industry-leading television businesses, including the successful releases of television series into the home video market. The sale of DVDs has been one of the largest drivers of the segment's profit growth over the last few years and Warner Bros.' extensive library of theatrical and television titles positions it to continue to benefit from DVD sales. However, the company has begun to see slower growth in DVD sales due to increasing competition, piracy, the maturing of the DVD format and the fragmentation of consumer time. Piracy, including physical piracy as well as illegal online file-sharing, continues to be a significant issue for the filmed entertainment industry. Due to technological advances, piracy has expanded from music to movies and television programming. The company has taken a variety of actions to combat piracy, individually and together with cross-industry groups, trade associations and strategic partners.

Time Warner's Networks group comprises Turner Broadcasting System Inc. (Turner), Home Box Office Inc. (HBO) and the WB Television Network (The WB Network). The Turner network, including such recognized brands as Turner Broadcasting System (TBS), Turner Network Television (TNT), Cable News Network (CNN), Cartoon Network and CNN Headline News are among the leaders in advertising-supported cable TV networks. In 1980, CNN introduced the idea of 24-hour television coverage. CNN is rated America's number one cable news source and is available to 90 percent of all US households and 1½ billion people around the world. The Turner networks generate revenues principally from the sale of advertising time and monthly subscriber fees paid for cable systems, direct-to-home satellite operators and other affiliates. Key contributors to Turner's success are its continued investments in high-quality programming focused on sports, network premieres, licensed and original series, news and animation, as well as a strong brand and operating efficiency. HBO operates the HBO and Cinemax multichannel pay television programming services, with the HBO ranking as the US' most widely distributed pay television network. HBO generates revenues principally from monthly subscriber fees from cable system operators, satellite companies and other affiliates. An additional source of revenue is the ancillary sales of its original programming, including such programs as The Sopranos, Sex in the City and Deadwood. The WB Network is a broadcast television network, whose target audience consists primarily of young adults. The WB Network generates revenues almost exclusively from the sale of advertising time.

The Time Warner's Publishing segment consists principally of magazine publishing and a number of direct-marketing and direct-selling businesses. Time Inc. publishes over 150 different magazines globally, including Time, Fortune, What's on TV and Sports Illustrated. It generates revenues from advertising, magazine subscriptions and news stand sales. Its growth is derived from higher circulation and advertising on existing magazines, new magazines launches and acquisitions. In 2006, the company sold Time Warner Book Group Inc. to Hachette Livre, a wholly-owned subsidiary of Lagardère SCA.

All Time Warner businesses face intense competition from the other leading media corporations and independent providers of specialized services within its product and segment portfolio. To remain competitive, Time Warner must continuously upgrade its business models and technological services.

Bertelsmann

Bertelsmann is an international media house based in Germany and operating in more than sixty countries.[28]

Bertelsmann was founded in the 19th century as a print and book publishing company. Since the 1950s, Bertelsmann has expanded into an increasing field of media by several acquisitions, including music labels in the 1950s and 1970s (Ariola and Arista). A book club was started in the 1950s. The publisher of newspapers and magazines Gruner + Jahr was acquired in the 1970s. RCA, in television, radio, TV and music production, was bought from GE in the 1980s. Including Windham Hill Records, all its music activities were bundled into the label BMG in the 1990s that entered a joint venture with Sony in 2004. In television and radio, Bertelsmann took over control with the leading private European company RTL in the 1990s, too. In 2000, it merged with British Pearson TV and became the RTL Group, which allowed it to enter the large American broadcast market. Random House, acquired in 1998, became the cornerstone of its book publishing activities in the US.

---

28 *www.bertelsmann.com.*

In 2007, Bertelsmann had revenues of $26 billion ($17 bn in 2001), of which 30 percent of earnings came from Germany, from other European countries 43 percent, 21 percent from the US, and 6 percent from the rest of the world.[29] The company includes the following business divisions, with annual revenues in 2007:

- *RTL Group:* includes television, radio and TV production within its operations – $7 billion. RTL is a leading broadcasting and TV production company, with holdings in 38 TV channels and 29 radio stations in ten countries, and worldwide presence in the content production sector.

- *Random House:* trade publishing – $3 billion. Random House is the world's biggest trade book publishing group, including more than 120 imprints.

- *Grûner + Jahr:* is a magazine publisher – $3 bio. The Gruner + Jahr printing and publishing company is Europe's biggest magazine publisher, publishing more than 300 magazines and newspapers in over 20 countries as well as online offers.

- *Bertelsmann Music Group (BMG):* BMG has 50 percent ownership of Sony Music. Sony-BMG now stands as the second largest music company in the world – $3billion. The BMG division consists of BMG Music Publishing and the Sony BMG Music Entertainment joint venture, uniting labels such as Arista, Columbia Records, Epic Record, Jive and RCA Records.

- *Arvato:* an international media and communications service provider of printing, mobile and other services – $6 billion.

- *Direct Group:* the club business of the company – $4 billion. The Direct Group division brings media to people, from books to DVDs via clubs, shops and online outlets.

---

29   Bertelsmann (2002-08). *Annual Reports 2001-07: www.bertelsmann.com.*

Vivendi

French Vivendi is a media conglomerate with activities in music, TV, cinema, mobile, internet, and games.[30]

Vivendi was founded in the 19th century under the name CGE, dealt for more than a century with water, energy and other resources. In the 1980s, CGE helped to found Canal+, the first Pay-TV channel in France, and in the 1990s, CGE began expanding into telecommunications and mass media. The deregulation of the French telecommunications market in 1998 made CGE divest most of its non-communications and media assets and change its name to Vivendi. Simultaneously, Vivendi began to acquire several media companies and launched digital channels in Italy, Spain, Poland, Scandinavia, Belgium and The Netherlands. Vivendi Universal Entertainment was created in 2000 with the merger of the Vivendi media empire with Canal+ television networks and the acquisition of Universal Studios from the Canadian company Seagram. To overcome disastrous losses in the early 2000s, Vivendi sold 80 percent of its stakes in Vivendi Universal Entertainment in 2006 to General Electric that formed NBC Universal. Since 2006, Vivendi has been expanding and upgrading its core businesses, including digital and consumer oriented distribution, the acquisition of innovative companies in new digital fields, content development, and new business models.

Vivendi is a world leader in entertainment with content creation and distribution at the heart of its businesses. The entertainment industry is a fast-growing sector driven by the development of leisure time (changing lifestyles, increased life expectancy, development of leisure activities, etc.), an increased desire for unique experiences, and by new technologies which provide quality digital content at any time and anywhere, at decreasing prices. Leisure activities are considered to be very important by more than one-third of the world population (almost half the population in developed countries, less in emerging countries and few in developing countries). Entertainment has become a key component of everyday life and one to which consumers allocate an ever-increasing budget. Vivendi's businesses all meet this growing demand and are positioned to make the most of this profitable and important source of growth. It is Vivendi's strategy to expand its business activities in content creation and distribution, as well as its digital services. Vivendi's businesses share many common denominations: they directly target consumers via strong brands, and they offer creative content based on subscription and digital technologies. The digitization of content, combined with the growing adoption of broadband distribution technologies, is creating major challenges and opportunities. Vivendi's strength

---

30   *www.vivendi.com.*

lies in anticipating consumer needs and meeting them, identifying future growth drivers for the group and reinforcing its businesses.

Total Vivendi revenues in 2007 were $27 billion ($33 bn in 2001, after merging with Universal).[31] 25 percent came from Universal Music, 20 percent from Canal+, 40 percent from SFR, 10 percent from Maroc Telecom, and 5 percent from Vivendi Games. In geographic terms, 60 percent stemmed from France, while the rest was almost equally divided between the rest of Europe, USA, Marocco, and the rest of the world. The revenues of Universal were equally divided between North America and Western Europe, however.

Vivendi is a major player in entertainment with business activities in music, television, cinema, mobile, Internet and games. The group's companies are all leaders in their respective fields:

- *Universal Music Group:* A 100 % Vivendi subsidiary, is the world's no. 1 record music company, selling more than one out of every four albums worldwide, with strong positions in North America and Western Europe. It also holds significant positions in the digital music market. By digital downloads via the Internet and mastertones, legal digital distribution of music has been expanding rapidly since 2005 and 2006 and has become a significant revenue stream. Revenue growth is driven by growth in downloads, via computer and mobile phones, the adoption of mobile personalization products and the monetization of music videos via downloads and ad-supported online streaming, mainly in the US, Western Europe and Japan. In 2006, Vivendi's Universal Music Group purchased Bertelsmann's BMG Music Publishing. Universal also signed an agreement in that year with YouTube, the leader in online sharing of original videos, giving YouTube and its users access to the thousands of Universal artist videos in all genres, including a copyright protection process. Universal has headquarters in Los Angeles and New York.

- *Groupe Canal+:* A 100 % Vivendi subsidiary, is the French leader in premium and theme channel distribution and programming with over 10 million subscriptions to its pay-TV offers, presenting films, sports events, news, documentaries, entertainment, lifestyle, series, and children's programmes. It is also a major player in the financing, acquisition and distribution of motion pictures in France and in Europe. Canal+ is also an expert in sports coverage,

---

31   Vivendi (2002-2008). *Annual Reports 2001-07: www.vivendi.com.*

having been granted exclusive rights to all League 1 (France) matches for the 2005-2008 seasons.

- *SFR:* A 56 % Vivendi subsidiary, is France's No. 2 mobile telecommunications operator and also owns 40.5 % of Neuf Cegetel, France's no. 2 fixed-line telecommunications operator. It offers mobile phone services on a subscription basis and via phone cards as well as mobile multimedia services (broadcasting of sound and pictures) and data transmission for consumers, professionals and companies in France. SFR is also active in the fixed line telecommunications sector through Neuf Cegetel.

- *Maroc Telecom:* A 51 % Vivendi subsidiary, is the leading mobile and fixed-line and internet access operator in Morocco.

- *Vivendi Games:* A 100 % Vivendi subsidiary, is the world's no. 1 player in the massively multiplayer online role-playing games (MMORPG) category. It is improving its position in the PC, console and handheld markets and has entered the high-growth casual online and mobile segments. The company maintains strong relations with strategic partners such as NBC Universal, Universal Music Group and the 20th Century Fox. With headquarters in Los Angeles, Vivendi Games is structured around four divisions, supported by global real sales: Blizzard Entertainment (in the subscription-based MMORPG market, known for World of Warcraft, the world's most popular game of its category); Sierra Entertainment (console, PC and handheld games for all platforms and across numerous genres: shooter, strategy, open world, etc.); Sierra online (casual online games for PC, Xbox and other platforms); Vivendi Games Mobile (action, strategy, casual and arcade games for the worldwide mobile market). Vivendi Games has expanded by acquiring several online and mobile developer companies.

- *Vivendi holds 20 % of NBC Universal:* A world leader in media with activities in film and television production, television channel distribution and amusement parks operations.

Liberty Media

Liberty Media Corporation (LMC) is a holding company that owns interests in a broad range of electronic retailing, media, communications and entertainment companies.[32] These interests are attributed to two tracking stock groups: the Liberty Interactive Group, which includes Liberty's interests in QVC (video and online shopping), Provide Commerce, IAC/InterActiveCorp, and Expedia (travel agency); and the Liberty Capital Group, which includes Liberty's interests in Starz Entertainment (provides premium programming by cable operators), News Corporation, and Time Warner, a.o. In 2007, Liberty had revenues of $9 billion.

Liberty Media Corporation was incorporated in 1991 on the Nasdaq stockmarket. In 1994 it merged with Tele-Communications and in 1999 with TCI Ventures. The same year TCI and AT&T merged and Liberty Media became a tracking stock at AT&T, and Liberty Media Group began trading on the New York Stock Exchange. In 2001, Liberty split from AT&T and began trading as a separate company on the New York Stock Exchange as LMC. In 2003, Liberty merged with Ascent Media Group and with Liberty Satellite & Technology. Its international businesses were spun off into Liberty Media International in 2004. In 2005, Liberty spun off its ownership in Ascent Media and Discovery Communications into a separate trade company Discovery Holding Company. The stock of this new company was distributed to existing Liberty shareholders. In 2006, Liberty completed its restructuring of the company and issued two new tracking stocks, Liberty Capital Group, which primarily represents its investment assets in media, telecom, and technology, and Liberty Interactive Group, led by QVC. Also in 2006, Liberty began implementing a strategy to convert passive investments into operating businesses.

Comcast Corporation

Comcast Corporation provides a wide variety of cable and other entertainment and communication products and services in the US, including video, high-speed Internet and digital voice.[33] Comcast's revenues are expanding rapidly in all three fields of communication. In 2006, Comcast had revenues of $31 billion ($8 bn in 2002), 63 percent in cable, 21 percent in high-speed Internet, 4 percent in digital phones and the rest in advertising and other income. 'On demand' viewership is growing exponentially. Half of Comcast's video customers take digital services with access to on demand. On

32   Liberty Media (2008). *Annual Report 2007: www.libertymedia.com.*
33   Comcast (2002-2008). *Annual Reports 2003-2007: www.comcast.com.*

demand access to content across multiple platforms, television, online and on demand, is driving the Comcast businesses. While the video customer market is maturing, there is plenty of room for expansion in the high-speed Internet and digital voice markets.

Comcast is the largest cable operator in the US serving some 23 million video subscribers, 11 million high-speed Internet subscribers and some 2 million digital phone subscribers, connecting more than one-third of all American homes.

The company manages its operations through two segments, Cable and Programming.

- *Cable:* The cable segment generates 95 percent of its revenues, primarily through subscriptions. It develops, manages, and operates broadband communication networks, including video, internet, telephone, and regional sports and news networks. The company's video services include basic and digital cable, video on demand, high-definition television, digital video recorders, premium channel programming, and pay-per-view programming. Its high-speed Internet service includes an interactive portal, Comcast.net, which provides multiple e-mail addresses, online storage and other value-added features and enhancements.

- *Programming:* The programming segment earns its revenues primarily from advertising. This content segment includes six national cable networks: E! Entertainment Television, Style Network, the Golf Channel, OLN, G4 and AZN Television. Comcast's other businesses includes a non-controlling interest in various programming entities in addition to Comcast Spectator. The programming entities include iN Demand, TV One, MGM, PBS KIDS Sprout, SportsChannel New England, New England Cable News, Pittsburgh Cable News Channel, Music Choice and Sterling Entertainment.

Comcast has continued its progression into the converged markets of telecoms, IT and entertainment. It has moved from being a cable provider to the largest national provider of integrated video, broadband and communications in the US in just 10 years and it aims to keep the momentum moving. The company has launched Comcast Digital Voice and VoIP service in 25 markets and will continue to roll this service out. Comcast is expanding the digitization of their TV services and with a large percentage of the US cable and broadband market (now with speeds up to 8MB), it is suitably positioned to take advantage of surging demand on the Internet video market. In 2007, Comcast continued to deepen subscriber relations with added value bundles of content and services. Key deals for the company that will enable it to increase its revenue base significantly over the next couple of years include the acquisition of 20 percent in MGM, and with Time Warner a joint acquisition of Cable Systems and the purchase of Susquehanna Communications. To develop communication and entertainment products for the wireless market, Comcast made joint ventures with Nextel Corporation, Time Warner Cable, Cox Communications and Advance Newhouse Communications.

DIRECTV

The DIRECTV Group is a US direct broadcast satellite television company.[34] DIRECTV, formerly known as Hughes Electronics, was formed in 1990. It reached one million customers in 1995. By way of acquisitions and organic growth, DIRECTV grew rapidly, reaching ten million customers in 2001, 15 million in 2005 and 16 million in 2007. It was sold to News Corporation in 2003, but in 2007 transferred to Liberty Media in return for Liberty's shares in News Corp. DIRECTV is the US industry leader in satellite TV or direct-to-home digital television services, and the second largest provider of multi-channel video programming distribution industry in the US It is also a leading provider of satellite television in Latin America. By way of satellites, DIRECTV provide its subscribers with access to hundreds of video and audio channels. DIRECTV had revenues of $17 billion in 2006 ($8 bn in 2001).

Gannett

Gannett Co. Inc. is a news and information company that operates primarily in the US and the UK.[35] It has been active in the business since the early 20th century. Gannett expanded by acquiring several regional US newspapers and developing an advanced printing business, too. In the 1960s, Gannett moved from being a regional newspaper group to a national publisher. Simultaneously, it acquired its first radio and television stations. Its growth continued through the 1970s and by 1980, Gannett owned 78 daily newspapers in more than thirty states, a national news service, seven television and fourteen radio stations (sold in 1997), including outdoor advertising companies in the US and Canada (sold in 1996), 21 weekly newspapers and a research firm. Its many newspapers and other media through the US adapted to the various local conditions of the continent.

Gannett is probably most known for its national newspaper, USA TODAY, that was started in the early 1980s. The newspaper quickly established itself with a two million daily circulation, the largest in the USA.

During the 1990s, Gannett continued to extend its newspaper business by acquisi-

---

34 DIRECTV Group (2008). *Annual Report 2007: www.directv.com.*
35 Gannett (2002-2008). *Annual Reports 2002-2007: www.gannett.com.*

tions in the US and UK, concentrating more and more on this core business, including TV stations and printing. It is the largest US newspaper publisher with a combined daily circulation of some seven million in the US and some half a million in the UK. Gannett television covers 18 percent of the US market. In 2007, it had revenues of $7.5 billion ($6 bn in 2001). The company also operates a number of Internet sites offering customized news and advertising to specific markets as well as an online business including several websites that offer news, entertainment, and advertising content. While there are problems in making newspapers profitable, Gannett is expected to focus increasingly on its Internet audience which numbered nearly 26 million unique visitors in January 2008, about 16 percent of the total US Internet audience, measured by Nielsen Ratings.

In 2006, Gannett announced a new strategic plan designed to adapt to the consumer and technology revolutions which took hold that year, and which began to change the marketplace for information, i.e. the impact of the Internet breakthrough in all fields of information production and distribution. Since 2006, Gannett has been carrying out a true transformation of the company to provide news and information on demand across all media, anywhere, anytime and in any form, taking advantage of the value of USA TODAY as a national brand and the ability of its newspapers and television stations to deliver local information. Gannett's relationship with its customers is being redefined. Gannett can no longer decide what its customers want and need, and deliver it as Gannett pleases. Customers have become the central focus of all that Gannett does. From product development, to content gathering, to advertising sales, the customer is put in first place, based on a technologically revolutionized digital business. This is the key strategic shift for Gannett.

Radio

The Global Radio Market

The radio market consists of global advertiser spending on radio stations, radio networks, and satellite radio as well as satellite radio subscriptions in the US and radio license fees and advertising spending in the rest of the world.[36]

---

36   PWC. Global Entertainment and Media Outlook, 268. An overview of the radio market and industry is given in Albarran, Alan B. and Patrick, W. Lawrence (2005). 'Assessing Radio Station Value: A Review of the Academic Literature and Analysis of Contemporary Industry'. *Journal of Radio & Audio Media*, 12:1, 3-13. Handy, David (2000). 'A Political Economy of Radio in the Digital Age'. *Journal of Radio Studies*, Vol. 7, No. 1, 213-234.

The radio market has been growing by six percent annually from $38 billion in 2001 to $45 billion in 2005 and a projected $59 billion in 2010 (Table 29). The US has the largest market, followed by Western Europe, led by Germany, UK, France and Italy, while the somewhat smaller Asian Pacific radio market is dominated by Japan. The rest of the world consists of small markets, although radio networks are found in all countries of the world and numbered in thousands.[37] The transition to digital radio formats will be the main cause of increasing spending towards 2010, particularly in the US.

Table 29

The Global Radio Market in $bn, 2001-2010

	2001	2005	2010
North America	19	22	32
USA	18	21	30
Canada	1	1	2
Western Europe	12	14	16
Germany	4	4	4
UK	2	2	3
France	2	2	2
Italy	1	2	2
Rest of WE	3	4	5
Eastern Europe	1	1	2
Africa and Middle East	0	0	0
Asia Pacific	5	6	7
Japan	4	4	4
Australia	1	1	1
Rest of Asia Pacific	0	1	2
Latin America	1	1	2
Total	38	45	59

Source: PWC. Global Entertainment and Media Outlook, 270, 286, 288, 295, 297, 299.

---

37   Johnston. Encyclopedia of International Media and Communications: 'Radio Broadcasting'. *www.wikipedia.org*: 'Radio network'.

USA

The overall radio market grew from $18 billion in 2001 to $21 billion in 2005, with a projected $30 billion in 2010, including terrestrial radio advertising rising from $18 billion in 2001 to $24 billion in 2010, and satellite radio subscription from nil in 2001 to $5 billion in 2010 (Table 30).

TABLE 30

The US Radio market in $bn, 2001-2010

	2001	2005	2010
Terrestrial Advertising	18	20	24
Local	14	16	19
National Spot	3	4	4
Network	1	1	1
Satellite Radio	0	1	5
Subscription	0	1	5
Advertising	-	0	0
Total	18	21	29

Source: PWC. Global Entertainment and Media Outlook, 274-275.

Terrestrial radio was one of the fastest growing advertising media during the 1990s, when consolidation reduced the number of sellers and made it easier for radio advertisers to buy radio time both within a market and across markets through large group owners such as Clear Channel, ABC and CBS. Consolidation also enabled group owners to package stations and selling them to advertisers as a group. Once the benefits of consolidation had been absorbed, there were no significant drivers to take their place. At the same time, cable operators were more aggressively selling time to local advertisers. Radio's share of radio/cable/out-of-home advertising fell from a five year peak of 67 percent in 2002 to 63 percent in 2005 and a projected 59 percent in 2010. In 2005, local radio advertising constituted 78 percent of the radio advertising market and national advertising 22 percent, which consists of national spot advertising (ads purchased in several markets in a single buy).

One development that will probably boost radio is the emergence of high-definition (HD) broadcasting, or digital audio broadcasting (DAB). HD radio provides near-CD quality sound and the ability to transmit information on the artist or song. The rapid take-up of satellite radio indicates that niche formats and superior quality appeal to listeners. Despite the fact that radio is generally available at no cost to the listener, satellite radio offered on a subscription basis is catching on. Listeners get access to significantly higher audio quality and more varieties of music than have been available on terrestrial radio, and they are willing to pay for the additional choice. The appeal of satellite radio was enhanced through sports deals with Major League Baseball, the National Football League, the National Basketball Association, and NASCAR. Looking ahead, satellite radio's prospects will be further improved by attracting celebrity hosts such as Howard Stern and Oprah Winfrey.

The structure and trends of Canadian radio are almost similar to those of the USA. Radio income is based on terrestrial advertising and to a small degree on an emerging satellite radio market. Digital radio broadcasting is expanding, as is the number of stations, creating a still more fragmented radio market. Local advertising generates much more income than national advertising. Total radio advertising will rise from $1 billion in 2001 and 2005 to $1.6 billion in 2010. Starting from nil in 2005, satellite advertising subscription will probably be $0.3 billion in 2010.

In Latin America, radio advertising, which is the only radio income, will rise from $1 billion in 2001 to a projected $2 billion in 2010. Mexico is by far the largest radio advertising market, including more than half the total Latin American radio market.

Western Europe

Radio spending in Western Europe will grow from $12 billion in 2005 to a projected $16 billion in 2010 (Table 31). In Western Europe, public radio license fees constitute the largest radio income, although radio advertising is catching up.

Next generation receivers and new digital broadcasting technologies will drive growth in most West European countries. Digital audio broadcasting (DAB) and digital radio mondiale (DRM) are the two principal digital technologies being introduced. DAB offers CD-quality sound while DRM is a digital technology with near-CD sound. As digital radio gets introduced throughout Western Europe, the number of radio stations will increase and advertisers will have more options. More channels, however, will also lead to increased fragmentation.

License fees are paid by households via government levies to help finance public radio stations. Growth is generally modest because fees depend on household growth and rate increases, which tend to be infrequent. Germany is by far the largest market for public radio license fees, followed by the UK and France. Except for Portugal and Ireland, public radio fees constitute an important part of total radio income in West European countries.

TABLE 31

The West European Radio market in $bn, 2001-2010

	2001			2005			2010		
	Advertising	Public License Fees	Total	Advertising	Public License Fees	Total	Advertising	Public License Fees	Total
Germany	1	3	4	1	3	4	1	3	4
UK	1	1	2	1	1	2	1	1	2
France	1	1	2	1	1	2	1	1	2
Italy	1	1	2	1	1	2	1	1	2
Rest of WE	1	2	3	1	2	3	2	2	4
Total	5	8	13	6	8	13	7	9	14

Source: PWC. Global Entertainment and Media Outlook, 286, 288.

In Eastern Europe, advertising is the major income source, except for Poland. The Russian radio market is expanding rapidly. East European growth in radio advertising will accelerate, but from a low level.

Asia Pacific

Asian radio, which consists of terrestrial advertising, public radio license fees, and a small satellite radio subscription market, will increase from $5 billion in 2001 to a projected $7 billion in 2010, based on a 60-40 share advertising and license fees income, respectively. Japan embraces half the advertising market and three-quarters of the public license fees market while the remaining license fees market is divided between Taiwan and Singapore. At a much lower level, Australia is second and China third in advertising. Japan is recovering from a setback in the early 2000s. The satellite radio market will still be very small in 2010.

Compared to developed countries, radio markets in Africa and The Middle East are small, although radio stations are large in numbers.

The Global Radio Industry and Clear Channel Communication

Most radio channels are part of leading television companies. Only a few companies specialize in radio transmission, such as American Clear Channel. Clear Channel

Communication is a diversified media company.[38] In 2007, it had revenues of $7 billion (with ups and downs the same level since 2000). In 2007, some half of its income stemmed from radio and almost a quarter from outdoor advertising (billboards and displays). Clear Channel clearly focuses on radio production and distribution by way broadcast, cable, satellite and wireless channels in mainly the US on the one hand, and outdoor advertising in the US and abroad on the other.

Clear Channel started transmitting in 1972 in San Antonio Texas and quickly spread throughout the US continent. In the 1980s, Clear Channel diversified into television. Since the 1980s, several radio and television acquisitions have been made. Clear Channel expanded rapidly during the 1990s, in the U.S as well as internationally in Canada, Western Europe, Oceania and elsewhere. In 2001, Clear Channel had radio operations in 65 countries, focusing on Australia, New Zealand and Mexico. An outdoor advertising division was developed in the 1990s, too. Since its peak performance in 2001, Clear Channel has had some setbacks and revenues declined until a new build-up started in 2005 and continued in the next years. By the end of 2006, Clear Channel owned and operated almost 1200 radio stations in the US and more than 200 international radio stations, 40 US television stations, and a large US and international outdoor business. In 2007, all its television stations and one third of all radio stations (its non-profitable stations) were sold, making radio and outdoor the two core businesses.

The company operates in two major segments:

-   *Radio broadcasting:* Clear Channel owns and operates radio stations in most US states and some nations abroad, providing programming and distribution for these stations, too. Its radio strategy centers on providing programming and services to the local communities in which it operates. By providing listeners with compelling programming, Clear Channel seeks to provide advertisers with an effective platform to reach their consumers. Its national radio coverage allows Clear Channel to deliver messages for specific audiences to advertisers on a local, regional and national basis. Most of its radio broadcasting revenue is generated from the sale of local and national advertising in the US. Clear Channel competes for audience, advertising revenues and programming with other radio stations owned by companies such as CBS, Cox Radio, Entercom and Radio One (each with approximately half a billion dollars in revenues in 2006).[39] It also competes

38   Clear Channel Communications (2001-08). *Annual Reports 2000-07: www.clearchannel.com.*
39   *www.coxradio.com. www.entercom. www.radio-one.com.*

with other advertising media, including satellite radio, television, newspapers, outdoor advertising, direct mail, cable television, yellow pages, the Internet, wireless alternatives, cellular phones and other forms of advertisement. Annual revenues of radio broadcasting in 2006 amounted to $3.7 billion.

- *Outdoor advertising:* Clear Channels outdoor business includes billboards (bulletins and posters) and displays (street furniture and transit) in the US and abroad in several countries, mainly Canada, Mexico, Chile, Peru, Australia and New Zealand, and minor markets in most Latin American and European countries. Clear Channel seeks to capitalize on its global network and diversified product mix to maximize revenues and increase profits, as well as by focusing on specific initiatives that highlight the value of advertising relative to other media. Clear Channel is working closely with clients, advertising agencies and other diversified media companies to develop more sophisticated systems that will provide improved demographic measurements of outdoor advertising. Advances in electronic displays, including flat screens, allow for alternatives to traditional methods of displaying clients' advertisements. Advertisements on a large number of displays may be linked through computer systems to change instantaneously and simultaneously. This is creating new advertising opportunities for clients, such as retailers that want to change advertisements frequently and on short notice. The outdoor advertising industry is fragmented, consisting of several larger companies involved in outdoor advertising, such as CBS, JC Decaux and Lamar Advertising Company, as well as numerous smaller and local companies operating a limited number of displays in a single or few markets. Clear Channel also competes with other media including broadcast and cable television, radio, print media, the Internet and direct mail. In 2006, about 40 percent of total revenues came from outdoor advertising (half from the USA and half from international markets).

Films

The filmed entertainment market consists of consumer box office spending for motion pictures plus spending on renting and purchasing home video products in both DVD and VHS formats.[40] It also includes online film rental subscription services, whereas

40   PWC. Global Entertainment and Media Outlook, 60.

music videos and movies distributed for TV are included in the chapters on Music and Television, respectively. In a wider sense, the movie industry also includes the film producers, the distributors, the actors, directors, screenwriters, cinematographers and the whole set up of technology producers of cameras, software, sound, light, special effects and other techniques and services.

Prior to the mid-1980s, the film industry had one major source of revenue: the movie theater.[41] Since then, the world has undergone a communication revolution, creating new markets that have become basic markets in themselves, such as home video, cable and pay-per-view and ancillary sales of merchandise goods. Taken as a whole, the majority of film admissions are registered during the first year after a film's release, some in the second year, but next to nothing in the third year. For many years, this rapid obsolescence of films from screens has been an economic characteristic familiar to distributors and exhibitors. The general consensus is, however, that the rate of obsolescence is accelerating due to the pressure of the increasing number of films on offer. This makes it even more difficult for less successful films to stay on screens and thereby preserve diversity in film production and access.

The basic problem with theatrical distribution is that it does not allow a film to take advantage of the so-called 'long tail' effect of the digital age.[42] The theory put forward by Chris Anderson says that products low in demand or sales can collectively make up a market share that rivals or exceeds the relatively few current bestsellers and blockbusters, if the distribution channels are wide enough. By offering broad access to vast catalogues, the Internet retail business is considered as the model of the long tail theory.

It is often said that films should be seen in cinemas. Recalling the economic facts that most films only last one year in cinemas and that bestsellers are a crucial part of box-office revenues, many opportunities to watch a wide selection of movies are left unfulfilled by the traditional forms of distribution. A British study shows that of 521 UK films released in 2003 and 2004, 68 percent were available through mainstream retail outlets, but just 21 percent had had a traditional video rental release. However, 78 percent could be rented on-line, thus demonstrating the capacity (and the longer exposure) available through this kind of distribution. The situation is supposedly the same when the video-on-demand distribution form reaches maturity. It demonstrates

41   Johnston. Encyclopedia of International Media and Communications: 'Film'. The European Audiovisual Observatory (2007). *FOCUS 2007. World Film Market Trends: www.obs.coe.int*. Pokorny, Michael and Sedgwick, Jon (2004). *An Economic History of Film*. UK: Routledge. Turner, Graeme (2002). *Film as Social Practice*. UK. Routledge.

42   Chris Anderson (2006). *The Long Tail: Why the Future of Business is Selling Less of More*. New York: Hyperion.

that on-line rental and most likely video-on-demand constitutes a real second chance for many more films than is the case currently. Another study illustrates the rapid emergence of video-on-demand in Europe, almost 150 operational services being identified at the end of 2006.

If you miss a film or want to view previously released movies, the video-on-demand services clearly gives you the opportunity to do so. This does not render theatrical exhibition obsolete. On the contrary, it gives the public access to the wide historic treasure of films that might lead to increasing diversity in demand for cinema movies, too. It is a win-win situation.

Since the mid-1990s, the number of films annually released in the EU has increased from 735 to 862, in the US from 646 to 699 and in Japan from 278 to 417. The average price of feature film production in the US is many times the size of that in Europe, reflecting a much larger audience for the American movies than for the European movies. Relatively, the US has more admissions, cheaper tickets and more screens than the Europeans and Japanese. The US film industry is also dominating the world film market.

The most watched films in 2006 in the US and Europe were Pirates of the Caribbean: Dead Man's Chest (Buena Vista)(45 million), followed by The Ice Age: The Meltdown (Fox)(40 million), The Da Vinci Code (Sony)(36 million) and Casino Royale (Sony)(26 million), Mission Impossible III (Paramount) and Superman Returns (Warner). Among the top 5 most viewed movies, national films are only to be found in a few cases, mainly from India and to some degree China, and Russia and Japan (Pirates, Da Vinci and Gedo Senki were the top 3). In Japan, all the top 10 Japanese titles are produced or co-produced by television networks. About half of the Japanese market is national, and almost half is international. Toho is by far the most widespread Japanese distributor (10 of top 20). In South Korea, the market share is almost one-third national and two-thirds US films. In Africa and the Middle East, all top ten films are of national or of regional origin, many produced in Nigeria.

The Global Film Market

The world filmed entertainment market rose from $64 billion in 2001 to $80 billion in 2005, with a projected $104 billion in 2010 (Table 32). The US film market is by far the largest, covering more than 40 percent of world total spending, and Canada accounts for 5 percent. Western Europe is second with a 25 percent share and Asia Pacific third with a 20 percent share. Compared to those regions, the Latin American as well as the Middle Eastern and African film markets are small, but in some cases, such as Nigeria, of significant size in numbers. All developed countries have film industries of their own, led by the USA in America, the UK in Western Europe, and Japan in Asia. Rather strong film industries exist in emerging countries such as China and India, and most developing countries also produce films. As mentioned, Nigeria even includes a large film industry. The film industry expands at almost the same pace in all parts of the world, i.e. about 5 percent annually.

TABLE 32

The Global Films Market in $bn, 2001-2010

	2001	2005	2010
North America	32	39	50
USA	29	34	44
Canada	3	5	6
Western Europe	16	21	27
UK	5	7	8
Germany	3	3	4
France	2	3	4
Italy	1	2	3
Spain	1	2	2
Rest of Western Europe	4	4	6
Eastern Europe	1	1	2
Middle East and Africa	0	0	0
Asia Pacific	14	17	21
Japan	7	8	9
China	1	1	2
South Korea	2	2	2
Australia	1	2	2
India	1	1	2
Rest of Asia Pacific	2	3	4
Latin America	1	2	2
Total	64	80	102

Source: PWC. Global Entertainment and Media Outlook, 60-113.

The filmed entertainment market consists of two major segments, box-office spending at cinemas (some quarter) and home video production, rentals and purchases (almost three-quarters) (Table 33).

TABLE 33

Global Box Office and Home Video Spending in $bn, 2001-2010

	2001	2005	2010
Box office	22	24	30
Home Video	42	56	74
Total	64	80	104

Source: PWC. Global Entertainment and Media Outlook, 60-113. Motion Picture Association of America (MPAA)(2007). *US Entertainment Industry. 2006 Market Statistics: www.mpaa.org*. The European Audiovisual Observatory, Focus 2007. World Film Market Trends.

Throughout the world, digital movies will be widely introduced within the next few years, including many modern cinemas and screens, too. This will further boost box office spending in developed and emerging countries. The introduction of high-definition DVDs, the emerging online DVD rental services, and film streaming services will stimulate home video sales and the rental market in North America, Europe and Asia Pacific, depending also on the consumer appeal of released movies.

USA

The US filmed entertainment industry is the largest in the world, accounting for more than 40 percent of the global filmed entertainment industry.[43] In the US and worldwide US films dominate box-office and home video revenues. Customers now have an exceptional amount of choice in cinemas, with a greater number of movies released each year. The number of US theaters is about 6,000 with six times that number in screens. Of the total US revenues in 2005 of $34 billion, some quarter came from box office tickets and almost three-quarters from home videos (Table 34). The top 10 movies attracting most people at box offices accounted for some quarter of total income. DVDs have gained huge popularity at the expense of VHS, which is about to disappear. The DVD has superior audio-visual quality and durability compared with VHS, and DVDs are also cheaper to manufacture and require less storage space. The total number of DVD discs shipped to dealers is constantly rising as is the number of titles available on DVD. In terms of theater classification, the miniplex segment had

---

43   MPAA. US Entertainment Industry. 2006 Market Statistics. ReportSURE, Global Media & Entertainment, 45-47.

Global Experience Industries

the highest share with 39 percent and the megaplex segment the lowest share with 9 percent, leaving 27 percent to single screen and 25 percent to multiplex. High definition DVDs and continued growth in TV shows on DVD will boost the home video market, but unit sales growth will moderate as the industry matures. Online rentals and digital streaming will enhance the market, but in-store rentals will continue to decline.

TABLE 34

The USA Film Market in $bn, 2001-2010

	2001	2005	2010
Box Office	8	9	11
Home Video	21	25	33
In-Store Home Video Sell-Through	10	17	23
In-Store Home Video Rental	10	8	6
Online rentals/Digital Streaming	-	1	4
Total	29	34	44

Source: PWC. Global Entertainment and Media Outlook, 63.

Changes are occurring in the way films are financed. High-budget films carry a high risk, and studios have sought to minimize that risk by entering into co-production deals with other studios or by pre-selling the rights for international distribution or other revenue streams. Private equity funding has become important to film financing. Private funds invest relatively small amounts in a large number of films, thereby spreading their own risk through diversification. For studios, private funding reduces their need to pre-sell rights or to enter into co-production arrangements, thereby increasing their potential profits. Another trend is the release of fewer films that are being marketed more effectively. The combination of new funding and fewer releases should allow more resources to be devoted to individual titles, thereby improving their chances to appeal to audiences.

A further development is the introduction of digital cinemas. In 2005, the US studios agreed on technical standards for digital films and equipment. The digital film projector provider, Christie, and the provider of digital film service content, Technicolor, have made deals with exhibitors to install digital projectors and end-to-end digital distribution solutions, and they have also made deals with studies to produce digital movies. Other companies such as Belgian Barco and US Eastman Kodak have provided digital equipment and digital solutions, too.

Digital movies substantially save costs of print duplication and transportation, thus freeing funds to be used for production of the film itself. Also, digital distribution allows films to be shown throughout the country at once. Currently, it is not economical to make prints to serve the entire country at once. Cinemas in smaller markets, therefore, have to wait until a film has played out in the major markets before they receive prints. In addition, digital prints do not wear out, scratch, or deteriorate, a problem encountered by cinemas after a film has been replayed several times. And further, digital films provide better picture and sound quality. The experience for cinema-goers, therefore, should be improved, which should also have a positive impact on admissions.

The goal is to convert approximately 15,000 screens, representing approximately 40 percent of all screens in the USA, to digital by the year 2015, and some 10 percent of screens are expected to be digital by 2010. Beginning in 2007, the impact of digital screens will gradually be felt, reaching box office spending of $11 billion in 2010.

Since the turn of the millennium, the declining VHS home video market has been more than offset by a rapidly increasing DVD market (Table 34). Total US video sales are being more than doubled from $10 billion in 2001 to a projected $23 billion in 2010, when VHS videos will virtually have disappeared from the market. TV programs represent a significant growth area for DVDs. The popularity of TV shows demonstrates that the underlying demand for home video content remains. The dramatically improved picture and sound of HD videos will most likely stimulate the market in the same way that the introduction of DVDs did in the late 1990s. It is believed that competing HD and Blue-ray formats will not slow the market, recalling that VHS and Beta formats coexisted during the 1980s until VHS won out. One format may ultimately become the industry standard but until then, video products will be released in both formats.

The online rental market for movies will increase. Netflix, Blockbuster, and Disney are among the providers of online rental services. Wal-Mart discontinued its online rental business and merged it with Netflix. Online rental services will have HD DVDs. The convenience of such services will expand the market. Annual spending on online rental subscriptions in the USA grew from zero in 2001 to $2 billion in 2005 and at least $3 billion in 2010.

The digital streaming services market is still small, but will accelerate through 2010. MovieLink and CinemaNow distribute films over the Internet via a broadband connection. These and other companies have made distribution deals with the major studios, giving them content to allow the market to grow. Bertelsmann is preparing to offer its own platform to enable consumers to download movies and music to their PCs. With the majority of Internet households now connecting through broadband, there is a significant potential for growth. Soon, computers will be connected to TVs, and Internet protocol television services will make the computer and TV experience more seamless. By 2010, downloads of digital streaming services will still be a relatively small component of the home video market at less than half a billion dollars.

The significant Canadian film market is very much dominated by US productions and companies, which embrace almost ninety percent of cinema movies. Like the US, the home video market is by far the largest and most expansive market. In Latin America, film spending has been rather small with estimated $2 billion through 2005 to 2010, divided between box office spending (most) and home video. Total market film value is much higher, however, as a consequence of widespread piracy in home videos. Brazil and Mexico are the two largest markets.

Western Europe

The West European filmed entertainment sector constitutes some quarter of the global filmed entertainment market.[44] DVD and video purchases account for a major part of the total filmed entertainment market, just like in the US. Growth in DVD sales is increasing rapidly, while box office growth has been slow due to a lack of any major films produced on the continent. The UK remains the most stable of European countries, while Germany, France, Spain and Italy witness less satisfactory performances in their box-offices. The West European film sector is likely to grow in the future. Leading motion picture companies in Europe are: UGC Cinema, Pathe Group, Time Warner Entertainment, United International Pictures and Walt Disney International. In UK it is: Universal Pictures, Walt Disney International, Time Warner Entertainment and Columbia Pictures. The majority of films and revenues come from American movies, just as American film companies dominate the European cinemas and home videos. New digital cinemas will turn the box office market in Western Europe around. The home video market continues to grow thanks to DVDs sales, but also boosted by online film subscription services that benefit from growing broadband subscriptions.

Filmed entertainment spending in Western Europe will increase from $17 billion in 2001, to $22 billion in 2005 and a projected $26 billion in 2010 (Table 35). While box office spending has been flat and is projected to grow only slowly from $7 to $8 billion in 2010, the home video market continues to grow from $10 billion in 2001 to $15 billion in 2005 and $18 billion in 2010.

---

44   ReportSURE. Global Media & Entertainment, 53-54.

TABLE 35

The West European Film Market in $bn, 2001-2010

	2001	2005	2010
Box Office	7	7	8
Home Video	10	15	18
In-store Home Video Sell Through	7	12	15
In-Store Home Video Rental	3	3	3
Online Rental/Digital Streaming	-	0	2
Total	17	22	26

Source: PWC. Global Entertainment and Media Outlook, 80, 83, 85, 87.

The UK is the largest home video market, constituting more than one-third of the total marked, followed by Germany and France at a much lower level. At almost the same size, Germany, UK and France cover half the West European box office market. UK is the dominant film market with almost $7 billion, more than twice the size of Germany and France at second and third place. Total box office spending is showing a moderate growth, except for a decline in Germany.

In 2006, US films had a market share in Europe of almost two-thirds, leaving some quarter to European films. The US share is only 44 percent in France but 74 percent in Germany and Italy, 71 percent in Spain, 81 percent in the UK, 90 percent in Austria, Switzerland and Benelux, and 80 percent in Scandinavia. In Russia, foreign movies cover three-quarters of the market. In the US, American movies embrace 90 percent of the market. In Canada, the US film market share is 88 percent, while in Australia the US market share is 86 percent. Films made in the UK, Germany, France, Italy and Spain covered more than 80 percent of total films produced in the EU in 2006. The top 25 films in the EU share almost 40 percent of total admissions in 2006. An increasing share of screens is in multiplexes and they attract the majority of admissions.

To reduce the dominance of US films in Western Europe, governments are seeking to both support local production and attract international producers by investment incentives and funding. Another development that should help the box office market is the proliferation of digital cinemas in several West European countries. By 2010, 7 percent of the screens are expected to be digital. Digital cinemas reduce distribution cost by 50 percent. Digital cinemas also allow new releases to be available sooner and provide a better quality that does not deteriorate after repeated screenings.

XDC, the leading digital cinema service company in Europe, is the main installer of digital screens in West European countries.[45] XDC is a member of the American EVS Group that provides digital broadcast equipment servers with associated control software and production network for television and motion picture communities.[46] EVS has its roots in sports television: Live Slow Motion system revolutionized live broadcasting in the early 1990s and grew up to a worldwide standard since then. The technology has evolved into a universal server platform capable of supporting HD, too. Other providers of digital cinema equipment are Irish Avica Technology and Austrian Cineplexx.

From a low level, the film market in Eastern Europe is expanding much more than in Western Europe. Russia is the largest market and growing fast to reach $1 billion by 2010, mainly caused by its box office expansion in new modern cinemas. The Middle East and Africa are small film markets, totaling half a billion dollars by 2010 (probably underestimated). Modern cinemas are spreading, however, in Eastern Europe and some Middle East and African countries, in particular South Africa. Piracy is proliferating in these regions.

Asia Pacific

Digital cinemas, modern theaters, and support of local films will boost the box office market in Asia Pacific. HD will enhance the sell-through market, but piracy will continue to limit growth. Online rentals will grow rapidly, cutting into in-store activity but boosting the overall rental market. Filmed entertainment in Asia Pacific expanded from $14 billion in 2001 to $16 billion in 2005 and a projected $21 billion in 2010. Box office expanded from $5 billion in 2001, with a projected $7 billion in 2010 and home video from $9 billion 2001 to a projected $13 billion in 2010 (Table 36).

---

45   XDC: *www.xdcinema.com.*
46   EVS Group: *www.evs-global.com.*

TABLE 36

The Asian Pacific Film Market in $bn, 2001-2010

	2001	2005	2010
Box Office	5	6	7
Home Video	9	11	13
In-Store Home Video Sell Through	3	5	6
In-Store Home Video Rental	6	6	6
Online Rental Subscriptions	-	0	1
Total	14	16	21

Source: PWC. Global Entertainment and Media Outlook, 96-100.

Japan is the dominant market in the region, covering half of total revenues.[47] Japanese box office receipts are fluctuating in up and down movements around $2 billion annually. Japans home video market is three times that size, mainly rental. Cinema complexes with multiple screens have made it easier to distribute films nationwide without going through a major distributor, leading to more indigenous films being shown. Animated movies, supported with a sound performance from the Japanese animation industry, are set to grow in the future. The leading film producing companies in Japan are: Toei Co, Toho Co, Nikkatsu Corporation and Shockiku Co.

In box office revenues, the Indian market is of almost equal size to Japan, the two covering some half of the total market in the Asia Pacific box-offices market.[48] India has the world's most productive movie industry, producing around 1000 movies each year. The Indian movie industry was worth $1.5 billion in 2005 and is expected to grow 20 percent annually. Domestic box-office revenues accounted for 78 percent of total industry revenue. The film industry constitutes two-thirds of the total Indian media and entertainment market. China, South Korea, Australia and India are of almost the same size in the filmed entertainment market, South Korea and India being the most expansive box office markets.

The sell-through market and home video in general is substantially lower than its potential because of high rates of piracy. In India, for example, pirated DVDs are estimated at three times the rate of legitimate DVDs. In China, piracy is blooming, too, as well as in the Philippines and Southeast Asia. HD video and reduced piracy

---

47 PWC. Global Entertainment and Media Outlook, 92. ReportSURE, Global Media & Entertainment, 67-68.
48 ReportSURE. Global Media & Entertainment, 70-71.

will stimulate the sell-through market. Piracy is even a greater problem for the rental market than for the sell-through market, because the picture and sound quality of video (pirated videos are often substantially poorer in quality compared with the legitimate product) are less important for films intended to be viewed once than for films which people would like to own. The total rental video market is flat, declining slowly in developed countries and rising slowly in merging countries, except for a rapid expansion in India, fueled by rising penetration from a very low level and increased spending per household. A growing online film rental market is on its way in developed countries of the region, reaching probably $1 billion by 2010.

Piracy

Piracy is the biggest threat, especially to the US motion picture industry.[49] A study of the costs of piracy found that:

- The major US motion picture studios lost $6 billion in 2005 in piracy world-wide.
- 80 percent of these losses resulted from piracy overseas and 20 percent from piracy in the US
- 62 percent of the $6 billion loss result from piracy in hard goods such as DVDs, 38 percent from Internet piracy.
- Piracy rates are highest in China (90 percent), Russia (79 percent) and Thailand (79 percent), followed by Poland (65), Mexico (61), Taiwan (54), Spain (32), India (29) and Italy (25). Losses are highest in Mexico, UK and France that return greater income to the US industry than developing markets such as China and Russia.
- The worldwide motion picture industry, including foreign and domestic producers, distributors, theaters, video stores and pay-per-view operators, lost some $18 billion in 2005 as a result of piracy, 11 bio. from hard goods and 7 bio. from the Internet.
- The typical pirate is aged 16-24 and male. 44 percent of the international Motion Picture Association's (MPA) losses in the US are attributed to college students.

---

49   MPAA (2006). *International Piracy Fact Sheets: www.mpaa.org.* MPAA (2006). *The Cost of Movie Piracy.*

The true cost of movie piracy to the US economy is probably far more than $6 billion. A comprehensive estimate reveals that total lost output among all US industries is annually $20 billion.[50]

The Global Film Industry

The film industry consists of the technological and commercial institutions of filmmaking, i.e. film production companies, film studios, cinematography, film production, screenwriting, pre-production, post production, film festivals, distribution, actors, film directors and other film personnel.[51] The expense involved in making movies almost immediately led film production to concentrate under the auspices of standing production companies. However, advances in affordable film making equipment and expansion of opportunities to acquire investment capital from outside the film industry itself have allowed independent film production to evolve, too.

The film industry to day spans the globe. The major business centers of film making are concentrated in the United States, China, India and Nigeria. However, most developed nations have film industries of their own. Distinct from the business centers are the locations where movies are filmed. Because of labor and infrastructure costs, many films are produced in countries other than where the company paying for the film is located. For example, many US movies are filmed in Canada, UK, Australia, New Zealand or in East European countries.

Roughly, the total global motion picture industry could be estimated at $250 billion in 2005, of which the US industry embraces at least $100 billion, Western Europe $75 billion, Japan $25 billion and the rest of the world, including Oceania, the rest of Asia, Eastern Europe, Latin America, Africa and the Middle East, $50 billion.

USA

Much like American popular music, American cinema has had a profound impact on cinemas across the world since the early 20th century.[52] Its history is sometimes separated into four main periods: the silent film era (c.1910-1930), the classical Hollywood

50 Siwek, Stephen E. (2006). *The True Cost of Motion Picture Piracy to the US Economy*. Institute for Policy Innovation: *www.ipi.org*.
51 Schement. Encyclopedia of Communication and Information: 'Film Industry'. *www.wikipedia.org*: 'World cinema'.
52 *www.wikipedia.org*: 'The Film industry', 'Cinema of the United States'.

cinema (c.1930-1950), The New Hollywood (c.1950-1980), and the contemporary period (after 1980).

The peaking silent era in the 1920s and the transition from the silent era to the classical Hollywood era in the late 1920s created a handful of American production companies and film industry conglomerates that owned their own studios, distribution divisions and cinemas. Five large companies, the 'Big Five', included 20th Century-Fox, MGM, Paramount, RKO, and Warner Bros. Their management structures and practices collectively came to be known as the 'studio system'. Although they owned few or no cinemas to guarantee sales of their films, Universal Pictures, Columbia Pictures, and United Artists were also considered leading film makers, making a total of eight 'major studios', or rather seven as United Artists was more a studio for independent producers. Minor independent studios operated simultaneously with the 'majors' and mostly filled the demand for B-movies. The Big Five's ownership of movie theaters was eventually opposed by independent producers, including Samuel Goldwyn, David O. Selznick, Walt Disney, and Walter Wanger. In 1948, the federal government won a case against Paramount in the Supreme Court, which ruled that the vertically integrated structure of the movie industry constituted an illegal monopoly. This decision hastened the end of the studio system and Hollywood's golden age.

The breakthrough of television in the 1950s brought finally the studio system to an end. Instead, movie studios were increasingly being used to produce programming for television. With the breakup of domination by 'the Studios' and the continued incursion of television into the cinematic audience, the major production companies gradually transformed into management structures that simply put together artistic teams on a project-to-project basis, which remains the norm today.

The original major studios did not disappear, except for RKO that was dissolved in the 1950s. The 'seven sisters' continued, however, as Walt Disney also became one of them. Later on, the seven sisters were taken over by the present media conglomerates. Columbia Pictures was acquired by Sony Pictures Entertainment. Walt Disney Productions is now the Walt Disney Company. 20th Century Fox Film Corporation became part of News Corporation. Metro-Goldwyn-Mayer is now owned jointly by Sony and Comcast. Paramount Pictures is now part of the Viacom conglomerate. Universal Pictures is now part of Universal Studios that is owned by NBC Universal, a unit of General Electric. Warner Bros. Pictures, now part of Warner Bros. Entertainment, is owned by the Time Warner conglomerate. These conglomerates own other film companies, for example Walt Disney also includes Touchstone Pictures, and they control most of the American film industry. Newer large film companies, such as New Line Cinema and DreamWorks Studios, have been acquired by Time Warner and Viacom, respectively.

The leading US film studios are also the leading film studios on a global scale. They produce much of the world's feature films and many of its recorded television programs. Through mergers and acquisitions, these film studios have developed into giant entertainment companies. They account for three-quarters of the film industry's revenues. These film producers also control the distribution market. In 2006, the distribution market share of North America in percent is: Sony/Columbia 18.6, Buena Vista 16.2, Fox 15.2, Warner Bros 11.6, Paramount 10.3, Universal 8.9, Lions Gate 3.6, New Line 2.7, Weinstein Company 2.5 and Others 10.5. Leading US exhibitors are Regal, AMC, Loews and Cinemark, and Digital Cinema Implementation Partners (DCIP).

The result of these mergers and acquisitions are conglomerates that produce content (i.e. film media) and distribute it through as many channels as possible. These corporations produce the films, distribute the films to cinemas as well as by way of DVDs and television, and they also own the TV channels and many cinemas and other outlets. With the increasing popularity of worldwide available cable television, digital video recorders, computer graphics and editing software, and the Internet, however, many small and medium-sized independent filmmaking companies have sprung up to fill the growing demand. Furthermore, the proliferation of digital technologies and the Internet have allowed the production and distribution of many films made for limited and specialized audiences. Small and medium sized companies have been increasingly in demand, too, because of the increase in the outsourcing of activities from the large film corporations, covering pre-production, production and post-production of films. Still, they retain only a minor share of the film market.

The film production in Canada and Latin America is mainly sold to and seen by local audiences, although not insignificant in major Latin American countries such as Mexico and Brazil, as well as in Canada.[53]

The Motion Picture Industry in Los Angeles

About 30 percent of the US motion picture industry is employed in the Los Angeles area.[54] The number of jobs is probably about 100,000. The production activities concern two out of three jobs, while the rest is employed in pre-production, post-production, distribution and exhibition. The seven majors of Hollywood are also the worldwide leading film companies: Walt Disney, Sony Pictures, MGM, Paramount, 20th Century Fox, Universal Studios, and Warner Bros. There are a vast number of

53   *www.wikipedia.org*: 'Cinema of Canada', 'South American Cinema'.
54   Camors, Carine. *The Motion Picture Industry in Los Angeles, May 12, 2005*: *www.iaurif.org*.

subcontractors in the Los Angeles area. Among the 459 movies released in 2003 in the USA, 194 were produced by the majors, covering 75 percent of the box office income whereas 265 were produced by numerous independents, covering 25 percent of the box office income.

Since the beginning of the 1990s, there has been a capital-intensive concentration of major groups. The major groups follow a strategy of vertical integration, tending to consolidate with broadcasters (TV channels, movie theatre owners, Internet providers, etc.). The process makes it possible to integrate the whole sector from design to broadcasting. Current mergers takes place between the producers of 'contents' (films, music, information) and the distributors of 'container' (broadcasting, cables, Internet network, TV, telecoms).

Three indicators make it possible to evaluate the income generated by the film industry: the box office revenues increased 60 percent over the last 10 years; the turnover generated by the film industry in Los Angeles reached $34 billion, 44 percent of the American turnover; the production costs reached $31 billion, 10 times more than in New York. Accordingly, the total US film industry revenues in 2003 amounted to $78 billion. Including its wider impacts, the Hollywood film industry generates probably twice or three times that amount, including hotels, catering, trade, car rental, business services, etc. However, the Hollywood film industry faces the consequences of piracy, too, that involves a loss of revenue (downloading via Kazaa, Emule, etc.). Nevertheless, the film industry of Los Angeles looks towards a prosperous future with projected growth in all markets.[55]

Western Europe

Every West European country has a movie industry of its own.[56] The largest film industries are found in the large countries, the UK, Germany, France, Italy and Spain, but smaller countries such as Sweden and Denmark have also developed well-known films. UK produces the most exported films, helped by the language of course, and including a range of popular TV series. German films are more rarely exported. Previously, French films were seen all over Europe, but today French movies are marginalized internationally. That goes for Italian and Spanish films, too, except for some Spanish films in Latin America.

---

55   Jehoshua Eliasberg, et al. 'The Motion Picture Industry. Critical Issues in Practice, Current Research, and New Research Directions'. *Marketing Science*, Vol. 25, No. 6, Nov.-Dec. 2006, pp. 638-661.
56   Lange (2001). *The Ups and Downs of European Cinema: www.obs.coe.int. www.wikipedia.org: Cinema of Europe.*

Leading European film companies are: UGC Cinemas (cinema chain in UK), Pathe Group, Time Warner Entertainment, United International Pictures and Walt Disney International. The American films and film producers provide most European movies shown in cinemas and on television.

Asia Pacific

Leading Japanese film companies are Toei Co., Toho Co., Nikkatsu Corporation, and Shochiku Co.[57] Japanese films have a long history throughout the 20th century, following the main lines of American and international motion pictures, marked by its national culture. In the 1950s, Japanese movies became known worldwide through Kurosawa's 'Seven Samurais' that is regarded as one of the greatest films ever made. Since then, several Japanese have won international rewards and, to a certain degree, also a market in the West. The Japanese movies are primarily seen in Japan and the rest of Asia. The Japanese film viewers are the largest spenders in the world.

In numbers launched, the Indian film industry is the largest in the world.[58] Movie tickets in India are very cheap, which allows a large public to regularly visit a cinema. Indian movies are popular in various parts of the world that count significant Indian communities. Compared to, for example, the US film industry, the revenues of the Indian film industry is small, about $3 billion annually. Centred in Bombay, the Indian film industry is often called 'Bollywood' (a melding of Hollywood and Bombay).

Since the start of reforms in the 1980s, China has become a rapidly growing film producer with international recognition.[59] Internationally known movies are 'Farewell my Concubine' and 'Raise the Red Lantern'. Many films are joint ventures and projects with international investment. Political censorship has caused several film producers to migrate to the US. Recent filmmakers often deal with the less romantic side of current China under capitalism.

Africa

Since the 1990s, the Nigerian film industry has risen to a significant size and employs thousands of people.[60] A couple of hundred home videos are produced every month and distributed mainly to the African world. Many movies of this so-called 'Nollywood' (a

---

57   *www.wikipedia.org*: 'Cinema of Japan'.
58   *www.wikipedia.org*: 'Cinema of India'.
59   *www.wikipedia.org*: 'Cinema of China'.
60   *www.wikipedia.org*: 'Cinema of Nigeria'.

melding of Hollywood and Nigeria) deal with the moral dilemmas and social problems facing modern Africans.

Music

On the demand side, the recorded music market consists of consumer spending on music through three different channels and two different formats, physical and online.[61] One is consumer spending on album and single sound recordings and music videos distributed in traditional formats and sold in record stores, including compact discs and cassette tapes. Two is licensed digital distribution services that provide electronic files for use on computers, iPod devices, and MP3 players. Three is mobile music, distributed to mobile phones through wireless carriers, including ring tones, ring backs, ring tunes or music video clips. On the supply side, the world music market consists of record companies, labels and publishers that distribute recorded music products internationally and that often control the rights to those products.[62] Some of these labels are independent companies, while others are subsidiaries of large corporations or media groups. The world music market is currently dominated by the 'big four' record groups, Sony BMG, EMI, Universal and Warner. Each of these corporations consists of many smaller companies and labels serving under different regions and markets.

The current forms of music recording and distribution are of rather recent date. During most of the 20th century, the gramophone record was the primary sound recording medium, mainly in the form of LP records.[63] The advent of the tape recorder in the 1950s called for a new and adequate recording format, namely the compact cassette.[64] Between the 1960s and early 1980s, the cassette was the second most common format of music recording. Both gramophone and cassette were analogue forms of recording. In the early 1980s, Sony and Philips launched the compact disc, an optical disc used to store digital data.[65] The CD spread gradually through the 1980s as an audio format alongside the LP and the cassette. During the 1990s, the CD displaced the LP and the cassette to such a degree that by 2000 it had become virtually the only music recording format. At the same time, the CD was made recordable allowing people to record

---

61   PWC. Global Entertainment and Media Outlook, 220.
62   *www.wikipedia.org*: 'World music market'.
63   *www.wikipedia.org*: 'Gramophone record'.
64   *www.wikipedia.org*: 'Compact cassette'.
65   *www.wikipedia.org*: 'Compact disc'.

digital music on their own. This was part of the digital revolution that made the CD the universal medium for sound and video recording and storing and the computer and the Internet the basis of an age of online recording and playing.

As a consequence of general digitization and the breakthrough of the Internet, a new development in music recording and business started in the 1990s. The audio file compression formats of MP3 and other such methods, similar to the JPEG image compression format, was invented and became a popular digital audio encoding format on the Internet.[66] Since the late 1990s, it enabled widespread file-to-file sharing of music, which was previously impossible. The free sharing of music reduced sales of music in CD as well as online formats and the major record companies reacted to this by pursuing against Napster and other providers of free peer-to-peer file sharing of music on the Internet and eventually against individual users of file sharing. Only the top of the iceberg was hit by these law-suits and in the early 2000s, music piracy by way of the Internet flourished to such a degree that perhaps more music was downloaded illegally than sold legally. In developing countries legal music sales are next to nothing, but also developed countries have high rates of illegal music downloads. Furthermore, illegal sales of illegal CD recordings spread throughout the world, too.

The free download of file-shared music and illegal sales of CD recordings caused CD sales to decline. The music industry reacted only slowly to these radical changes of technology and market, however, and even though cooperated efforts of record companies and governments to some degree have reduced these massive copyright violations, piracy is a thriving business worldwide.[67] More efficient perhaps than law-suits at fighting piracy is the fact that the music industry is finally beginning to develop strategies and business models that are adapted to an online age. The online technology of the Internet, computers, mobile phones and new playing technologies such as Apple's iPod (replacing the popular Sony walk-man of the cassette and early CD age) are not only here to stay. They have become the foundation of music recording and distribution. And file-sharing is possible, with or without the law. In the end, the music industry will have to build new business models on the fact that free music downloads will prevail and can only be reduced to a certain degree. In fact the potential sources of music income have multiplied. One example is the synergy benefits of cooperating with mobile phone service providers that have made ring tones and tunes a profitable business.

---

66   The International Federation of Phonographic Industry (2008). *IFPI Digital Music Report 2008: www. ifpi.org*. The Recording Industry Association of America: *www.riaa.org*.

67   OECD (2005). *Working Party on the Information Economy. Digital Broadband Content: Music*. Paris: OECD.

The Global Music Market

The widespread music piracy makes it difficult to accurately estimate the global music market. According to official recordings of music sales of CDs and music videos as well as online and mobile music recordings, the world music market declined from the late 1990s until 2005 when spending began to rise and is projected to continue doing so from $37 billion in 2005 to $48 billion in 2010 (Table 37). The world market is almost equally divided between the US, Western Europe and Asia Pacific, while markets in the rest of the world are small. Mobile music and licensed digital distribution services drive spending and is steadily replacing the physical market. Digital distribution is fueled by rising broadband subscriptions, new services and content and attractive pricing. Upgrades to third generation wireless networks that support high-capacity applications of music and the migration from ring tones to higher-priced ring tunes will drive the mobile music market. On the whole, physical formats will increasingly be replaced by digital distribution.

TABLE 37

The Legitimate World Music Market in $bn, 2001-2010

	2001	2005	2010
USA	14	12	15
Canada	1	1	1
Western Europe	14	13	17
Eastern Europe	1	1	1
Middle East and Africa	0	0	0
Asia Pacific	8	9	12
Latin America	1	1	2
Total	39	37	48

Source: PWC. Global Entertainment and Media Outlook, 220-263. The IFPI market data are about ten percent lower: *www.ifpi.org.*

Rising broadband penetration is facilitating the digital distribution of music. Since the turn of the millennium, broadband subscriptions have skyrocketed in developed countries and by 2010, the majority of households in developed countries and increasing numbers in developing countries will have access to this mode of distribution. As more music is being available for digital distribution, the market is growing. The record companies are now looking to digital distribution music as sources of growth rather than as the cannibilization of their physical product. Although revenues are lower for digital distribution, there are substantial cost savings as well. Moreover, tracks can readily be released digitally which generate incremental revenues with little incremental costs. The demand for digital format album downloads is also growing as consumers are becoming accustomed to getting music digitally. The subscription market uses the flat-rate pricing model that consumers have become accustomed to in the wireless and Internet access markets. While the physical music market is in a long-term decline, by 2010 the joint digital music and mobile markets will almost reach the same size as the physical market.

The mobile music market is growing, too. While the market for mobile phones is mature in developed countries, the number of mobile phone subscribers is increasing rapidly in developing countries. With mobile music, there is also a public element to demand, because users are making a statement when the phone plays a ring tone or ring tune that others can hear, including ring backs that the caller can hear. Also there is no competition from free peer-to-peer file servers in the mobile market. Since 2005, ring tunes are becoming increasingly popular at the expense of ring tones in the mobile music market. Ring tunes face competition from iPods and other mobile devices for full-length songs, far more music and better sound quality than that of a mobile phone.

TABLE 38

The Global Physical, Digital and Mobile Music Markets in $bn, 2001-2010

	2001			2005			2010		
	Physical	Digital	Mobile	Physical	Digital	Mobile	Physical	Digital	Mobile
USA	13.7	0	0	11.2	0.7	0.4	8.5	4.9	1.4
Canada	0.9	0	0	0.7	0	0.1	0.6	0.3	0.2
Western Europe	14.0	0	0,1	10.7	0.2	1.5	8.6	3.1	4.2
Asia Pacific	8.2	0	0,2	6.6	0	2.1	5.2	1.0	5.8
Rest of World	2.1	0	0	2.5	0	0.4	2.8	0.2	1.2
Total	38.9	0	0,3	31.7	0.9	4.5	25.7	9.5	12.8

Source: PWC. Global Entertainment and Media Outlook, 220-263.

The legal physical, digital and mobile music markets are dominated by North America, Western Europe and Eastern Asia (Table 38). In Eastern Asia, mobile markets led by Japan and South Korea as well as Australia and New Zealand are the world's most developed mobile markets, followed by Western Europe. The US is somewhat behind

Global Experience Industries

in the mobile market, but is taking the lead in digital distribution with Western Europe catching up and Asia Pacific left somewhat behind. The licensed digital distribution is growing since 2005 with the advent of new services, particularly in Japan. The physical distribution of music is declining in all major regions, reflecting on the one hand the growth of digital distribution, and on the other hand lower sales because of piracy. In Asia, Japan embraces more than two-thirds of the physical music market and half the total market. Japan is the world's second largest music market after USA. In Western Europe, the UK is the largest single market covering one-third of the total, and the third largest in the world, and including Germany and France two-thirds of the total music market. Legal music markets in the rest of the world are only small markets, including Eastern Europe, Africa and the Middle East as well as Latin America. Like in Asia, piracy rates are very high in these regions. The continuous spread of broadband access and mobile phones will fuel digital and mobile music distribution in most developing countries, although prevalent piracy is not likely to disappear. The majority of music in developing countries is estimated to be of pirated origin, compared to one-fourth in developed countries.

On the content side, rock is still the king of music and the music industry, followed by pop, rhythm and blues, Rap, Hip hop and other popular genres. Together they comprise some 90 percent of all music sales, leaving only small portions to classical music and jazz.[68]

Piracy

The European Recorded Industry Association (ERIA) estimates the world trade of pirate discs to be worth $4.5 billion in 2005.[69] At the same time, almost 20 billion songs were illegally downloaded on the Internet in 2005. It is estimated, that more than one in three of all music discs purchased around the world is thought to be an illegal copy. This also illustrates the vast potential for legitimate music. Pirate CDs sales outnumbered legitimate sales in 2005 in a total of 30 markets. DVD music video piracy is also expanding, as well as illegal peer-to-peer music uploading. Well-known engines of copyright infringement are Grokster (now shut down by the US Supreme Court) and Kazaa (found infringing by the Australian Federal Court). In 2006, the Belgian and Swiss authorities had closed down Razorback, at that time the world's biggest eDonkey P2P server. One new development in file sharing technology is Bit-

---

68   IFPI (2007). *The 2007 Recording Industry in Numbers: www.ifpi.org.*
69   IFPI (2006). *Piracy Report 2005: www.ifpi.org.* Siwek, Stephen E. (2006). *The True Cost of Sound Recording Piracy to the US Economy.* Institute for Policy Innovation: *www.ipi.org,*

Torrent, which was designed to distribute large amounts of data between users without consuming costly server and bandwidth resources. Action has recently been taken by Swedish authorities against one of the largest BitTorrent services in the world – The Pirate Bay. Other tools of illegitimate music downloading are LAN based file-sharing networks at universities, digital stream ripping, and Bluetooth transfers from mobile phone to mobile phone.

The poor music sales in developing countries, and the stagnating or even declining sales in developed countries, indicate that the value of the illegitimate music market is much higher than estimated by ERIA. Probably, the illegitimate music market is at least as large as the legitimate music market, reaching a total of almost $100 billion (Table 39).

TABLE 39

The Global Legitimate and Illegitimate Music Market in $bn, 2005

	Legitimate	Piracy	Total
USA	12	4	16
Canada	1	0	1
Western Europe	13	4	17
Eastern Europe	1	3	4
Middle East and Africa	0	3	3
Asia Pacific	9	40	49
Latin America	1	5	6
Total	37	59	96

Source: PWC. Global Entertainment and Media Outlook, 220-263. RIAA (2006). *2005 Commercial Piracy Report: www.riaa.com.* IFPI (2001-2007). *The Recording Industry 2000-2006 Piracy Reports: www. ifpi.org.*

Who are the music pirates? Probably they are true music lovers, since they invest so much energy in getting access to music. Perhaps the anti-piracy measures by law enforcement just hit the core consumers of the music industry. Using the stick against illegitimate music downloads may even increase piracy tendencies, whereas positive incentives might reduce piracy. At least that is what is indicated by investigations into the field.[70]

---

70 Sihna, Rajiv K. & Mandel, Naomi (2008). 'Preventing Digital Music Piracy: The Carrot or the Stick?' *Journal of Marketing*, Vol. 72, Issue 1, 1-15.

The Global Music Industry

The music industry is a term used to describe a range of music-related businesses and organizations.[71] In a narrow sense, the music industry refers only to the businesses and organizations that record, produce, distribute, and market recorded music (e.g. music publishers, recording industry, record production companies). This corresponds to the International Standard Industrial Classification (ISIC) that includes sound recording and music publishing activities. When the term is used more broadly, it refers to a range of sub-industries that come from a number of different industrial classifications, including information and communication (which includes sound recording and music publishing activities, programming and broadcasting activities, e.g., radio stations), education (e.g., music training schools), arts, entertainment and recreation, and manufacturing and retail sales (e.g., musical instruments). In this broad sense, the term usually also encompasses not-for-profit organizations such as musician unions and writers' copyright activities and performance rights organizations.

In a more restricted sense, the music industry consists of record companies, labels and publishers that distribute recorded music products internationally and that often control the right to those products. Some music labels are independent, while others are subsidiaries of larger corporate entities or international media groups. There are four major record labels. The world music market is currently dominated by the 'Big Four' record groups: Sony BMG, EMI, Universal and Warner, each of which consists of many smaller companies and labels serving under different regions and markets. In 2005 these four big companies accounted for 82 percent of the US music market: Universal (France based) 32, Sony BMG (Japan/Germany)(Sony 14, BMG 12) 26, Warner (USA based) 15 and EMI (UK based) 10 percent. On the global market, the 'big four' covered almost three-quarters of world music recorded sales. Scores of independent minor and medium sized record labels around the world account for the remaining quarter of the world market share.

The predominant business model of the consolidated music companies is to create, produce, market and sell music hits to secure profitable businesses for the large companies. In search and selection of such hits, little room is left to niche or innovative music titles. Modern recording and communications technologies have improved opportunities for independent record companies to rise, however. For instance, instead of the often costly marketing of new music, the breakthrough of virtual communities

---

71 Bishop, Jack (2005). 'Building International Empires of Sound: Concentrations of Power and Property in the Global Music Market'. *Popular Music and Society*, 28:4, 443-471. Vlachos, Pavlos, Vrechopoulos, Adam and Pateli, Adamantia (2006). 'Drawing Emerging Business Models for the Mobile Music Industry'. *Electronic Markets*, 16:2, 154-168.

has given easy and cheap access to a multi-million audience, such as MySpace. Still, the 'big four' control the majority of the world music market.

Universal Music Group

Universal Music Group (UMG), formerly MCA Music Entertainment Group, is the largest business group and family of record labels in the recording industry, with a quarer of the world market share.[72] UMG has some of the world's biggest artists in popular music, including Elton John, Diana Ross and U2, and holds strong positions in classical music, too. UMG owns one of the largest music publishing businesses of the world, the Universal Music Publishing Group (owning more than one million music copyrights).

Universal Music used to be the music company attached to the film studio Universal Pictures. The present organization was formed when its parent company Seagram purchased PolyGram and merged it with UMG in 1998. Seagram merged with Vivendi SA in 2000 to form Vivendi Universal (now Vivendi SA). In 2006, the group became 100 percent owned by French media conglomerate Vivendi when Vivendi bought the last 20 percent from Matsushita, the group's sole owner from 1990 to 1995 and co-owner from 1995 to 2006. In 2007, UMG purchased BMG Publishing, to become Universal Music Publishing Group. Revenues in 2007 were $6 billion ($9 bn in 2001).

Warner Music Group

Warner Music Group originated in the 1920s, also as a publishing company that was founded to acquire music copyrights as a means of providing inexpensive music for films.[73] Amongst the historic compositions in which publishing rights are controlled by Warner Music Group are the works of Cole Porter, Richard Rodgers and Lorenz Hart. Its printed music operation, Warner Bros. Publications, was sold to Alfred Publishing in 2005. Warner Music's roots in what became Time Warner date back to the founding of Warner Bros. Records as a division of the Warner Bros. movie studio in 1958. After Warner Bros. became Warner Bros.-Seven Arts in 1967, it purchased Atlantic Records, now the Warner Music Group's oldest label. When its successor Kinney National Company bought Elektra Records in 1970 and then became Warner Communications in 1972, it assembled three labels into a group then known as WEA (Warner-Elektra-Atlantic), a

---

72   *www.umusic.com.* Vivendi. Annual Report 2001 and 2007: *www.vivendi.com.*
73   *www.wmg.com.* Time Warner. Annual Report 2007: *www.timewarner.com.*

name that was also used as a label outside the US In 1987, it was announced that Warner Communications were to merge with Time Inc. to form Time Warner. To reduce its debt, Time Warner sold the company in 2004 to a group of investors led by Edgar Bronfman, Jr. In 2007, Warner Music Group had revenues of $3.4 billion.

Sony BMG

Sony BMG Music Entertainment, Inc. is the result of a 50/50 joint venture between Sony Music Entertainment (part of Sony) and BMG Entertainment (part of Bertelsmann) that was completed in 2004.[74] It includes ownership and distribution of several recording labels, including Columbia, Epic, Providen, RCA, Sony, and Zomba. In 2006, it signed a content deal with the popular video sharing community YouTube. Sony BMG had revenues of $6 billion in 2007 (half Sony, half Bertelsmann). In 2008, Sony bought Bertelmann's stakes and got full control of the company.

EMI

The EMI Group is a British music company.[75] It includes the record company EMUI Music which operates several labels, and EMI Music Publishing, both based in London. Annual revenues in 2007 were $3 billion. It includes labels such as Parlophone, HMV and Columbia. EMI originated in the 1930s. In the 1960s and 1970s, EMI was the world's best-known and most successful recording company, including artists such as The Beatles, The Beach Boys, the Hollies, Cilla Black and Pink Floyd. EMI has grown by mergers since the 1980s. In 2006, an offer to buy Warner was rejected, followed by an offer in 2007 from Warner to buy EMI. Its labels include for example, Angel, Apple, Capital, Virgin, and Mute.

Alfred Publishing

Three companies dominate the global market of music publishing: Alfred Publishing, Universal Music Publishing and BMG Music Publishing. All three embrace every aspect of written music for any kind of music on a global basis. While the two latter named are part of two of the four music giants, Alfred Publishing is the only one to stand alone.[76] Compared to the recording music corporations, the publishing companies are small. Alfred Publishing is a family-owned company, which started in the 1920s in New York

---

74   *www.sony.net. www.bertelsmann.com. www.sonybmg.com.*
75   *www.emi.com.*
76   *www.alfred.com.*

and moved to Los Angeles in 1975. Overall sales were just $12 million in the 1980s. In the 1990s, Alfred expanded internationally and established branches in Australia, Asia, UK and Germany and sales doubled to $25 million. In 2005, Alfred acquired Warner Bros. Publications and increased its sales to $60 million. Alfred's publications include thousands of prints, CDs, DVDs and software covering a full range of titles and styles, including educational titles for every instrument.

The Broader Music Sector

The recorded music industry is helping to drive a much broader music sector, woth more than $130 billion globally, three times the value of the recorded music industry (Figure 30). The global industry is a catalyst of many commercial uses of music. It is the principal investor in music talent, too. Music is also a crucial part of the media and entertainment sector and worth far beyond $1 trillion. Furthermore, music is a key driver behind the increasing broadband subscriptions. Accordingly, music is important to several other industries.

FIGURE 30

The Global Broader Music Sector in $bn, 2006

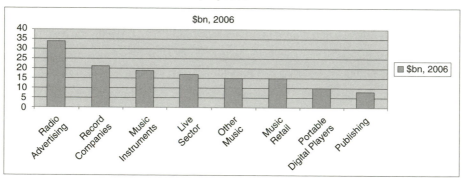

Source: IFPI. *The Broader Music Sector: www.ifpi.org.*

The largest sector underpinned by recorded music sales is the global commercial radio advertising market, worth $34 billion in 2006. Record companies provide radio stations with the content they need to attract the audience that advertisers want to reach. Although total physical and digital music sales are stagnating or even falling, revenue streams continue to grow. Live performance is a fast growing sector worth $17 billion, merchandising and sponsorships are accounting for an increasing share of revenues. Portable digital music is an expanding sector as is publishing at $10 and $8 billion, respectively.

7. Games

Toys

The Global Toys Market and Industry

Manufacturers and retailers of toys face a current generation of children and youth who are decisively different from previous generations.[1] The children of today have more money and they have great influence on the consumption habits of their parents and family as a whole. Furthermore, they grow up faster causing the children's market to shrink. Simultaneously, the current young generation is born into the age of the computer, the Internet, and the mobile phone, which they consider a natural part of their lives and they thoroughly know how to use the potentials of the new technologies. The Internet has become increasingly important to the sales of children's products, too.

Developments in computer and communications technologies put pressure on manufacturers from two sides. Partly, they change the perception of toys, partly they affect the way products become known and distributed. In addition, the knowledge content of products is growing which for several reasons causes developing costs to skyrocket. Children's preferences have become more and more unpredictable, and the life cycle of products is getting shorter and shorter. In particular, the toy industry is moving more and more towards electronic toys. As a result, toy manufacturers enter licensee agreements with providers of global hits such as Star Wars and Harry Potter, benefiting from spill-over effects from existing products and ideas and cooperating with multimedia producers. The money follows the idea. Finally, caused by the growing knowledge requirements to members of current societies, it is increasingly required that the products help develop children by including a learning element in toys. All these trends are global, i.e. all children in developed and emerging countries follow the same patterns of development and companies compete in the same global markets. This has made manufacturers and distributors consolidate into a few globally leading corporations.

To the toy industry, these new trends mean that the lines between traditional toys and electronic toys are blurring, and even towards other industries that focus on children. And in addition, these industries market an increasing number of products to this consumer group. Accordingly, as their competitive environment is changing and becoming more intense they have to widen their competences as well as interact more closely with customers to know their preferences and develop new products accordingly. While the toy industry companies is faced on the one hand with increasing

---

1   International Council of Toy Industries: *www.toy-icti.org*.

competition and demanding children that develop a grown up consumer pattern earlier than they used to do, on the other hand this trend is somewhat upset by the economic growth in emerging countries such as China, India, Eastern Europe and Russia.

TABLE 40

The Global Toy Market in $bn, 1996-2010

	1996	2001	2005	2010
North America	19	21	22	25
USA	18	20	21	23
Canada	1	1	1	2
Western Europe	13	12	17	18
UK	3	3	4	4
Germany	3	2	3	3
France	3	2	3	3
Rest of Western Europe	5	5	7	8
Eastern Europe	1	1	2	4
Asia Pacific	15	15	17	21
Japan	9	8	7	7
China	3	3	5	8
Oceania	1	1	1	1
Rest of Asia	2	3	4	5
Latin America	2	3	4	5
Middle East	1	1	1	1
Africa	0	0	1	1
Total	52	55	64	75

Source: *www.toy-icti.org*. 2010 is estimated.

Still, traditional toys and electronic games may be seen as two different markets (the electronic games market and industry is dealt with in the chapter on Video Games). Total global spending of the traditional toys market amounted to $63 billion in 2005, up from $55 billion in 2000 (Table 40). The majority of toy sales are concentrated in developed countries, mainly the US (one-third), and Japan, Germany, UK and France (also one-third). Annually, each child in developed countries spends on average almost $300 on toys. In developing countries, it is about $10 per child. The growing middle classes in emerging countries such as China will eventually spend more on toys, however. Besides, much of Western toy production has been outsourced to China and other emerging and developing countries. This has increased the importance of the Asian market.

By product category, dolls, outdoor toys, pre-school toys, games and puzzles have the largest sales, while learning and building sets make somewhat smaller sales groups.[2] Retail channels are dominated by large stores in the US, followed by toy specialists, while the toy specialists and large stores in Europe more equally divide sales. A minor share is sold by mail order or Internet.

The traditional toys market is growing little, mainly in emerging markets, whereas the electronic toys market continues to grow in developed countries. The world toy industry is dominated by a handful of companies placed in the US, Japan and Western Europe. The toy industry is marked by convergence within a wider media and entertainment sector, too. Manufacturers of traditional toys (Mattel, Hasbro, Bandai and Lego) are challenged by producers of video games coming from the electronic and computer games industry (Sony, Nintendo and Microsoft) and the content providers originating in the software industry (Electronic Arts) and media industry (Time Warner, Disney and Vivendi). The content production is also based on licensee agreements with the motion picture industry on global hits (Star Wars, Lord of the Rings, Harry Potter, James Bond, The Godfather) and is competing with the movie industry, too (Hollywood). The toys and games industry is also related to providers of learning software (Riverdeep Learning Co.). Retail is based on department stores (Mal-Wart, Target) and toy shops (Toys 'R' Us) as well as book shops and electronic consumer chains.

Mattel

For decades American Mattel has been the world's leading toy company.[3] The Barbie doll is probably its most well-known product. In 2007, Mattel had revenues of some $6 billion.

The Barbie doll made her debut in the late 1950s. The 1950s started a new era in child entertainment with the breakthrough of television and the popular Disney figures, already being introduced before the war. Since then, Mattel as well as other toy companies used television to market its products. During the 1960s, Mattel extended the doll family with, for example, Barbie's boyfriend Kenn. Since the 1960s, Mattel began to diversify into other spheres of children's leisure time, such as amusement

---

2   *www.toy-icti.org.*
3   *www.mattel.com.* Mattel (2008). *Annual Report 2007: www.mattel.com.*

parks, book publishing, play cars (Hot Wheels), and film production. Around 1980, an attempt to turn the new video games technology into a success failed and was given up. During the 1980s, action-men were the big hit (Hit Man). Mattel continued to expand in the 1990s, acquiring first of all the leading pre-school toys company Fisher Price (Winnie the Pooh and Sesame Street). Mattels merged with several toy companies in that decade, including British Games, Spear & Sons, Tyco Toys (pre-school), Pleasant Company (American Girl for 7-12 years). Furthermore, Mattel achieved licensees to the most watched American television network Nickelodeon, and in 2000 toy licensees to Harry Potter.

In 2001, Mattel made a year long agreement with the leading interactive companies Vivendi Universal Publishing and THQ to develop and publish gaming, educational and productivity software, based on strong Mattel brands such as Barbie, American Girl, Hot Wheels, and Fisher Price. Computer animated films were introduced in 2001. The early 2000s saw the beginning of more innovative ways of playing, for example 'the ello Creation System'. With ello, girls can create anything they can imagine, including fancy figures, inventory, jewelry, houses, etc. In 2003, locations in New York and Chicago were introduced, filled with everything that girls love, a magical place for girls, family and friends for playing and creating memories. At the same year, a museum for Hot Wheels cars opened in Los Angeles and a full fashion collection of Barbie couture for grown ups as well as girls was launched, too.

Mattel has continuously increased its efforts to profit from its strong brands by diversifying into all kinds of media, which reached not only children, but also their parents, and by being more end more innovative. Mattel has made several licensee agreements with globally popular movie figures, such as Warner Bros.' Batman, Superman and Harry Potter, including Disney's figures. Simultaneously, Mattel is expanding globally beyond North America and further into Europe, Latin America and Asia. From just one-third in 2000, the international market share increased to more than half in 2007, mainly in Europe but also much in Latin America. Since 2006, all the Mattel brands have been consolidated in one division, Mattel Brands Division. Most toys are produced on Mattel's own factory units in East and Southeast Asia and Mexico, using third party subcontractors for non-strategic components, too.

Mattel competes with the other international toy companies such as Hasbro, Bandai and Lego, and some smaller national companies, of which the two latter are larger than Mattel in Japan and Europe, respectively. Moving into electronics and media as a consequence of changing patterns of demand, Mattel also competes with video games producers and providers of consumer electronics. In 2007, American Wal-Mart, Target and Toys 'R' Us took care of almost half its total sales. Most of the other half is being sold through international department stores and toy shops.

Hasbro

The Hasbro company was started between the two world wars.[4] Parker Brothers, that later merged with Hasbro, launched its world famous Monopoly game in 1935. After the Second World War, Selchow and Righer, another company to merge with Hasbro later on, launched SCRABBLE that turned out to be the best selling game ever. Hasbro's first major toy success was Mr Potato Head in the 1950s, followed in the 1960s by the toy for girls Easy Bake Oven. In the 1970s, its first action figures were introduced which developed into great successes in the 1980s. The popular figure for girls 'My little Pony' was also marketed in the same decade, as was TRANSFORMERS, including play cars and planes.

In the 1990s, Hasbro expanded even more. In 1991, Tonka was acquired including its well-known products Tonka, Play-Doh, Easy Bake Oven and Monopoly and several licensees such as Star Wars and Batman. The various toy companies were consolidated into Hasbro Games in 1992. Since the mid-1990s, Hasbro expanded into the electronic games market and developed a secondary product line, merging with several companies such a Rush Berry and its successful interactive Cap Candy line. Since the late 1990s, Hasbro also took advantage of an increasing demand for role playing games, such as Dungeons & Dragons and POKEMON, as well as Magic card games.

Since the turn of the century Hasbro, like other large companies, has increasingly focused on creating value from its well-known brands in toys, card games (Monopoly and Trivial Pursuit) and role playing games (Dungeon & Drakons), as well as license agreements with leading entertainment corporations such as Disney (films and Disneyland) and Lucas (Star Wars). While Hasbro is marketing products for pre-school, early-school and tween school ages, it has been especially keen on focusing on the tween group. Hasbro is planning to expand its games segment and go into new categories, such as a toothbrush that includes a music player. Most of its sales are in the US, almost two-thirds, and just like Mattel its three largest customers are Wal-Mart, Target and Toys 'R' Us. One-third is sold outside the US. Its three large segments are US Toys, Games and International. Like Mattel, Hasbro is competing with leading international toy companies as well as makers of video games and consumer electronic products as a consequence of changing demands as 'children are getting older younger', moving away from traditional toys and games at a younger age than previously.

In 2007, Hasbro had revenues of $4 billion.

---

4   *www.hasbro.com*. Hasbro (2008). *Annual Report 2007: www.hasbro.com.*

Namco Bandai

In 2005, Namco merged with Bandai, making it the leading Japanese toys company.[5] Both companies have been producing toys and entertainment products since the Second World War. Bandai's main characters are action figures meant for boys and inspired by the Japanese history, including Gundam, Power Ranger, Masked Rider and Ultraman that have been turned into television series, too. As a result of declining demand caused by the low Japanese birth rate and changing demand patterns, Bandai is trying to develop products for older segments and create new business areas, such as life-style products. Half of Bandai's income stems from its long-time popular characters (toys, video games and other animated films), while the other half comes from licensees (Disney, Warner Bros., Cartoon Network, WiZ Entertainment Japan) and a minor share from amusement parks and game halls. In 2007, Bandai had revenues of $2.5 billion, of which 80 percent came from Japan.[6]

Namco's main products are home video software and amusement facilities. In particular, Namco is a leading developer and publisher of wireless games content, such as Pac-Man. Namco is also a distributor of video game ringtones. Games are mainly sold to be played on leading consoles such as Playstation and Nintendo. Namco had revenues in 2007 of $1.5 billion, of which three-quarters stemmed from Japan.

Namco and Bandai merged to meet the new challenges of a declining birth rate and the technological and business development of the global entertainment industry. By combining Namco's content production and amusement facilities with Bandai's characters, Namco Bandai wanted to create a global entertainment company. So far, they have just had some success outside Japan, namely in North America with Namco's mobile games.

Lego

The name "LEGO" is an abbreviation of the two Danish words 'leg godt', meaning 'play well'.[7] It is the name of the company as well as its basic idea. Play is a fundamental part of childhood and personal development. Play stimulates one's fantasy, conceptual development and creativity. That is why the Lego-corporation provides a long line of products, all based on the idea of learning and developing by way of playing. For decades, the Lego brick has been sold in more than one hundred countries and is

5   *www.namcombandaigames.com. www.bandai.com. www.namco.com. www.bandainamco.co.jp/en.*

6   *www.bandainamco.co.jp*: Bandainamco (2008). *Annual report 2007-08: www.bandainamco.co.jp.*

7   *www.lego.com.* Lego (2008). *Annual Report 2007: www.lego.com.*

found in most homes in developed countries. The Lego brick has been awarded the prize as the toy of the 20th century.

The Lego Group was founded in 1932 by Ole Kirk Christiansen. The company has passed from father to son and is now owned by a grandchild of the founder. Today, Lego is the world's fourth largest manufacturer of toys (after Mattel, Namco Bandai, Hasbro). MGA Entertainment (pre-school toys, mainly the popular fashion doll Bratz), and Leap Frog (learning products) are somewhat smaller (revenues about $0.5 billion). Its business idea is still based on the original Lego brick. Current Lego products are developed to suit all ages and stages of development, from kindergarten toddlers, schoolchildren and teenagers to young-at-heart adults. One can also build with virtual bricks on one's computer as well as use the bricks for classroom teaching. The brick is meant for constructing things.

The Lego-company and its brick products have passed through different stages throughout its fifty year long history. As early as the 1950s, Lego introduced its basic idea of learning through play, the 'Lego System of Play', and the Lego brick with its new interlocking system. During the 1960s, the Lego brick was made movable by adding wheels, engines and gear. A second age started in the late 1960s, when the Lego brick systems were being adapted to different ages, introducing the large Lego Duplo bricks to the youngest. At the same time, the Legoland Park opened in Billund. Legoland offers adventures for children and fun and enjoyment for the whole family. A third age began in the 1970s with the first Lego figures that made role play and personality a part of Lego play.

In the late 1970s, a new business model was introduced when the different products were organized around a child's needs and abilities at each stage of life, continuously aiming for optimum stimulation of his creativity and imagination. Simultaneously, a new dimension was added to the Lego system of play. Lego had already established popular figures and as the next step, Lego began to focus on stories, themes and role play, including action figures in space. During the 1980s in cooperation with American MIT, Lego started to integrate computers into its products by blending physical and virtual worlds through its Lego Technic Computer Control, which later paved the way for Lego robots. In the 1990s, Lego stepped into its fourth era, making intelligence and behavior integral features of Lego products, and robot technology an integrated part of the Lego construction system. Lego Mindstorms enabled children to create and program intelligent Lego models. Through First Lego League and in cooperation with American First organization, a worldwide tournament was held where children competed in designing robots and participating in a series of scientific and technical projects. A new version of the Mindstorms robot of 2006 enables consumers in just half an hour to build and program a robot.

In 1998, the Lego Group made a licensee agreement with Lucasfilm that gave the group the right to develop, manufacture and market a new series of Lego sets based on themes from the original Star Wars movies. In 2001, Lego launched its first complete story with Binacle. Lego combined its construction toys with action figures and movie themes to invite children to tell how they see the story and the action developing. Since then, storytelling based on licensee agreements with world film hits has been an integrated part of Lego product development, including for example Batman, Lord of the Rings and Harry Potter, just like the other toys companies. Based on movie characters and other characters, mini figures were developed to populate the stories.

Besides its products, the Legoland Parks have become a vital part of the Lego business. Today, Legoland Parks are found in Denmark, UK, Germany, California. In 2005, Legoland was sold to Merlin Entertainments, a member of the Blackstone Group. Merlin has the know-how and investment capital to expand Legoland world-wide in combination with its other entertainment facilities. Lego is still a large shareholder in Legoland, however.

In order to have contact to its fans and consumers around the world, Lego has created a virtual Lego universe on its official website. Lego.com is a place where children, parents and Lego fans of all ages can play, exchange information and learn about Lego values and ideas through games, stories, activities and experiences. The website has become very popular and tops the list of family and children's sites on the Internet. Other Lego communities include the Lego Club for children in the 6 to 12 age group, with a couple of million members. Members can show each other pictures of their favorite building work and draw inspiration for future play. A new Lego BrickMaster club aims especially at children aged seven years and upwards that are the most enthusiastic members. Finally, the LegoFactory group gives the children the opportunity to build virtual models on the computer, and then have the bricks sent by post. If children look for inspiration and advice, they can be inspired by the designers and designs of adult fans on this site. A growing number of adults have set up communities, too, in which they share their Lego hobby. Based on research in the field of play and learning and technological developments in collaboration with MIT, Lego Education has developed ideas on how to use the bricks and technologies to learn the concepts of science through practical exercises. The robotic tournament is part of Lego Education.

The Lego products have always targeted boys, but through CLITKITS in 2003 a new building system was launched that enabled girls to create their own interior and personal design. This is obviously inspired by Mattel's similar initiatives.

Since 2004, Lego has been enforcing a new seven year long strategy to regain its profitability and momentum. The aim of the strategy is to 'rebuild the company and revitalize the Lego brand as a synonym for creative building fun and role play.' As part of this strategy, the whole supply chain has been reorganized to increase productivity and cut down costs, including outsourcing of the bulk of its production sites to low-cost countries in Eastern Europe and Mexico, close to its two main markets Europe and the US. Faced with increasing pressures from consumers, customers and competitors, just like all other toy manufacturers, Lego is determined to bind consumers, fans and retailers even closer to the organization. Lego continues to supply excellent play products to children and new products and product lines have been centered on the classical product idea, the Lego brick. Also the development and production time from concept to final product on the retailer's shelf has been dramatically reduced.

Lego is facing the same challenges as other manufacturers of traditional toys. Competition on prices is intensive in retail outlets. Huge department stores develop their private labels, often cheaply produced in China. Continuously, consumers prefer electronic products to traditional toys and at an early age, children loose interest in toys and turn to new technologies such as mobile phones. Furthermore, changing fashions result in ever shorter lifecycles of existing products. To meet these challenges, Lego has implemented its new strategy to cut down on costs and time-to-market. In addition, Lego is focusing much more on its core customers, instead of the larger mass markets, such as for example Sony, by mobilizing its users, brands and visions.

As a consequence of its reorganization and sales of Legoland, Lego's revenues declined from almost $2 billion in 2000 to $1.2 billion in 2005 and $1.5 billion in 2007, while turning a deficit into a surplus.[8] Lego's products are sold through department stores and toys shops, similar to the other large toy companies.

Toys 'R' Us

Toys 'R' Us is one of the leading retailers of toys with more than 1,500 stores world-wide.[9] Almost half of the stores are in the US and some half in the rest of the world. The company sells virtually all kinds of toys to children of all ages. Since its start in 1948 in Washington D.C., Toys 'R' Us has been a retailer based on an increasing number of supermarket stores. In the 1980s, the company diversified into clothing and started its first international stores. Currently, Toys 'R' Us has stores in the US, Japan, Australia, Canada, UK, France and Portugal.

In the 1990s, Toys 'R' Us diversified into being a baby's products retailer and

---

8   *www.lego.com*: Lego (2002 and 2008). *Annual Report 2001 and 2007.*
9   *www.toysrus.com.*

specialty store chain, having now opened 250 stores in the US. In 2001, it opened its international flagship store in New York City that quickly established itself as 'The Center of the Toy Universe'. The changing definition of traditional toys since the late 1990s has made Toys launch innovative products appealing to today's tech-generation of kids, from digital cameras and iPod accessories to musical instruments. In 2005, Toys 'R' Us was taken over by an investor group to secure capital for future developments. Revenues in 2007 were $13 billion ($11 billion in 2001).[10]

Kompan

Danish Kompan is probably the world's leading specialist in play equipment solutions for outdoor playgrounds.[11] Kompan was started in 1970 and the name 'Kompan' is derived from a Danish word meaning 'companion'. Throughout the 1970s and 1980s, Kompan expanded internationally in Western Europe and the US by merger and organic growth. Kirkbi Invest of the Lego-corporation became the majority shareholder. Kompan continued to grow internationally in Europe, America and Asia throughout the 1990s and the 2000s. Lack of capital for a truly international breakthrough made Kompan accept an offer to purchase from Nordic Capital in 2005. In 2006, Kompan moved its production and distribution facilities to a new production facility in the Czech Republic, while headquarters remained in Denmark. A process started to consolidate the global playground industry.

Kompan's first product line, Kompan Moments, provided pre-school children with play facilities for climbing, rocking, sliding, swinging, hiding and other universal play themes, including trains, ships and castles that inspire the children's imagination and role-modeling play as well as stimulating their senses and concepts. Even today, Kompan's products for toddlers are built on the concepts of the original Moments line, mainly built in materials of wood. Moments have also been developed to fit school children, applying steel, plastic and rubber materials, too. Through the acquired French Sporadix, Kompan gained access to an open sport and playing ground for tweens and teenagers that works as a place for physical and social activities. Increasingly, Kompan's own products have been extended with third-party products, such as climbing nets, security tiles, benches, beds and skate ramps. Sales of spare parts and services to its many playgrounds around the world make up an increasing share of total sales.

A vital part of the Kompan-corporation is Kompan Play Institute. This is a know-

---

10   *www.toysrus.com.*
11   *www.kompan.com.*

ledge center researching children's play and development as a basis of developing the company's products. Its knowledge is made available to customers, too.

Over the past recent years, Kompan has undergone a transformation from a traditional woodworking company to a modern industrial group using a wide range of materials. Its supply chain has been optimized and customer oriented, including outsourcing of facilities to a low-cost country. Product developments and business opportunities have been maximized and speeded up to meet the challenges of a future global market. Its customers are mainly public authorities.[12] Kompan is looking to strengthen its position in a number of segments and continue to consolidate the somewhat fragmented play equipment industry. In geographic terms, 80 percent of revenues stem from Europe, 12 percent from the United States and 8 percent from Asia. In 2007, Kompan had revenues of $0.2 billion.

Video Games

'A video game is a game that involves the interaction with a user interface to generate visual feedback on a video device'.[13] The 'video' in a video game, however, traditionally refers to a raster display device with the popular use of the term 'video game'. It now implies any type of display device. The electronic systems used to play video games are known as platforms, including video game consoles, video game handheld PDAs and cell phones, and PCs. The main separations between platforms are their design, technical capabilities, and available video games. The user interface to manipulate a video is generally called a game controller, which varies across platforms. For instance a dedicated console controller might consist of buttons and a joystick, such as Playstation. The original dedicated device, the so-called 'Arcade game', was only designed to play one game, for instance the previously popular Pac Man. Computer games allow the player to use a keyboard and a mouse simultaneously. Currently, the interactive dimension is developing rapidly, as is the case with convergence between the many dedicated and non-dedicated devices for playing games. While CDs used to be the dominant format of the 1990s and DVDs in the early 2000s, online distribution is rapidly expanding to become probably the dominant distribution form of the 2010s. For instance the world's most sold video game 'World of Warcraft' may be reached and played over the Internet.

---

12   Kompan (2008). *Annual Report 2007: www.kompan.com*.
13   Schement. Encyclopedia of Communication and Information: 'Video and Computer Games'. *www.wikipedia.org*: 'Video game'.

Video games were first introduced as a commercial entertainment medium in the 1970s, becoming the basis of an expanding entertainment industry since the 1980s in the United States, Japan and Western Europe. Today two decades later, the video game industry is a profitable multi-billion dollar business. The devices to play video games have developed from the simple dedicated devices of the 1980s to the advanced and interactive online consoles, portables, and PCs of the 2000s, based on a few leading companies, such as Sony, Nintendo and Microsoft, and including several large content providers (for example Electronic Arts and the three console producers) and numerous minor game developers. Previously, the video game industry was most widely spread in Japan, with a higher market share of total entertainment than in the USA and Western Europe. Currently, however, the video game industry is becoming a true global industry and converging in devices, content and business.

The breakthrough of the Internet, the broadband expansion, and the rapid spread of mobile phones since the turn of the millennium have paved the way for new kinds of video game applications and business models. While the so-called 'console games' continue to dominate the video game industry, two other video game segments are expanding quickly to reach considerable revenue sizes: 'casual games' and 'serious games'.

Unlike console games, which are large and require millions of dollars to develop, as well as skills and dedicated consoles to play, casual games are small low-cost productions that are easily played on any computer.[14] Casual game players also vary from the predominantly young male console player, as the typical casual gamer is older and female. The casual game market springs from the widely used Microsoft's Solitaire that came free with Windows and Nintendo Game Boy's free Tetris. Casual games are often computer simulations of common games that used to be sold by traditional toy companies. Puzzles, word, card and board games are the most popular casual genres, but increasingly popular also are crime stories and games, for example, in kitchens and supermarkets. The Internet is the primary distribution channel for casual games, often for free or a very small fee, including iPod games made available via the iTunes store. Mobile casual games are gaining wide popularity, too. Casual games are distributed via gaming portals, such as Big Fish Games and PlayFirst, but also available at major retailers, including Wal-Mart and Carrefour. Around the world, more than 200 million people play casual games each month over the Internet. The casual game industry is worth $2-3 billion in 2007 and the market is growing 20 percent a year. As a consequence of its growth and widespread attraction, the leading console and

---

14   *www.casualgamesassociation.org*. 'Casual Game'. *www.wikipedia.org*: 'Casual game'.

game providers of Sony, Nintendo, Microsoft, Electronic Arts a.o. have included casual games in their portfolio.

While console games and casual games are meant for entertainment, the primary aim of serious games is for non-entertainment purposes.[15] There is no single definition of serious games, but it is generally held to include all kinds of non-entertainment applications, such as games for training, learning, advertising, and simulation. Long before the term 'serious games' came into use with the 'Serious Game Initiative' in 2002, games were being developed for non-entertainment purposes. Airlines and military units started to use simulation games in the 1980s. Computer games were developed for education, as well as economic, business and policy purposes, too. It took until the late 1990s, however, before technology was adequately developed to allow the use of games in wide areas of society. Since the beginning of the 21th century, computer games have been increasingly applied in military operations, medical education, emergency training, airline, ship and train simulations, machinery instructions, building, matters of business and policy planning and organization, school education, advertising, edutainment, etc. In fact, all social activities may be dealt with by serious games and the serious games industry is projected to continue its growth in the years to come. Leading companies in, for instance, military, business and airline simulations are partnering closely with related industries and customers, such as 3D Learning Solutions (military training/Lockheed), knowledge Dynamics (business simulations/ Microsoft), Forterra (virtual collaboration/IBM). The global serious games market was estimated at $10 bn in 2007, i.e. one-third the size of the console games market and four times the size of the casual games market.[16]

In this context, the focus will be on console games and to some degree on casual games. Serious games will not be dealt with further here, as they make-up a field of their own moving into practically all non-experience industries. The console games industry continues to dominate and drive the video game industry, and as the casual games industry continues to expand and mature, consolers and their developers and distributors are increasingly targeting this industry, too.

Video console games are generally categorized into genres. Due to a general lack of commonly agreed-upon genres or criteria for the definition of genres, similar to for example literature's divide into poetry, drama and prose and their many subdivisions, classification of games is not always consistent even to the end of arbitration. One commonly used list contains for example: action (Hit Man), adventure (Legend

---

15   *www.wikipedia.org*: 'Serious game'. Serious Games Initiative: *www.seriousgamesinitiative.org*.
16   Future-Making Serious Games: *http://elianealhadeff.blogspot.com*.

of Zelda), fighting (Street Fighter), role-playing (Final Fantasy), multiplayer online games (World of Warcraft), simulation games (mainly for professional applications, such as flight, military, and economics, such as Flight Simulator, Sim City), educational (Carmen Sandiego), sports (NBA Jam), racing (Gran Turismo), and strategy (Age of Empires). Video games are made by developers, who used to do this as individuals or in small teams. But since the 1990s, development commonly requires a large team of designers, programmers, artists, composers, musicians, producers and directors.

The leading organization within the computer and video game industry is the American Entertainment Software Association (ESA) (previously the Interactive Digital Software Association, IDSA), most of the publishers in the gaming world (or their American subsidiaries) are members of ESA: Activision, Atari, Capcom, Crave Entertainment, Disney Interactive Studios, Eidos Interactive, Electronic Arts, Her Interactive, id Software, Konami, LucasArts, Microsoft Corporation, Midway Games, Namco Bandai, Nintendo, NovaLogic, SEGA, Sony Computer Entertainment, Square Enix, Take Two Interactive, THQ, Ubisoft, Vivendi Games, Warner Bros. Interactive, and Wild Tangent. Important also is the International Game Developers Association.[17]

Within the last decade, the revenues of video games have become almost as large as those of films.[18] The video game upstart is not just a competitor to movies, it is also a cooperator. Once, video games and movies were two separate media. Within recent years, however, these two media have melted and today you rarely see a Hollywood movie or TV series that is not launched with a matching video game. Movies as well as TV series melt with the new game universe. Often it is even difficult to see the difference between film, game and reality. Furthermore, computer animation has become a widespread tool, for instance, simulate parts of war scenes that otherwise would have been extremely expensive to stage (for instance, Gladiator).

Although many video games are based on stories of their own (such as Hit Man and World of Warcraft), there is a strong symbiosis between movies and video games. Earlier on, the video game was just one product in a line of numerous merchandise in the wake of a new film, and the content merely replicated the manuscript of the movie. But today, the video games are much more than replicates. Current games provide a content of their own, telling the story in a different way. For example, that was the case in Star Wars, which developed some of the loose ends of the story into new layers and characters. The melting of the two media was even more complete in the making of 'The Matrix' as a film and a video game. In the case of The Matrix, the production was

---

17   International Game Developers Association: *www.igda.org*.
18   *www.wikipeadia.org*: 'Video game industry'.

based on both film and game from the very start and the actors did not know whether the individual scene was made for the game or the movie. As a consequence, the game contained much more than the movie. In order to keep the attention of the audience, a film manuscript does not allow digressions. In a video game, on the contrary, parallel actions and extra dimensions might be added to the story. The 2005 version of King Kong is another example of the simultaneous direction of film and video game.

Movie hits turned into video games include films for the young as well as the grown up audience, for example 'King Kong, The Lord of Rings, Star Wars, Harry Potter, Godfather, James Bond, and The Da Vinci Code'. Popular TV series are being turned into video games, too, such as 'Desperate Housewives', 'The Sopranos' and 'The Simpsons'. Video games have also been turned into movies, such as 'Tomb Raider' and 'Halo', two of the world's most popular games.

Apart from movies, sports are another large content provider. For instance Electronic Arts have dedicated a division to develop and distribute sports games including all US leagues (NFL, NBA, etc.), FIFA 2006 World Cup and UEFA Euro 2008, NASCAR, Golf tours, Tennis tours, etc.[19]

The Global Video Game market

Worldwide, the video game is very popular and perhaps the most popular of all games. For example, half the Americans are playing video games.[20] The video game market reflects consumer spending on console games (including handheld games), PC games, online games, and wireless games.[21] The category excludes spending on hardware and accessories used to play the games. These will be dealt with when describing the companies of the video game industry. It must be noted, however, that numbers only include the legitimate market. Just as in movies and music, the legitimate video game industry is also hit by piracy, but perhaps not as much as the music and films industries.

---

19   *www.easports.com.*
20   *www.igda.org.*
21   PWC. Global Entertainment and Media Outlook, 368

TABLE 41

The Global Video Games Market in $bn, 2001-2010

	2001	2005	2010
North America	6	9	14
USA	6	8	13
Canada	0	1	1
Western Europe	5	8	14
UK	2	2	4
Germany	1	2	3
France	1	1	2
Rest of Western Europe	2	2	4
Asia Pacific	8	10	17
Japan	4	4	5
South Korea	2	2	5
China	0	1	2
Rest of Asia Pacific	2	3	5
ROW	1	1	1
Total	21	27	46

Source: PWC. Global Entertainment and Media Outlook, 371, 379, 386, 392, 395.

During the 2000s, the global video games market has grown at some ten percent com-pound annual rate from $21 billion in 2001 to $27 billion in 2005, with a projected $46 billion in 2010 (Table 41). Asia Pacific is the largest market, growing from $8 bil-lion in 2001 to $10 billion in 2005 and $17 billion in 2010. While the US market has increased from $6 billion in 2001 to $8 billion in 2005 and a projected $13 billion in 2010, the West European market has increased from $5 to $8 billion, with a projected $14 billion, respectively.

TABLE 42

The Global Video Game Market in Segments in $bn, 2001-2010

	2001	2005	2010
Console/Handheld Games	15	17	24
PC Games	6	4	4
Online Games	0	3	9
Wireless Games	0	3	10
Total	21	27	47

Source: PWC. Global Entertainment and Media Outlook, 371, 378, 385, 392, 395.

The growth of the console/handheld market the largest segment of the industry is dependent on the cycle of the new game consoles (Table 42). The introduction of Microsoft's Xbox 360 in 2005 and Sony's Playstation 3 and Nintendo's Wii in late 2006 and early 2007 will stimulate the market in the next few years. They are fueling demand for the online market, too, as the new consoles are able to play games with other people. The online market will also be spurred by the growth of broadband connections worldwide, which provides for a more enriching video game experience. As consumers replace their current wireless handsets with new ones capable of down-loading games, the wireless game industry will experience significant growth. The movement toward 3G facilitates the development of more-advanced games and will also spur demand. The market for PC games will continue to deteriorate as consumers turn their attention to newer technologies.

USA

The overall US video game market is growing fast from some $6 billion in 2001 to some $8 billion in 2005 and a projected $13 billion in 2010 (Table 43). Console/handheld games continue to dominate the market, growing from $5 to $6 and $8 billion in 2001, 2005 and 2010, respectively. Online games and even more wireless games are the fastest growing group, increasing from almost nil in 2001 to $2 billion each in 2010. The PC game market continues to decline. Sales in consoles follow the cycle of console generations, the second generation being launched in 2000 and the third in 2005-2007. Hit games and movies are the most popular content played on the three consoles.

TABLE 43

The US Video Game Market in Segments in $bn, 2001-2010

	2001	2005	2010
Console/Handheld Games	5	6	8
PC Games	2	1	1
Online Games	0	1	2
Wireless Games	0	1	2
Total	6	8	13

Source: PWC. Global Entertainment and Media Outlook, 371.

With the growth of the video game industry, advertisers are turning to games as a means of reaching the male 18 to 34 demographic group, which is the core user of video games. The business model of product placement has evolved with the growing popularity of the video game industry. Originally, game developers would pay advertisers for the opportunity of having products placed in their games in order to give them a more realistic feeling. The next stage was the inclusion of products at no charge, as both sides agreed that it was an opportunity for cross promotion. The current model has advertisers paying for the privilege of being included in games.

With the advent of online games, a dynamic advertising model was developed, which allows ads to be changed at will and enables advertising to be geared to specific demographic or geographic targets. Massive Inc. is one of the companies that pioneered this method of advertising. Its Video Game Advertising Network enables advertisers to place their ads by using the Internet, and it can update the ads every time the player goes online. The system can also monitor the number of times that the ads are seen. The use of in-game advertising is growing significantly with the introduction of the new generation of console games and provides an incremental revenue stream for video game developers.

The online game platform enables players to download games and game content and to compete against each other via the Internet. The PC platform was traditionally the only means of playing games online but is gradually being surpassed by the new consoles. There are a number of free online sites on Google, Yahoo, MSN and Electronic Arts' sites, with most of their revenues coming from advertising. These sites reach millions of game players.

Massive multiplayer online games are played by thousands of people worldwide simultaneously, with games continuing for weeks or months. The games, usually played by younger males, involve role playing in fantasy worlds. Players usually pay for the initial copy of the game and then pay a monthly subscription fee to play online. The online market is driven by significant growth in the number of broadband subscribers. Revenues are achieved through subscription fees and digital distribution of content. The number of US online video game subscribers is increasing rapidly from 1 million in 2001 to 6 million in 2005 and a projected 16 million in 2010, while the online video game penetration of broadband households is doubling to reach some twenty percent in 2010. Simultaneously, the online video game market increased from a very low level in 2001 to $2 billion in 2010.

With the maturing of the wireless industry, carriers are looking for other sources of revenue beyond voice. The downloading of digital content including music and video games is proving to be a significant revenue source for carriers. Almost all new mobile phones are Internet enabled, thereby enhancing the potential for downloading games. As individuals upgrade their existing handsets for newer models, the number of game-capable handsets will increase dramatically. Playing games on cell phones has become a mass market phenomenon, with consumers spending more in 2005 downloading video games than on downloading ring tones. The demographics of wireless gamers are different from those of console players. Wireless players are generally more casual players and include a higher percentage of women and older adults. Players can pay monthly charges to play a game or can pay a higher, onetime fee to download the game permanently. The number of wireless game subscribers increased dramatically from 1 million in 2001 to 16 million in 2005 and a projected 76 million in 2010, spending $0.1 bn in 2001, 1 $bn in 2005 and a projected $2 bn in 2010.

In Canada, the video game market follows the same lines of development as in the US. Console/handheld games continue to be the largest video game segment in Canada. Canada has one of the highest broadband penetration rates in the world, spurring growth in the online game segment. The wireless market will show growth as people exchange their phones for more advanced ones that are capable of downloading games. The video game market has grown from $0.4 billion in 2001 to $0.7 billion in 2005, and a projected $1.3 billion in 2010 (console/handheld $0.5, PC $0.1, Online $0.4, Wireless $0.3 billion).

In Latin America, piracy of video games is widespread, limiting the growth of the legitimate industry. As a result of lack of competition from the newer online and wireless technologies, PC games are relatively more important in Latin America and are not showing declines evident elsewhere in the world. The overall legitimate video game market was just half a billion dollars in 2005 and is projected to be less than $1 billion in 2010. As a consequence of piracy, the real value of the video game market in Latin America is several times higher. In North America, piracy is also a reality within the video game market, adding probably a quarter to the total legitimate numbers.

Western Europe

The overall West European video game market increased from $5 billion in 2001 to $8 billion in 2005, with a projected $14 billion in 2010 (Table 44). Like in the USA, console/handheld games continue to be the largest segment of the video game market, having increased from $4 billion in 2001 to $5 billion in 2005 and a projected $7 billion in 2010. Console/handheld games will expand less, however, than online and wireless games, which rose from almost nothing in 2001 to a projected $3 billion each in 2010. From $1.7 billion in 2001, the PC games market remains flat at $1.5 billion from 2005 to 2010.

TABLE 44

The West European Video Game Market in Segments in $bn, 2001-2010

	2001	2005	2010
Console/Handheld Games	4	5	7
PC Games	2	1	1
Online Games	0	1	3
Wireless Games	0	1	3
Total	5	8	14

Source: PWC. Global Entertainment and Media Outlook, 378.

The UK has the third largest video game market in the world, following the markets of the US and Japan. UK has a significant game development industry, with more than 150 game studios. These studios develop approximately 15 percent of the world's games. British companies are beginning to cooperate with Asian countries in the development of games appealing to Asian tastes. The British game market is expected to maintain its dominance in Western Europe, rising to $2.4 billion in 2005 and $4.5 billion in 2010. Germany is the second largest European market. The PC game market in Germany which used to be stronger than the console game market has declined in recent years, falling behind the console market. Simultaneously, the expanding universe of broadband subscribers in Germany spurs the growth of the online market. Germany will maintain its position as the second strongest European game market, growing to $2 billion in 2005 and $3 billion in 2010. France is the third largest European game market, though significantly behind UK. France, however, has the largest online video game market in Western Europe. Spain and Italy are in fourth and fifth place, respectively. Italy has a number of small companies developing games. Italian game companies are often subsidiaries of large foreign companies. The games developed locally are often soccer related. The Netherlands' video game market in sixth place continues to be dominated by PC games, but online and wireless games are growing, as is the console game market, spurred by the new generation of consoles. The Irish video game market in seventh place is growing and has produced several successful game companies. At a smaller level, this is also true in Denmark, for example.

Just as in the USA, the online and wireless game markets are growing rapidly in Western Europe, driven by the spread of broadband subscribers and new cell phones. The number of online video game subscribers has been increasing from virtually nil in 2001 to 4 million in 2005 and a protected 16 million in 2010 (including a smaller share of subscribers in Eastern Europe, Middle East and Africa). Simultaneously, the number of wireless game subscribers has skyrocketed from almost nothing in 2001 to 16 millions in 2005 and a projected 76 millions in 2010 (including a smaller share of subscribers in Eastern Europe, Middle East and Africa).

The official video game market in Eastern Europe, Africa and the Middle East is almost negligible. Piracy is widespread and the real value of the video game markets in these regions is a multiple of the official numbers. In Western Europe, piracy is less but not insignificant, adding probably a quarter to the legitimate numbers.

Asia Pacific

After a slow start in the early 2000s, the Asian Pacific video game market is increasing fast from $10 billion in 2005 to a projected $17 billion in 2010 (Table 45). Console/handheld games continue to be the most important segment of the market, growing from some $5 billion in 2005 to almost $8 billion in 2010. The online and wireless game markets are increasing much faster to reach $4 billion each in 2010. PC games will continue to decline from some $2 billion in 2001 to some $1 billion in 2005 and 2010.

TABLE 45

The Asian Pacific Video Game Market in Segments in $bn, 2001-2010

	2001	2005	2010
Console/Handheld Games	6	5	8
PC Games	2	1	1
Online Games	0	2	4
Wireless Games	0	2	4
Total	8	10	17

Source: PWC. Global Entertainment and Media Outlook, 385.

Japan is the second largest video game market in the world, after the USA. It is the home of two out of three major console manufactures, Sony and Nintendo, making the console/hand-held game segment relatively more important than in other countries in the region. The new generation of consoles will make the Japanese game market expand in the next few years. South Korea has the highest percentage of broadband subscribers in the region, and, in the world, too. It is therefore no surprise that the online segment of the market is very important in South Korea. In the period from 2005 to 2010, the South Korean game-industry has been projected to increase strongly from $2 to $5 billion.

In China, online gaming is the dominant segment of the market, outpacing console, PC, and hand-held gaming combined. The reason for this is the rampant piracy in the country. PC games are duplicated and sold on the streets, leaving little incentive for console manufactures to enter the market. Online games in China are stored on servers, thereby eliminating the threat of piracy. Gamers pay to play on an hourly or monthly basis. As in the case of South Korea, most Chinese gamers play in one of the thousands of Internet cafés. Massive multiplayer online role-player games constitute the dominant form of the online games in China, though casual games are expected to become more important as the number of game players increases. Local content has the most appeal, with South Korea being the only country to successfully export games to China, such as Legend Mir II, developed by Wemade Entertainment of South Korea. World of Legend, developed by Shanda Entertainment, is the most popular domestic game.

Asia Pacific has a high concentration of broadband subscribers, making it the prime territory for online games. South Korea represents the strongest market for online gaming in the world in terms of penetration. Taiwan is also a major online gaming market. By contrast Japan has lagged behind these other countries in the online area, with most Japanese preferring console and hand-held games. Multiplayer games are the most popular online games, but there is a substantial audience for simpler games played by the more casual player, downloaded for free from Google, Yahoo and MSN browsers. The online market is expected to be driven by the increase in the number of broadband connections as well as the emergence of cheaper PCs and the increased downloading of additional game content.

The number of online video game subscribers in Asia Pacific increased from 2 million in 2001 to 15 million in 2005 and a projected 49 million in 2010. The number of wireless game subscribers increased from almost nothing in 2001 to 48 million in 2005 and a projected 193 million in 2010.

In conclusion, the widespread piracy in China and elsewhere in Asia Pacific makes the official aggregate spending much lower than the real spending and furthermore, it obstructs the development of a much larger video game market. The combined legitimate and illicit video games world market might add up to $100 billion, or double the size of the legitimate market.

The Global Video Game Industry

Games are continuously being improved in matters of graphics and animation, making them increasingly realistic. Because massive investments and large size of development teams are required to create modern high-end games, this predominant segment of the game industry has been highly consolidated for quite some years. That is particularly the case in consoles and platforms, but increasingly in game development, too. These large consoles and games are sold in stores. A different type of game market has emerged, however. This is the so-called 'casual game' that has become extremely popular.[22] While advanced titles typically are played for hours and require time and skill to master, the casual games are simple and easy to learn and play.[23] There are thousands of casual games available on game portals on net. Casual games are usually developed by independent developers, although large studios are also beginning to show interest. Casual games can be bought for a small price or even accessed freely, based on advertising income. Between these two game segments a third game segment may be emerging, so-called MOR (Middle of the Road). Such games tend to be more advanced in graphics and content, but can be played from anywhere over the net. While game developers often concentrate on development, they may outsource the hardware part and buy a license to en existing engine or use a free one. This is the case with expensive game engines used for large games that are being played on, for instance, PlayStation, but also for inexpensive and free engines. In spite of a proliferating game market, large games played on consoles and pc's still dominate the game market, as do the leading console providers and to a lesser extent, game developers.

Sony

Japanese Sony is one of the world's largest media conglomerates with activities in North America, Western Europe and Asia.[24] It is a leading manufacturer of electronics, video, communications, video games and IT products for the consumer and professional

---

22   International Game Developers Association (2006). *2006 Casual Games White Paper: www.igda.org*.
23   *www.wikipedia.org*: 'Casual game'.
24   *www.sony.net. www.wikipedia.org*: 'PlayStation'.

markets. Sony's three core business segments are electronics, games, and entertainment (motion pictures and music).

Since the Second World War, Sony has created a leading global position within consumer electronics and electronic media. In the 1950s and 1960s, Sony built a strong Japanese market position in audio visual products and conquered the American market in the 1970s, including radio, television, recorders and gramophone players. Sony expanded into Western Europe and Asia, too, and became a worldwide based company. Since the 1970s, Sony has also marketed video recorders. In the 1980s, Sony launched its successful Walkman and CD players and CD discs in cooperation with Philips, as well as its computer games, hardware and software. In the 1990s, Sony developed digital cameras and television and the DVD recorder to replace the VCR. Sony also established its entertainment division in the 1990s by acquiring in 1989 the famous American film studios of Columbia Pictures and its large treasure of movies. In 2004, Sony BMG was a result of a 50/50 joint venture with Bertelsmann, acquiring one of the big four music companies of the world. In electronics, Sony is a leader in still and motion cameras, moving from analog to digital technologies in the 1990s. Sony is also the world's leading provider of professional electronic equipment to cinemas and television studios.

In 2007-2008, Sony had revenues of $89 billion, almost equally divided in four shares between Japan, USA, Europe, and Other.[25] Unlike most Japanese companies that are mostly based on their domestic market, Sony is a truly globalized corporation. Its activities include:

- Consumer electronics (65 percent, of which radio is 10 percent, video 21 percent, television 23 percent, information and communications 18 percent, semi conductors 4 percent, components 16 percent, other 10 percent),
- Games (12 percent),
- Motion pictures (12 percent),
- Financial services (9 percent),
- Music (3 percent).

In the game segment, Sony continues to hold a high share of the world console market, although PS2 was six years in its business cycle until PS3 was launched in early 2007 and is expected to fuel sales of games hardware and software. Since the launch of PS2 in 2000, many facilities have been added to the device. The new PS3 version is meant

---

25   Sony (2008). *Annual Report 2007-08: www.sony.net.*

for the Internet age and for interactivity. Via its hardware, users are able to download a variety of content as well as access online games and services over the network, like any television set. With the aim of providing support for the development of software to PS3, Sony acquired a couple of companies and developed programming tools and middleware for game software developers. To strengthen its own software development capabilities it combined its development studios in Japan, the US and Europe to form a worldwide studio group. The studios will further accelerate the creation of global hit titles and titles adapted to the taste of consumers in each region. The worldwide studios group will work with content creators around the world to strengthen its software portfolio. In 2006, there were more than 500 titles to PlayStation 2 worldwide. In 2007, numerous titles were released for sale around the world to PS3.

Nintendo

Nintendo is a multinational Japanese corporation that since the 1970s and particularly the 1980s has been one of the world's leading video game producers.[26] Through thirty years, Nintendo has marketed several generations of consoles and video games. The handheld consoles and video games based on Game Boy is its core product. In 2006, Nintendo launched its seventh generation video game console the Wii that is interactive and Internet based. Wii is a wireless controller that may be used as a handheld device. Nintendo DS is the current portable game console. Technology has developed enormously through all these years, including new interfaces, easier communication and increased capacities. Nintendo combines hardware and software competences in-house.

Nintendo's consoles and video games are sold all over the world. It has been calculated that Game Boy and later versions are found in 40 percent of all American homes. In recent years, the video game market in software has been flat because of the increasing trend to develop content based on sports games and films. Nintendo is seeking to meet these challenges by appealing to people of all ages around the world to play video games. In geographic terms, some half of Nintendo's sales are in Japan, some quarter in America, and virtually all the rest in Europe, mainly Western Europe.[27] In 2006-2007, Nintendo had total revenues of $8 billion ($5 bn in 2005-06). Revenues were flat during 2000/01-2005/06, until the release of the new Wii generation console in 2006 fuelled sales.

---

26 *www.ninetendo.com. www.wikipedia.org*: 'Nintendo and Wii'.
27 Nintendo (2007). *Annual Report 2006-07.*

Microsoft

Microsoft is the world's leading provider of office software (Windows).[28] In 2007, Microsoft had revenues of $60 billion.[29] More than 75 percent of its income stems from Windows client, server, tools and office, 2 percent from business solutions, 5 percent from internet services, 1 percent from mobile services and 10 percent from home and entertainment.

Microsoft's 'home and entertainment' business unit includes Microsoft Xbox video console system, PC games, CPxG (consumer software and hardware products) and TV platform products for the interactive television industry. The success of the video game consoles is determined by console innovation, the portfolio of video game content, online offerings, and the market share of the console. In 2005, Microsoft launched a new version of its console, Xbox 360. During 2005 to 2007, almost 500 games have been released to Xbox 360. Xbox 360 is number three in the world after PlayStation 3 and Wii. Microsoft entered the console market late, compared to its two competitors.

While Microsoft in its Windows client, server, and office systems is competing with numerous leading IT providers, such as HP, IBM, Apple, Sun, Linux, Google, AOL and Yahoo in its internet services, Oracle, SAP and others in its business solutions, Nokia and others in its mobile services – its main competitors in the video game business remain Sony and Nintendo. Microsoft also competes with many companies that have achieved licenses to develop software to the Xbox console, i.e. Acclaim Entertainment, Activision, Atari, Capcom, Eidos, Electronic Arts, Sega, Take-Two Interactive, Tecmo, THQ and Ubisoft.

Electronic Arts

Electronic Arts (EA) is an independent American developer, marketer, publisher, and distributor of computer and video games.[30] Established in 1982, the company was a pioneer of the early home computer games industry. In the late 1980s, EA began developing games in-house and started supporting consoles in the early 1990s. During the 1990s, EA expanded by acquiring several successful developers. In the 2000s, EA has become the world's largest third-party publisher of interactive entertainment software for the three leading consoles of Sony (PlayStation), Nintendo (Game Boy, GameCube, Wii and Nintendo DS), Microsoft (Xbox and Xbox 360) as well as PC and games for mobile phones and the Internet. EA also publishes titles for the two

---

28   www.microsoft.com.
29   Microsoft (2008). *Annual Report 2007.*
30   www.electronicarts.com. www.wikipedia.org: 'Electronic Arts'.

smaller consoles Sega and Matsushita. Since 2006, EA is increasingly focusing on exploiting the opportunities of mobile technologies as well as the increased capacities and online capabilities of the newly launched versions of the Sony, Nintendo and Microsoft consoles.

By combining diverse media – such as computer animation, video, photographic images, motion capture, 3D face and body rendering technologies, computer graphics, and stereo sound with contributions from storywriters, film directors and musicians – EA uses technology and creativity to develop mainstream entertainment through an interactive medium.[31] Currently, EA's most successful products are sports games (NFL, NBA and FIFA), games based on popular movie licensees (The Lord of the Rings, Harry Potter and Godfather) and games from long-running franchises (e.g. Need for Speed, The Sims, and Burnout). In 2006, EA had 24 titles that sold over 1 million copies.

From its headquarters in Redwood California, EA runs several studios in USA, Canada, UK and Japan and has sales organizations in most developed countries of the world and some emerging countries.[32] In EA's main markets in North America and Western Europe, its products are sold through mass retailers (like Wal-Mart), electronic specialized shops (like Best Boy) and specialized software shops (like GameShop) on CD and DVD formats. Online versions are sold via EA's website. Being well established in the Atlantic community, EA is seeking to expand its business in Japan and the rest of Asia Pacific. In 2007, EA had revenues of almost $4 billion. Revenues have more than doubled since 2000, but they have been flat since 2004. The majority of its sales are almost equally divided between North America and Western Europe, leaving a minor share to Asia.

The EA business is dependent on several relationships for hardware platforms and content. EA has licensee agreements with Sony, Nintendo and Microsoft that authorizes it to develop and distribute DVD-based software products and online content that is compatible with the consoles of these three companies. In 2006, almost half of EA's revenues stemmed from titles to Sony's PlayStation platform, almost 20 percent from Microsofts Xbox platform and 5 percent from Nintendo's platforms. EA has agreements to distribute its wireless applications through more than 90 carriers in over 40 countries. Furthermore, EA has content licensee agreements with major sports leagues and associations (like NFL, NBA, FIFA, UEFA, NASCAR, PGA Tour) as well as media entertainment conglomerates (like Warner, Viacom, Fox).

---

31 *www.electronicarts.com.*
32 Electronic Arts (2008). *Annual Report 2007: www.electronicarts.com.*

The highly competitive software game business is characterized by a continuous introduction of new titles and the development of new technologies. EA's competitors vary in size and cost structure from very small companies with limited resources to very large, diversified corporations with greater financial and marketing resources than EA. The video games business is driven by hit titles, which require ever-increasing budgets for development and marketing. As a result, the availability of significant financial resources has become a major competitive factor in developing and marketing software games. Competition is also based on product quality and features, timing of product releases, brand-name recognition, quality of in-game content, access to distribution channels, effectiveness of marketing and price.

The software games segment may be viewed as a part of the overall entertainment market and industry. For the leisure time and spending of consumers, EA compete with other forms of entertainment, such as motion pictures, television and music. The large software and media companies are increasing their focus on the software games segment of the entertainment market and competing directly with EA. For quite some time, large software companies such as Microsoft, Sony and Nintendo have published products that compete with EA. Diversified companies such as Time Warner, Viacom, Fox and Disney are expanding their software game publishing efforts, too.

EA also competes with numerous companies that, like EA, are licensed by the console manufacturers to develop and publish software games that operate on their consoles. Among others, these competitors include Activision, Atari, Capcom, Koei, Konami, LucasArts, Midway, Namco, Sega, Take-Two Interactive, THQ, Ubisoft and Vivendi Games. Together with the increasing game publishing efforts of the above-mentioned large software and media publishers, this makes the video games industry an intensely competitive market.

In addition to competing for product sales, EA face heavy competition from other software companies to obtain licensee agreements granting it the right to use intellectual property included in its products. Some of these content licenses are controlled by the diversified media companies, which in some cases have decided to publish their own games based on popular movie properties, rather than licensing the content to a software game company like EA, for instance expanding Vivendi Games, acquiring several game developers, including Activision in 2008.[33] The market for software games is characterized also by significant price competition.

Competition is also intense and rising in the wireless entertainment applications market. Current and potential competitors include major media companies, traditional

---

33   *www.vivendi.com.*

video game publishers, wireless carriers, wireless software providers and other companies that specialize in wireless entertainment applications. Primary competitors in this market are Disney, Gameloft, Infospace, Mforma, Namco, Sony, Sorrent, THQ, VeriSign and Yahoo. The online games market segment is also highly competitive and characterized by frequent product introductions, new business models and new platforms. As the proportion of households with broadband connection increases, new competitors are expected to enter the market and existing competitors are expected to allocate more resources to develop online games. Current and potential competitors in the online game market include major media companies, traditional video game publishers, and companies that specialize in online games, including Vivendi Games, NC Soft, Sony, Atari, Yahoo, Popcap, Real and MSN.

In conclusion, EA, like other software game developers and publishers are increasingly adopting new mobile and online technologies on the one hand, while on the other, they are being put under heavy competitive pressure from large software and content providers in the IT and entertainment industry that control the platforms and content of their software games. This shows the continuous blurring of boundaries and consolidation within the entertainment industry.

Gaming

The term gambling or gaming is referring to 'wagering money on an event with an uncertain outcome with the primary intent of winning additional money'.[34] Typically the outcome of the wager is evident within a short period of time. The term 'gaming' refers to activities that have been specifically permitted by law. Because many religious authorities generally disapprove of gambling, and because gambling can have adverse social consequences, most legal jurisdictions limit gambling to some extent. Some Islamic nations prohibit gambling, while most other countries regulate it.

There are three variables common to all forms of gambling or gaming: the initial stake (determines the scale of the bet), the predictability of the event (determines the frequency of success), and the odds between the two parties to the wager (determines the payout if successful). The expected value, positive or negative, is a mathematical calculation using these three variables.

---

34   *www.wikipedia.org*: 'Gambling'. On the wider economic aspects of gambling, see Nottingham Trent University (2002). *The Economics of Gambling*. UK: Routledge.

There are basically three types of gaming or gambling: casino gambling, non-casino gambling, and fixed-odds gambling games. 1. Casino gambling games are games offered in a casino. Casino games include beatable games, i.e. the outcome can to some degree be predicted, such as a blackjack, poker, slot machines, and sports betting. 'Unbeatable' casino games, i.e. games with only negative outcome, include for example baccarat, pachinko, and roulette. 2. Non-casino gambling games take place outside of casinos and include for instance bingo, card games, coin-tossing and dice-based games, for instance Backgammon. 3. Fixed-odds gambling frequently occur at many types of sporting events. In addition many bookmakers offer fixed odds on a number of non-sports related outcomes, for example the direction of financial indices, the winner of television competitions, and election results. Horse or greyhound racing is one of the most widespread forms of gambling, too. Betting on team sports has become an important industry in many countries, particularly in soccer and football. Worldwide, a large business of casinos, bookmakers and lotteries has emerged to meet the demands of a growing passion for gambling or gaming. The United States has the largest gambling market, dominated by casinos, followed by the UK that is more keen on sports betting and lotteries. In the Orient, Macau has risen to become the Asian Las Vegas in casinos.

The Global Gaming Market

Casino and other regulated gaming consist of betting activities conducted within brick-and-mortar casinos, including:[35]

- Land-based casinos, riverboats, dockside casinos, tribal casinos, slot parlors, racinos (slots at racetracks), and limited-stakes casinos,
- Online gaming at Internet casinos, virtual poker rooms, and other online sites in countries where it is legal.

Total spending represents gross gaming revenue, which is the amount wagered minus the amount returned to the winning players. In the case of virtual poker rooms, revenue consists of charges to the pot in each game. Online gambling is illegal in the USA, among other reasons for fear of unhindered money laundering, and in Australia, although WTO claims that this is a violation of the General Agreement on Trade in Services, but legal in most member states of the EU and Caribbean countries. However, much illegal online gambling occurs for instance in the USA.

---

35   PWC. Global Entertainment and Media Outlook, 564.

Global legitimate revenues of casino and other regulated gaming amounted to $55 billion in 2001 and $82 billion in 2005 and are projected to reach $125 billion in 2010 (Table 46). The United States is by far the largest legitimate gaming market, covering two-thirds of world total. All markets of the world are expanding, most in Asia Pacific, but also the West European market is growing fast. These two regional markets are almost of equal size, constituting together one-third of world total. The legal gaming market in the rest of the world is insignificant, except for Canada with a well-developed gaming market equivalent to the USA. In industry terms, the world industry revenues may amount to as much as 250 billion in 2005, of which online revenues accounted for 4 percent.[36] Other estimates on online gaming are much higher.

TABLE 46

The Global Gaming Market in $bn, 2001-2010

	2001	2005	2010
USA	38	53	75
Canada	2	3	5
Western Europe	7	11	18
UK	1	3	7
France	2	3	4
Germany	1	2	2
Rest of Western Europe	3	3	5
Asia Pacific	7	12	23
China/Macau	2	5	12
Australia	2	2	3
Rest of Asia Pacific	3	5	8
ROW	1	3	4
Total	55	82	125

Source: PWC. Global Entertainment and Media Outlook, 567, 574, 583, 587, 591.

Online gaming is expanding rapidly in all regions, fueled by the popularity of online poker and rising broadband penetration. Online gaming in the USA is not included, however, because it is illegal to host an online gaming site in the US New bricks-and-

---

36   Stewart, David O., et al. (2006). *An Analysis of Internet Gambling and Its Policy Implications.* An AGA White Paper.: *www.americangaming.org*.

mortar casinos will boost growth in each region, with the greatest development in Asia Pacific as the introduction of Las Vegas-style casinos in Macao solidifies that territory as a major casino gaming destination. New casinos in South Korea and in Singapore, Japan, Taiwan, Thailand, and the Philippines during 2006-2010 will contribute to growth in Asia Pacific. A Las Vegas-style casino is also expected in Spain. The new Gambling Act of 2005 in the UK is opening up that market, too. Likewise, new casinos will boost revenue in South Africa. In the USA, increased convention activity, new casinos, and continued capital reinvestment will fuel the Las Vegas market. In Canada, new and upgraded casinos in the western part of the country will boost revenue. New casinos in Chile will contribute to growth in Latin America.

USA

The US gambling and gaming industries are big business. They include casino, lottery, betting (horse racing and sports), bingo and slots. Not only has gambling or rather gaming, stressing its legitimacy gained ground in the past decade, but it is also being turned into a legitimate social activity alongside other forms of entertainment.[37] The United States has been the center of this remarkable change, having repercussions not only on the games and entertainment industry but on the American society as such. More than one-third of total American entertainment industry revenues stem from the gaming industry.

Since the mid-1980s, revenues of the gaming industry, including online gaming, have increased ten-fold to reach $100 billion in 2006 (10 percent from online gaming), doubling within the recent decade.[38] Two-thirds of the revenues come from the casino industry and a quarter from lotteries. The rest is shared between betting and bingo. The casino industry is the largest and the most expansive part of the gaming sector and its influence stretches throughout all gaming industries. In 2005, every fourth adult American visited a casino. Online gaming is becoming increasingly popular, although it is still prohibited in the US.[39] Driven from obscure places in Canada, the Caribbean or the UK, in 2005 perhaps 4 percent of all adults gambled online and the number of online players continues to rise. Poker is booming, too, and in 2005 every fifth adult American played poker, mostly with family and friends and some for money in casinos. [40] Poker, casino games and sports betting dominate online gaming. Often

---

37   Fr. Mc Gowan (2001). *Government and the Transformation of the Gaming Industry.*
38   American Gaming Association (AGA). *Industry information: www.americangaming.org.*
39   Stewart, et al. An Analysis of Internet Gambling and its Policy Implications.
40   AGA (2006). *2006 State and the States. The AGA Survey of Casino Entertainment.*

lotteries and bingo are related to charity activities. All in all, three out of four adult Americans take part in some gaming. One percent is doomed 'gaming addicts'.[41]

TABLE 47

The US Gaming Market in $bn, 2001-2010

	2001	2005	2010
Nevada	9	12	17
Atlantic City	4	5	6
Tribal Casinos	13	23	33
Regional Casinos	12	14	19
Total	38	53	75

Source: PWC. Global Entertainment and Media Outlook, 567.

The US has four centers of casino gaming, Las Vegas, Altantic City, tribal casinos, and regional casinos.[42] Increased convention traffic and tourism, new casinos, and continued capital reinvestment will continue to fuel casino gaming in Nevada. Atlantic City will benefit from revenue growth in table games, but increased competition in the region will cut into slot machine revenue. Tribal casino revenues will grow by an effort to attract an expanded and more diversified market base, but changing regulatory provisions could limit expansion. New casinos and slot parlors in Pennsylvania will add to overall regional revenues, and states such as Ohio are expected to once again test gaming as a resource for funding education initiative.

The US gaming market increased from $38 billion in 2001 to $53 billion in 2005, with a projected $75 billion in 2010 (Table 47). Most revenues are made in tribal casinos, about 40 percent, followed by regional casinos and Nevada, while Atlantic City is smaller and less expansive than the other casinos. Regional casinos are casinos outside Nevada, Atlantic City and tribal casinos.

Canada's casino and online gaming market is growing from $2 billion in 2001 and $3 billion in 2005 to $5 billion in 2010.[43] Much of the world's online poker activity is processed in Canada by Mohawk Internet Technologies (MIT), a tribal company licensed by the Kahnawake Gaming Commission. MIT hosts 200 sites even though

---

41   Gambling industry: *www.gambling.com*.
42   PWC. Global Entertainment and Outlook, 566-571.
43   PWC. Global Entertainment and Media Outlook, 590-591.

online gaming sites are not permitted in Canada. MIT claims it operates on sovereign tribal ground, and so far the government has not taken any action against MIT.

Legitimate gaming in Latin America is a small business, indicating quite some illicit gambling.

Western Europe

In Europe, Asia Pacific, Africa and Latin America, governments are mostly more restrictive towards gambling than in North America. Often a state monopoly runs gaming, although for instance the EU is seeking to deregulate the gaming industry in Europe. While non-American countries are very reluctant to accept casinos, betting and lotteries are pervasive activities. Even the Internet is becoming acceptable as a gaming channel. Still, the gaming industry is regulated in most countries, except in the UK.

In Western Europe, new casinos will boost revenue, but the presence of relatively few Las Vegas-type venues will prevent the region from becoming a major destination market.[44] The emergence of new online outlets and rising broadband penetration will fuel online gaming. The EU will require member states to open up markets to competition, but regulatory restrictions will continue to limit growth in many countries. The West European gaming market has increased swiftly from $7 billion in 2001 to $12 billion in 2005 and a projected $20 billion in 2010 (Table 48).

TABLE 48

The West European Gaming Market in $bn, 2001-2010

	2001	2005	2010
Casino Gaming	6	9	13
Online Gaming	1	3	6
Total	7	12	20

Source: PWC. Global Entertainment and Media Outlook, 575.

In Western Europe, France and the UK have the largest single markets at $3 billion each in 2005, with Germany coming third at half that size. France has approximately 200 casinos, one of the highest totals in the world, most of which are located in coastal resort towns. More than half of the total UK gaming revenue is generated by online

---

44   PWC. Global Entertainment and Outlook, 572-580.

gaming, a sector that will continue to grow rapidly now that domestic sites are permitted. The casino market will be enhanced by the introduction of one new-style large casino and up to 16 smaller venues from 2007.

Casinos in Western Europe, and for that matter in Eastern Europe and the Middle East and Africa, are generally small and have not become tourist attractions as they have in the United States and Asia – except for Dubai that is building a huge gaming center. Few have hotel and convention facilities. Instead, many are located in private clubs or are restricted to spas and resorts. Casino resorts exist in a few countries, such as Portugal and Austria, and new casinos will open in the next few years in Spain and the Netherlands. The UK will be the fastest growing gaming market, because many of the restrictions on casino gaming have been lifted or relaxed by the Gambling Act of 2005, although it will not permit true Las Vegas-style casinos. Total casino gaming revenues in Western Europe amounted to $6 billion in 2001, $9 billion in 2005 and a projected $13 billion in 2010.

Online gaming occupies an unusual legal niche. Some countries prohibit online gaming sites from being hosted domestically but do not prohibit people from visiting such sites located in other countries. Consequently, online gaming is legal in a number of West European countries. Online gaming is growing rapidly, fueled by online poker and an expanding number of broadband households. With a broadband connection, the play speeds up and stimulates interest. There is also an emerging market through interactive television and through mobile phones that access the Internet. Online gaming rose from $1 billion in 2001 to $3 billion in 2005 and a projected $6 billion in 2010. The UK is by far the largest online gaming market, constituting almost two-thirds of total. Germany is the second largest online market at a much lower level.

Under the new UK Gambling Act, online sites are being permitted for the first time to locate in the UK, and they are allowed to advertise and promote their sites.[45] The act also permits any licensed gambling site in the EU to advertise and market its services in the UK. The UK is attracting online gaming companies, including PartyGaming's introduction to the London Stock Market.

Gaming markets in Eastern Europe are expanding rapidly, especially in Russia that has become a major market with more than 50 casinos and 70,000 slot machines in Moscow alone. So far South Africa is the only country in the Africa/Middle East region with legalized casino gaming.

---

45   The Gambling Commission (2007). *Annual Report 2006: www.gamblingcommission.gov.uk.*

Asia Pacific

Big spenders are making Macau an international gaming center and will drive overall revenue in Asia Pacific.[46] Competition for tourists will lead to the introduction of casinos in a number of countries and sustain growth at double-digit rates through the remainder of the decade. Online gaming will grow rapidly, spurred by mobile devices and rising broadband penetration.

TABLE 49

Asian Pacific Gaming Market in $bn, 2001-2010

	2001	2005	2010
Casino Gaming	6	10	19
Online Gaming	1	2	4
Total	7	12	23

Source: PWC. Global Entertainment and Media Outlook, 583.

Casino gaming spending increased from $6 billion in 2001 to $10 billion in 2005, with a projected $19 billion in 2010. Online gaming has expanded rapidly, too, from $1 billion in 2001 to $2 billion in 2005 and to a projected $4 billion in 2010 (Table 49).

Macau, which now is part of China, dominates the region with an increase from $2 billion in 2001 to $6 billion in 2005 and a projected $12 billion in 2010. Gaming is prohibited at mainland China. Macao's gaming market will expand as new Las Vegas-style casinos will open in the next few years. Macao constitutes almost two-thirds of the total Asian Pacific gaming market. Australia is the second largest market in the region with $ 2 billion in 2005 and a projected $3 billion in 2010. South Korea is the third largest at $1 billion in 2005, almost doubling up to 2010. The Malaysian gaming market is no. four and the Philippines no. five, but growing rapidly to become the fourth largest regional market. Other countries, such as Singapore, are planning to create expanding gaming markets, too.

In addition to generating growth for themselves, the new casinos in Macao are stimulating other countries to build new casinos to attract tourists, including South Korea, Singapore, the Philippines, Taiwan, and Thailand. All these countries are working on legalizing casino gaming. That is also the case in Japan, where in order to attract foreign tourists casinos are expected to open in 2009.

---

46   PWC. Global Entertainment and Outlook, 581-585.

Online gaming is illegal in some countries. Others prohibit domestic sites. The promotion of online gaming is often illegal. The online gaming in Asia Pacific totaled almost $2 billion in 2005 and a projected $4 billion in 2010. As in other regions, growth has been explosive, driven by a rapidly expanding broadband market. Nevertheless, even through Asia Pacific has many more broadband households than Western Europe, online gaming is smaller in scope, because it is illegal in China and other large broadband markets. The ability to access the Internet through mobile devices is also stimulating the market, as is the growing interest in poker and in online and mobile entertainment in general.

The Global Gaming Industry

The various sub-sectors of the gaming industry are being consolidated on national and regional levels and to some degree globally. In its two main markets, the US and Western Europe, consolidation is based on casinos in the US and on betting and lotteries in Western Europe. Online poker is the most expansive segment of the gambling industry, led by Pokerstars, Party Poker and Full Tilt Poker.[47] Traditional leaders of the gambling industry are moving into the popular online poker gambling, too, including other online gambling, as gambling is rapidly moving from brick to online. The following companies take part in this consolidation process, including providers of IT and online gaming systems.

Harrah's Entertainment

In the 1930s, Harrah's opened its first bingo hall in Reno, Nevada.[48] After the Second World War, Harrah's began a remarkable expansion in the casino and hotel industry, first in Las Vegas and since the 1970s throughout the US and Canada, and in recent years in Australia, UK, Spain, Slovenia, Singapore and the Bahamas, too. In 2005, Harrah's made its largest acquisition by merging with Caesars Entertainment, starting a new era by redefining its gaming and entertainment business into a unique combination of properties, hotels, casinos, international relations and high-performing activities and competences among its 85,000 employees. The core of Harrah's activities is located in Las Vegas and Atlantic City. In 2007, Harrah's had total revenues of $10 billion, of which $8 billion came from casinos. An increasing share of income comes

47   *www.pokerstars.com. www.partypoker.com. www.fulltiltpoker.com.*
48   *www.harrahs.com.*

from hotels, conferences, restaurants and non-gaming entertainment. Today, Harrah's is one of the largest casino entertainment providers in the world. Competition in the casino industry is increasing, however, in the US as well as the rest of the world, with currently few new markets opening for expansion.

MGM Mirage

MGM Mirage is one of the world's leading casino and hotel companies also based in Las Vegas.[49] Just like Harrah's, MGM Mirage has expanded throughout the US and abroad and runs many casino and hotel resorts. A large developing project is going on in Macau, China. MGM Mirage is also engaged in a large city developing project in Las Vegas. In 2007, MGM Mirage had revenues of $7 billion, respectively, of which some half came from casinos.[50] MGM Mirage is transforming its business to a wider entertainment environment based on its many and future resorts in Las Vegas, Atlantic City, Detroit and Macau. MGM Mirage is reviewing its most valuable assets, land, management and brands, expanding into other regions of the world, including the Middle East.

TabCorp

TabCorp is the leading Australian gaming and entertainment group and fourth in the world in its field.[51] In 2007, TabCorp had revenues of $4 billion, based on three equal sized business areas, casinos, games, and wagering as well as a small media division. TabCorp's activities are based on four casinos, 43 restaurants, 1,400 hotel rooms, three theaters, conference facilities and entertainment and convention centers. TabCorp aims at creating value for its customer through every contact, in the casino, at a hotel, restaurant or bar, online or telephone, at a wagering or gaming venue or through its media channels. TabCorp focuses on the racing industry and other sporting activities.

Ladbrokes

British Ladbrokes is one of the world's leading sports betting and gaming companies.[52] Together with William Hill, Ladbrokes is the largest betting company in the UK and

49   www.mgmmirage.com.
50   MGM Mirage (2008). *Annual Report 2007*.
51   www.tabcorp.com.
52   www.ladbrokesplc.com.

the largest retail bookmaker in the world. It also operates online gaming websites offering sports booking, poker, casino, games, bingo and backgammon. From its UK base, Ladbrokes is expanding internationally into mainland Europe and, for instance, China. Ladbrokes has been in the bookmaking business for more than a hundred years. In 2007, Ladbrokes had revenues of $2bn. Football and horse racing are its main segments, increasingly based on online betting. Online poker is the most expanding segment.

William Hill

Along with Ladbrokes, William Hill is the UK's largest betting company and one of the largest in the world.[53] Through William Hill, one can bet on almost any sporting activity, try one's luck in Hill's online casino, test one's nerve on its online poker room, or play bingo. In 2007, William Hill had a turnover of $2 billion.[54] For decades, William Hill has been expanding organically and by mergers. Since the turn of the 20th century, it has, in addition to retail and telephone channels, increasingly based its activities on the Internet. Its biggest competitors in UK are Ladbrokes and Coral.

Arena Leisure

Arena Leisure is the UK's leading gaming operator in horse racing, including ownership of seven horse racing tracks and hospitality facilities ensuring "that our customers enjoy the experience of a day at the races".[55] Arena Leisure has television and radio rights for transmission from the races, too.

SportingBet

British SportingBet is a leading international bookmaker firm for horse races and dog races, offering bets in most other sports, too.[56] From its British base, SportingBet has expanded into Continental Europe, North America and Australia. In 2007, SportingBet had revenues of $4 billion.

---

53   *www.willhill.com.*
54   William Hill (2008). *Annual Report 2007: www.willhill.com.*
55   *www.arenaleisureplc.com*
56   *www.sportingbet.com.*

Betandwin

Betandwin is a large international Austrian betting company in Vienna.[57] With Betandwin you can bet on the results of more than fifty sports in twenty countries, as well as on poker, casino and games. Betandwin is a leading European provider of sports gaming and also a leader in online games. Every day, a bookmaker group is calculating the odds of its five thousands games. Betandwin is also an important sponsor of leading European football clubs such as Juventus, Bordeaux and Werder Bremen and international sports events. Besides sports, Betandwin also offers all kinds of online gaming within poker, casino, lotteries, slots and cards, for computers as well as mobile phones. Since 2005, and in particular 2006 by acquiring Ongame, Betandwin has moved into a position as a leading global online gaming company with strong market positions in North America and Europe, and is expanding in Asia, too. In 2007, more than $300 billion were spent on betting with Betandwin, while the group had net revenues of $2 billion.[58]

Lottomatica

Lottomatica is one of the world's largest lottery operators and market leader in the Italian gaming industry, with multi billion wagers in 2005 and 2006, half in lotteries and half in games.[59] Its games and services are distributed through an extensive European online network. The Lottomatica Group achieved net revenues of $1 billion in 2007. Similar lottery companies are found in most countries of the world.

Multimedia Games

Multimedia Games is the leading provider of gaming technology to Native American tribes.[60] By way of its broadband, multi-channel communications network thousands of online slots, video lottery and games are available throughout several US states, mainly based on Native Americans.

57   *www.betandwin.com*
58   *www.bwin.com.* Betandwin (2008). *Geschäftsberichte 2007: www.bwin.com.*
59   *www.lottomatica.com.*
60   *www.multimediagames.com.*

CryptoLogic

Based in Toronto, Canada, CryptoLogic is a leading software developer to the rapidly expanding Internet gaming industry.[61] Its software licenses are sold to online gaming companies around the world. CryptoLogic offers a complete online gaming solution, including more than 150 casino tables and slot games, player-to-player poker, multi-player bingo, multi-languages, multi-currencies, multi-platforms (download, not-download, wireless), as well as an integrated proprietary e-cash management system and multi-language customer support. The UK and Continental Europe are its main markets, because online gaming is still prohibited in the US. CryptoLogic had revenues in 2007 of approximately $0.1 billion.

The world market of Internet gaming is growing quickly from $5 billion in 2001 to $12 billion in 2005, with a projected $24 billion in 2010, of which poker casino each encompasses one quarter. Most revenues stem from the consumer companies, such as Intercasino, William Hill, Linewoods Casino, Ukbetting, Ritz Club Online, Betfairpoker, SunPoker and PokerPlex. There are between 2000 and 3000 sites on the Internet, offering online gaming services from casino games (blackjack, roulette, slots) to sports and horse racing, bingo and lotteries and poker.

GTech

American GTech is a leading provider of integrated technologies to run the expanding gaming markets.[62] GTech delivers end-to-end lottery services and lottery game content, including system design, implementation, support, and network internationally. GTech embraces the whole value chain of gaming, including payment systems and other services needed to run gaming systems. In 2007, GTech had revenues of $1 billion, half from the US and half from abroad.

Scientific Games

American Scientific Games is a leading provider, globally, of technology and marketing in lottery, pari-mutuel and telecommunications.[63] Scientific Games offers a full line suite of online and instant lottery products, integrated systems and services and

---

61   www.cryptlogic.com.
62   www.gtech.com.
63   www.scientificgames.com.

operates the online lottery systems for several countries in America and Europe and Australia. In 2007, Scientific Games had revenues of almost $1 billion.[64]

64   Scientific Games (2008). *Annual Report 2007: www.scientificgames.com.*

8. Design

Design

Design may be defined as applied arts, engineering, architecture, and other such creative activities.[1] Design is a matter of developing and implementing a plan for a creative endeavor that leads normally to a commercial product. It might also include processes that can be seen as the results of design. In its widest sense, every human creation may be considered a product of design, including the making of our societies. In this context, we shall use the term 'design' in a more restricted sense that corresponds to a common view of design, namely as the combined aesthetic, functional, and commercial aspects of making an object to be marketed in the market place. Designing normally requires a designer to do the research, thinking, modeling, and adjustment of the object. While engineering is applied design with emphasis on function and the utilization of math, physics and chemistry, the aesthetic perspective of design is dominant in applied arts and architecture. In this context, design is used in the latter sense of the word. More specifically, the term design embraces architecture and interiors, industrial design, graphic design, fashion and other applied arts. Fashion will be dealt with separately because of its wide application. Although we stress the importance of design as a creative and aesthetic process, it is always closely related to the materials and production methods applied in the making of the products as well as business considerations. Design is a creative activity but it is also based on a multidisciplinary knowledge that unites in the production process.

The History of Design

Everything is designed.[2] The world is human made and a result of designing. Today, the engineer, the architect and the designer have made the resources of the world available to us. Not only articles for everyday use such as tables, chairs, plates, flatware and toothbrushes are being designed, but also the production, transportation and communication means of society, including plants, bridges, engines, cars, computers and telecommunications, even towns and landscapes are designed. Design is placed right in the middle of modern business and working processes, including all the pro-

---

1   *www.wikipedia.org*: 'Design'.
2   Ida Engholm, Anders Michelsen (1999). *Designmaskinen – design af den moderne verden.* Copenhagen: Gyldendal (The Design Machine – Designing the Modern World).

cesses of turning nature's raw materials into the high value enriched products of our modern lives.

Specialized professions and industries have emerged to handle an increasing number of increasingly advanced design tasks, including architects, urban planners, interior designers, industrial designers, graphic designers, etc. Today, these skills and professions cannot stand alone. When dealing with design tasks in current complicated and dynamic societies, many professions and competences work together, including knowledge of manufacturing, materials, psychology, environment, aesthetics, marketing, business, etc. The final design object is a synthesis of all these perspectives. This symbiosis of industrial societies and design has been going on for more than one hundred years.

Modern design was born with modern industrial societies and industries of the early 20th century. Almost from the start, mechanization and functionalism dominated modern design. Eventually, all sides of societies were being based on mechanized or even automated mass production, including a high division of labor, rationalization, standardization and assembly lines, as well as mass consumption and mass organization. Companies, governmental agencies, public organizations, and households were all considered machines that had to function in the most rational way. As a consequence of this systematic organization of social activities, productivity and wealth increased and people were able to buy more and more of the increasing number of marketed products, including cars, houses, electronics, inventory, food, clothing, etc. While the engineer took care of the transformation of nature into mass produced products, it was the task of the designer to form the products, buildings and inventory according to their functions and in harmony with their surroundings. In this way, the perspective of the engineer was combined with an aesthetic dimension. The ideal was that form followed function, but the designer made sure that functions cooperated with their human context. Throughout most of the 20th century, virtually everything was designed according to such functional premises. Leading international designers such as the Americans Frank Lloyd Wright and Raymond Loewy and, in particular, French Le Corbusier and designers of the German Bauhaus school, added an avant-garde perspective to it all, inspired by the new artistic trends between the two World Wars.

While modern design was formed during the first half of the 20th century, it did not take-off until the breakthrough of post-war industrial expansion and welfare societies. Modern designers were put to work as never before, designing infrastructure, engines, plants, housing, shopping malls, public institutions, cars, electronics, furniture, apparel, inventory and other consumer products that entered modern life in thousands since the 1960s. In the new Western consumer societies, design was formed by the general wealth that spread from the US to Western Europe, Japan and Oceania. American management and marketing were universally adopted, accompanied by American lifestyles, entertainment and a new youth culture. A reverse influence also took place, although to a lesser degree, as the refined and diversified European functional design, for example the artistic and colorful Italian design and the elegant Danish design of furniture and other applied arts, appealed to well-off people in the US. However, the relaxed American lifestyle was adopted everywhere and eventually became the predominant expression of the post-war world.

In the new welfare society, people were surrounded with thousands of products and infinitely more things than by previous generations. Form continued to follow function, but continuously the life cycle of products shortened. In the affluent society, people could afford more than products for simple survival and daily needs. And one always had the option of choosing between similar products. Increasingly, on the supply side, the enormous supply of competing goods made companies differentiate their products.

During the 1960s and 1970s, a new trend gradually emerged in product designing. A symbolic dimension that referred to the cultural and social world of consumers was being introduced in design. Often symbols were taken from the expanding mass media and mass culture. In one way, designers joined with marketing to seduce consumers. In another way, symbolism was a reaction to a rather boring and uniform functionalism. Deep down under the surface of markets, a roaring economic crisis called for a radical reform of traditional mass producing and consumption methods. Social and environmental problems caused by modern industry and life only added to an emerging general crisis in Western societies. Anti-capitalist movements of the 1960s and 1970s protested against the repressing, un-ethical, dull and deadlock nature of traditional industrial societies. In doing so, they even abstained from any kind of modern design. These changes in the 1960s and 1970s paved the way for postmodernism since the 1980s and 1990s.

Since the 1980s, design thinking and practice changed. Instead of pure functionalism, products were designed to communicate meanings and feelings in accordance with human life. Designers were inspired by the huge number of cultural symbols and expressions in cities that interacted with the way consumers found their identities in an increasingly individualized world. Furthermore, the socialist and grass-root movements of the 1970s that looked for more alternative ways of life made people in general and professional designers in particular look for more humane housing and user friendly products as well as improved environments. For example instead of tearing down old houses, they were being renovated to create more diversified accommodation. Individualization was the common slogan, dissociating with uniform mass production. At the same time, postmodernism was formed by the expanding supply of mass media, information and entertainment that created a reality of its own.

The breakthrough of globalization in the 1990s accompanied by the widespread use of computers and the Internet made it clear that the industrial age was being radically transformed. By way of flexible adaptation to rapidly changing markets and use of digital technologies, customized and knowledge-based ways of manufacturing and distribution replaced traditional mass production. As a consequence, wealth increased and more people got access to an even wider selection of goods than in the golden industrial age. The cycle of products became shorter and shorter, while buyers helped by the Internet took command of markets. This put design in a crucial position to differentiate products and attract customers to the individual companies and products.

The design and designers of the 1990s and 2000s added cultural dimensions to products that appealed to feelings of romance, sensitivity, elegance, style, self-confidence, influence and/or playfulness. It was a kind of 'sampling-technique' that picked and mixed forms, colors, and symbols from all kinds of context, including nature, city, business, culture and entertainment. Postmodern design did not simply follow function the way that modern design did. Based on many tools, postmodern design endeavored to connect products with the individual current life style of people who wanted to feel good and unique, but also complying with an age of environmental and ethical standards. Functions are still important and in some ways more important than ever, because of intense competition and increasing environmental ethical demands. At the same time, all products must contain an esthetic-based meaning appealing to different groups and individuals. Design is everywhere, from the functional dimension of products and businesses to the symbolic value added to products. In the end, design has become so competitively important that the way consumers experience the cultural dimension of a product is often decisive for their choice.[3]

Because design has become an integrated part of everything, it is also difficult to separate and measure design as a sector and industry of its own. Leaving out engineering in this context, design is considered a combination of aesthetic oriented professions and companies primarily within the fields of architecture and interior design, industrial design and graphic design, and fashion. They have all one thing in common, namely that they support the value-creation process of other industries. Architects and interior designers work in housing industries, as well as industries that manufacture furniture and other inventory. Industrial design is applied to all other manufacturing industries. Graphic design typically addresses the media and entertainment industries, but also any other industry dealing with communication values such as advertising. Fashion

---

3   Verganti, Roberto and Del'Era, Claudio (2002). 'Radical design-driven innovation. The secret of Italian design': *www.eu-design.net*.

is related to clothing, shoes, accessories and other personal items of which clothing is the crucial sector. Some of these designers are employed in large entreprises, while others work in companies of their own.

Architectural Design

An architect is primarily involved in the design of buildings or urban landscapes, as opposed to the engineering and management knowledge required to construct it.[4] As the two parties of architects and engineers are interdependent, some large companies include both dimensions. Generally speaking, however, most architectural firms deal exclusively with the design process and leave the engineering to other specialized companies. Interior design is a particular branch of the architectural profession. While large firms may offer interior design as part of their services, it is more often based on specialized companies. Interior designers may even move into related industrial product design, designing for example furniture and illumination. The predominant trend is that the leading group of architectural firms provides external as well as internal design for their customers.

Within dimensions of space, architects combine functions, materials, and aesthetics to a unified whole according to customer needs and wishes. Architects cooperate with engineers, the materials industry, and the authorities to make design, industry and communities form a synthesis. New materials, new technology, new cultural trends and the overall economic conditions are channeled into the designs of architecture.

In historical perspective, the modern architect was born with the industrial age.[5] The pre-modern architect was a generalist, combining the artist, the architect and the engineer in one person. With the consolidation of knowledge in scientific fields and the rise of new materials and technology, the architect began to lose ground on the technical aspects of building. He therefore concentrated on the aesthetic field. Because architecture was an applied science, the architecture kept close relations with the material and technological dimensions of building, however. The breakthrough of mass production and mass consumption at the turn of the 20th century gave rise to modern architecture. Throughout the 20th century, a modernist tradition of functionalism prevailed in Western architecture. The general idea was that form followed function.

---

4   *www.wikipedia.org*: 'Architecture'.
5   David Raizman (2003). *History of Modern Design*. London: Laurence King.

A reaction to the rather rational and boring expression of modernist architecture emerged slowly during the 1960s and 1970s and took-off in the 1980s.

Postmodernism, as it was called to signify its dissociation with modernism, stressed the importance of the aspect of human behavior and feelings in the housing and working environments of people. In postmodern architecture, diverse cultural elements and lively expressions were put together to create a more human and inspiring context, including the potentials of new materials and product designs. Instead of the uniformity of the modernist vision, an urban patchwork of old, new, and renovated buildings, promoting a diversity of uses best experienced from street level, became the new vision for urban planning. This included breaks of green and other aspects of a more wide human-scaled urban structure. The famous American architect Robert Venturi called it a 'messy vitality' over 'obvious unity'. Unity is boring, while diversity is equivalent to vitality. A way of presenting the postmodern view was to look at Las Vegas. Along the Strip in Las Vegas, the huge, extravagant neon signs dominated the visually insignificant casinos. Architecture became an insubstantial and even 'antispatial' form of pure information.

The globalization of economic, political, social and cultural affairs since the 1990s made these postmodern trends spread in a mixture of diversity and convergence. Still, modernist functionalism did not disappear as the core of buildings and urban planning, but a cultural dimension was added to all physical expressions of architecture. Furthermore, the demand for total solutions by leading clients such as large corporations and public organizations and communities, made architectural companies diversify into the engineering, designing, planning and management aspects of architecture. In some way, the leading group of international architect-firms in the early 21th century has returned to the general approach of pre-modern architecture. Including Japan, Western societies and companies dominate all parts of present-day architecture and its business.

The Global Architectural Services Industry

Architectural services are an established industry in all developed countries and worldwide. Globally, there was an estimated one million architect-firms with total revenues of $95 billion in 2005 (Table 50), occupying about one million people. Developed countries account for more than three-quarters of world total, led by the United States, Western Europe, and Japan. The architectural industry consists of many small firms and a few large companies in each country. In the USA, for example, two percent of its c.100,000 architect-companies account for half the industry's revenues.[6] The majority of firms occupy less than 50 persons. Other developed countries present a similar structure. In small countries such as Denmark, for example, the predominance of minor architectural firms is even more the case. 10 percent of the architect firms account for half the $1 billion Danish architectural industry's revenues, while the remainder revenues are shared between about 600 smaller firms. A few large and internationally oriented firms drive the Danish architectural industry, however.[7]

TABLE 50

The Global Architectural Services Industry's revenues in $bn, 2001-2010

	2001	2005	2010
North America	27	32	38
USA	25	30	35
Canada	2	2	3
Western Europe	27	27	32
Germany	7	7	8
UK	4	4	5
France	4	4	5
Italy	3	3	4
Spain	2	2	2
Rest of Western Europe	7	7	8
Eastern Europe	2	2	4
Asia Pacific	25	25	32
Japan	14	14	15
China	3	3	5
South Korea	2	2	3
India	1	1	2
Australia	1	1	2
Rest of Asia Pacific	4	4	5
Africa	3	3	3
Latin America	5	6	8
Total	89	95	117

Source: Barnes Reports (2007). *Worldwide Architectural Services Industry: www.barnesreports.com.*

6   US Census Bureau (2007). 'Architectural Services'. Statistical Abstract: *www.census.gov.*
7   Statistics Denmark. 'Produktstatistik for arkitektvirksomhed 2005'. *Nyt fra Danmarks Statistik nr. 412,* 20. september 2006 (Product Statistics of Architect firms): *www.dst.dk.*

In spite of some differences, national architectural industries are worldwide based on the same divide between a few large prize-winning architects and the many small bread-and-butter architects. At the same time, a consolidation process is taking place across the US, Japan, Germany, the UK, and France, as well as small developed nations such as Denmark and Sweden. The consolidation process is fueled by national and global economic growth. In developed and emerging countries such as China, an increasing number of large architectural tasks are being allocated by tender and this has led to a growing internationalization and dominance of a leading group of firms based in developed countries. Across developed countries, internationalization is taking place, too. For example, the British Norman Foster designed the new German Reichstag in Berlin and the American Frank Gehry the new Guggenheim Museum in Bilbao.[8] Measured on their export share, however, architectural services have still a long way to go before this industry is truly internationalized, as less than 10 percent of total revenues in all developed countries, even the USA, stems from export and based on rather few large companies. Internationalization and even globalization has come late in this industry, but it is beginning to take-off.

Large national and international building projects are typically designed by one of 500 to 1000 globally leading architect companies. In some cases, the companies combine engineering and architecture, for example American AECOM Technology Corp. in California, The New Berger Group in New Jersey, and British Atkins.[9] Total revenues are therefore much larger than specialized architectural firms. Leading American architect companies are Gensler in California, Kohn Pedersen Fox Associates in New York, Swanke Hayden Conell Architects in New York, Wemberley Allison Tong Goo in Hawaii, Callison in Washington, and Acquitectonica in Florida. Leading West European architectural companies are, among others, British AEDAS, Foster & Partners, RMJM, and Broadway Malayan, German gmp-Architekten von Gerkan, and Marg und Partner, and Swedish SWECO FFNS and White Architects.[10] Suomitomo Mitsui Construction is a large Japanese architect and engineering company. American architectural companies and combined engineering and architect companies dominate world export of architect assignments, followed by British companies.[11]

---

8   Howkins. The Creative Economy, 91.
9   McGraw Hill Construction ENR. *The Top 200 International Design Firms.* July 2006: *www.construction.com.*
10 Eurostat (2008). *European Business. Facts and Figures,* 383: *http://epp.eurostat.ec.europe.eu.*
11 McGraw Hill Construction ENR, July 2006.

Gensler

Headquartered in San Francisco, Gensler is one of the largest US architect-companies.[12] Gensler occupies more than 2000 employees and had revenues of some $400 million in 2007. About 10 percent of its revenues are international and the remaining 90 percent stems from its domestic market.[13] Since the 1960s, Gensler has expanded to become a leading American architect firm. Even though architectural design and drawing remains its core area, Gensler has diversified into other fields of architectural design and counseling, including building facilities, interior design, management, branding, and urban planning. It is Gensler's aim to cover the whole cycle of buildings and estates from strategic planning to implementing and facility management. Gensler is a multidisciplinary architectural company because its customers are mainly large corporations and public organizations that require total solutions, including a full perspective on building, interior design and planning.

Foster + Partners

Headquartered in London, British architects Foster + Partners had revenues in 2007 of c. $100 million and more than 600 employees.[14] Just as Gensler, Foster + Partner designs large building projects, including management counseling and all other parts of the total planning and implementing process. Foster has designed buildings and complexes within virtually all industries, from education and research to arts, retail, sports and manufacturing. The majority of these projects are located in London, such as London City Hall and St. Mary Axe, but Foster has also fulfilled several international tasks, including the Smithsonian Institute in New York, Free University in Berlin and Beijing Airport. High tech buildings with much steel and glass are a characteristic feature of many Foster projects.

AEDAS Architects

AEDAS is another large British company.[15] It is centered in Hong Kong and London, including large branches in New York and Beijing. In 2007, AEDAS had revenues of almost $150 million and more than 1300 employees. Like Gensler and Foster, it

12   *www.gensler.com*
13   Gensler (2008). *Annual Report 2007.*
14   Eurostat. European Business. Facts and Figures, 383. *www.fosterandpartners.com.*
15   *www.aedas.com.* Eurostat, European Business. Facts and Figures, 387.

embraces all aspects of architecture, including design, interior, implementation and facility management as well as urban planning.

RMJM

RMJM is a third large and international British architectural company.[16] Its programmatic website presentation is characteristic of the multidisciplinary dimensions of the leading group of companies that gradually is consolidating international architecture: "RMJM is a UK-based, international architectural practice. Our design-led work connects people and places, context and culture to create dynamic modern architecture that enhances our daily lives. RMJM believes in a 'more than architecture' approach: a collaborative process encompassing planning, engineering, art and sustainable urban and landscape design". The RMJM clients are virtually the same as any other international architect-firm, namely corporate offices, airports, universities, governmental projects, community housing and urban planning etc. RMJM is a business of $100 million and 600 employees.

gmp

gmp von Gerkan, Marg und partner is a leading German architectural company.[17] Gmp has been involved in building projects for most German and some large international companies, governmental agencies and public institutions, including offices, airports, hospitals, malls, hotels, sports centers and apartments. In its philosophy, gmp states some vital characteristics of present architectural trends. Gmp is searching for 'simplicity and the creation of uniformity within variety and variety within uniformity'. Gmp wants to develop a design identity from the specific conditions of locations and task, rendering a structural order to its designs. In 2007, gmp had revenues of approximately $50 million and occupied 300 employees.

WECO

SWECO is the largest Nordic combined engineering and architectural company dealing with environmental, technical and architectural tasks.[18] Its architectural group had revenues of about $50 million in 2007 and occupied 300 employees. From its base

---

16   *www.rmjm.com*. Eurostat, European Business. Facts and Figures, 387.
17   *www.gmp-architekten.de*. Eurostat, European Business. Facts and Figures, 387.
18   *www.sweco.se*. Eurostat, European Business. Facts and Figures, 383.

in Sweden, SWECA has expanded its markets into other Scandinavian countries and into Eastern Europe and Russia.

Throughout West European countries are found many medium sized architect firms with a couple hundred employees and revenues of about $50 million, such as White Architects in Sweden and Danish C. F. Moller.[19] All these firms are expanding into neighboring countries and into emerging nations such as China.

Industrial and Graphic Design

While design of buildings and interiors were dealt with under the term 'architecture', the term 'design' includes mainly industrial design and graphic design, leaving fashion to be a field of its own. According to ISDA (Industrial Design Society of America) Industrial design may be defined as the 'service of creating and developing concepts and specifications that optimize the function, value and appearance of products and systems for the mutual benefit of both user and manufacturer'.[20] In this sense of the term 'industrial design', it is a dimension of virtually all manufactured parts of modern industrial societies. Industrial design is more or less the applied arts of the modern world. It is the synthesis of industrial engineering, economic forces and consumer behavior and culture that is put in commercially produced objects, most intended for personal use, which over time has become an increasing component of the material world.[21] Today, all products are designed from an engineering as well as an aesthetic perspective.

Industrial Design

As the industrial leader of the world since the early 20th century, industrial design is very much an American story.[22] But all other developed countries have followed suit and adopted the idea of adding extra values of function and aesthetics that corresponds to human behavior and appeals to changing human values. The story of industrial design began in the USA between the two World Wars when manufacturers increasingly

---

19   *www.white.se. www.cfmoller.com.*

20   *www.wikipedia.org*: 'Industrial design'. Industrial Designers Society of America: *www.idsa.org.*

21   Meikle, J. L. (2005). *Design in the USA*, 17. Oxford: Oxford University Press. Bürek, Bernhard E. (2005). *Design: History, Theory and Practice of Product Design*. Basel: Birkhäuser.

22   Votolato, Gregory (1998). *American Design in the Twentieth Century.* Manchester: Manchester University Press. Meikle, Design in the USA.

tried to differentiate their products by way of certain shapes and colors. In particular, they addressed the growing middle classes that demanded consumer durables such as cars, the most important durable, radios, and later on television, washing machines, vacuum cleaners, refrigerators, stoves, lighting, telephones and other electrical goods that invaded the households of the 1920s and 1930s. In addition, designed pots and pans, china and glasses, dinnerware, furnishings, and wallpaper became part of middle class homes. This was the initial marriage of industry and art. Lowey was one of the leading pioneers of industrial design. He started his famous design career in the 1930s, designing refrigerators for Sears, Roebuck and Co. and styling railway locomotives. The interaction of function, materials, style, and color was introduced.

The focus on industrial design became ever stronger in the postwar era. The material abundance of America and eventually all Westerners fueled the production of goods and the wish to differentiate products by way of design. Furthermore, modern lifestyles spread rapidly and required more functional and organic design, inspired by German and Scandinavian designers. This was most clearly seen in interior designs and furnishings, such as with the American furniture designer of the early postwar decades Herman Miller. American cars, however, continued to focus on interior comfort and exterior luxury.

Until the 1960s and 1970s, industrial design had first and foremost given shape to the machine age. The economic, political, social, and cultural upheavals and crises since the late 1960s indicated the end of Fordism, Keynesian Economics, and the traditional welfare state, however. The functionalism of modernism that so to speak had been the design expression of the industrial and governmental rationalism was about to give way to a different approach to human affairs. Increasingly, cultural significance crept into the design of industrial products. In the beginning, this trend was only marginal and overshadowed by the predominant trend of people to show off material abundance and functional elegance of, for example, the Scandinavian style.

The leftist and student movements of the 1970s dissociated themselves from commercialism, material abundance and the mismanagement of nature and human values. Counterculture values were being introduced into traditional corporate cultures. This was only one design trend, however. Scandinavian functionalism, Italian extravagance in colors and artificial materials added a mood of elegance and playfulness to it all. This was a reflection of multiple lifestyles that gradually began to replace the stylistic coherence that had marked American design. The decline of the American automobile industry in the 1970s was almost symbolic of the changing of the guard, as the automobile industry had been a vital part of industrial design throughout the 20th century.

The 1980s saw industrial design grow remarkably in importance. While design so far had been just a necessary part of product development and marketing, it became considered now as the key to industrial competitiveness. The well established American design profession of hundreds of consultant offices and thousands of in-house designers moved from the back seat to the front seat of the American industry as it sought to regain its international competitiveness. The business importance of design was seen in many cases. A famous international example of successful redesign was the introduction of Swatches that saved the Swiss watch industry.

Dissatisfaction with modernism affected architecture and city planning before it reached design in the 1980s. Quickly, designers of postmodern furniture and consumer goods abandoned any traditional notion of functionalism. Even the idea that there was one right form of each type of machine, or the importance of timeless perfection as the mark of good design, was all considered a bore and replaced by flashy, colorful designs. Instead of 'form follows function', the new ideal might be called 'form follows emotion'. The transition into the age of the computer and high-tech did not lead designers to worship technology as in the machine age. The importance of computers as a driving force behind social and cultural change was, so to speak, taken for granted. The high-tech style played with artificial forms, surfaces, and textures out of context, and put them in familiar arrangements serving as metaphor of something already known.

The consumer culture and technology was not simply rejected or criticized in the modernist tradition of looking for progress and a cultural regeneration capable of changing the world according to a rational design. It was a matter of broadening awareness, shaking things up and setting up fresh opportunities as well as creating warmness and making people feel good. A new language and ways of communication emerged that combined different materials and motives from many cultures and ages, a synthesis of function, fun, and inspiration emerged. As industrial designers were, so to speak, the humanizers of the machine and things for their users, they had to adapt to broad social and cultural changes that took place since the late 20th century. That included computers and the transition of the industrial age into an information age that stressed immaterial and intellectual labor instead of physical labor. So a computer had not just to be understandable, but also had to be considered a natural part of everyday life and therefore must be felt playful and personal, and above all welcoming.

The design of the Machintosh computer of the mid-1980s made it a true personal computer that was user-friendly and invited the user to play, too. The achievement of the original Mac was seamless integration of hardware and software and the user's simultaneous interaction with both. In the late 1990s, the new iMac design shook up the design world once more restoring the original Mac's integration of computer and monitor in a colorful translucent plastic surround. However, Apple's computers still suggested the coherence of the information age as a progressive extension of modernity. It was not a new vision but a realization of the fact that new techniques overlapped rather than replaced old techniques and offered new opportunities for all, not just for professionals.

By the mid-1990s, a new technology began to replace the physical computer, the Internet. Through millions of websites and webpages, every one of them consciously designed by someone, the digital and virtual age rapidly overtook the physical age of the computer. The opening of the cyberspace made millions of users proliferate in behavior and views that served to make a postmodern world even more fragmented. At the same time, rapid technological advances in software and communications capacity over the Internet made it possible to move easily from 3D images generated on the computer to actual physical prototypes of products intended for manufacturing and marketing. The immediacy of such digital designing, unmediated by model-makers or tool-and-die makers, was unprecedented. The profound gap between the designer and maker of the industrial age was about to disappear. Form and function might finally coalesce as the process of designing merged with the products of design. This integration might even include the user. The computer and the Internet turned the passive consumer into a personal creator of his own world, either as an individual or in relationship with designers and business units that introduced user based innovation. An explosive proliferation of subcultures spread across cyberspace and the real world and finally dissolved the modernist vision of rational, universal coherence. At the same time, however, globalization made the basis of products and the behavior and minds of people around the world converge, opening the road to cultural transitions across nations.

Graphic Design

Graphic design is the process of communicating visually, using text and images to present information or promote a message.[23] Graphic design practice embraces a range of skills and crafts, including typography, image development and page layout. Graphic design is applied in communication design and fine art. Like other forms of communication, graphic design often refers to both the process (designing) by which the communication is created, and the products (designs) such as creative solutions, imagery and multimedia compositions. Graphic design was traditionally applied to static printed media, such as books, magazines and brochures. Since the advent of the PC and interactive user interfaces, graphic design has been utilized in electronic media, often referred to as interactive design, or multimedia design.

---

23   *www.wikipedia.org*: 'Graphic design'.

In some sense, graphic design is as old as human kind, spanning from the caves of Lascaux to the neons of Times Square. The increasing commercialization of visual expressions and the digitalization of information and communication continue to blur the distinctions between advertising, graphic and fine art. Furthermore, they all share the same elements, theories, principles, practices and languages, and sometimes the same clients. While fine art may still keep some distinctive features, advertising and graphic art is converging to one visual way of marketing products.

Modern graphic design is a child of the industrial age. Just like fine art, modern design of the early 20th century was a reaction to the historical romanticism of the 19th century. With the breakthrough of mass production and the rational functioning of modern societies, human beings called for a new visual language. In graphic design, just as in industrial design, functionalism became the new visual language. Since the 1930s and particularly after World War II, a booming postwar economy in America created a vast demand for graphic design, mainly advertising and packaging. The emigration of many German Bauhaus designers to the USA brought its 'mass-produced' minimalism to America and applied it to create popular advertising and logo designs, including posters and corporate identity.

The reaction to minimalism, functionalism and the severity of modernistic design, and accordingly the origin of postmodern graphic design, came slowly in the 1960s and 1970s. Most of this reaction was marked by the anti-capitalist movements of those days. Critical designers claimed that design is not a neutral and value-free process and they rallied against the consumerist culture that was purely concerned with selling things and tried instead to introduce a humanist dimension into graphic design. Simultaneously, new features and styles began to appear in movie titles, posters, T-shirts, etc., such as the famous 1973 'I Love NY' ad campaign. In these cases, the graphic design was no longer simply a visual expression of the form. The visuality of products and communications appealed to people's feelings.

In the 1980s, graphic design experienced a true breakthrough, similar to industrial design. Within few years, the competitive importance of the visual side of the ad, the package, the consumer product, cars, airplanes, and other machines was realized and moved to the forefront of business. A graphic design dimension was added to all products and life. The arrival of the PC and desktop publishing and the introduction of graphic art software applications in the mid-1980s introduced a generation of designers to computer image manipulation and eventually 3D image creation that had previously been very difficult to do. Computer graphic design enabled designers to instantly see the effects of layout and typographical changes without using any ink in the process, and to simulate the effects of traditional media without requiring a lot of space. Still, in spite of all technological development, including the emergence and spread of the Internet since the 1990s, graphic design is based on the imagination and skill of designers.

Some of the well-known designers are the following: For decades, Paul Rand (died in 1996) designed many well-known corporate logo designs, including IBM, UPS and ABC.[24] Donald Young has since the 1950s specialized in the design of logotypes and trademarks for numerous American firms and organizations, including GE, Hilton Hotels, University of California, and Mattel Toys. The German designer Erik Spiekermann is known for his typefaces, including typefaces as parts of corporate design programs, such as ITC Officina. The American designer Paula Scher has designed many music album covers, along with British Peter Saville and American Stefan Sagmeister. British Alex Rutterford is known mainly for his music videos. Patrick Nagel (died 1984) was an American designer famous for many well-known commercial designs, such as the album cover of Duran Duran, and projects for Lucky Strike, Intel and Budweiser. Milton Glaser is best known for his Bob Dylan poster and 'I Love New York' logo. American Chip Kidd has designed many innovative book covers. Tibor Kalman (died in 1999) is best known for his work for Benetton Colors magazine and its focusing on multiculturalism and global awareness.

Karlssonwilker, Inc. is a New York City design firm founded in 2000 and staffed by young graphic designers Jan Wilker of Germany and Hjalti Karlsson of Iceland. The two met while working with Stefan Sagmester. Major clients include Warner Brothers, Universal Music, MTV, L'Oreal and Capital Records. British Alan Fletcher (died 2006) is known for several corporate logos, including Reuters and Novartis. Shepard Fairey is a contemporary American designer wellknown for posters, such as Walk the Line, and t-shirts, prints and CDs. Roger Cook, in Cook and Shanosky Associates, is a known American graphic designer that produces all kinds of corporate communications, such as corporate identity, advertising, annual reports and brochures, including for example IBM, Black & Decker, Volvo, AT & T, New York Times and Bell Atlantic. New Yorker Deanne Cheuk is a young designer and art director, as many graphic designers are, contributing to numerous magazines, including The New York Times Magazine, and corporations such as Nike and Sprint. Japanese Moori Chack is famous for his Chax product line, especially Gloomy Bear that is an antithesis to the cute animals of Disney. David Carson is a wellknown American designer, having worked for many international corporations, such as Pepsi Cola, Nike, Microsoft, Budweiser, Armani, American Airlines and Levi Strauss. British Neville Brody is known for his typefaces, record cover designs, newspaper and magazine designs, innovative packing

---

24   *www.wikipedi.org*: 'List of graphic designers'.

and corporate identity as well as his ability to create new visual languages. Saul Bass (died in 1996) is best known for his animated motion picture title sequences for some of Hollywood's greatest filmmakers, most notably Alfred Hitchcock, Otto Preminger, Stanley Kubrick and Martin Scorsese. He also designed the AT&T logo.

The Global Design Market

According to official statistics of the US, more than half a million people were employed in some kind of design work.[25] One-third worked in independent design companies, while two-thids were employed in large corporations. Just as in UK, the majority of American design firms are small with little international extension. Large numbers of designers are mainly concentrated in leading multinational corporations that provide transportation means, pharmaceutical products, foodstuffs, electronics, media and entertainment to the US and global markets. It is through these American corporations that industrial design has got its widespread importance. The number, and importance, of independent design companies is increasing however, as a consequence of the global outsourcing and growing use of external design competences. Similar to other nations, the official US statistics probably underestimate the total number of US designers and design companies. Design is as important in the US as in the UK. Based on the size of the US economy compared to the UK economy, the number of people occupied in US design might amont to almost 1 million, with a total turnover of at least $100 billion. That corresponds to just under one percent of US total GDP in 2005.

Worldwide the design industry is concentrated in the large industrial countries of North America, Western Europe, and Eastern Asia. The US includes some one-third of world total, as does Western Europe, and Japan about 10 percent. Almost three-quarters of the global design industry and market of an estimated $300 billion is based in the US, Japan, Germany, UK, France and Italy (Table 51). Just as in the US and UK, the majority of design activities take place in-house of large corporations, although independent design firms get an increasing share of the design market as a consequence of global outsourcing. Much design activity is concentrated in the metropolises of the world, such as New York, Los Angeles, London, Paris, Milan and Tokyo, with significant design centers in Berlin, Madrid, Antwerp, Amsterdam, Stockholm, Copenhagen, and Sydney, too, as well emerging centers in Moscow and Beijing.

---

25   USCensus Bureau (2007). 'Design Services'. *Statistical Abstracts*: *www.census.gov*.

TABLE 51

The Global Design Services Market in $bn, 2001-2010

	2001	2005	2010
North America	95	106	127
USA	90	100	120
Canada	5	6	7
Western Europe	100	110	125
UK	20	23	27
Germany	20	20	22
France	18	20	22
Italy	18	20	22
Rest of Western Europe	24	27	32
Asia Pacific	65	72	83
Japan	30	32	34
China	10	12	15
South Korea	10	10	12
Australia	5	6	7
Rest of Asia Pacific	10	12	15
Rest of the World	10	12	15
Total	270	300	350

Source: *www.designcouncil.org. www.bls.gov. www.census.gov.* Estimates.

Design is a growing national and global business. Encompassing architectural, graphic, industrial, and fashion design services, it is estimated to grow from $270 billion in 2001 to $300 billion in 2005 and $350 billion in 2010. Western and Japanese companies and markets will continue to dominate world design, although emerging markets such as China, Russia, India and Brazil will increase their market share from a low level.

The Global Design Industry

UK

To my knowledge, the UK is the only country that has performed a thorough investigation of its design industry.[26] The UK research covers all designers, including not only design consultancies but also in-house teams that are not included in official statistics, as well as freelances. The many designers that are self-employed and freelances are also under-represented in official statistics. Consequently, the total number of consultancies is far higher than previously estimated. The official category of speciality design has also critically important exclusions. For example, it does not cover product and industrial, or web and exhibition design. Furthermore, this investigation includes designers with supervisory responsibilities, such as design managers in in-house design teams and creative directors in design consultancies.

The UK research uses these definitions:
- Design business: design consultancies and freelances, and in-house design teams in non-design businesses with 100 or more employees
- Freelance: freelances and all other design partnerships and businesses that do not employ staff other than the principals
- Large business: employing more than 250 people
- Medium business: employing 50 to 250 people
- Small business: employing fewer than 50 people
- SME: small and medium-sized enterprise employing fewer than 250 people.

The range of design disciplines has been grouped into a few relevant groups:
- Communications design: graphics, brand, print, information design, corporate identity
- Product and industrial design: consumer/household products, furniture, industrial design (automotive design, engineering design, medical products)
- Interior and exhibition design: retail design, office planning/workplace design, lighting, display systems, exhibition design
- Fashion and textiles design: fashion, textiles

---

26   UK Design Council (2006), *The Business of design. Design industry research 2005: www.design-council.org. uk.* All other investigations of national design industries fail to include more than companies registered as design firms, leaving out designers employed in corporations as well as many design consulting companies and small design firms that are not caught by the rough classifications of official statistics.

- Digital and multimedia design: website, animation, film and television idents, digital design, interaction design
- Other: advertising, aerospace design, building design, engineering design, landscape design, jewellery design, mechanical design, etc.

Design clients have been bracketed into the following key industry groupings:
- Primary, utilities and construction: agriculture, forestry and fishing, mining and quarrying, electricity, gas and water supply, sewage, refuse disposal and sanitation, building, transport and communication
- Manufacturing: fuel processing and production, manufacture of chemicals and man-made fibres, metal goods, engineering and vehicles industries, other manufacturing industries
- Professional business services: banking, finance and insurance, real estate, renting and business activities
- Retail, wholesale and leisure services: wholesale and retail trade, personal household goods, hotels and restaurants, other community, social and personal service activities.

The total British design sector in 2005 was made up of some 12,000 consultancies, some 47,000 self-employed, freelance and non-employing designers, and some 77,000 in-house designers in nearly 6,000 businesses with more than 100 employees. Some 185,000 people work in the design industry. They generated £11.6 billion in annual turnover in 2004-2005, equivalent to $23 billion. Almost one-third of all companies are located in London, including four out of ten large design consultancies. Two-thirds of all in-house designers work in private companies. In-house designers are more evenly spread across the country, although London has a disproportionately large share of these design teams. More than three-quarters of all design businesses have a turnover of less than £100.000 ($0.2 million) per year. Most designers are young men under 40 year. The UK design industry services clients in every major industrial sector. One in six design businesses say their main competitor is from outside the UK. Almost 9,000 designers left design businesses in 2004 but twice as many were recruited. Almost one-third of all businesses have been in business for less than three years. A lack of long-term perspective seems to prevail in the majority of design firms.

So, the UK design industry comprises mainly small, young businesses employing a handful of designers. Large design consultancies are relatively rare and the design industry is overwhelmingly characterized by very small businesses, particularly in interior and exhibition design, but less so in product and industrial design that has more medium-sized design businesses than average. In-house teams tend to be larger than consultancies. Half of in-house teams comprise five or more designers, while only a quarter of consultancies do so. Three percent of all companies in the design industry occupy more than 1000 employees with a turnover of more than £1 million ($2 million), 3 percent occupy 250 to 1000 employees with turnover between £0.5-1 million ($1-2 million), 2 percent occupy 50 to 250 employees with a turnover between £0.25-0.5 million ($0.5-1 million), 2 occupy percent 10 to 50 employees with a turnover between £0.1-0.25 million ($0.2-0.5 million) and 85 percent occupy less than 10 employees with turnover of less than £0.1 million ($0.2 million).

The UK design industry includes a wide range of disciplines. Designers are creating everything from consumer electronics to corporate identities, interiors to interactive interfaces and fabrics to Formula 1 cars. Many consultancies and freelances work across more than one discipline. For example, half of all businesses in communications also work in digital and multimedia design. In-house teams dominate product and industrial design. In other areas, design businesses generally work in just one discipline. Turnover in the three main groups are: Design consultancies: £5.1 billion ($10 billion), Freelance designers: £2.0 billion ($4 billion), and In-house design teams: £5.5 billion ($11 billion). Unfortunately, the investigation of the British design industry does not allow us to measure the size of each design group, such as industrial design and graphic design. Industrial design is by far the largest single part of the design industry, however, because it is working with all other industries.

IDEO

IDEO is one of the world's largest design companies.[27] Headquartered in California, IDEO has offices in other places in the USA, in the UK, Germany and China. In 2007, IDEO occupied c.500 employees that include experts within design, technology, social science and business strategy. By visualizing new ways of development, media and digital interaction, as well as supporting organizations in changing their culture and building new competencies to obtain continued innovation, IDEO provide consulting services to companies, governmental agencies and organizations within education and the social sector. IDEO's clients include the largest international corporations within several industries, such as Procter & Gamble, McDonald's, Nokia, SAP, BMW, and Airbus.

---

27 *www.ideo.com*. The strategies and methods of IDEO are thoroughly described by IDEO's general manager in Tom Kelley (2001). *The Art of Innovation*. New York: Random House. Tom Kelley (2005). *The Ten Faces of Innovation*. New York: Random House.

Design Continuum

Based in Massachusetts and with offices in Milan and Seoul, Design Continuum is another large international design consulting firm.[28] Design Continuum provides strategic and holistic design solutions to mostly large companies in sectors such as pharmaceutical, computer, and interactive industries. Its consulting is based on competences within design, social behavior, environment, corporate branding and business strategy. In 2007, Continuum occupied approximately 150 employees.

Smart Design

Smart Design is a large designer company, based in New York.[29] Just like the above-mentioned designer companies, Smart Design designs consumer products and brands and provides strategic and holistic design solutions mostly to large companies, including HP, Acer, Coco-Cola and Kellogg's.

Among other large design companies you find: fuseproject, ZIBA, Lunar Design, Pentagram, Herbst LaZar Bell (HLB), RKS Design, Antenna Design N.Y., and Ralph Appelbaum.[30] Most of these design firms are multidisciplinary, covering the total process of design support, while some have specialized in certain industries, such as Appelbaum in exhibitions and museums, and Antenna in transportation, computers and consumer electronics.

Fashion

The term 'fashion' usually applies to a prevailing mode of expression.[31] Inherent in the term is the idea that the mode will change more quickly than the culture as a whole. In this sense, fashion is a sort of art and cultural phenomenon that is common to many fields of human activity and thinking. Fashions change. They rise and they fall with the social dynamics of each age and fashion is an integral part of history, particularly Western history. Roughly, fashion changes with the pace of social development. The change of fashions, therefore, accelerated with the breakthrough of modern societies

---

28   *www.dcontinuum.com.*

29   *www.smartdesignusa.com.*

30   *www.fuseproject.com. www.ziba.com. www.lunar.com. www.pentagram.com. www.hlb.com. www.rks.design.com. www.antennadesign.com. www.raany.com.*

31   Smelser and Baltes. International Encyclopedia of the Social & Behavioral Sciences: 'Fashion'. *www.wikipedia.org:* 'Fashion'.

in the 20th century. Today, the global and rapid changes of developed countries make fashions change more often than ever. Although, fashion is part of many and eventually almost every part of present day societies, including such fields as music, dance, economics, politics, entertainment, management, etc., fashion has always been and is still mainly attached to clothing.

Just as all design industries, modern fashion design was an integral part of the breakthrough of mass production and mass consumption in the early 20th century.[32] This was not obvious in the beginning of fashion thinking and practice, because fashion originated in the new born Parisian 'haute-couture' that dressed the upper classes, mainly women, in fashionable and expensive costumes. As the middle classes of the expanding industrial societies also demanded modern clothing appropriate to their new urban lifestyles, a 'ready-to-wear' (or 'prêt-a-porter') dimension of fashion developed along side haute couture. Large British, German, French and American department stores quickly saw the commercial potential of the new Parisian haute-couture, too, and pretty much stole the designs and turned them into less expensive ready-to-wear clothes. Eventually, the growing demand for ready-to-wear fashion clothes created a distinction between the two modes of production and a growing market for ready-to-wear apparel in North America and Western Europe. However, the haute-couture did not disappear. On the contrary it became a fashionable art and business addressing the upper bourgeoisie and the new group of famous movie stars. At the same time, haute-couture developed into a high-profiled way of marketing fashion design. Instead of following the lead of customers as previous dressmakers used to do, the new designers were able to dictate to their customers what they should wear. This was the beginning as well as the breakthrough of modern fashion design.

Since the inter-war period, well-known fashion houses established themselves in the leading Western cities of Paris, London, Berlin, New York and Milan. A major figure of the pre-war age was the French Coco Chanel that promoted chic and progressive designs for women. Although menswear was never in the forefront of fashion, there was a growing mood of informality, too, in particular among the Americans. The true breakthrough of ready-made fashion design and industry did not come until the 1950s and 1960s, however. The booming Western societies brought welfare to the majority of people and now most of them wanted to dress-up in accordance with fashion. The Parisian haute-couture lost its grip of fashion. A fashionable way of dressing was part of the new rising incomes and democratization of life. People, especially women

---

32   Gertrud Lehnert (2000). *Geshichte der Mode des 20. Jahrhunderts.* Köln: Könemann (A History of 20th Century Fashion). English, Bonnie (2007). *A Cultural History of Fashion in the Twentieth Century: From the Catwalk to the Sidewalk.* New York: Palgrave-Macmillan. *www.wikipedia.org*: 'Fashion design'.

and the young ones, could choose freely among the growing number and versions of clothing that was marketed by the expanding ready-made apparel industry. Next in line, fashion diversified into shoes, handbags, jewelry and other so-called accessories that became an increasingly important part of a total outfit.

The relaxed and anti-consumption styles of the young cultural revolution of the 1960s and 1970s paved the way for a more diverse and often American ready-to-wear fashion style. Across the Atlantic, the internationalization of fashion increased and since the 1990s, fashion design was uplifted to even higher levels. The globalization and expanding economies of the developed as well as emerging countries of America, Europe and Asia Pacific, created new grounds for ready-to-wear fashion. Everybody looked to the leading and dynamic centers of fashion in the Western capitals, inspiring new designers in smaller developed countries to take advantage of a growing demand for fashion clothes. In doing so, each group of designers added new national features to the global fashion markets. For example, the elegant and colorful styles of Italy were accompanied by the relaxed and comfortable fashion of Scandinavia and the eastern inspired fashion design of Japan.

At the turn of the new millennium, the industry of fashion design became increasingly an integral part of large global fashion corporations. These corporations did not just expand geographically into all major markets of the world and reorganize on a global scale. They diversified into still more fields of outfitting and modern lifestyles, including clothing, shoes, jewelry, handbags, watches, glasses, perfume, cosmetics, etc. And the diversification did not stop here. They turned their interest towards leisure, luxury, gastronomy and other parts of modern lifestyles that increasingly came under the spell of fashion. In the background of these worldwide consolidating corporations, room was left for small and innovative fashion designers to develop and market their original designs to an audience that was highly receptive to innovations.

The Global Textile and Clothing Sector

The textile and clothing sector is one of the largest economic sectors of the world. In developed as well as developing countries, millions of people are employed in textile and clothing companies. The textile industry played a crucial role in the industrial revolution of Western societies in the 19th century and today it is particularly important to enable a 'take-off' in developing countries. In developed countries, the textile and clothing industries have retained much of their economic importance. Globalization has created a new kind of internationally interlinked relation between the various links of the textile and clothing supply chain. Based on cooperation and competition, an increasing flow of goods is imported and exported across all regions and nations of the world.

After more than forty years of import quotas, trade in the textile and clothing sector was liberalized from 1 January, 2005.[33] Liberalization was controversial because both textile and clothing contribute to employment in many developed countries, particularly in regions where alternative jobs may be difficult to find, such as parts of Southern Europe and Southern USA. On the other hand, textiles and clothing are among the sectors where developing countries have the most to gain from multilateral trade liberalization. In fact, the starting point of the global liberalization of trade in the mid-1990s was, so to speak, a deal between developing and developed countries. By accepting to include services and intellectual property rights into this so-called 'Uruguay Round', the developed countries accepted a gradual liberalization of trade in textiles and clothing to be fulfilled by 2005.

Textiles and clothing are closely related both technologically and in terms of trade policy. Textiles provide the major input to the clothing industry, creating vertical linkages between the two, but textiles are also widely used in other industries such as the manufacturing of furniture and cars. International trade in the two sectors is regulated by the multilateral Agreement on Textiles and Clothing (ATC within WTO), while bilateral and regional trade agreements typically link the two sectors through rules of origin accompanying preferential market access.

At the micro level, the two sectors are increasingly integrated through vertical supply chains that also involve the distribution and sales activities. Indeed, the retailers in the clothing sector increasingly manage the supply chain of the clothing and textiles sectors. This development probably started with the establishment of shopping malls such as Wal-Mart in the United States in the 1970s. Wal-Mart insisted that suppliers implemented IT for exchange of sales data, adopted standards for product labeling and methods of material handling. By ensuring quick replenishment of apparel, it allowed retailers to offer a broad variety of fashion clothes without holding a large inventory. This approach has spread throughout the industry in the United States as well as elsewhere (and to other industries), shifting the competitive advantage of suppliers from being mainly a question of production costs to becoming a question of costs in combination with lead time and flexibility. In turn, this development has favored suppliers close to the major markets, including regional agreements giving these suppliers preferential access to the market. As a consequence, Latin America has indeed gained market shares in the United States at the expense of Asia, while Central and Eastern Europe have gained market shares in the EU. Even though China and India is likely

---

33 Nordås, Hildegunn K. (2004). *The Global Textile and Clothing Industry Post the Agreement on Textiles and Clothing: www.wto.org.*

to increase their market shares, clothing is increasingly considered a perishable good where time to market matters. This will be disadvantageous for producers in more remote locations, particularly in fashion-segments of the clothing industry.

The textile and clothing sectors can be seen as a supply chain consisting of a number of discrete activities. Increasingly, the supply chain from sourcing of raw materials via design and production to distribution and marketing is being organized as an integrated production network where the production is sliced into specialized activities and each activity is located where it can contribute the most to the value of the end product.

The Global Fashion and Apparel Market Segments

Fashion apparel may be separated in the following market segments.[34] 'Haute Couture' is the so-called 'make-to-measure' fashion where each piece of clothing is commissioned. This is the highest-priced category of fashion. Today, haute couture is more like art or 'show pieces' than real 'wearable fashion'. Haute couture is for the most part often driven by prominent creative persons in one of the large traditional fashion houses, such as Karl Lagerfeld (Gucci) or John Galliano and Heidi Slimane (Christian Dior). Haute couture is made for rich people, including movie stars, representing mainly marketing value to these houses.

Below haute couture, 'prêt-a-porter', or 'ready-to-wear' suits are the first level of industrially produced clothing. Ready-to-wear clothes are designed by the major fashion houses in limited numbers. Often ready-to-wear clothes are called 'high fashion' collections, that twice a year point to the new fashion trends. Ready-to-wear clothes are often designed by well-known designers that outline the seasonal models that are being further elaborated by the staff of the fashion houses, including for example Armani, Jacobs and Prada. In addition to their main collections, they also market cheaper versions of their design. Just like haute couture, ready-to-wear houses are concentrated in the fashion capitals of the world.

At the mid-high priced level just below prêt-a-porter, one finds the 'premium' market segment. Mid-high priced clothes are being produced in larger numbers than prêt-a-porter. A team of designers develop the designs that are presented at retail stores. Mid-high priced companies include for example Lacoste, Levi Strauss and Brooks

---

34   FORA (2005). *Brugerdreven innovation i dansk mode* (User-Driven Innovation in Danish Fashion). Copenhagen: FORA.

Brothers, but companies addressing this market segment are found in all primary and secondary fashion centers of the world.

The truly mass produced fashion clothes are found at the 'mid-price' market segment. These mid-price companies use retail stores of their own as well as shop-in-shops in chain stores. Unlike high-priced fashion, mid-priced collections are mainly based on successive replacement of products rather than seasonal renewals. Designers in these companies are rarely known, but to promote the companies and in an emerging attempt to upgrade towards higher segments, famous designers such as Karl Lagerfeld (H & M) are sometimes hired to design an individual collection. Mid-price companies include for example Gap, H & M, Etam, Marks & Spencer and Bestseller. To a high degree, mid-price companies collect information on sales and consumer preferences as well as emerging consumer behavior as a basis of innovation.

'Budget' is the low-price market segment based on mass production and mass distribution of clothes. Often it is large retail stores such as Wal-Mart, Target, and Carrefour that organize the whole supply chain from manufacturing in low-cost countries to sales in their own stores.

To meet changing consumer demands, all segments are seeking to upgrade to higher levels of fashion: Budget to Mid-price and Mid-price to Premium and Premium to High fashion and High fashion to Haute couture.

The Global Fashion Industry

Fashion used to be restricted to clothes, but within recent years, fashion has spread to virtually all aspects of personal apparel. It includes bags, jewelry, watches, glasses, perfumes, cosmetics, and even luxury wines and alcohols. Sports equipment has been caught by the extension of fashion trends, too. For instance in 2007, PPR the world's second largest fashion company acquired the large German sports equipment company Puma. The enormous expansion of fashion into more and more fields of human life makes it difficult to measure the fashion industry, separating it from the many related sub-sectors that are being gradually included in the fashion industry. Although functions clearly are important to products such as watches and glasses, the fashion value added to these goods has become crucial to their market value. In the end, all the above-mentioned products marketed by large fashion corporations are fashion-driven and would be unsaleable without their fashion design and image.

Luxury may also be considered part of the fashion industry.[35] In the last twenty

---

35   Luxury Briefing, July-August, 2006: *www.luxury-briefing.com*.

years, the luxury industry has witnessed the greatest transformation of its history. It evolved from an artisan activity to a genuine industry and from family-owned businesses into publicly quoted global organizations. The luxury world has become a much larger and more complex marketplace than it used to be. The constant increase of wealth in Western societies and access to more disposable income, and the rise of a wealthy class in emerging markets as well as the invention of the Internet have created an environment that offers endless opportunities for luxury brands.

A luxury good, in contrast to normal goods, is a good for which demand increases more than proportionally as income rises, and in reverse drops in demand in the case of declining income.[36] Certain manufactured goods attain the status of 'luxury goods' due to their design, quality, durability or performance that are remarkably superior to the comparable substitutes. Thus, virtually every category of goods available on the market includes a subset of similar products whose 'luxury' is marked by better quality and appearance in all respects. There are also goods that are perceived as luxurious by the public, simply because they tend to signify the purchasing power of those who acquire them and as such assume the role of status symbols. A luxury brand is a brand under which the majority of its products can be called luxury goods. LMVH is the largest luxury good producer in the world with over fifty brands, including Louis Vuitton. Other luxury market leaders include PPR and Richemont. These luxury corporations include all or most of the above mentioned parts of the fashion industry, including apparel, footwear, accessories, jewelry, cosmetics, perfume, exclusive wine and alcohol.

Apparel fashion drives the fashion accessories.[37] Accessories such as bags, belts, scarves, jewelry, hosiery, etc. change their look as clothing fashion changes. In recent years, accessories have become an ever more vital part of the fashion industry. Personal apparel is surrounded by more and more accessories which are considered a necessary part of dressing, because they define the style and character of the wearer, in particular women while men's fashion is changing much less.

The design, production and marketing of fashion accessories are not a single business, but several. Each category of accessories is produced in its own industry, and these industries are as diverse as the merchandise itself. Some, such as shoes and hosiery, are large and dominated by big producers. Others, such as gloves, handbags, jewelry, scarves, and millinery are the domain of small firms. The accessories industries as a whole, however, do have several elements in common:

---

36 *www.wikipedia.org*: 'Luxury good'.
37 Kitty G. Dickerson (2000). *Inside the Fashion Business.* 7th Ed., 323. New Jersey: Prentice Hall.

-   All are extremely responsive to fashion and quick to interpret incoming trends, and there success depends on how well they reflect the look of the apparel with which they will be worn
-   All present a minimum of two new seasonal lines a year
-   All domestic accessory manufacturers, as is the case with other segments of the fashion industry, are confronted with increasing competition from imports
-   Almost all major accessory producers have entered licensed agreements with leading apparel designers to produce and market styles bearing the designer's name.

Industry revenues and retail sales in the fashion industry are huge. They include fashion clothing for men, women and children, as well as shoes, accessories, jewelry, cosmetics and luxury goods. Total revenues amount to several hundred billion dollars. In 2000, total US clothing, shoes and accessories spending exceeded $200 billion and cosmetics about $50 billion.[38] Total world fashion spending might be an estimated $750 billion, one-third in North America, one-third in Western Europe and one-third in the rest of the world.

As mentioned, the fashion industry may be divided into three market segments. At the high-end, you find luxury and exclusive ready-to-wear clothing as well as accessories, jewelry, cosmetics and wine and liquor. Leading corporations include LVMH, PPR and Richemont. The mid-price segment includes the largest share of fashion companies around the world, such as Gap and Levi Strauss in the US, Debenhams and Marks & Spencer in UK, Hugo Boss in Germany, Zara in Spain and H & M in Sweden. The mid-price segment may be subdivided into the somewhat more expensive premium brand (Hugo Boss) and cheaper mid-price (H & M). At the low-end of so-called budget companies, you find the huge department stores of the world, such as Wal-Mart, Carrefour and Tesco.

LVMH

French based LVMH (Louis Vuitton. Moët Hennesy) is the world's largest fashion corporation, or rather world leader in fashion luxury.[39] In 2005, LVMH had revenues of nearly $26 billion and in 2007. 40 percent came from fashion and accessories, including watches and jewelry, 15 percent from perfume and cosmetics, 25 percent from wine

---

38   Dickerson. Inside the Fashion Business, 210, 283, 325, 352.
39   *www.lvmh.com*. LVMH (2008). *Annual Report 2007: www.lvmh.com*.

and liquor and 25 percent from selective retailing. In geographic terms, 15 percent of sales were in France, 22 percent in the rest of Europe, 26 percent in US, 17 percent in Japan and 7 percent in the rest of the world.

LMVH was formed in 1987, when leather goods producer Louis Vuitton merged with luxury wine and liquor producer Moët Hennessy. In 1996, LVMH merged with the Dior luxury fashion house that became a leading shareholder. Since 1987, the holding company LMVH has merged with more than sixty companies and luxury brands, developing a global luxury and fashion conglomerate.

With LVMH, fashion and luxury have become fused. LVMH addresses the market segment that wants the "most refined qualities of Western 'Art de Vivre' around the world. LCMH is synonymous with both elegance and creativity. Our products, and the cultural values they embody, blend tradition and innovation, and kindle dream and fantasy". The company is dependent on its creative resources, its unique brands and technological innovation. LMVH's business units are based on well-known brands often with a long history.

Within the largest business unit 'Fashion & Leather Goods', Louis Vuitton is the lead name. Louis Vouitton originated in the 19th century as a producer of leather goods for travel such as suitcases, bags and accessories. In modern times, Louis Vuitton diversified into ready-to-wear apparel, shoes, watches and jewelry. Louis Vuitton's image of excellence is reflected in its association with major events such as the America's Cup. Louis Vuitton has several manufacturing units around the world, an international logistic center, hundreds of exclusive shops in more than fifty countries, although most of its eleven thousand employees are occupied in France.

The Louis Vuitton business unit includes several well-known brands, such as French Celine, Kenzo, Givenchy, Spanish Loewe, American Marc Jacobs and Donna Karan, British Thomas Pink, Italian Fendi, StefanoBi and Emilio Pucci. All of these companies started within leather goods or ready-to-wear clothes. From this starting point, they expanded internationally since the 1970s and diversified into a wide portfolio of fashion and accessories. Since the late 1980s, when they were acquired by LVMH, they all continued under their original brand.

Christian Dior in Paris is the principal brand of the 'Perfume & Cosmetics' business unit. Since the Second World, Dior has been a leading provider of perfumes and cosmetics to women. Just like other fashion and luxury houses, Dior expanded internationally and diversified into ready-to-wear apparel and accessories, besides its increasingly successful brands of perfume and cosmetics. In addition to Dior, many other perfumes and cosmetics brands are included in the LVMH corporation, such as Guerlain, Givency, Kezon, La Broche et Dupont, BeneFit Cosmetics, Fresh, Makeup For Ever, Acqua di Parma and Perfumes Loewe.

In the somewhat smaller 'Watches & Jewelry' business unit, TAG Heuer is the great brand. TAG Heuer has been a leading Swiss watch maker for almost one-hundred-and-fifty years, producing world famous luxury watches and advanced sports watches and chronographs. TAG Heuer is corporate partner and official timekeeper of the Team McLaren Mercedes in Formula One, partnering with world number one golfer Tiger Wood as well as other leading partnerships. Zenith is a similar well-known Swiss watch brand included in the LVMH corporation, including luxury watches marketed by Dior, Fred and Chaumet in Paris, Omas in Bologna, and De Beers in London.

The 'Selective Retailing' business unit (Distribution Sélective in French) is based in San Francisco. Since the 1960s, this group has created a leading position within the international travel business in the Asia Pacific region, selling liquor, tobacco, and cosmetics at airports, large hotels and restaurants as well as on board cruise lines of Carnival and Royal Caribbean. Cooperating in particular with Japanese tour operators and American cruise lines, the retailing group has built a large business in the Asia Pacific region.

Since the 18th century, Moët & Chandon has been one of the world's favorite champagnes, including for example the Veuve Cliquout. Moët & Chandon also includes the famous brandy Hennessy.

Placed at the high-price end, LVMH competes with the two other leading luxury and fashion conglomerates, French PPR and Swiss Richemont.

PPR

PPR (Pinault-Printemps-Redoute) is a French international holding company, specializing in luxury, fashion and retailing similar to LVMH.[40] PPR started in the timber and building material businesses in the 1960s. In the early 1990s, PPR moved into retail, especially since the take-over in 1994 of La Redouce and Fnac. It continued to expand into retailing by merging with an increasing number of retail chains, including home furnishing, books and magazines, sports, home shopping in Europe and the US. PPR entered the luxury and fashion goods sector in 1999 by acquiring the world famous brand Gucci, including Yves Saint Laurent and YSL Beauté and Sergio Rossi. Since the turn of the century, PPR has continued to build and expand its multi-brand luxury group and its strong positions in retailing. Mergers in luxury and fashion included Bottega Venta and Balenciaga and PPR signed partnership agreements with fashion houses Stella McCartney and Alexander McQueen. Based on the world famous Gucci Group

---

40   *www.ppr.com.* PPR (2008). *Annual Report 2007: www.ppr.com.*

as well as other well-known brands, PPR has established a strong global presence in the high-growth luxury goods market. In retail, PPR enjoys leading positions in the more stable and mature consumer markets, such as fashion, accessories and beauty care in shops around the world. Half of its revenues stem from France, and half from the other developed markets in North America, Western Europe and Asia Pacific.

In 2007, PPR had revenues of $25 billion. 20 percent of revenues came from luxury goods and 80 percent from retail.

The core of PPR's fashion and luxury sector is the Italian fashion house Gucci. Gucci started as a producer of leather goods between the two world wars. After the Second World War, Gucci became probably the world's most famous luxury brand. The Gucci company expanded internationally throughout Western Europe, North America and Asia Pacific. Since the 1970s, Gucci started a process of diversification into clothing, accessories, perfumes and cosmetics, including gradually the whole portfolio of fashion. Internal family and economic problems in the late 1990s made Gucci sell to PPR.

PPR's large retail group includes Conforama, the number one in furnishings and home appliances in France and number two in the world. Fnac is a leading French and international retail store of books, CDs and DVDs as well as technological and multimedia products. CFAO is a leading distributor of automobiles and pharmaceutical products in Africa and French overseas departments and territories. Redcats is number three world wide in home shopping, based on ready-to-wear fashion clothes, with La Redoute, the leading French women's ready-to-wear retailer, as its flagship.

Through its Gucci Group, PPR is targeting the high-price market segment and through its retail group the mid-price segments. In 2007, PPR made a remarkable merger, when acquiring German sports clothing and equipment company PUMA. PUMA the high-profiled sports brand strengthens PPR's position in the sporty styles clothing sector and makes it more visible in the market.

Richemont

Headquartered in Geneve, Richemont is the third leading global luxury holding company.[41] In 2007, it had revenues of $4 billion. Richemont was founded in 1988 by the South African billionaire Anton Rupert. Since then, Richemont developed into a multi-brand luxury company by way of several acquisitions. Its core business is watches and jewelry, including companies such as Cartier, Van Cleef & Arpels, Piaget,

---

41   *www.richemont.com*. Richemont (2008). *Annual Report 2007.*

Vacheron Constantin and Baume et Mercier. Half its sales stem from jewelry, one-fourth from watches and the rest from writing instruments, leather and accessories, etc. In geographic terms, 42 percent of revenues come from Europe, 22 percent for Asia Pacific, 21 percent from America and 15 percent from Japan. Richemont sells its products from several hundred of its own shops as well as through franchise partners. With the exception of Chloé, Richemont is not established in clothing fashion. In 2007, Richemont and Ralph Lauren formed a joint venture, the Polo Ralph Lauren and Richemont Watch and Jewellery Company.

Armani and Other Fashion Houses

Based on fashion clothing, the core of modern fashion, several companies compete in the upper end of the mid-price market segment, premium. That include among others Armani, Hugo Boss, Ralph Lauren and Tommy Hilfiger. The line between these fashion houses and the luxury segment upwards and the mid-segments downwards is no longer as sharp as it used to be. The mid-segment includes such fashion houses as Gap, Debenhams, Marks & Spencer, Zara and H & M.

The Italian designer Giorgio Armani broke through in the 1970s with luxury collections for men and women.[42] Since then, Armani has created several internationally well-known fashion lines. Just like other fashion houses, Armani expanded internationally and diversified into an increasing portfolio of fashion, accessories and personal care products, including cosmetics and perfume. Armani established restaurants in Milan, New York and other cities, too, for providing a unique gastronomic experience. From his luxury starting point, Armani moved into the much larger markets of ready-to-wear, taking advantage of his strength in an increasing number of sectors. Since the turn of the century, the Armani strategy aimed at leading not only international fashion but in a wider sense to be a lifestyle trend setter across multi-sectors, at the cost of watering-down the brand, however.[43] In 2007, Armani had revenues of $3 billion.

Ralph Lauren is connected with the Polo label.[44] He established his fashion company in New York in 1967 by acquiring the Polo label. Since the 1970s, he increasingly diversified his brand into a wide collection of men's, women's and children's clothing as well as inventory design, accessories and perfume. He aimed at redesigning the American fashion style into something exclusive and refined. During the 1990s, the expanding sports style was integrated more and more into his products and Ralph

---

42   *www.giogioarmani.com.*
43   VentureRepublic (2007). *Giorgio Armani – the Ultimate Fashion Brand: www.venturerepublic.com.*
44   *www.ralphlauren.com.*

Lauren became the official provider of clothing for the American team in America's Cup. The strategy is to extend the Ralph Lauren brand into a global lifestyle brand. In 2007, Ralph Lauren had revenues of $4 billion.

German Hugo Boss markets a men and women collection in business and relaxed styles.[45] It is an international company selling its products from thousands of points of sale in one hundred countries. Boss had revenues in 2007 of $2 billion.

Tommy Hilfiger in New York is a fashion house of similar size as Hugo Boss.[46] Hilfiger has diversified into sports clothing, shoes, sun glasses, perfumes, bags and watches.

In the low-mid-price segment, American Gap is one of the largest firms.[47] Its several thousand shops in North America, Western Europe and Japan sell men's, women's and children's fashion clothes brands such as Gap, Banana Republic and Old Navy. In 2007, Gap had revenues of $16 billion, the majority of which was based in North America. Gap's products are at the low-end of mid-price, coming close to budget-level.

Zara, H & M, Marks & Spencer are the three large West European mid-price fashion houses, based in Spain, Sweden and UK, respectively with revenues in 2007 around $10 billion.[48] Like Gap, these three companies are very much based on their own retail stores around the world, mainly Zara and H & M, while Marks & Spencer is mostly British based. They address women primarily but their collections cover men and children, too. Below the size of these three companies, you find several medium sized fashion houses such as Bestseller in Denmark ($2 billion in revenues), Van Heusen in the US ($2 billion in revenues), Debenhams in UK ($3 billion in revenues).

Finally, the budget segment includes the huge department stores of the world, including Wal-Mart, Carrefour and Tesco. They organize all parts of the value chain themselves, manufacturing, logistics and sales. Just as the mid-segment in one way is catching-up to the high-price segment, the budget segment is catching-up to the mid price segment. More and more people want fashion clothes, but most want them as cheap as possible. This discount movement is also the reason for a flourishing black market of fake designer clothes, accessories, watches, sun-glasses, etc., mostly produced in China – the global value of which is huge.

---

45   www.hugoboss.com.
46   www.tommy.com.
47   www.gap.com.
48   www.zara.com. www.hm.com. www.marksandspencer.com.

Fine Art

There is no authoritative definition of art. In this context, art is defined as 'fine art'. 'Fine art' includes visual arts such as painting, sculpture, and printmaking, excluding performing arts that are dealt with above.[49] The word 'fine' denotes that the object of fine art is art itself. Contrary to applied arts such as craft and design, fine art is not characterized by any clear usefulness. Art may be defined as pieces of work made with the intention of stimulating the human mind and senses, and the quality of artwork is assessed by the impact it has on people. 'Masterpieces' of art are often highly stimulating to the human mind.

The line between fine art and applied art is not as clear as it may seem, however. Some pieces of applied art such as furniture, lightning, ceramics and other design products have become classics and put into museums and/or traded, and just as high value has been attributed to some pieces of fine art that end up in museums and/or traded at auctions. Even fine art often has goals other than pure creativity. The purpose of art may be to communicate political or philosophical ideas, but fine art is also commercialized, and today this is increasingly the case. Many artists work as designers, too. Furthermore, artists have to make a living and in the end, artwork is created to be sold. Even pre-modern artists made their artwork for money, hired by members of the upper classes to create paintings, sculptures, castles, churches, etc. It makes sense, however, to keep the distinction between fine art and applied art, although it is hard to draw a sharp line between the two of them – probably because of greater aesthetic and historic value and less functional value in fine art compared to applied pieces of art.

Fine art is no divine piece of work. It is marked by its time and its purpose. In pre-industrial ages, art was made to praise the Lord or the commissioners of a painting, a sculpture or a building. The artists of the early industrial age of the 19th century were primarily concerned with the ideas of truth and beauty. With the breakthrough of the mass production and mass consumption of modern societies and the horrors of World War I in the early 20th century, art lost, so to speak, its ideals and innocence. Art became critical of modern societies and its means of human destruction in war and work. Life was meaningless and absurd, as many artists liked to present it after another disastrous World War. During the 1960s and 1970s, some artists engaged themselves in the anti-capitalist movements of the time. Art became political.

As early as the 1980s, however, many artists were captured by postmodernism and contributed to make this new trend emerge. Postmodernism has many faces and

---

49   Smelser and Baltes. International Encyclopedia of the Social & Behavioral Sciences: 'Art'. *www.wikipedia. org*: 'Art' and 'Fine art'.

cannot be given one clear and all-inclusive definition, except maybe as a reaction to modernism. In art, it was no longer a matter of cultivating one big idea or story. There were many stories to tell and they could be told and mixed as wished. Furthermore, the seriousness and darkness of modernism was replaced with warm and gay colours. Life was not so bad after all. This was one kind of post modern art. Another trend in postmodern art was the adoption of relativist and nihilist ideas that dismantled the enlightenment project of modernism. To some of these artists as to other people, progress in living conditions and democracy was no longer an option. At the same time, modernism did not disappear in art and some considered postmodernism to be just a kind of 'late modernism' that brightened up modernism to suit the conditions of another age. Since the turn of the millennium, the relativism and nihilism of postmodernism seem to have vanished, however, facing the realities of a globalizing world. Increasingly, fine art has become a part of life, just as design and other creative expressions of the human mind.

Fine artists are painters, sculptors, glassmakers, ceramists, and the like, that produce works of art they try to sell or as commissioned tasks. An increasing number of buildings have been decorated by artists, including new churches, concert halls, office buildings, governmental buildings, universities, housing quarters, etc. Decorations may include sculptures, facades, windows, and interior paintings.

Fine art is not just made for the sake of pure art. It is also a business and a market. The fine art market is unusual in that it deals in original works that are unique or rare. Although an increasing number of new pieces of art are made to meet a growing demand for art as decoration and inspiration in open places, company buildings, offices and households, the fine art market is to a high degree a second-hand market.[50] Whereas the whole point of all other experience industries is to multiply and sell as many copies as possible, the art dealer's objective is to emphasize scarcity. As a result, the purchaser of a piece of art normally buys only the object and not the copyright to it. The artist retains the copyright which is secured by his signature. Unlike the US, artists in the European art market qualify for a percentage of the sale price, each time a piece of art is sold. In some cases, however, copies of works of art are made. That is when publishers, for example, make posters of a painting, involving fees for copyright.

The fine art market may be subdivided into two parts, the primary art market of new works of art, and the secondary art market dealing with second hand pieces of art, including antiquarian books, antiquities, paintings, drawings, etc. While sales of new art are often based on commission or sold through galleries, most secondary pieces of

---

50   Howkins. Creative Industries, 91-93.

art are traded at auctions. Leading auctioneers are Christies, the world's largest auctioneer, and Sotherby, and Bonhams & Butterfields. Art dealing is a business done by art dealers. In recent years, the price of works of art has been rising as a consequence of growing demand for art. The low barriers to entry and the low start-up costs allow many thousands of dealers to operate, some of them just over the Internet. That art is a big business may be seen by the French Groupe Serveur's Artprice.com database that includes 370,000 artists, more than 2 million works of art, 21 million auction prizes, 270,000 auction catalogues and 2,900 auction houses around the world.[51] It is the private art market that is expanding, and this includes rich people who go for the very expensive paintings and other pieces of art, the many medium-priced works of art, and the larger art market in the low end. Art is not exclusively for art collectors. Art has become a part of people's surroundings in their houses and at their working places.

Overlapping the commercial market is the stately world of museums and galleries with collections of paintings and other kinds of art. Their main business is normally to guard the heritage and celebrate new work. Most museums and many galleries around the world are based on governmental funding or other forms of support, because they take care of the national heritage and are considered to be of unique cultural value. The largest museums of the world, also based on the number of visitors, are the Louvre in Paris, British Museum in London and the Museum of Modern Art in New York. All over the world, art museums are being upgraded. Even medium-sized towns invest in building and creating fine museums of art, because they are considered important tourist attractions.

Works of art are mostly sold at auctions and through galleries. The professional market of art is very much dominated by New York and London. Almost three-quarters of the world market of art is concentrated in these two cities. Buyers from other countries often buy through a dealer in one of these two cities. The next largest centres are Paris and Geneva. The world's largest auction house is Christie's in London with revenues of $5 billion.[52] Christie's global sales also include other items than works of art, including exclusive jewellery, cars and wines. Christie's has salesrooms around the world in such places as New York, Los Angeles, Paris, Milan, Amsterdam, Geneva, Hong Kong, Tel Aviv and Dubai.

The US market is the largest and most dynamic art market in the world (Table 52). There are a quarter of a million artists and an even larger group of people working in

---

51   *www.artprice.com.*
52   *www.christies.com.*

administrative and management jobs in galleries and museums. The total global fine art market was estimated at $27 billion in 2001, $32 billion in 2005, with a projected $40 billion in 2010. In 2005, the US art market was worth about $13 billion, almost half the world market. The UK art market is the next largest market with its $7 billion. France, the rest of Western Europe (except Germany and Italy), Japan, the rest of the developed world (Canada, Oceania, South Korea, Hong Kong and Singapore) and the developing and emerging world (China, India, Russia, Brazil, etc.) are third with each $2 billion, and Germany and Italy with each $1 billion in fourth place. Except for France and Italy, all other regions are likely to increase sales in fine art through 2010.

TABLE 52

The Global Fine Art Market in $bn, 2001-2010

	2001	2005	2010
USA	12	13	14
UK	6	7	8
France	2	2	2
Germany	1	1	2
Italy	1	1	1
Rest of Western Europe	2	2	3
Japan	1	2	3
Rest of Developed World	1	2	3
Developing and emerging World	1	2	4
Total	27	32	40

Souce: Kusin & Company: *www.kusin.com. www.artprice.com.* Estimates.

The activities of American art dealers may illustrate the nature of the art market and its activities, including mainly the professional market that addresses collectors.[53] Dealers may be distinguished from auctioneers and art consultants by their financial commitment to art, artists and collectors of art. This commitment fosters a deep knowledge of particular fields of art. There are as many different types of dealers as there are types of art to collect. Primary-market dealers identify new talent. These dealers regularly visit artists' studios and participate in international art fairs. Primary-dealers also function as supporters of contemporary artists by providing stipends and encouragement.

---

53   *www.artdealers.org.*

By committing them to emerging artists, they identify tomorrow's talent and make a long-term investment in these artists' futures.

Secondary market dealers handle works of art that are appearing on the market for resale on behalf of collectors and institutions. Often these dealers specialize in a particular period, equal to that of art historians. They are the experts that decide on authenticity and the quality of pieces of art, which makes them a vital resource not just for collectors, but also for curators, scholars, auctioneers and art consultants.

Public museums and galleries offer the greatest free art show in any country, making an unequalled opportunity to browse and study the widest collection of art. This may be a guide for collectors and art dealers in purchasing a single work or in the formation of an entire collection.

Crafts and Hobbies

Craft works are artistic works meant to be sold individually in art galleries and auctions or as mass products to tourists.[54] In addition, many people make crafts for their own use and not for sale, i.e. as a hobby. There is no clear distinction between art and crafts, but a workable divide may be made between fine art done by professionals and sold at often high prices and crafts made by amateurs and half professionals. Crafts include a number of specialized trades, such as ceramics, glass, textiles, wood work, metal work, furniture, jewellery, toys and music instruments. All businesses are small with few or no employees. Many people dealing with crafts have complementary incomes, for example from teaching and in third-world countries from any kind of supplementary income.

The US crafts and hobbies industry had revenues of about $25 billion in 2001 and $30 billion in 2005, growing to $35 billion in 2010 (Table 53).[55] The US industry is estimated at one-third of world total, similar to the West European share. Revenues in US crafts were only an estimated $15 billion in 2005, and $2 billion in the UK. Worldwide the crafts industry is considerable because of its importance to third world people. Total world revenue estimates were almost $100 billion in 2005.

---

54   Howkins. The Creative Industries, 94-95.
55   *www.craftandhobby.org.*

Table 53

The Global Crafts and Hobbies Market in $bn, 2001-2010

	2001	2005	2010
USA	25	30	35
Western Europe	25	30	35
Japan	10	10	15
Rest of Developed Countries	10	10	15
Developing Countries	10	15	20
Total	80	95	120

Source: Howkins. The Creative Industries, 94-95. Craft and Hobby Association: *www.craftandhobby.org*.

9. Family and Religion

Family

A family consists of a domestic group of people, typically affiliated by birth or marriage.[1] In modern societies, family ties are only those recognized by law. According to an article of the Universal Declaration of Human Rights by the UN, the family is the natural and fundamental group unit of society and is entitled to protection by society and the State. A family may be defined as a unit of two parents or a single parent family rearing their children and caring for each other. In Western and developed countries, the nuclear family of father, mother and children has been the predominant unit since the breakthrough of modern industrial societies. Family patterns have changed to a certain degree in recent decades, however. While the importance of the nuclear family is declining, although still the most widespread family unit, the share of single parent families has been increasing for decades mainly caused by the rise of divorces. A growing number of people choose to live as singles, too. Furthermore, many married couples live without having children. Among the nuclear families some practice an extended family pattern, including grandparents, uncles, aunts, and cousins.

In traditional and pre-industrial societies, the economic function of the family was vital to its existence and to ensure the continuous maintaining of a certain class status, families seldom married outside their class. The economic role of the family has gradually diminished as industrialization and economic growth progressed, becoming much smaller in current developed countries, although it remains important in family based businesses. While the economic role of families has declined, the importance of its caring and loving dimension has increased. In the end, modern families are based on love and reproduction of human beings.

In economic terms, the family constitutes a household.[2] Normally the terms family and household are treated as synonymous, but in fact it only refers to all persons living in the same dwelling. In developed countries, a household is based on the same structure as families, i.e. either a nuclear family, a couple without children, one parent families or singles. In income terms, there is a divide between couples with two incomes and singles with one income, particularly single parents. Roughly, household incomes in developed countries may be divided into three groups: there is one well-off third with top incomes, one-third with middle incomes and one-third with low incomes. Except for the difference between one or two incomes, total household income often depends

---

1   Smelser and Baltes. International Encyclopedia of the Social & Behavioral Sciences: 'Family', 'Families'.
     www.wikipedia.org: 'Family'.
2   Smelser and Baltes. International Encyclopedia of the Social & Behavioral Sciences: 'Household',
     'Household Production'. *www.wikipedia.org*: 'Household'.

on education, race and gender and increases with the age of income holders. The level of state subsidized education, medical and social care is also important to the structure of household incomes, especially to the low income group. Finally, there is a great deal of difference between the various parts of large countries such as the United States, UK, Germany, France and Italy, while the smaller and highly developed countries of Scandinavia, Benelux and Switzerland contain more even levels of household incomes. In the US, for example, with an income average in 2005 at $44,000, New Hampshire topped the list with a median income of $57,000, while West Virginia with $32,000 bottomed the list.[3]

The United States, for example, had 113 million households in 2005 with a total income of $4.3 trillion. Compared to total US GDP of $13 trillion in 2005, it means that household spending constitutes one-third of all American economic activities, while business to business trade accounts for two-thirds of all spending. The consumption of families is not only the basics of everyday life but also a vital part of the total economy. Roughly, this commercial pattern applies to all developed countries. Shopping is a daily activity that may turn into an experience at weekends, spending time at shopping malls. Investigations into tourism and travel patterns show, for instance, that shopping is the most popular attraction and way of spending your time off (see chapter on Tourism).

Marriage

In most societies, marriage is an important social institution. Marriage is a contract and close relationship between two persons that includes governmental, social, and religious recognition.[4] In the most frequent form of marriage, a man and a woman is united as husband and wife. Other forms of marriage also exist, for example polygamy and marriage between two persons of the same sex. In developed countries, polygamy is not allowed and same-sex marriage is only hesitantly being accepted in some countries. Restrictions on marrying close relatives are adopted in virtually all societies. Most often people marry because they want to form a family and have children. Other reasons may include legal stability and equal rights, for example to children and property, legitimate sexual relations, social recognition or the public declaration of love. A marriage is usually celebrated with a wedding ceremony. The act of marriage usually creates obligations between the individuals involved. Marriage may be costly to enter

---

3   US Census Bureau, 'Households'. Statistical Abstract.
4   Smelser and Baltes. International Encyclopedia of the Social & Behavioral Sciences: 'Marriage'. *www.wikipedia.org*: 'Marriage'.

and to leave. It implies that the benefit from marriage exceeds the benefit from being apart. Divorce as the dissolution of a contract entails financial obligations between the spouses, such as alimony and partition of property.

Marriage is found in virtually every society. While most non-Western societies have a broader definition of family that includes an extended family network, the nuclear family is the core unit in Western cultures. Many religions encourage marriage and some even condemn non-marriage relations between man and women. Previous religious control of marriage disappeared with the secularization of developed countries. In spite of Western secularization, many couples include a Christian ceremony in their marriage contract. While Islam recommends marriage highly, Buddhism neither encourages nor discourages marriage, although it includes ethical rules on married life. Hinduism sees marriage as a sacred duty including religious and social obligations. Although castes are legally forbidden in India, marriage is often directed by unwritten laws to prevent marriage between castes.

Relatively, fewer people marry while more people divorce.[5] This is the main trend of post-war development in developed countries. The marriage rates continue to drop and the divorce rates continues to rise, although at a slower pace than during the primary restructuring period of c.1960 to 1990. Changes always start out first in the United States and then some years later in other developed countries.

People marry for many reasons, including love, sex, children and money. Probably, they get divorced for the same reasons. Let us take a look at marriage from an economic perspective, dealing with the benefit you gain from sharing your life with another. Love may change your utility function, because it makes you care about the well-being of the one you love. Usually, sex complements love. Sex also offers utility, given the right partner. Sex may be bought in a relatively well-functioning market, too, but just for the act and not for love. Another characteristic of sex is that it involves certain risks, such as disease and pregnancy. It may be for these reasons that sex is often associated with marriage. Since around 1970, the introduction of the birth control pill and its legal distribution among unmarried women has probably contributed to reduce the frequency of marriage.

Generally, people have children because they feel a biological imperative and that they enjoy kids, too. Regardless of the reasons, children raise the utility of an individual in an economic model. A child provides utility at the same time to both parents and is therefore a public, not private, good. The benefit that one parent gets from spending

---

5   Friedberg, Leora and Stern, Steven N. 'Economics and Marriage and Divorce'. Bowmaker, Simon W. (Ed.)(2005). *Economies Uncut*, 137-167. Cheltenham, UK: Edward Elgar.

time with the child is not diminished by the benefit the other gets from spending time with the child. Since kids cost about the same whether they live with one or two parents, it is from this perspective prudent to live together. Living together as married couples includes other public goods. Kitchens can be used to provide two meals about as easily as one, and the two of them can share the same heating, lighting and air conditioning. The same applies to home decor and home entertainment, that is, if you do not have completely different tastes. Another common good is time that can be used to produce a public good, for example clean house and polite kids. Unlike the former examples, the ladder utility is not based on money but on time. It is a non-market utility or household production, whereas the former cases are market activities. By splitting household work between the two spouses, one could work in the market while the other one performs the household work. Another option would be that both worked and paid someone else to do the household work. This is possible for almost anything except giving birth to a child (although a 'brooding mother' is also an option). So, marriage comprises a number of potential gains from a more efficient use of time and resources. Of vital importance, too, is the family value of caring and happiness brought to grown-ups as well as children.

Divorce

In developed countries, half of all marriages end in divorce.[6] Actually, half of all marriages in the world end in divorce. In Islamic countries, divorce is difficult without the consent of the husband. According to an annual British study of the causes of divorce, the main reasons are: extra-marital affairs, family strains, abuse, mid-life crisis and addictions to, for example, alcohol, gambling, work and the like. The majority of divorce cases are petitioned by women and take place within 5 to 15 years of marriage. While divorce is accepted in Protestant, Orthodox, Islamic, and Judaic religions, it is not condoned by the Roman Catholic Church. Islam discourages divorce, too.

Divorce is a legal act with economic consequences for both parties, because it leads to the creation of two households rather than one with consequent increased costs. In most cases where children are involved, women are awarded child custody and the men awarded alimony. Women often suffer financially from a divorce due to lower income and a greater role in rearing children. On the other hand, a divorce often has negative economic consequences for men, too, that is rarely discussed openly. Many governments provide some kind of welfare system to divorced mothers and their children.

---

6   Smelser and Baltes. International Encyclopedia of the Social & Behavioral Sciences: 'Divorce'. *www. wikipedia.org*: 'Divorce'.

Divorce is often one of the most traumatic periods in a person's life. Separation and divorce are frequently associated with depression and conflict, especially when complicated by child custody. Divorce has often long-term economic, social, physical, and mental health impacts on adults and children, too, although it is difficult to determine and agree on the full extent of such effects. The question is whether it is better or worse to be adults and children in a family of unhappily married adults who decide to divorce, or whether it is better to be part of an unhappy family that does not divorce? In practice, this is almost impossible to determine, also because it is often a matter of long-term effects. Most long-term effects seem to be of a negative kind, but you may also find positive effects, such as a learning process of how to do things right.

The Value of Families

While the total spending value of families and households may be estimated roughly to be one-third of world GDP, about $15 trillion, the added value within families is very difficult to measure, because the household is a non-market economy, the value creation of which is not included in the GDP. Making a monetary evaluation of the household economy would require an estimate of the revenues and spending in case all activities of the household were to be bought in the market. But what is the value of love, child care, shared experiences, cleaning, cooking, mending, etc.? A study of the value of household production is going on in many countries. It is based on measuring of labor time and valuation of income. Household production may be defined as 'those unpaid activities which are carried on, by and for the (family) members, which might be replaced by market goods, or paid service, if circumstances such as income, market conditions, and personal inclinations permit the service being delegated to someone outside the household group'.[7]

Almost three-quarters of day and night is spent on non-productive activities, primarily personal care (sleeping, washing, etc.) and secondly mass media use and entertainment, recreational activities and learning. The remainder quarter of the day is almost equally divided between work outside the household that is measured in the national statistical accounts and non-accounted household work and care of household members. So, during a week a family works as many hours doing unpaid household work as outside paid work. The survey shows that men spend more time on paid work than women, while women spend more time on unpaid housework than men. The pattern was the same for all grown up ages. Not surprisingly either is that

---

7   Sylvester Young. 'Income from Households' non-SNA production: A Review', 2002: *www.ilo.org*.

young people spend less time on paid and unpaid work than adults and more time on non-productive activities.

In the US, women spend almost four times as much time on housework as men, including cooking, cleaning, and washing and care of children, while men are more active than women in home maintenance and shopping, paying accounts, etc. The pattern of time usage by sex and by age is probably representative for developed countries in general, but in some countries such as Scandinavia the time spent is more evenly divided between the two sexes.

The United Nations statistical classification system includes a category (07) for 'unpaid care-giving services to household members', subdivided into 'childcare', 'adult care' and 'working time'. The EU are dealing with the importance and measuring of household activities, too.[8] The European average is based on some differences between Eastern and Southern Europe on the one hand and Northern Europe on the other (Table 54). In the former case, men mainly do paid work outside the household while women primarily do work in the households. In Northern Europe, paid and unpaid work is more equal for the two sexes. The inclusion of all persons aged 20 to 74 (including those retired) and across the whole year including working days and weekends as well as holidays explains that the time spent on paid work is significantly less than a normal working day.

TABLE 54

Average Time Use of European Men and Women Aged 20 to 74 in Hours per Day, 2000

	Men	Women
Paid Work, Study	4	2
Domestic Work	2	4
Travel	1	1
Sleep	8	8
Meals, Personal Care	2	2
Free Time	5	5
Total	22	22

Source: EU. 'How is the time of women and men distributed in Europe?' *Statistics in focus. Population and Social Conditions*, 4/2006: http://epp.eurostat.ec.europa.eu. Numbers are rounded and therefore, they do not add up to 24 hours.

---

8   Eurostat (2004). *Guidelines on Harmonised European Time Use Survey: http://epp.eurostat.ec.europa.eu.*

The cases of Italy and UK may show the difference between time usage in Southern and Northern Europe (Table 55). In Italy, women spend much more time on food preparation than in UK where food preparation is more evenly shared. While Italian women spend four times as much time doing domestic work, UK women spend twice as much time as men doing housework. Time spent on child care and shopping is more evenly divided, whereas men solely take care of house repairs and gardening.

TABLE 55

Daily Domestic Activities of Men and Women in UK and Italy in %, 2000

	UK		Italy	
	Men	Women	Men	Women
Food Preparation	19	22	12	25
Dish Washing	7	7	5	11
Cleaning and other upkeep	14	20	15	28
Laundry, Ironing and Handicrafts	3	11	0	11
Gardening	9	3	16	2
Construction and Repairs	12	2	6	0
Shopping and Services	17	15	23	11
Childcare	9	13	12	9
Other Domestic Work	10	7	11	3
Total Domestic Work	100	100	100	100
Hours and Minutes per Day	02:18	04:15	01:35	05:20

Source: EU. How is the time of women and men distributed in Europe.

On average, the family man and woman spend 3 hours each day, seven days a week, 365 days a year on household activities. Accordingly, each family spends half as much time doing unpaid housework and childcare as it spends on paid work outside the family. Compared to paid work in the marketplace, most household work involves low paid activities; doing cooking, cleaning, mending, child care, etc. Furthermore, two parent families are probably only half of all households. Therefore, the total value of domestic activities is not simply half the total income in national accounts. If this was the case in, for example, the United States, the value of household work in 2005 would be $2,000 billion. Total value of unpaid household activities in the United States may be an estimated $500 billion. Compared to total US GDP of $13 trillion, it makes and additional 4 percent. Worldwide, this would add up to $2,500 billion (Table 56).

TABLE 56

Global Household Activities in $bn, 2001-2010

	2001	2005	2010
North America	450	550	655
USA	400	500	600
Canada	50	50	55
Western Europe	400	500	600
Germany	90	100	110
UK	80	90	100
France	70	80	90
Italy	60	70	80
Rest of Western Europe	100	110	120
Eastern Europe	100	125	150
Asia Pacific	750	975	1200
Japan	150	175	170
China	250	325	300
India	150	175	150
Rest of Asia Pacific	200	200	180
Middle East and Africa	150	175	200
Latin America	150	175	200
Total	2000	2500	3000

Source: Estimated 4 percent of GDP. CIA. World Fact Book.

Family and household activities include vital parts of economic, social and human life. It embraces several specialized markets, such as marriage, children, love, divorce, sex, social care, food, cleaning, gardening, and maintenance. In economic terms, the non-market household activities add an estimated 4 percent to world GDP. In addition, families and tax payers in general spend money on child care, schooling, social care of handicapped and old people, health care, etc. Total consumer spending includes one-third of world GDP. Across these economic figures, one can only guess the value of family care and love that mostly involves non-market activities. What would be the result if children were brought up outside their biological parents and adults did not enjoy the benefits of living with their loved-ones? Maybe love and caring should add a few extra percent to world GDP!

Religion

'Religion may not be bought and sold like fish and chips, but there are parallels'.[9] Religion is a commodity that is produced and consumed in a competitive marketplace. Some of us choose to believe, and others do not. Some of us choose to be Catholic, others Protestants, others Muslim, and still others Hindu or Buddhist. Religion is supplied and marketed by firms called churches, synagogues, mosques, or temples. Each must choose production technologies and set prices. They must compete among themselves and with secular firms for the time, attention and money of potential adherents.

A religion is a set of beliefs and practices organized in communities, involving codified beliefs, rituals and scriptures as well as personal faith.[10] In one way religion is a matter of belief in some supernatural universe and God that promises eternal life to believers and in another way, religious belief is part of your inner feelings and behavioral attitudes. The nature and expressions of these beliefs are not universally uniform but differ according to the historical and current social context of each congregation and individual person. In contemporary societies, religion is considered to be a private matter that must accept the rules of a secular world. Secularized modern societies will not tolerate that religion seeks to undermine reason and take command. At least, this is the case in developed countries and most developing countries. Besides the existence of religious organizations, an ethical code of charity and humanity may be considered to be the historical heritage of religions on modern societies. In some parts of the world, in particularly Islamic countries, strong groups and whole nations have made religion a set of moral codes to rule the ways of life, however. This has made religion even more economically important.

Even though we live in a secularized world based on reason and science, the majority of the world population consider themselves to be believers and to be part of some religion.[11] As human beings, we have one vital shortcoming, namely that of being mortal. Religion offers us the chance to become immortal and thus bring rewards that could not otherwise be obtained in our physical world. As a consequence, the demand for religion is as basic as the wants it seeks to satisfy.

Moreover, the advance of science and reason will not necessarily undermine religion. While science can be tested right or wrong and proofs its usefulness in practical

---

9   Stonebraker, R. J. 'Economics and Religion'. Bowbaker, *Economies Uncut*, 264-290.

10   Smelser and Baltes. International Encyclopedia of the Social & Behavioral Sciences: 'Religion'. *www.wikipedia.org*: 'Religion'.

11   Gallup International Association (2000). *Gallup International Millennium Survey: www.gallup-international.com*.

life, the existence of God cannot be verified in some scientific or practical test. But neither can we prove that supernatural beings do not exist. As the philosopher Pascal put it some hundred years ago, 'Let us weigh the gain and loss in wagering that God is … If you gain, you gain it all. If you lose, you lose nothing. Wager then, without hesitation that He is'.[12] So, to invest in religion is a perfectly rational reaction to eternal risk. Because religion in this way does not conflict with science, there is no logical reason to expect it to disappear. Although religion springs from a demand for an afterlife, it can also offer worldly benefits. Belief and religious adherence may provide people with a sense of purpose in life and even create present happiness. In addition, church attendance can lead to strong social networks of importance to your business and carrier as well as to your mental and physical well-being, for example by discoursing drugs abuse. Adherence to a specific church society may serve some kind of insurance function in matters of happiness as well as income, too, particularly where governmental social insurance is lacking.[13] Religion is also a strong driver of charity to the benefit of people in social and medical need and distress. Often charity is linked to missionary work to make people convert to Christianity or Islam. You are charitable because you believe in charity but also to ensure immortality for converters and strength to your church.

The religions of the world compete in the marketplace of promising a hereafter life. The religions that are likely to prosper are those that promise the greatest benefits to theri own followers, and in particular to people who are the most faithful. If a religion offers the same rewards to all, it is less attractive. Consumers will either spend little or no time and money pursuing religious activities if they promise no additional gain. This has created problems for liberal Protestant churches that cannot bring themselves to promise heaven to their members and hell to non-members. Furthermore with little to offer, it is not surprising that atheists have made little headway in religious markets.

Some three-quarters of humanity adhere to one of the five world religions.[14] Christianity is the largest world religion encompassing about 33 percent of the world population. Islam is second with about 20 percent, followed by Hinduism with about 14 percent, the Chinese folk religion and Buddhism each with 6 percent. The remainder consists largely of non-religious people. The two large world religions Christianity and Islam are growing, the former mainly in Eastern Europe and Asia, and the latter primarily in Asia and Africa. In developed countries especially in Western Europe, it

12   Pascal. Pensées. Here based on Stonebraker. 'Economics of Religion', 265.
13   Dehejia, DeLeire, and Luttmer. 'Insuring Consumption and Happiness through Religious Organizations', August 2005, RWP05-047: *www.harvard.edu*.
14   The Heritage Foundation: *www.heritage.org*.

has become more and more difficult to recruit priests and monks. In general, the global landscape of religions has become more diverse. In some parts of the world especially developing countries, religious activities are growing even to the degree of fanaticism, while many developed countries suffer from declining adherence to religions. Interest in religious matters does not seem to have declined, however, but the changing pattern of lifestyles and thinking in a rapidly developing globalized world may call for different ways of practicing religion. It should also be born in mind that religion is dealing with matters of eternal importance to the human heart, such as those moments when everyday life is suspended, moments of deep sorrow, death and suffering.

Theories of the relationship between religion and economics are, roughly speaking, of two kinds. One, the so-called 'secularization theory' or 'modernization theory' states that as economies develop and get richer, people become less religious.[15] Two, 'the religion market model' speaks about the way governments interact with religion, making it difficult or easy for people to practice their religion. While there is some validity in the secularization theory, there is also support for the religion market model. For example, monopoly churches as the Anglican Church in England and the Lutheran churches in Scandinavia do not just lead to bad religious practices. A positive relationship probably springs from the fact that state religion is accompanied by state subsidizing, whereas government regulation also seems to have a negative effect on religious participation and beliefs. Former communism is the most radical case of negative relationship, but the rise in religious activity in post-communist countries also shows that even long periods of dictatorial repression of religion does not wipe out interest. Although the two theories of the interactions of religion and economics may explain religious activities to a certain degree, they have problems in explaining the wide and perhaps even growing religious activities of the United States. But maybe it is simply that a free market in religion goes well with a free market economy.

The relationship between religion and economic performance interacts both ways.[16] On the one hand, a nation's economic and political development affects its levels of religiosity measured by the extent of individual religious participation and beliefs and the role of organized religion in a country's political, legal, and social structure. On the other hand, the nature and extent of religiousness influence economic performance and the nature of political, legal, and social institutions. In the former case, economic development causes individuals to become less religious according to the so-called 'secularization theory'. This theory also claims that religiosity would

---

15   Robert Barro. 'Religion and Economic Growth': *www.economics.harvard.edu/barro/papers*.
16   Barro and McCleary. 'Religion and Political Economy in an International Panel', Harvard University, May 2002, and November 2003: *www.economics.harvard.edu/barro/papers*.

decline with state monopolized churches and increase in countries with competing religions.

Religion can also have a negative or positive impact on economic development. According to Max Weber, religion would stimulate economic growth if it looked favorably on the accumulation of wealth (Christianity) and vice versa (Islam). Religion may also influence a country's openness and willingness to interact with outsiders in domestic and international business. The religious view of work ethic is also important to the economic effects of religion, such as the strong Protestant work ethic. Religion may also encourage thrift and investment that leads to economic growth and in another respect to be productive by discouraging participation in 'sinful' activities, such as gambling, sex outside marriage and over consumption of alcohol and other drugs. In these ways, the interaction between religion and economic performance makes an integral part of a nation's culture in a wider sense.

Religion and business may have something to learn each other.[17] Churches might be managed much better and there is a lot to be learned from business in this respect. Business on the other hand has a number of moral problems that they need to learn to deal with in a better way. Furthermore, religion deals with deeply rooted sentiments. It is a very strong resource that may be cultivated for the benefit of capitalism and for the religious dimension of life. 'Treat people as you want them to treat you', is a Christian ethical saying. In general and bearing in mind the words of Pascal from the 17th century that men never do evil with greater pleasure than when they do it with religious conviction, or the current religious extremists, religious people may hardly be considered good and better people than non-religious human beings. Religion is ambiguous.

After all, the conclusion is that religion may be seen as a market phenomenon with a supply side and a demand side. The demand side is believers, adherers and members of religious congregations and churches throughout the nations of the world. About 85 percent of the world population can be considered part of religious communities. On the supply side, churches, graveyards, education and research in religion as well as priests and other employees in religious churches, mosques and other institutions may either be subsidized by the state, private funding or by congregation members, or perhaps some combination of these three sources of funding. While many European churches are state subsidized, American and most African and Asian churches are based on private funding.

---

17   Laura Nash and Scotty McLennan (2001). *Church on Sunday, Work on Monday. The Challenge of Fusing Christian Values with Business Life.* San Francisco: Jossey-Bass.

Whether privately or stately subsidized, the churches and mosques and other re-ligious communities and sites of the world have to be served by priests of some kind. For example, members of the Catholic Church are served by approximately 400,000 priests.[18] But what are the revenues and spending of some 2 billion Christians, some 1 billion Muslims, 1 billion Hindus and the other religious groups of 5 billion world adherents to some religion? What are the benefits of religious institutions in matters of social charity, education, church attendance, religious networks and mental strength and support of beliefs? What is the importance of religious ethics in everyday life, in business, in politics, in education and science? Will it be possible to make a total sum of this complicated arithmetical problem? It may be possible to make qualified estimates, but they will be very difficult and uncertain. Based on state-subsidized revenues and spending, the market of world religion economy may be estimated at 1 percent of total world GDP. In 2005, global GPD was nearly $45 trillion, and 1 percent will be $450 billion, the majority of which is spent in developed countries (Table 57). In addition, religion and religious institutions include non-market activities such as ethics, social networks, religious feelings, etc., the value of which is hard to measure!

TABLE 57

The Global Religious Market in $bn, 2001-2010

	2001	2005	2010
USA	100	100	105
Canada	5	5	5
Western Europe	90	100	105
Eastern Europe	10	15	20
Asia Pacific	135	150	170
Middle East and Africa	40	50	60
Latin America	25	30	35
Total	400	450	500

Source: Maddison. The World Economy: Historical Statistics, 259-261.
CIA. World Fact Book. Estimated 1 percent of world GDP.

Although these quantifying analyses of religious attendance and beliefs bring useful insights into parts of the relationship between religion and economy, much remains to be said on this subject that cannot be quantified. In general, the importance of

---

18   Eternal Word Television Network: *www.ewtn.com*.

religion in modern societies is deeply rooted in the changing nature of capitalism and cultural dimensions of life in an increasingly globalized and technological based world. The importance of welfare, democracy, fear of violence, ethical and environmental considerations of the future of human life, the searching for meaning in a secular and individualized humanity – all such dimensions of modern life are to be taken into consideration to evaluate the importance of religion in a modern world. In the end, it is difficult to determine whether it is religion or other cultural factors that are decisive.

10. Sex and Drugs

There is much more to the world economy and the experience economy than the activities measured in the some two hundred national GDPs of the world. Much revenues and spending are not included in the official accounts. There are three sources of 'parallel' economy. One is crime, i.e. economic activities that do not correspond to legal production and services recorded in the official economy, but simply are based on burglary, robbery, drug dealing, trafficking, etc. We have already discussed the extensive piracy in music and films as well as fashion brands. Two is non-market household production and services within families, which were included in the chapter on 'family'. Three is a 'shadow economy', i.e. all market-based production of goods and services that are deliberately concealed from public authorities to avoid: taxes, payment of social security, meeting legal labor market standards and complying with certain administrative procedures. The shadow economy will shortly be discussed in general and more particularly in the case of the sex industry. Finally, crime will be dealt with in relation to drugs, including legitimate tobacco. Although they all may be said to have some consciousness expanding impact, the category 'drugs' will neither include medication of the pharmaceutical industry, nor alcohol, wine, beer, and coffee of the food and beverage industries that all may be considered integrated parts of the 'functional' or 'knowledge' economy. The border between these fields of economy and the experience economy is neither stable nor permanent, however. For instance, an increasing part of the food and beverage industries are upgrading their experience dimension.

The Shadow Economy

On average, the size of the 'shadow economy' is an additional 40 percent to GDP in developing countries and about 15 percent of GDP in developed countries. Including the 'shadow economy', global GDP would be an estimated a quarter larger (Table 58).[1] The driving forces behind the shadow economy in developed countries are the increased burden of taxation and social security contributions, combined with labor market regulation. In developing countries, the informal economy is practiced by maybe half the adult population as a simple means of survival for individuals and families. Furthermore, the shadow economy seems to reduce corruption in developed countries and increase corruption in developing countries. The informal economy or

---

1   Because of the nature of the case it is difficult to measure the shadow economy and therefore, the extent and size of the shadow economy is also debated, see for instance The Shadow Economy: *www.shadoweconomy.eu*. I have chosen the widest estimates.

the shadow economy includes home-based workers making, for example, garments, street traders, itinerant job workers on building sites or road works, waste collectors and the like. It also includes sexual activities, corruption, and any other economic activity that is concealed from public authorities and therefore neither taxed nor accounted for in national statistics. These activities are performed by single persons or micro enterprises within or outside the household sector. A large informal economy signals a weak state, such as is the case in many parts of the developing world, for example Latin America and Africa. In the case of China, a strong state seems tacitly to accept a comprehensive violation of international patents and intellectual property rights.[2]

TABLE 58

The Global Informal Economy in $bn, 1990-2010

	1990	2000	2005	2010
North America	750	1000	1100	1200
Western Europe	1000	1500	1650	1800
Eastern Europe	500	1000	1250	1500
Asia Pacific	2250	3500	4.000	4500
Middle East and Africa	750	1000	1250	1500
Latin America	750	1000	1250	1500
Total	6.000	9000	10.500	12.000
Developed Countries	2000	3000	3500	4000
Developing Countries	4000	6000	7000	8000

Source: Schneider, Friedrich. 'Shadow Economies and Corruption all over the World: What do we Really Know?', IZA DP, no. 1043, 2004, no. 2315, 2006: *www.iza.org*. Numbers are rounded.

The Sex Market and Industry

The sex industry comprises two dimensions. One is the so-called 'porn industry' that provides pornographic entertainment for adults on video films, Internet etc.[3] Depend-

---

2   Fernández-Kelly, Patricia and Sheffner, Jon (2006). *Out of the Shadows: The Informal Economy and Political Movements in Latin America*. Princeton: Princeton University Press. Portes, A. and Haller, W. (2005). "The Informal Economy". Smelser, N. J. and Swedberg, R. (Eds.)(2005). *Handbook of Economic Sociology*, 2nd Ed. Princeton: Princeton University Press.

3   Smelser and Baltes, International Encyclopedia of the Social & Behavioral Sciences: 'Sex' *www.wikipedia. org*: 'The Sex industry'.

ing on what is pictured, a divide is often made between pornography (all) and erotica (some). Two is prostitution that is the sale of sex for money. Both, pornography and prostitution function as legitimate industries and markets in many countries, while one or the two of them is prohibited in other countries. Whether legitimate or illegal, the sex industry is found in all countries of the world. Products of the porn industry are primarily produced in developed countries, mainly the United States, while prostitution is found everywhere. The money and demand for purchased sex in the developed countries has created a heavy sex trafficking of women from poor countries to rich countries.[4]

Pornography

What is pornography? A broad definition might be: a depiction of sexual activity with the goal of sexual arousal with the viewers.[5] It is distinct from erotica in the sense that the latter use sexually-arousing images mainly for the artistic purpose. The line between 'erotica' and 'pornography' is often highly subjective, however. While some define pornography as merely erotica, others would perceive it as obscene and therefore quite different from erotica. The definition of obscenity differs between persons, cultures and eras. This leaves legal actions against pornography open to wide interpretation and in addition, a lucrative business for lawyers.

Pornography may use any media for depicting sexual acts, including literature, photos, sculpture, ceramics, painting, animation, sound recording, film, video or video game. When sexual acts or sexually stimulating activities such as live shows, stripping and lap dancing are performed for a live audience, however, it is not pornography as such, but just another part of the sex industry. Historically, every art and publishing medium has been used for pornography, too, and in recent history it has even been part of the driving forces of new media technologies, such as DVDs and the Internet. Furthermore, the porn film industry produces more titles per year than Hollywood. Because porn plays in few theaters and it is difficult to rent porn videos in many countries, most distribution is by sale. Movie rental stores such as Blockbuster and other large video-rental firms avoid porn.

Mass-distributed pornography is as old as the printing press, even as old as mass produced ceramics of antiquity. As soon as photography was invented in the 19th

---

4   There are thousands of studies on prostitution, see the database: Routledge: Studies on Women and Gender Abstracts. A non-moralist approach that considers sex trafficking to be just part of a globalization process is: Agustín, Laura Maria (2007). *Sex at the Margins. Migration, Labour Markets and the Rescue Industry*. London: Zed Books.
5   Smelser and Baltes. International Encyclopedia of the Social & Behavioral Sciences: 'Pornography'. *www.wikipedia.org*: 'Pornography'.

century, it was being used to produce pornographic images. The same story is true of motion pictures since the early 20ᵗʰ century and computers, video, satellite TV, DVD and the Internet of the late 20ᵗʰ century. With the maturing of animation software and computer capabilities since the turn of the millennium, digital manipulation of source photographs and completely computer-generated pornography has been a growing segment of the porn industry. Furthermore, this technological development has made it possible to melt live and animated images into one-and-the-same feature film, such as Lord of the Rings, but is yet to be applied to pornography.

The creation of highly realistic computer-generated images creates new ethical dilemmas. As opposed to authentic pictures, synthetic images of torture, rape, adult sex with a child and other criminal acts may cause problems in law enforcement and challenges the traditional notion of evidence. Faked pornographic photos of celebrities show the possibility of using fake images to blackmail or otherwise harm other people. Furthermore, the spread of synthetic images that do not record actual events, challenges some of the conventional criticism of pornography.

Internet entrepreneurs operate pornographic Internet sites, including conventional photographic and video pornography and even interactive video game-line entertainment. Due to the international character of the Internet, consumers in countries where pornography is illegal can easily access such material from another country where it is legal. The low cost of copying and delivering digital data boosted the formation of circles of people swapping pornography. With the advent of peer-to-peer file sharing applications such as Kazaa, pornography swapping has reached new heights. Prior to that, the Usenet news service was a popular place for pornographic swapping. Free pornography became available en masse from other users and is no longer restricted to private groups. Large amounts of free pornography on the Internet are also distributed for marketing purposes to encourage subscriptions to paid content.

Since the late 1990s, 'porn from the masses for the masses' seems to have become another new trend. Inexpensive digital cameras, increasingly powerful and user-friendly software, and easy access to pornographic source material have made it possible for individuals to produce and share home-made porn for next to nothing. Despite adult filters on most Internet search engines, porn sites are easily found on the Internet.

Although there is no official industrial production coding in the SIC (Standard Industrial Classification), it clearly makes sense to talk of a 'sex economy', including the marketing of legal and illegal porn through various media along with other activities such as prostitution, stripping, lap dancing, telephone sex and chat lines.[6] Besides the

---

6   Cameron, Samuel. 'Economics of Pornography'. Bowmaker, *Economics Uncut*, 171-192. Peter G. Moffatt.

actors and models providing porn services, the porn industry generates employment and revenues in writing scripts and literature, photography, cameramen, film directors, marketing, website design, sales, legal and economic advice, management and other ancillary services. Accordingly, the sex industry generates multiplier effects of creating additional economic activity in other and related industries. Where there is specialization of the sector, this could be important to local economies, for example sex tourism in Thailand and Amsterdam. A local specialization in porn production can also be a valuable source of export earnings due to demands in other countries, reflecting national differences in legal regulation and availability of porn, for example in Hollywood the home of the porn film industry.

The porn sector or adult industry, because nobody in the business calls it porn, is a very diverse one in terms of the size distribution of firms. Due to the development of technology, there are now one-person firms in the form of people who may provide still pictures, film clips or even interactive sexual performances via webcams. There are also small firms distributing almost 'home-made' porn without trained actors or scriptwriters. Although they might be called amateurs, they are still addressing the sex market. At the other end of the scale, there are corporations such as Playboy, a multi-product firm supplying magazines, DVDs, its own TV channel and a website. For short or full-length feature-films, there are large companies in the same way as in regular movie production, including an annual Oscar-style award ceremony for porn movies.

Due to the restricted field of consumption, these firms cannot make nearly as much money as the mainstream film sector. Just like in any other industry, however, some operators will make large profits, whilst many others will struggle for survival or go out of business. Porn is supplied in a dynamic technologically progressive industry and therefore there will be 'first-mover advantages' to producers who establish a niche market or perfect a delivery method. Wages are generally higher to compensate for the psychic costs of being in a disliked business. Some use porn films as a stepping stone to a career in mainstream movies, too, and are therefore willing to accept lower wages.

In general, there are few entry barriers to the porn industry. The main obstacle to new producers of pornography is finding consumers. In the case of films, this problem has decreased due to the emergence of DVDs and pay-TV channels, because in many parts of the world porn films are not allowed in conventional movie theatres. Barriers to entry in pornography may in fact be lower than in some other niches of the sex

'Economics of Prostitution'. Bowmaker, *Economics Uncut*, 193-228.

industry such as prostitution, because it is based on 'looking' and not on 'participating'.

Opposition to pornography comes generally from sources such as law, religion and feminism. Distribution of obscenity is a Federal crime in the United States and also illegal in most of the 50 states. Child pornography is illegal as well as animal pornography. In practice, the line between obscenity and erotica is not easy to draw, bearing in mind the First Amendment's freedom of speech and press. Some religious groups consider pornography to being immoral and a violation of the sacred family. They may even claim that viewing pornography is addictive and destructive in the same way as alcohol. Feminist critics of pornography consider it demeaning to women. They believe that most pornography contributes to the male-centered objectification of women and is likely to encourage rape and other violence against them. No research has verified any clear connection between pornography and sexual crime, however. The opposite may even be the case that easy access to porn reduces the number of rapes in a country. Furthermore, there is always the matter of culture which may be seen from two perspectives. In some national or wider cultures, a patriarchal or macho view of women may consider rape or sexual assaults acceptable in some cases and something that is allowed to pass unchallenged. Other nations that have developed a more equal view and practice of the two sexes will be less tolerant with sexual assaults.

As for the types of pornography, it may be divided into 'softcore' porn where male genitals are hidden and 'hardcore' porn where all parts of sexual intercourse and genitals are shown. The depiction of intercourse is predominantly dealing with man and women sexual acts. Adults having sex with children, which is prohibited, is much more rarely seen in pornography, which is also the case for lesbian and gay pornography.

The Porn Industry

In the United States, the hard- and softcore porn industry was not particularly large before the advent of modern technologies such as Video and DVD, pay-TV, high computer capabilities and the Internet. Over the past few decades, a large industry for the production and consumption of pornography has come into existence, due to the emergence of the VCR, the DVD, pay-TV channels and the Internet, but also as a consequence of more tolerant social attitudes. Most heterosexual and lesbian porn film studies as well as gay porn studios are found in the United States. Europe and Asia, including Japan and Thailand have many porn film studios, too.

The porn industry also includes many cartoons and magazines, including Playboy, Penthouse and Hustler which are all part of large porn corporations producing and selling videos, magazines, clothing and sex toys from their own chain of stores and even include casinos. As well as the porn industry, there is a large amount of non-commercial pornography. Various Usenet groups are focused on non-commercial pornographic photographs. Erotic works of literature are as old as literature itself, including for example Ars Amatoria (Ovid), Kama Sutra (Vaysayana), Decameron (Boccacio), Fanny Hill (John Cleland), Lady Chatterley's Lover (D. H. Lawrence), Tropic of Cancer (Henry Miller) and Story of O (Pauline Réage).

The US porn industry is by far the largest and most developed region in the world.[7] In the United States, distribution of pornography changed radically since the 1990s with the breakthrough of videotape, cable television and later on DVDs and the Internet. Distribution of pornography is a large industry that involves major entertainment companies such as Time Warner and AT & T in the US (which profits from pornography through its cable channels and the in-room movies provided by hotel chains). American pornography refers mainly to the Internet, adult movies, publications (books and magazines such as Playboy, Penthouse and Hustler) and pay-per-view broadcasting. The so-called portable porn market is in its initial stage in the US.

There are over 40 adult movies studios in the US featuring heterosexual scenes, which is more than any other country. The industry includes manufacturers of adult products, distributors, suppliers, retail store owners, wholesalers, cable TV buyers and foreign buyers, including several hundred companies. The production is concentrated in San Fernando Valley in Southern California and Las Vegas in Nevada. The world's largest adult movies studio, Vivid Entertainment, generates about $100 million a year in revenue, introducing more than 60 films annually that are sold in video stores, hotel rooms, on cable systems and on the Internet. Vivid's two largest regional competitors are Wicked Pictures and Digital Playground. Colorado-based New Frontier Media and Spanish Private Media Group are the only two adult video companies traded publicly. Vivid as well as Playboy, Penthouse and Hustler each run their own TV channel, showing porn movies. Subsidiaries of the large media conglomerates such as News Corporation's Direct TV and Comcast are the largest porn sellers.

Pornography is edging its way from the margins into the mainstream, partly with help of some of America's biggest and most respected companies, but mainly because pornography is the entertainment of choice for millions of Americans.[8] Who is profiting from porn, who is consuming it, and what is its future? The mainstream corporations that are making big money on porn is: hotel chains, such as Marriott, and Hilton (businessmen's hotels) that all offer in-room X-rated movies delivered to the hotel by one of the two major distribution companies, LodgeNet or On Command.

---

7   www.wikipedia.org: 'Pornography in North America'.
8   www.pbs.org. Public Broadcasting Service.

The telecom companies make good money from subscribers on their broadband, too, for example AT & T.

A lot of the revenues are made by several small producers in Hollywood that are setting up movies costing no more than $5,000 to $15,000.[9] Playboy spends about $100,000 per film. The business process is like this. You produce a show for a few thousand dollars to be sold as home videos. These home videos seldom show up in the home video rental store, however. Chains such as Blockbuster and Hollywood Entertainment will for the most part not carry adult entertainment on videos. So you have to go to the mom-and-pop stores for that and the whole chain of adult stores around the country. Concerning pay-per-view, most of the good stuff will be sold through Playboy that is going to run eight channels or New Frontier that runs three channels. They will carry most of the adult entertainment programming. All keep testing the limit to see how far they can go, however. Gradually everybody has become more liberal as to porn. And things that were not permissible 10 years ago now are accepted by society.

Over the years, many law suites have tested the legitimacy of pornography. Most famous and of greatest importance as the basis of court decisions are probably Miller v. California in 1973 and Larry Flynt/Hustler v. Falwell in 1986. In the first case, the US Supreme Court determined what constituted obscene material, i.e. government had the right to restrict access to pornography. Marvin Miller was one of the West Coast's largest mail-order businesses dealing in sexually explicit material. He was found guilty by Californian courts for knowingly distributing obscene material. The question was whether this distribution of pornographic material was protected under the First Amendment's freedom of speech and print or not. The Supreme Court established a three-pronged test, the so-called 'Miller Test', to identify obscene materials: lacking political, artistic, literary, and scientific value; violating community standards for obscenity; having the sole purpose of appealing to one's prurient interests. While the case demonstrated that hardcore pornography and child pornography enjoy no First Constitutional Amendment protection, it also recognized that individual communities had different values and opinions on pornography.

Since then the states can pass their own laws on pornography and the Miller Test has been enforced very heterogeneously. In the second case, referring to the First Amendment of free speech and print, Hustler was not sentenced for parodying Falwell having sex with his mother. Larry Flynt has probably contributed to the rise of the sexual revolution in the US by publishing the sexually open and crude humor of the

9   *www.pbs.org.*

Hustler magazine. Prosecution for and tolerance of pornography varies widely from state to state and city to city in the US. In other cases, for example child pornography, the emergence of virtual pornography animation and pictures has made it difficult for the Supreme Court to reach a final decision on the matter, for want of clear evidences to distinguish between reality and virtuality.

In Canada, the porn industry is mainly situated in Montréal, the third largest porn producing city in the world after Los Angeles and Amsterdam. Japan has a large and highly developed culture and industry for pornography, too.[10] The attitude towards nudity and sex is rather relaxed, because Japan is little influenced by Christian ethics. In Japan the production and distribution of sexual films started in the 1960s, the so-called 'pink films'. The 1970s was the era of big-studio software pornography in Japan. The big-studios took over the pink film market and consolidated the Japanese porn film industry. Unlike Western porn films, porn films in Japan were shown in mainstream theaters. The widespread private ownership of VCRs in the 1980s changed adult entertainment in Japan. The adult video captured the adult entertainment market from the theatrical erotic films. Some porn women rose to become media stars. The Japanese porn industry developed similar to Western pornography and into all kinds of media and genres. Japan has several adult studios, porn magazines, publishers and porn stars. Porn is restricted in Japan by a law that forbids obscenity, too, but the definition of obscenity is controversial and has given reason to many lawsuits over the years. Mainly it is prohibited to show genitals and intercourse, but the legal practice is being increasingly relaxed on the subject. Many Japanese porn movies are being exported.

While the pornography industry is somewhat limited in Latin America and mainly developed in Brazil, it is a rising industry in Asia Pacific outside Japan. Hong Kong and Thailand produce a lot of porn products, mostly print. The porn industry is also considerable in Australia and to some degree New Zealand. Porn is illegal in many countries, including Vietnam, India, Indonesia, Iran, Pakistan and the Middle East, except in Israel.

Europe is the third largest porn market in the world. Hardcore pornography is dominated by a few pan-European producers and distributors, the most notable of which is Private Media Group.[11] Most European countries also have national porn producers with varying potentials of international competitiveness, including France, Germany, UK, and Italy. Women in European pornography typically have a so-called

---

10   *www.wikipedia.org*: 'Pornography in Japan'.
11   *www.wikipedia.org*: 'Pornography in Europe'.

'more natural' look than in American pornography, with less emphasis on breast implants. The once popular chic pornography has in most cases been replaced by a more hardcore style, including lead producers such as French Pierre Woodman. Throughout Europe, and also in the US, ostensibly private 'stolen' videos featuring celebrities (TV and music stars) having sex are very popular on the Internet and on the black market. Since the turn of the millennium, East European countries such as Russia, Ukraine, Hungary, the Czech Republic and Romania have become rising stars in the European and actually world porn industry, as it has become the destination of several Japanese and American producers. In the Islamic world, only Turkey allows porn production and distribution. Most Turkish porn producers are located in Germany, although they recruit their performers from Turkey.

Based on American estimates (Table 59), the global porn market has grown from $3 billion in 1990 to $15 billion in 2005, with a projected $27 billion in 2010.

TABLE 59

The Global Porn Market in $bn, 1990-2015

	1990	2000	2005	2010
USA and Canada	1	4	6	11
Magazines	½	1	1	1
Adult Video	½	1	1	2
Pay-per-view	0	1	2	3
Internet	0	1	2	3
Video Games	0	0	0	1
Mobile Phones	0	0	0	1
Western Europe	1	2	3	5
Eastern Europe	0	0	1	2
Asia Pacific	1	2	3	5
Middle East and Africa	0	0	1	2
Latin America	0	0	1	2
Total	3	8	15	27

Source: *www.pbs.org*. Non-US markets are estimated.

Global Experience Industries

Prostitution

Prostitution may be defined as providing sexual services for money. By far the largest part of this industry is the sale of sex by female prostitutes to male clients.[12] Prostitution is as old as pre-industrial agrarian countries and empires. Prostitution was wide spread in ancient Greece and Rome. Although it was prohibited by the Roman Catholic Church, it was more or less tolerated in pre-industrial Europe in order to prevent greater evils, such as rape and masturbation. Regardless of the laws, prostitution existed everywhere in pre-modern times. Since the early 20th century, prostitution was being prohibited in many countries, for example the US where it used to be legal. After the Second World War, the new Islamic states made prostitution illegal, as did the communist states. Even Western countries began to fight prostitution. Since the 1990s, globalization and liberalization has made migration easier and many women from poor countries travel, forced or voluntarily, from south to north and east to west to supply the sex demands of men in rich countries, or for that matter men in all countries, who can afford it.[13] Each year millions are trafficking in this way. Millions of women in developing countries, who migrate from the countryside to cities to seek their luck often end up in prostitution as their only way of making a living.

The Prostitution Industry

There is an enormous variation in the types and prices of sexual services.[14] At the bottom end of the spectrum, we see street-girls who normally deliver outdoors or in clients' cars for less than $100. At the top end, we see high-class escorts who might charge $1000 or more for a lengthy session in luxurious surroundings. Why is the variation in price so much higher than in most other services? First, there is a good deal of variation in the quality of services. Second, high prices are used by both parties of the transaction as a 'screening' device. High-class providers use high prices to attract the best and richest customers. Wealthy clients are attracted by high prices because of their signal quality.

Formal entry barriers to prostitution do not exist and neither do real barriers at the low-end of the market, except for threats of violence from incumbents and their associates. At the high-end, informal barriers are much higher. However, the entry

---

12 Smelser and Baltes. International Encyclopedia of the Social & Behavioral Sciences: 'Prostitution'. *www.wikipedia.org*: 'Prostitution'.

13 Agustín. Sex at the Margins.

14 Peter M. Moffatt, 'Economics of Prostitution'. Bowmaker, *Economics Uncut*, 193-228.

decision is normally more difficult to make than in other professions, because of feelings of sin or social stigma. But when the threshold is crossed, preferences may change
because of the economic benefits.

The most commonly occurring market structure in prostitution is a collection of
sole traders acting independently and competitively. Some informal price agreements
may occur, however. As soon as the enterprise takes on a third party gainer (pimp)
the enterprise change status from sole trader to small firm. The extent of sole prostitutes and prostitutes working for a pimp or in brothels differs widely from country to
country and region to region. While most British prostitutes seem to work on their
own, brothels are more common in Germany and Australia, for example.

Prostitution occurs in different forms and contexts: street prostitution, brothel
and massage parlors, escort agencies or call girls and sex tourism. Street prostitutes
find their clients while waiting at street corners or other outside places. The sex is
performed in the customer's car, in a nearby alley, or in a rented room. Escort agencies
often maintain websites and can be contacted by telephone. An escort is sent to the
arranged meeting point and the agency charges a fee for its services. Some agencies are
large businesses that even take credit cards. Some escort girls work alone. Sex tourism
is simply traveling for sexual intercourse, such as from Europe to massage parlors in
Thailand and from various parts of the US to brothels in Nevada.

Another difference between different forms of sex work in Western countries is
the legality. Street-based sex work is illegal in many countries. Illegal sex immigrants
are another kind of problem. Within the EU people can freely travel and work without attention from authorities. In political and police circles, there is much focus on
illegal immigrants from Latin America and Asians in the US, Asians in Australia, and
Eastern Europeans in the EU. Human trafficking is not restricted to the sex industry,
however. Hundreds of industries are involved in illegal migration.

There is no simple answer to the question whether prostitution is legal in a given
country or not. There are different approaches to decriminalization and legalization
of prostitution. In some countries, for example Switzerland and Singapore, not only
is prostitution fully legal, but also the operation of third parties such as 'pimps' is
permitted. Prostitution is legal in another group of countries, but third party gainers
are not allowed, including Australia, Germany, Hungary and the Netherlands. Many
other countries appear to have ambiguous systems, for example China, Japan and the
United States, where prostitution is illegal but tolerated, and in the USA it is legal
in certain counties within the state of Nevada, but illegal everywhere else. In some
countries, prostitution is simply illegal.

At one end of the legal spectrum, prostitution carries the death penalty in some
Muslim countries. At the other end, prostitutes are tax-paying and unionized profes-

sionals in the Netherlands and brothels are legal and may advertise their businesses. The legal situation in Germany, Switzerland, and New Zealand is similar to that in the Netherlands. Australia has much the same rules. The Australian Brothel Daily Planet is even listed on the Australian Stock Exchange. In Japan, prostitution is legal to a certain degree. In the UK, street prostitution and brothels are illegal, but associated activities are legal, however, the laws are practiced in much different ways throughout the country. While street prostitution is illegal, government regulated brothels are legal in Turkey. In the US, prostitution is illegal, but most activities around it are not. Regulated brothels are legal in several counties of Nevada and prostitution is not illegal in Rhode Island. In Canada, prostitution is legal, but most activities around it are illegal. Prostitution is legal in Brazil. In Denmark, prostitution is legal, but it is prohibited to profit from it. Prostitution is illegal in Thailand, in practice it is widespread.

Generally, prostitution is found in all countries. It is legal in many countries, but also illegal in another large group of countries. Pimps are prohibited in practically all countries of the world, as is child prostitution. Regardless of the law, all kinds of prostitution are to be found everywhere, and in some cities it has become a large industry. Sex tourism is often related to child prostitution, mainly in South East Asia and Latin America. Prostitutes, particularly street prostitutes, are at high risk of becoming victims of violent crimes, and also have a higher risk of occupational mortality then any other group of women.

Human trafficking is the fastest growing form of modern slavery and is the third largest and fastest growing criminal industry in the world.[15] Poverty and war are the main reasons of human trafficking. Women engage with traffickers, often connected to travel agencies, modeling agencies and employment offices. Other women are simply kidnapped. Once overseas, it is common for their passport to be confiscated by the trafficker and to be warned of the consequences should they attempt to escape. The market for traffickers is created a) by men who will pay to have sex with foreign women; b) the demand for cheap unskilled labor. According to the International Labor Organization (ILO), at least 2-3 million people were trafficked in 2005. Thousands of children are sold into the global sex trade every year, too. Often they are kidnapped, and sometimes they are sold by their own families. The problem is especially alarming in South East Asia and India.

The political attitudes to prostitution fall into one of the following categories: 1) It should be abolished and made to disappear, because it is immoral and degrading and an exploitation of women. This is the prevailing attitude in the US, Turkey, Sweden

---

15   Factbook on Global Sexual Exploitation: *www.uri.edu/artsci*.

and Norway. Feminists have been eager proponents of this attitude and reasoning. 2) Prostitution should be regulated and considered a legitimate business. 3) Prostitution should be made completely legal so that it is no longer an underground activity. 4) Prostitution is labor like any other activity, and as in Australia and New Zealand, the sex industry should not be subject to any special regulation of laws.

The total world number of prostitutes is estimated at some 31 million people, of whom more than ninety percent are women (Table 60). Approximately 1 out of 1000 women is a prostitute in developed countries, and 1 out of 100 in developing countries. Moneywise a single prostitute in a developed country makes as much money as ten prostitutes in a developing country. That makes about 1000 prostitutes for every million inhabitants in developed countries and 10,000 for every million inhabitants in developing countries. With some one billion inhabitants, the number of prostitutes in, for example, India is estimated at 10 million.[16] This relationship seems to apply around the world, based on international calculations. Including related businesses, each prostitute makes an annual income of an estimated $100,000 in developed countries, and $10,000 in developing countries. In Thailand, a center of international sex tourism, research on prostitution concluded that the year 2000 there were 2.8 billion prostitutes in a country with 62 million inhabitants, i.e. almost 1 out of 30 persons.[17] Of the 2.8 million, 2 million were adult females, 0.8 million boys and girls under the age of 18 years and 20,000 male prostitutes.

The world prostitution industry is much larger than normally considered. Because of the wide gap between official numbers and actual numbers, a very high level of revenues and prostitutes is reached. Domestically and internationally, poverty in developing countries makes prostitution a way of living. Thailand is a center of sex tourism and that causes a migration of children and young females from the country side to the sex industry around Bangkok. Furthermore, a comprehensive trafficking in young females is going on from South East Asia and the Philippines to Japan, Australia, New Zealand, South Korea, Taiwan, Hong Kong, and North America. From Nepal, thousands of young females are exported, often by force, to India and other Asian countries to serve in the prostitution industry. Thousands of young females migrate from Bangladesh to Pakistan, for example. Illegal 'sex slave' trade is going on between poor Asian countries to rich people in the Middle East, too. China and India are the two large prostitution markets of Asia. Sex trafficking is taking place from Eastern Europe and Africa to Western Europe and from Latin America to North America.

16 Factbook on Global Sexual Exploitation: *www.uri.edu/artsci.*
17 The Nation. 03.01.2004: *www.nationmultimedia.com,*

TABLE 60

Global Number of Prostitutes, 2005

	2005
North America	270.000
USA	250.000
Canada	20.000
Western Europe	350.000
Germany	100.000
UK	60.000
France	50.000
Italy	50.000
Rest of Western Europe	100.000
Eastern Europe	250.000
Asia Pacific	23.520.000
Japan	150.000
China	10.000.000
India	10.000.000
Australia	20.000
Thailand	2.000.000
Indonesia	500.000
The Philippines	500.000
Rest of Asia Pacific	500.000
Middle East and Africa	5.000.000
Latin America	2.000.000
Total	31.390.000

Source: EU. Sex Work and Sexual Exploitation in the European Union: *www.ex.ac.uk/~warupman/ undergrad/aac*: World Sex Guide: *www.worldsexguide.org*. CIA. World Factbook. Coalition Against Trafficking in Women: *www.catw-ap.org/facts*. Based on anthropological studies in the field, trafficking and prostitution is also shown to be a voluntary living strategy by many women: Austin, Sex at the Margins.

In 2005, an estimated 31 million prostitutes and other directly related persons made revenues of $125 billion, two-thids in developed countries and one-third in developing countries (Table 61). In the next decade, the prostitution industry is projected to grow more in developing countries than in developed countries, reaching an equal size of revenues in the two parts of the world by 2010.

TABLE 61

The Global Prostitution Market in $bn, 1990-2010

	1990	2000	2005	2010
North America	16	27	29	29
USA	15	25	25	27
Canada	1	2	2	2
Western Europe	20	35	35	40
Germany	6	10	10	11
UK	3	6	6	7
France	3	5	5	6
Italy	3	5	5	6
Rest of Western Europe	5	10	10	11
Eastern Europe	2	4	5	6
Asia Pacific	26	46	50	53
Japan	10	15	15	16
China	5	10	12	13
India	5	10	11	12
Australia	1	2	2	2
Thailand	2	3	4	4
Indonesia	1	2	2	2
The Philippines	1	2	2	2
Rest of Asia Pacific	1	2	2	2
Middle East and Africa	2	4	4	5
Latin America	2	4	4	5
Total	68	118	125	138

Source: EU. Sex Work and Sexual Exploitation in the European Union. World Sex Guide. CIA. World Fact Book. Coalition Against Trafficking in Women: *www.catw-ap.org/facts*.

Drugs

Some drugs are illegal, such as opium and heroin, coca and cocaine, cannabis, LSD, amphetamine and ecstasy.[18] As demand for these drugs is high, a large criminal business has emerged to reap the exorbitant profits of the illegal drugs trade. While most

18   United Nations Office on Drugs and Crime (2007). *World Drug Report 2007: www.unodc.org*.

of the drugs are cultivated by farmers in third world countries in the Far East, the Middle East and South America, most drugs are consumed in developed countries in North America and Western Europe and increasingly in emerging nations such as Eastern Europe and China, too. Drugs may also be produced synthetically. The use of drugs is also widespread in developing countries, such as coke in Latin America, chat in Eastern Africa and heroin in Asia. In economic terms, however, drug abuse in developing countries is not important, although it has a significant bearing on local economies. Organized crime in all parts of the world has quickly rushed to take control of production, distribution and sales.

Illegal Drug Trade

The drug trade is a worldwide black market of producing, distributing, packaging and selling illegal psychoactive or conscience expanding substances. Crime, violence and many social problems have followed in the wake of drug trafficking and use, but in spite of many governmental efforts to fight illegal drugs the massive economic profitability of the trade has made it a tough nut to knack. The fight against drugs in the West has not been lightened by the fact that the producing countries of the drug markets in developing countries are inclined to turn a blind eye to the drug trade, often corrupted by crime cartels. As for drugs such as alcohol and tobacco, the production, distribution and consumption of alcohol is prohibited in the Islam world, whereas alcohol elsewhere in the world is considered like any other beverage. Illegal trade of tobacco is motivated primarily by heavy taxation in developed countries. Tobacco smuggling is therefore a profitable business, too. In Western countries, an anti-smoking movement is cutting down consumption of tobacco, however, while consumption is rising in emerging and developing countries.

In the US, marijuana and crack (cannabis and cocaine) are the illicit drugs most easily purchased by users across the country.[19] They are followed, in descending order, by heroin, ecstasy, powder cocaine, and methamphetamine. Marijuana remains the country's most widely abused illicit drug. Heroin is the drug associated with the most serious consequences, including overdose deaths. Heroin is a very expensive and profitable drug, but also popular in many circles looking for an intense rush.

A large global business is based on the production, distribution and sale of heroin. A number of processes are involved in the manufacturing of heroin.[20] First, the opium

---

19   Office of National Drug Control Policy. *Pulse Check: Trends in Drug Abuse*, January 2004: *www.white-housedrugpolicy.gov*.
20   *www.wikipedia.org*: 'Opium' and 'Heroin'.

poppies cultivated by farmers are being refined into opium. Next, morphine is being refined into heroin that is a much stronger drug than opium. The production of opium poppies, opium and heroin refining is mainly taking place in the 'Golden Triangle' of South East Asia (Myanmar/Burma, Thailand, Laos and Vietnam), the 'Golden Crescent' (Afghanistan and Pakistan) and Mexico and Columbia in Latin America. While the Golden Triangle used to be the main provider worldwide of opium, Afghanistan has taken over this position, constituting a large part of this country's export. The decline of the Golden Triangle is also a consequence of the death penalty for trafficking in heroin in several countries. All links in the herointrade profit enormously from this business: farmers gain much more from cultivating opium poppies than from ordinary wheat and corn farming; local states achieve higher taxes or bribes to officials and politicians; middle men are paid to take care of transportation and smuggling into receiver countries; crime organizations profit heavily from running all chains of the business right to the end user.

According to the United Nations World Drug Report, the value of the global illicit drug market for 2005 was estimated at $15 billion at the production level, at $100 billion at the wholesale level, and at $350 billion based on retail prices, taking seizures and other losses into account.[21] In 2000, the total value of global trade in illegal drugs was estimated at $400 billion. Although consumption is worldwide, major consumer nations are the countries of North America and Western Europe. Major producer countries include Afghanistan (opium), Bolivia and Columbia (cocaine) and Mexico (cannabis).

Not all these drugs are illegal in all countries. In particular, cannabis is legal in some countries, such as Spain, Switzerland and the Netherlands and decriminalized in several countries throughout the world, including some states in the US, most of Australia, Russia and many Latin American nations. All the other narcotics are forbidden all over the world, and some countries such as Singapore even use the death penalty as punishment for drug trading. Whether drug prohibition or drug liberalization have a positive or a negative impact on drug consumption and the size of illicit drug trade is not clear.[22]

A hundred years ago, the opium trade was the worst drug problem and world production was several times larger than today. Of a population of 450 million, China

---

21 UN. *World Drug Report 2007: www.un.org*.
22 Bowmaker, Simon W. and Heiland, Frank (2005). 'Economics of Drug Addiction', in Bowmaker, *Economics Uncut*, 11-43. Miron, Jeffrey A. (2005). 'Economics of Drug Prohibition'. Bowmaker, *Economics Uncut*, 44-67. Thornton, Mark, et al. (2005). 'Economics of Drug Liberalization', in Bowmaker, *Economics Uncut*, 68-98.

had an estimated 25 million opium users in the early 20th century. A hundred years later this number is less than 10 million in all Asia. To day, many more use other drugs. The total number of people using illicit drugs is now 5 percent of the world's adult population (4 percent cannabis and 1 percent amphetamine, cocaine and opiates). Cannabis remains by far the most used drug in the world, and cannabis is everywhere and usage is increasing. While a licit but very addictive substance such as tobacco is used by 28 percent of the world's adult population, true drug addictives encompass less than one percent of the world adult population.

Opiates are used most widely in Asia and Europe, but Africa is the prime user of cannabis and America of cocaine and also cannabis. The war against opium cultivators and heroin producers in Asia has obviously succeeded in South East Asia, but not in Afghanistan. Generally speaking, the production and consumption of cannabis, cocaine and opiates seem to have stabilized. After years of massive increases in the 1990s, this is also the case for amphetamine and ecstasy. Synthetic drugs are being produced in both developed and developing countries.

There are currently three production centers for opiates which supply three distinct markets. One trafficking flow is from Afghanistan to neighboring countries, the Middle East and Europe. A second trafficking flow goes from Myanmar/Laos to neighboring countries of South East Asia (notably China) and to Oceania (mainly Australia). A third trafficking flow goes from Latin America (Mexico, Columbia and Peru) to North America (mainly USA). Most global opiate seizures take place in the countries surrounding Afghanistan. The gram retail price of heroin is more than $100 in the US and $75 in Europe. 16 million, 0.4 percent of all adults, are heroin or opiate abusers, half in Asia, one-fourth in Europe and on-sixth in America. Heroin abuse is increasing in Asia and declining in Western Europe and USA.

Half of all cocaine bush cultivation takes place in Columbia, one-third in Peru and the rest in Bolivia. Some two-thirds of global cocaine is produced in Columbia and the rest in the other two countries. The retail cocaine price per gram in USA is $100 and in Europe a little less. Most cocaine is used in North America, Western Europe and South America. There are 6 million users in USA, 3 million in Western Europe, and 2 million in South America. The market is almost stable.

Cannabis is a plant that grows virtually in every region of the world. Contrary to opium and coca, the cultivation of cannabis is not concentrated in certain places but found everywhere, which makes it difficult to estimate global cultivation. Herb production seems to be on the rise worldwide. Almost half of the global cannabis production is estimated to take place in North Africa, mainly Morocco, and one-fourth in Middle East and South Western Asia. Cannabis herb and resin remain the most widely trafficked drugs worldwide. The main trafficking routes go from Morocco to Spain, from Mexico to USA, from Afghanistan and Pakistan and Central Asia to Russia. The main destination of cannabis is Western Europe, of which 80 percent is estimated to originate in Morocco. The second largest destination of cannabis resin is the Middle East region, supplied mainly from Afghanistan and Pakistan and to a lesser degree from Lebanon. Some goes to Eastern Africa and Canada, too. North Africa that makes up the third largest market is predominantly supplied by cannabis resin produced in Morocco. Nepal is a source country for cannabis resin to India and Jamaica and to some other American countries. Cannabis remains by far the most commonly used drug in the world, used by an estimated 162 million in 2004. Relatively, cannabis use is most prevalent in Oceania (15 percent of the adult population), and then North America and Africa (c. 10 percent). Cannabis use has been rising since the late 1990s, mainly in Russia and Africa.

Amphetamine production and consumption seems to be stable. In Asia, most amphetamine is produced in China, Myanmar and the Philippines. In America most is produced in Mexico and USA. In Oceania most is produced in Australia. World-wide, most amphetamine is produced in Europe, mainly the Netherlands, Poland and Belgium, but also Lithuania, Estonia, Bulgaria and Germany. Production sites seem to move to Eastern Europe, however. Amphetamine production remains limited in South America and Africa. Ecstasy is mainly produced in North America, Oceania and East and South East Asia and to a lesser degree in Europe, primarily the Netherlands. Most Amphetamine abusers are found in developed countries, but the number is rising in emerging countries.

Organized Crime

Organized crime or criminal organizations are groups or operations run by criminals, most commonly for the purpose of generating a monetary profit.[23] Mafias are such criminal organizations. Gangs may develop into organized crime, too. Organized gangs or mafias are sometimes referred to as a mob. Terrorist organizations are po-litically motivated crime organizations. In the United States, the act of engaging in organized crime is referred to as racketeering. Organized crime is characterized by a few common qualities. On the one hand, a crime organization is similar to an ordinary business organization, including durability over time, hierarchy, profit goals, capital accumulation, and reinvestment. On the other hand, a crime organization is based

---

23   Smelser and Baltes, International Encyclopedia of the Social & Behavioral Sciences: 'Crime', 'Organ-ised Crime'. Benson, Bruce L. and Bowmaker, Simon W. (2005). 'Economics of Crime', in Bowmaker, *Economics Uncut*, 101-136.

on illegal methods, such as the use of violence, political corruption, tax evasion, and illegal trade in drugs and women.

Criminal organizations keep illegal actions secret, and its members communicate by word of mouth, telephone, or Internet. Many organized crime groups have legal fronts, such as licensed gambling, building construction or trash hauling. Criminal activities include drug trafficking, human trafficking, prostitution, money laundering, fraud, black marketeering, theft, protection rackets in shopping districts, political corruption and violence, extortion, murder for hire, hijacking, insider trading, and terrorism, and even the lucrative business of producing and distributing fake high fashion branded goods.[24] For a criminal organization to prosper, some degree of support is required from the society in which it lives. Therefore, it is often necessary to corrupt some of its politicians and officials, including judges and police officers. Criminals are financed by customers inside any local society, providing drugs, prostitutes, black market products and similar services. Working without much paperwork and formal procedures, criminal organizations are usually more flexible than legitimate organizations. They are quick to capitalize on new markets and when caught by authorities, they often reorganize quickly. Crime is as much globalized as legitimate business, and criminal organizations easily cross frontiers. This is especially true of organized groups engaged in the illegal arms trade, drug and human trafficking. Online crime is the newest growth sector. The Internet makes it easier for criminal organizations to cross boundaries and in addition to operate from anywhere. Furthermore, organized crime using the Internet is much harder to trace down for the police, also because police forces and other law enforcing agencies generally operate on a national level.

In the past, criminal organizations often competed violently for expansion. Today, criminal organizations increasingly cooperate rather then compete. This has led to the rise of global criminal organizations such as Mara Salvatrucha in America, originating in El Salvador, The Sicilian Mafia in the US that has links to the other Italian mafia groups, the Irish Mob, the Japanese Yakuza, and the Russian Mafia – groups that all are working internationally, too. Other leading international crime organizations include the Columbian drug cartels that control the cocaine smuggling from Columbia to the United States, the Chinese Triads, and the Brazilian Primero Comando da Capital. Terrorist organizations such as Hezbollah, Al Qaeda and IRA are also engaged in criminal activities such as drug and women trafficking and money laundering as the means of financiering their terrorist activities, for instance from the Triple Frontier in

---

24   Saviano, Roberto (2007). *Gomorrah*. New York: Farrar, Straus and Giroux.

Latin America[25]. The FBI estimates that global organized crime annually makes one trillion dollars. The rise in cooperation between criminal organizations has meant that law enforcement agencies increasingly have to work together. The FBI is the leading agency in fighting global crime and cooperates with other law enforcement agencies within the US and internationally.

Tobacco

Tobacco is an agricultural product processed from the fresh leaves of the tobacco plant.[26] It is most often used for smoking and is commercially available in the form of cigarette or cigar, smoking pipe or water pipe. Tobacco can also be chewed or sniffed. As tobacco contains nicotine, regular tobacco users become addicted and dependent on this drug. Long term tobacco use can damage the lungs and the circulatory system, carrying risks of developing cancer. Many jurisdictions and organizations have enacted smoking bans in order to prevent the damage to public health caused by tobacco smoking.

Native Americans used tobacco before Europeans arrived in North America in the 16th century and the Europeans brought tobacco smoking and chewing back to Europe, where it became immensely popular.[27] As a consequence, tobacco growing spread in the US. Eventually a tobacco industry developed in the US and Western Europe to process the leaves into cigars, cigarettes, pipe tobacco, chewing tobacco, and snuff. Since the late 19th century, a large-scale US industry and to some degree West European industry came to dominate world tobacco production and distribution. To day, the tobacco industry is a global industry heavily dominated by giant private and state-owned companies.

The tobacco industry in the United States has suffered greatly since the mid-1990s, when it was successfully sued by several US states. The suits claimed that tobacco causes cancer, that companies in the industry knew this, and that they deliberately understated the significance of their findings, contributing to the illness and death of many citizens in those states. A group of tobacco companies had to pay a large sum to the states that sued. Since then, new individual suits followed, which the tobacco industry won in the most cases, however. Lawsuits against the tobacco industry are primarily restricted to the United States due to differences in legal systems in other countries.

---

25 *www.wikipedia.org*: 'Triple Frontier'.
26 Smelser and Baltes. International Encyclopedia of the Social & Behavioral Sciences: 'Tobacco'.
27 WHO (2007). *The Tobacco Atlas: www.who.int./tobacco*

Many parties are involved in the tobacco industry and the impacts of smoking. On the supply side, the tobacco industry is a large business of growing, manufacturing, distributing, marketing and selling tobacco. On the demand side, more than a quarter of the world's adult population, consume tobacco, i.e. some 1 billion people. The negative effects of tobacco smoking include the involvement of the health sector and insurance companies, but the families of the cancerstruck person are to a very high degree also involved. Non-smokers are also claimed to be in danger from passive tobacco use. As a consequence, a strong anti-smoking movement has emerged in developed countries around the world that has led to restrictions on tobacco sale, advertising and smoking. The UN World Health Organization has even passed a treaty on tobacco control. All these initiatives have made life difficult for the tobacco industry. One consequence is a less offensive marketing. Another consequence is an increasing outsourcing of production to developing countries that take a more relaxed attitude to smoking. While demand for tobacco is decreasing in developed countries, the tobacco industry is benefiting from a growing demand in developing countries, however. Today most tobacco production takes place in China, followed by India and Brazil, while the US is only in fourth place. High taxes on cigarettes have led to a considerable smuggling business, too.

Tobacco is grown in more than 100 countries.[28] China is the world's leading producer of tobacco. Other principal suppliers are the United States, India, Brazil, Turkey, Zimbabwe and Malawi. Tobacco products are consumed all over the world. At least 75 percent of cigarette smokers are to be found in developing countries. Most tobacco is used for smoking, and over 80 percent is used for cigarettes. China accounts for 30 percent of world production and consumption of cigarettes by volume. At 12 percent of total, the United States is the second largest producer. Other principal cigarette suppliers are Japan, Russia, Indonesia, Brazil and Germany. Following many decades of steady growth, in the 1990s the growth of world demand for tobacco came to a halt. Since then, demand in developed countries is declining, while growth in developing countries has slowed down. The world cigarette market is becoming more concentrated by company. Taking advantage of a globalized and open world economy, the tobacco companies have reacted to the stagnation in demand in their traditional markets in developed countries by consolidation of the industry, exploring new markets in developing countries and raising productivity. Governments face a dilemma. They have an economic and social interest in tobacco. It provides jobs, tax revenue and in

---

28 Liemt, Gijsbert van (2002). *The World Tobacco Industry: Trends and Prospects.* Working Paper, ILO: *www.ilo.org*. WHO. The Tobacco Atlas.

some countries export earnings. But tobacco also creates governmental expenditure for smoking-related illnesses. In practice, governments cope with these conflicting pressures by discouraging demand in several ways, including raised tax on cigarettes.

Leading tobacco companies and their global market percent shares include: China National Tobacco Co. (CNTC)(33), Altria Group, USA (17, Philip Morris), British American Tobacco (BAT)(16), Japan Tobacco (9), Reynolds Tobacco, USA (2), Imperial Tobacco, UK (2), Altadis, France and Spain (2), Gudang Garam, Indonesia (1.4), TEKEL, Turkey (1.3), ITC, India, and Gallaher, UK (each 1.0). As a consequence of the increasing consolidation and globalization of the tobacco industry, trade flows of cigarettes in particular are explained by corporate strategies. The companies can concentrate production in fewer places and determine which market is being supplied from where. Three groups, CNTC, Altria and BAT control two-thirds of the world cigarette market. Former state-monopolies have in some cases come under the control of the large multinationals.

In addition to taking over competitors, tobacco companies have tried to reduce their dependence on traditional, slow growing or declining markets through diversification by market segment, target group, tobacco product, non-tobacco product and geographical region. In part, diversification has been achieved through mergers and acquisitions. Through several acquisitions, for instance Altadis has become the world's leading company in premium cigars. Food products are a favorite for tobacco companies seeking to diversify. For example, Philip Morris owns Kraft and Miller breweries. A large part of Altadis' earnings originate in its logistics division. By mergers and acquisitions and organic growth, tobacco companies diversify into new and expanding markets in the emerging countries of Eastern Europe, Latin America and in particular the Far East,

Women and young people are prime target groups of the tobacco industry, because fewer women than men smoke and many women see smoking as a symbol of women's liberation and, in addition, some women believe that smoking keeps them slim. The tobacco industry targets women by using seductive images of vitality, slimness, emancipation, sophistication and sexual allure. They also create feminized brands for women, such as 'Glamour' and 'Vogue', and cigarettes which are extra-slim, light colored or menthol. The number of women smokers has been increasing for some time, particularly in developing countries, and women's smoking rates are higher than those of men in some developed countries. A likely future scenario is the convergence of male and female smoking prevalence. Young people are the other main target group, because they are potential new smokers. New products include roll-your-own cigarettes by supplying tobacco and cigarette paper to the market.

Worldwide the tobacco industry employs hundreds of thousands of people. As a consequence of slow market growth, consolidation and higher productivity, this number is unlikely to grow. Tobacco growing gives work to millions of people, however, and continues to be a labor-intensive activity in developing countries. In cigarette production, most people are employed in China, and next India and Indonesia. Productivity is much lower in these countries than in the United States, for example, where the number of employees has been rapidly declining for years, as in all other developed country. The majority of tobacco is grown in developing countries. By merging with non-American companies, US enterprises are being indemnified from future litigation.

The world market in cigarettes amounted to almost $500 billion in 2005, and the total tobacco world market was $600 billion.[29] According to the WHO, there are around 1.3 billion smokers in the world, of which 1 billion are men. This represents about one-third of the global adult population and out of these 1.3 billion people, 1 billion live in developing countries. While half of all males in developing countries smoke, less than one-third in developed countries do so. Every fourth woman in developed countries smokes, but only every tenth woman in developing countries smokes. This smoking pattern is the reason why tobacco companies target women and young people. Worldwide 15 billion cigarettes are smoked each day. For decades since the end of Word War II, the annual world cigarette production and consumption multiplied from 1.6 trillion in 1950 to 5.5 trillion in 1990. Since 1990, cigarette production remains on this level.

As mentioned, there has been a shift in the tobacco market from developed countries, where people are stopping smoking, towards developing countries where sales are continuing to rise. Tobacco companies consequently have been expanding their international operations in Eastern Europe, Asia Pacific, Latin America, Arab nations and Africa for some time. The Asia Pacific region is the fastest growing tobacco market in the world, including China, Indonesia, Pakistan and Vietnam. The tobacco industry has been able to enter these new markets through the privatization in many countries of previously state-owned tobacco companies. This expansion is often accompanied by a lack of regulation around tobacco, especially with respect to marketing to youth and lack of health warnings. Advertising in developing countries tends to reflect the aspirations of the poor to emulate Western nations. The results are increased consumption and therefore a corresponding impact on human health. The six largest cigarette consuming nations of the world and their percent shares are China (18), USA (4), Russia (4), Japan (3), Indonesia (2), and Germany (1).

Tobacco smuggling has become a major worldwide problem. Cigarettes are the

---

29   Action on Smoking and Health: *www.ash.org.uk.*

world's most widely smuggled legal product. It is estimated that sales of contraband cigarettes via the Internet could represent around 10 percent of the US market. In the UK, approximately 15 percent of the cigarette market is comprised of smuggled goods. In China, around 95 percent of foreign cigarettes are contraband, equivalent to an estimated $2.4 billion loss in taxes per annum. Smuggling reduces the price of cigarettes, increases demand and undermines national tobacco tax policies and as a result, harms health by increasing overall tobacco use. Approximately one-third of internationally traded cigarettes are eventually sold illegally with the avoidance of duty, amounting to $200 billion in addition to legitimate numbers. Furthermore, the national and global economic costs of tobacco-related illness are at least as high as the revenues of the tobacco industry and markets, straining governmental budgets on health services.

11. Conclusions

The result of investigations into the many different industries of what is called 'the experience economy' shows first of all that it is growing more rapidly than the general economic growth. Its share of world GPD is approximately 10 percent and gradually growing (excluded the illegal and informal economy shares) (Table 62).

TABLE 62

The Global Experience Industries in $bn, 1990-2010[1]

	1990	2001	2005	2010
Tourism	875	1500	1700	1905
Sports	100	175	200	250
Newspapers	175	325	350	400
Books	125	200	225	250
Business Information	75	150	175	225
Magazines	100	175	200	225
Television	300	500	600	800
Radio	50	75	100	125
Internet	0	125	300	500
Advertising	350	600	700	900
Films	75	125	150	200
Music	75	125	150	200
Performing Arts	75	150	175	225
Crafts and Hobbies	50	80	95	120
Toys	50	100	100	125
Video Games	25	75	100	125
Gaming	50	100	150	250
Design	75	150	175	200
Family	1000	2000	2500	3000
Religion	300	400	450	500
Sex	50	125	150	175
Drugs	500	1000	1100	1300
Total	4.475	8.255	9.845	12.000
* Illegal and informal share	2.000	4.000	5.000	6.000

Source: A summary of previous chapters. Numbers are rounded.

---

1   Most figures are estimates based on added market spending and industries' revenues. In some industries,

Compared to manufacturing industries, the experience industries are more domestic based than part of international trade. While at least one-third of manufacturing goods are exported and imported, the internationally traded share of experience products is about ten percent. Some sub-sectors are more international than others, for example tourism, whereas design is predominantly based on domestic markets. Internationalization and even globalization is increasing and the export and import share of experience industries and products is on the rise. However, generally speaking, markets of experience goods are less internationalized than markets of merchandize products.

In geographic terms, the global experience industries are highly concentrated in developed countries (Table 63). USA is the centre of virtually all experience industries and markets, including more than one-third of world total. Western Europe is next in line with a quarter global share. Japan, other developed Asian Pacific countries such as South Korea and Australia and increasingly emerging China include the lion's share of the rest of the world.

TABLE 63

Regional Shares of Global Experience Industries in %, 2005

	2005
USA	35
Canada	2
UK	5
Germany	5
France	5
Italy	5
Spain	3
Rest of Western Europe	5
Eastern Europe	2
Japan	8
China	5
Rest of Asia Pacific	15
Latin America	3
Africa and Middle East	2
Total	100

Source: Summary of previous chapters. Numbers are estimated.

---

where piracy is widespread, numbers are almost doubled. Other numbers not included in official statistics are Family, sex and drugs.

Looking at developments and structure of the many included experience industries, some common characteristics may be outlined. First, the business world of human experience is growing and areas that used to be outside the market are being increasingly commercialized. That is a consequence of the general dynamics of capitalism on the one hand and, on the other hand, the increasing wealth of developed and merging societies of the world. Furthermore, experience industries tend to grow at a faster rate than general economic growth. Second, changing demographics are also expected to have a positive impact on the market. Growth in the number of young people in Asia Pacific and Latin America will contribute to advertising growth in those regions, while large increases in the number of people in their prime earning years in all regions will contribute to end-user spending growth. In developed countries, low birth rates result in an aging population that live longer than people used to. Therefore, the economic importance of middle-aged and old people is increasing in the Western world.

Third, the revolutionary developments of digital technologies are changing the way consumers demand leisure, entertainment, and other experience-based products. It is challenging companies to come up with new business models to adapt to radical changes of technology and consumer behavior, while creating many new business opportunities that hardly existed just two decades ago. Fourth, piracy still continues to cut into legitimate sales. Although aggressive enforcement of laws and aggressive actions taken by industry trade associations seem to have slowed piracy down somewhat, such defensive measures will never solve this problem. Instead, the music, film and other industries will have to develop new business models adapted to consumer behavior in the age of the Internet and mobile phones. Fifth, globalization has opened the road to consolidation and the making of much more professional organizations that are able to move and mobilize their huge resources around the world and its markets. Sixth, this is part of a much more dynamic and innovative world economy including all other sectors of society in a way never seen before. Seventh, consolidation of the experience industries is not stopping at the gates of the individual industry. Media conglomerates and other large corporations are crossing an increasing number of industry boundaries within media and entertainment that is currently including a significant share of the experience economy. Cross-industry consolidation is also on the move based on service producing industries, particularly in tourism and design. In both respects, consolidation is based on a holistic and global strategic approach intending to combine content, media, arena and performance as a consequence of converging content, technologies and businesses as well as changing distribution channels (broadband, internet, wireless, satellite, and digital terrestrial). This is also reflected by the activities of large investor groups entering the experience industries to expand and unite them. Eight, although political regulations are being downsized, they continue to interfere with several experience industries throughout the world.

Behind consolidation, there is continuously room for innovation and profiting from niches that are considered of little interest to large corporations or maybe new business opportunities that have not been located. This is a dynamic dimension of current developed and emerging societies that is fueling capitalism, including the experience economy, and paving the way for new innovative companies. The sources of innovation are even being democratized as a consequence of easy business and user access to information and marketing through the virtual communities of the Internet. The leading and consolidating companies of the experience industries are also very innovative. Only by being innovative are these companies able to remain leaders of their industry. One part of this innovation process is to scan the market for new and successful firms which are consequently often acquired.

The wider economic effects of the experience economies are huge (Figure 32). Each company and industry is served by several other industries, such as IT and telecommunications, consumer electronics, business services, transportation, construction, and governmental agencies. Parts of this related sector are included in the experience industries when the majority of their revenues stem from the experience economy, while the remaining share of related industries are considered just part of a wider experience-based economy that may add up to be double the size of the experience industries in a narrow sense. As the experience dimension is growing more rapidly than the economy as such, the experience industries are relatively expanding their scope on behalf of the rest of the economy.

FIGURE 32

The Experience Economy Sector in $bn, 2005

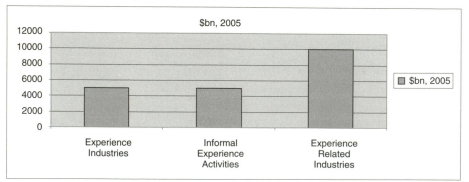

Source: Estimates based on the text above.

Finally, it should be noted that the experience economy and many of its industries are more exposed to fraud, piracy, black-market activities and other illicit methods than the rest of the economy. This is particularly the case in developing countries, but it is common in developed countries as well. From entertainment to fashion, sex, drugs and tobacco, illegal production and trade even tend to dominate developing countries and are widespread in developed countries, too. If this informal economy was included in official statistics, the total revenues of many experience industries and markets would double in size. Consequently, the experience economy and business is crossing the line from the white market to the grey and even black markets. In time, the reasons for this, such as taxes, regulations, poverty, technology, etc. may reduce the illicit activities of the experience economy, if supported by economic growth, relevant business models and governmental procedures. If not, they will just grow in size and economic importance. What we probably know is that the experience industries on average are likely to grow annually five percent in the foreseeable future, e.g. more than the general economic growth.

TABLE 65

Large Companies of the Experience Industries

	Tourism	Sports	Pub-lishing	Audio-visuals	Games	Design
Sabre	x					
Amadeus	x					
Travelport	x					
Expedia	x					
Carlson Wagonlit	x					
American Express Bus.Tr.	x					
BCD Travel	x					
TUI	x					
Thomas Cook	x					
Carnival Corporation	x					
Royal Carribean	x					
Star Cruises	x					
InterContinental Hotels	x					
Accor	x					
McDonalds	x					
Nike		x				
Adidas		x				
Hearst			x			
Google			x			

	Tourism	Sports	Pub-lishing	Audio-visuals	Games	Design
Yahoo			x			
WPP			x			
Omnicom			x			
Interpublic			x			
NBC Universal			x	x		
News Corp.		x	x	x	x	
Viacom			x	x	x	
Walt Disney	x	x	x	x	x	
Vivendi			x	x	x	
Time Warner			x	x	x	
Bertelsmann			x	x	x	
Sony			x	x		
EMI				x		
Mattel					x	
Hasbro					x	
Namco Bandai					x	
Lego					x	
Toys 'R' Us					x	
Nintendo					x	
Microsoft					x	
Electronic Arts					x	
Harrah's Entertainment					x	
MGM Mirage					x	
Ladbrokes					x	
William Hill					x	
SportingBet					x	
bwin					x	
LVMH						x
PPR						x
Richemont						x
Armani						x

Source: The text above. (x) Main activity.

Each leading experience-company is based on one or a few industries (Table 65). Media conglomerates are the most widely diversified companies. In matters of content applications, the experience industries are clearly converging. Sport is for instance an important vehicle of tourism, sports, television, radio, Internet, newspapers, books, magazines, and advertising. The digital revolution and the globalization of business as well as easy consumer access to all media have prompted convergence and cross media consolidation, too. Furthermore, as a consequence of the breakthrough of the Internet and virtual social networks, users and small firms may easily market themselves online, thereby developing new business models. Established companies seek to meet these challenges of a globalized online-age in several ways. One, is the enforcement of copyrights against piracy. Two, is a stronger and wider use of their brand names. Three, is a determined move onto the Internet. Four, is the acquisition of innovative companies. Five, is a continuous consolidation process on a global scale. Six, is a change in business models. Seven, is a reorganization of the value chain.

Finally, sources of change and innovation may be widely drawn from the mega-trends of economic, technological, political, social and cultural developments. Besides globalization and digitization, that includes a continuous search for personal identification in local, national, regional and global cultures, there is a longing for values of democracy, ethics, improved environment, authenticity and social relations.

References

AARP Magazine: www.aarpmagazine.org.

ABC: www.disneyabctv.com.

Access America: www.accessamerica.com.

Accor Hotels: www.accor.com.

AC Nielsen: www.acnielsen.com.

Action on Smoking and Health: www.ash.org.uk.

Adidas (2002-2008). *Annual Reports 2001-2007*.

Advertising: www.wikipedia.org.

Advidsson, Adam (2003). *Marketing Modernity. Italian Advertising from Fascism to Postmodernity*. UK: Routledge.

AEDAS Architects: www.aedas.com.

Air Transport World (2006). *World Airline Financial Results 2005:* www.atwonline.com.

Albarran, Alan B. and Patrick, W. Lawrence (2005). 'Assessing Radio Station Value: A Review of the Academic Literature and Analysis of Contemporary Industry'. *Journal of Radio & Audio Media*, 12:1, 3-13.

Alcatel: www.alcatel.com.

Alfred Publishing: www.alfred.com.

Aller: www.aller.dk.

Allianz: www.allianz.com.

Allmax Travel: www.amxtravel.com.

Amadeus: www.amadeus.com.

Amadeus Global Travel Distribution (2005-2006). *Annual Report 2005-2006*.

American Hotel & Lodging Association: www.ahla.com.

American magazines: www.wikipedia.org.

Amer Sports: www.amersports.com.

Amer Sports (2006-2007). *Annual Reports 2005-2006:* www.amersports.com.

American Association of Publishers: www.publishers.org.

American Express (2006-07), *Annual Report 2005-06:* www.americanexpress.com.

American Express – Travel: www.itn.net.

American Gaming Association: www.americangaming.org.

American Gaming Association (2006-2007). *2006 and 2007 State of the States. The AGA Survey of Casino Entertainment*.

American Hotel & Lodgning Association. www.ahla.com.

Americans for the Arts (2006). *Arts & Economic Prosperity III. The Economic Impact of Non-Profit Arts Organizations:* www.artusa.org.

Anderson, Chris (2006). *The Long Tail: Why the Future of Business is Selling Less of More*. New York: Hyperion.

Answers.com: www.answers.com.

Architecture: www.wikipedia.org.

Arena Leisure: www.arenaleisure.com.

Arts: www.wikipedia.org.

Artprice: www.artprice.com.

Association of Event Organisers: www.aeo.org.

The Association of American Publishers: www.publishers.org.

ATAG (2008). *The Economic & Social Benefits of Air Transport 2008*. www.atag.org.

AT & T: www.att.com.

Agustín, Laura Maria (2007). *Sex at the Margins. Migration, Labour Markets and the Rescue Industry*. London: Zed Books.

Australasian Special Events: www.specialevents.com.au.

AVIS: www.avis.com.

AVIS Budget Group: www.avisbudgetgroup.com.

Axel Springer: www.axelspringer.de.

Bandai: www.bandai.com.

Barnes Reports (2007). *Worldwide Architectural Services Industry:* www.barnesreports.com.

BCD Holdings: www.bcd-nv.com.

Beck, Ulrich and Beck-Gernsheim, Elisabeth (2002): Individualization. London: SAGE Publications.

Benson, Bruce L. and Bowmaker, Simon W. (2005). 'Economics of Crime'. Bowmaker, *Economics Uncut*, 101-136.

Bernstein, Alina (2002). 'Meeting the Industry: An Interview with Alex Gilady'. *Sport in Society*, 5:3, 115-138.

Bertelsmann (2004-2008). *Annual Reports 2003-2007:* www.bertelsmann.com.

Best Trip Choices: www.besttripchoices.com.

Betandwin: www.betandwin.com.

Betandwin (2007). *Gechäftsberichte 2006*.

Bishop, Jack (2005). 'Building International Empires of Sound: Concentrations of Power and Property in the 'Global Music Market'. *Popular music and Society*, 28:4, 443-471.

Blackstone Group: www.blackstonegroup.com.

Blomberg: www.blomberg.com.

Blue Guides: www.blueguides.com.

Bonhams and Butterfield: www.bonhams.com.

Bonn, Mark A., et al. (2008). 'Heritage/Cultural Attraction Atmospherics: Creating the Right Environment for the Heritage/Cultural Visitor'. *Journal of Travel Research*, vol. 45, 345-354.

The Bonnier Group: www.bonnier.com.

English, Bonnie (2007). *A Cultural History of Fashion in the Twentieth Century: From the Catwalk to the Sidewalk*. New York: Palgrave-Macmillan

Bonner Publications: www.bonnierpublications.com.

Bowmaker, Simon W. and Heiland, Frank (2005). 'Economics of Drug Addiction'. Bowmaker, *Economics Uncut*, 11-43.

Bowmaker, Simon W. (Ed.)(2005). *Economics Uncut*, 137-167. Cheltenham, UK: Edward Elgar.

The Broader Music Industry: www.ifpi.org.

Bureau of Labor Statistics: www.bls.gov.

Bürek, Bernhard E.(2005). *Design: History, Theory and Practice of Product Design*. Basel: Birkhäuser.

Business Week: www.businessweek.com.

Cameron, Samuel. 'Economies of Pornography'. Bowbaker, Economies Uncut, 171-192.

Camors, Carina. *The Motion Picture Industry in Los Angeles*. May 12, 2005: www.iaurif.org.

Carlson (2008). *Annual Report 2007:* www.carlson.com.

Carlson Wagonlit: www.carlsonwagonlit.com.

Carnival Cruise Lines: www.carnical.com.

CBS Corporation: www.cbscorporation.com.

CBS Corporation (2002-2008). *Annual Reports 2001-2007*: www.cbscorporation.com.

Cendant Group: www.cendant.com.

C.F. Moller: www.cfmoller.com.

Cheaptickets: www.cheaptickets.com.

Cheyne, Jo, Downes, Mary, and Legg, Stephen (2005). 'Travel Agent vs. Internet: What Influences Travel Consumer Choices?'. *Journal of Vacation Marketing*, vol. 12, 41-57.

Christensen, Jens (2000). *IT and Business. A History of Scandinavian Airlines*. Aarhus: Aarhus University Press.

Christensen, Jens (2001), 'Globalisering og industrialisering – to århundreders perspektiv', *Den Jyske Historiker*, no. 94-95, 142-186 (Globalization and Industrialization – a Two Centuries Perspective).

Christie's: www.christies.com.

CIA (2001-2008). *World Fact Book 2001-2008*. www.cia.gov.

Cinven: www.cinven.com.

Clear Channel Communications: www.clearchannel.com.

Clear Channel Communications (2001-2008). *Annual Reports 2000-2007:* www.clearchannel.com.

ClickZ. *The US Online Travel Market*. 10.11.2004: www.clickz.com.

Coalition Against Trafficking in Women: www.catw-ap.org/facts.

Comcast Corporation: www.comcast.com.

Comcast Corporation (2005-2007). *Annual Reports 2004-2006: www.comcast.com.*

Convention Industry Council: www.conventionindustry.org.

Cox Radio: www.coxradio.com.

Craft and Hobby Association: www.craftandhobby.org.

Crafts Council and Arts Council of England & Wales (2004). *Making it into the 21th Century. A Socio-Economic Survey of Crafts Activities in England and Wales, 2002-2003:* www.craftassoc.com.

Creative London: www.creative.london.uk.org.

Cruise Copenhagen: www.cruisecopenhagen.com.

Cruise line International Association (2006). *CLIA 2006 Cruise Market Profile:* www.cruising.org.

CryptoLogic: www.cryptologic.com.

Dale, Christie (2001). 'The UK Tour-Operating Industry'. *Journal of Vacation Marketing*, vol. 6, 357-367.

Dallan, Timothy J. (2005). *Tourism Shopping, Retailing, and Leisure*. Tonawanda, New York: Channel View Publications.

Dankort: www.dankort.dk.

De Agostini: www.deagostini.it.

Dehejia, DeLeire, and Luttmer. 'Insuring Consumption and Happiness through Religious Organizations', August 2005, RWPO5-047: www.harvard.edu.

Deloitte (2006-2008). *Football Money League*, Febr. 2006, Febr. 2007, and Febr. 2008.

Deloitte (2007). *Hospitality 2010*. www.deloitte.com.

Dentsu: www.dentsu.com.

Dentsu (2008). *Annual Report 2007-2008*: www.dentsu.com.

Desbordes, Michael (2001). 'Innovation Management in the Sports Industry'. Lessons from the Salomon Case'. *European Sport Management Quarterly*, 1:2, 124-149.

Design Continuum: www.dcontinuum.com.

Deutsche Telekom: www.telekom.de.

Dickerson, Kitty G. (2000). *Inside the Fashion Business*. 7th Ed. New Jersey: Prentice Hall.

DIRECTV Group: www.directv.com.

DIRECTV Group (2001-2008). *Annual Report 2000-2007*: www.directtv.com.

Divorce: www.wikipedia.org.

Dolnicar, Sara and Leisch, Friedrich (2003). 'Winter Tourist Segments in Austria: Identifying Stable Vacation Styles using Bagged Clustering Techniques'. *Journal of Travel Research*, vol. 42, 281-292.

Dolnicar, Sara and Laesser, Christian (2007). 'Travel Agency Marketing Strategy: Insights from Switzerland'. *Journal of Travel Research*, vol. 46, 133-146.

Dow Jones: www.dj.com.

Doyle, Gilliam (Ed.)(2006). *The Economics of Mass Media*. Mass., USA: Edward Elgar Pub.

Drewry (2005). *The European Ferry Business*. www.drewry.co.uk.

Dun & Bradstreet: www.dnb.com.

Dyreson, Mark (2003). 'Globalizing the Nation-Making Process: Modern Sport in World History'. *International journal of the History of Sport*, no. 1, 91-106.

Ebookers: www.ebookers.com.

Economist: www.economist.com.

Egmont: www.egmont-magasiner.dk.

Egmont: www.egmont.com.

Electronic Arts: www.ea.com.

Electronic Arts (2008). *Annual Report 2007.*

Eliasberg, Joshoshua, et al. The Motion Picture Industry: Critical Issues in Practice, Current Research, and New Research Directions. *Marketing Science*, vol. 25, no. 6, Nov.-Dec., 638-661.

EMI Group: www.emi.com.

Engholm, Ida, og Michelsen, Anders (1999). *Designmaskinen – design af den moderne verden (The Design Machine)*. Gyldendal: Copenhagen.

Entercom: www.entercom.

Ericsson: www.ericsson.com.

Eternal Word Television Network. Global Catholic Network: www.ewtn.com.

ETC, 'New Media Review, 2006: www.etcnewmedia.com.

EU (2003). *Structure, Performance and Competitiveness of European Tourist Enterprises.*
www.sete.gr.

EU (2004). *Family Life and Professional Work.*

EU/Leidner, Rüdiger (2004). *The European Tourism Industry*. EU: Bruxelles. http://ec.europa.eu.

EU (2006). *Energy and Transport Figures 2005*: http://circa.europa.eu.

EU. 'How is the Time of Women and Men Distributed in Europe'. *Statistics in Focus. Population and Social Conditions*, 4/2006: http://epp.euostat.ec.europa.eu.

EU (2006). *ICT and e-Business in the Tourism Industry*. Sector Report no. 8/2006: www.union-network.org.

EU/Leidner, Rüdiger (2007). *The European Tourism Industry in the Enlarged Community*. Bruxelles: EU: www.europe-travelers.eu.

Eurazeo (2007-08). *Annual Reports 2007-08*: www.eurazeo.com.

Eurofound: www.eurofound.europa.eu.

European Audiovisual Observatory (2001). *The Ups and Downs of European Cinema*: www.obs.coe.int.

European Audiovisual Observatory (2007). *FOCUS 2007. World Film Market Trends:* www.obs.coe.int.

European Travel Commission (2005). *City Tourism & Culture. The European Experience:* www.etc-corporate.org.

Europäische Reiseversicherung: www.erv.de.

Eurostat (2001). *European Implementation Manual on Tourism Satellite Accounts.* http://circa.europa.eu.

Eurostat (2004). *Guidelines on Harmonised European Time Use Survey:* http://epp. eurostat.ec.europa.eu.

Eurostat (2008). *European Business. Facts and Figures:* http://epp.eurostat.ec.europa.eu.

Eurostat (2008). *Panorama on Tourism:* http:// epp.eurostat.ec.europa.eu

EURATEX (2004). *European Technology Platform for the Future of Textiles and Clothing:* www. euratex.org.

EVS Group: www.evs-global.com.

Expedia: www.expedia.com.

Extraordinary Events: www.extraordinary-events.com.

Facebook: www.facebook.com.

Factbook on Global Sexual Exploitation: www. uri.edu/artsci.

FactSet: www.factset.com.

Falk, Gerhard (2005). *Football and American Identity.* New York: The Haworth Press.

Fashion History: www.fashion-era.com.

Fernández-Kelly, Patricia and Sheffner, Jon (2006). *Out of the Shadows: The Informal Economy and Political Movements in Latin America.* Princeton, New Jersey: Princeton University Press.

Fetscherin, Marc and Krohmayer, Gerhard (2004). 'Business Models for Content Delivery. An Empirical Analysis of the Newspaper and Magazine Industry'. *International Journal on Media Management,* 6:1, 4-11.

Le Figaro: www.lefigaro.fr.

First Choice: www.firstchoice.com.

Fodors: www.fodors.com.

FORA (2005). *Brugerdreven innovation i dansk mode (user-driven innovation in Danish fashion)*

Foster + Partners: www.fosterandpartners.com.

France Telecom: www.francetelecom.com.

Frankfurter Allgeime Zeitung: www.faz.net.

Friedberg, Leora and Stern, Steven N. 'Economics of Marriage and Divorce'. Bowmaker, *Economics Uncut,* 137-167.

Full tilt Poker: www.fulltiltpoker.com.

Fuseproject: www.fuseproject.com.

Gambling Industry: www.gambling.com.

Gannett: www.gannett.com.

Gannett (2001-2008). *Annual Reports 2000-2007:* www.gannett.com.

GAP: www.gap.com.

Gensler: www.gensler.com.

Gensler (2008). *Annual Report 2007.*

Georg von Holtzbrinck: www.holtzbrinck.com.

Gmp: www.gmp-arkitekten.de.

Galileo: www.galileo.com.

Gallup Inernational. *Gallup International Millennium Survey:* www.gallup-international.com.

Gamblin: www.wikipedia.org.

Gilmore, James H. and Pine II, B. Joseph (2007). *Authenticity. What Consumers Really Want.* Boston, Mass.: Harvard Business Publishing.

Giorgio Armani: www.giorgioarmani.com.

Goig, Ramón Lllopåis (2008). 'Identity, Nation-State and Football in Spain. The Evolution of Nationalist Feelings in Spanish Football'. *Soccer & Society,* no. 1, 56-63.

Goldfarb, Avi (2004). 'Concentration in Advertising-Supported Online Markets: An Empirical Approach'. *Economics of Innovation and New Technology,* vol. 13, Issue 6, 581-594.

Govers, Robert, Go, Frank M., and Kumar, Kuldeep (2007). 'Promoting Tourism Destination Image'. *Journal of Travel Research,* vol. 46, 15-23.

Gratton, Chris and Solberg, Harry Arne (2007). *The Economics of Sports Broadcasting.* New York: Routledge.

Grüner + Jahr: www.grunerjahr.com.

GTech: www.gtech.com.

Gudis, Catherine (2004). *Buyways, Billboards, Automobiles, and the American Landscape*. UK: Routledge.

Hachette: www.hachette.com.

Handy, David (2000). 'A Political Economy of Radio in the Digital Age'. *Journal of Radio Studies*, vol. 7, no. 1, 213-234.

HarperCollins: www.harpercollins.com.

Harrah's Entertainment: www.harrahs.com.

Hartley, John (Ed.)(2005). *Creative Industries*. MA, USA: Blackwell Publushing.

Hasbro: www.hasbro.com.

Haymarket Publishing: www.haymarketgroup. co.uk.

Hearst Corporation: www.hearst.com.

HenH & M: www.hm.com.

Herz: www.hertz.com.

Herbst LaZar Bell: www.hlb.com.

The Heritage Foundation: www.heritage.org.

HolidayAutos: www.holidayautos.com.

Holtzbrinck: www.holtzbrinck.com.

Hoovers: www.hoovers.com.

Houghton Mufflin: www.hmco.com.

Hotwire: www.hotwire.com.

Howkins, John (2001). *The Creative Economy*. Penguin Books: London.

Hugo Boss: www.hugo.com.

Hyde, Kenneth F. and Lawson, Rob (2003). 'The Nature of Independent Travel'. *Journal of Travel Research*, vol. 42, 13-23.

IAB Internet Advertising (2002-2008). *Revenue Reports 2001-2007*.

IDEO: www.ideo.com.

IMS Health: www.imshealth.com.

Industrial Design Society of America: www. idsa.org.

Informa Plc: www.informa.com.

Information Week, 2006.

InterContinental Hotels Group (2008). *Annual Reports 2007*: www.ichotelsgroup.com.

International Association of Exhibitions and Events: www.iaem.org.

International Council of Cruise Lines (2005-2006). *The Cruise Industry 2004-2005*: www.iccl.org.

International Council of Toy Industries: www. toy-icti.org.

International Federation of the Phonographic Industry (2001-2008). *The Recording Industry 2000-2007 Piracy Report*: www.ifpi.org.

International Federation of the Phonographic Industry (2007). *The Broader Music Sector*: www.ifpi.org.

International Federation of the Phonographic Industry (2007). *The 2007 Recording Industry in Numbers*: www.ifpi.org.

International Federation of the Phonographic Industry (2008). *Digital Music Report 2008*: www.ifpi.org.

International Festivals and Events Association: www.ifea.com.

International Game Developers Association: www.igda.org.

International Game Developers Association (2006). *2006 Casual Games White Paper*: www.igda.org.

International Special Events Society: www.ises. org.

International Telecommunication Union (2006). *Digital Life. ITU Internet Report 2006*. www. itu.int.

International Telecommunication Union (2007). *The Information Society*. www.itu.int.

Internet World Stat: www.internetworldstat. com.

Interpublic: www.interpublic.com.

Interpublic (2008). *Annual Report 2007*: www. interpublic.com.

Jamal, Tazan and Kim, Hyounggon (2005). 'Bridging the Interdisciplinary Divide: Towards an Integrated Framework for Heritage Tourism Research'. *Tourist Studies*, vol. 5, 55-83.

The Japan Newspaper Publishers & Editors Association: www.pressnet.or.jp

Jensen, Rolf (1999). *The Dream Society*. New York: MacGraw-Hill.

Johnston, Donald H. (Ed.)(2003). *Encyclopedia of International Media and Communications*, vol. 1-4. San Diego, Cal.: Academic Press. *Journal of Sport & Tourism*, vol. 11, no. 1, 2006.

Jun, Hyon Soo, Vogt, Christine A., and Mac
Kay, Kelly J. (2007). 'Relationships between
Travel Information and Travel Product
Purchase in Pretrip Contexts'. *Journal of
Travel Research*, vol. 45, 266-274.
Jupiter Media Corporation: www.jupitermedia.
com.
Jyllands-Posten: www.jp.dk.

Kayak: www.kayak.com.
KEA/EC (2006). *The Economy of Culture in
Europe*. Bruxelles: EC.
Keeble, Richard (Ed.)(2005). *Print Journalism.
A Critical Introduction*. Abingdon, UK:
Routledge.
Kelley, Tom (2001). *The Art of Innovation*. New
York: Random House.
Kelley, Tom (2005). *Ten Faces of Innovation*. New
York: Random House.
Khosrowpour, Mehdi (Ed.)(2005). *Encyclopedia
of Information Science and Technology*, vol. 1-5.
Hershey, PA: Idea Group Reference.
KK-Stiftelsen (2003). *Upplevelsesindustrien* (The
Experience Industry). Stockholm.
Kompan: www.kompan.com.
Kompan (2008). *Annual Report 2007*.
Kuoni (2007-2008). *Annual Report 2006-2007*:
www.kuoni.com.
Kusin & Company: www.kusin.com.
Kwortnik, Jr. Robert (2006). 'Carnival Cruise
Lines: Burnishing the Brand'. *Cornell
Hospital Quarterly*, vol. 47, 286-300.

Lagardère: www.lagardere.fr.
Lange. *The Ups and Down of European Cinema.
08.11.2001*: www.obs.coe.int.
LEGO: www.lego.com.
LEGO (2007-2008). *Annual Reports 2006-2007*.
Liberty Media Corporation: www.libertymedia.
com.
Liberty Media Corporation (2002-2008).
Annual Reports 2001-2007: www.
libertymedia.com.
Libreros, Marion, Massieu, Antonio, and
Meis, Scott (2006).'Progress in Tourism
Satellite Account Implementation and
Development'. *Journal of Travel Research*,
vol. 45, 83-91.

Liemt, Gijsbert van (2002). *The World Tobacco
Industry: Trends and Prospects:* www.ilo.org.
LMVH: www.lmvh.com.
LMVH (2006-2008). *Annual Reports 2006-2007*.
Lonely Planet: www.lonelyplanet.com.
Lunar Design: www.lunar.com.
Luxury Briefing, July-August 2006: www.
luxury-briefing.com.
Luxury Goods: www.wikipedia.org.

Maddison, Angus (2003). *The World Economy:
Historical Statistics*. Paris: OECD.
Maddison, Angus (2001). *The World Economy: A
Millennium Perspective*. Paris: OECD.
Marks & Spencer: www.marksandspencer.com.
MarketingVOX: www.marketingvox.com.
Markusen, Ann, Wassall, Gregory H., deNatale,
Douglas, and Cohen, Randy (2008).
'Defining the Creative Economy: Industry
and Occupational Approaches'. *Economic
Development Quarterly*, vol. 22, 24-45.
Markussen, Carl H. (2003). *Trends in the US
Online Travel Market, 2000-2002:* www.crt.
dk.
Markussen, Carl H. (2008). *Trends in European
Internet Distribution – Travel and Tourism
Services:* www.crt.dk.
Mastercard: www.mastercard.com.
Mattel: www.mattel.com.
Mattel (2006-2008). *Annual Reports 2005-2007*.
Mazanec, Josef A., Wöber, Karl, and Zins,
Andreas (2007). 'Tourism Destination
Competitiveness: From Definition to
Explanation?'. *Journal of Travel Research*, vol.
46, 86-95.
McCabe, Scott (2005). 'Who is a Tourist?: A
Critical Review'. *Tourist Studies*, vol. 5,
85-106.
McComb, David (2004). *Sports in World History*.
Abington, UK: Routledge.
McGovern, Richard (2001). *Government and
the Transformation of the Gaming Industry*.
McGraw-Hill: www.macgraw-hill.com.
McGraw Hill Construction ENR. *The Top 200
International Design Firms*. July 2006: www.
construction.com.
Mechikoff, Robert A. (2006). *A History and
Philosophy of Sport and Physical Education*

from the Ancient Civilization to the Modern
World, 4th Edition. New York: McGraw-Hill.

Meikle, J. L. (2005). *Design in the USA*. New
York: Oxford University Press.

Missiroli, Antonio (2002). 'European football
Cultures and Their Integration: The 'Short'
Twentieth Century'. *Sport in Society*, 5:1,
1-20.

MGM Mirage: www.mgmmirage.com.

MGM Mirage (2008). *Annual Report 2007*.

MGM Mirage Events: www.mgmmirageevents.
com.

Michelin: www.michelin.com.

Microsoft: www.microsoft.com.

Microsoft (2008). *Annual Report 2007*.

Milman, Ady (2001). 'The Future of the
Theme Park and Attraction Industry: A
Management Perspective'. *Journal of Travel
Research*, vol. 40, 139-147.

Miron, Jeffrey A. (2005). 'Economics of Drug
Prohibition'. Bowmaker, *Economics Uncut*,
44-67.

Moffatt, Peter G. 'Economics of Prostitution'.
Bowbaker, *Economics Uncut*, 193-228.

Le Monde: www.lemonde.fr.

Mondial Assistance Group: www.mondial-
assistance.fr.

Motion Picture Association of America (2006).
International Piracy Fact Sheets: www.mpaa.
org.

Motion Picture Association of America (2006).
The Cost of Movie Piracy: www.mpaa.org.

The Motion Picture Association of America
(2007). *The U. S. Entertainment Industry.
2006 Market Statistics:* www.mpaa.org.

Motorola: www.motorola.com.

Muehlfeld, Katrin and Sahib, Padma Rao
(2007). 'Completion or Abandonment of
Mergers and Acquisitions: Evidence from
the Newspaper Industry, 1981-2000'.
Journal of Media Economics, 20:2, 107-137.

Multimedia Games: www.multimediagames.
com.

MySpace: www.myspace.com.

MyTravel (2006). *Annual Report 2005:* www.
mytravel.com.

Namco: www.namco.com.

Namco Bandai: www.namcobandaigames.com.

Nash, Laura and McLennon, Scotty (2001).
*Church on Sunday, Work on Monday. The
Challenge of Fusing Christian Values and
Business Life*. San Francisco: Jossey Bass.

The Nation, 03.01.2004: www.
nationalmultimedia.com.

National Restaurant Association: www.
restaurant.org.

NBC Universal: www.nbc.com. www.nbcuni.
com.

New Media Review (2006). *The Online Travel
market*. www.etcnewmedia.com.

News Corporation (2002-2008). *Annual Reports
2001-2007:* www.newscorp.com.

New York City: www.nycvisit.com.

The Nielsen Company: www.nielsen.com.

Nintendo: www.nintendo.com.

Nintendo (2008). *Annual Report 2007*.

NFL Team Valutations: www.forbes.com.

Nike (2001-2008). *Annual Report 2000-2007*.

Nokia: www.nokia.com.

Nordås, Hildegunn K. (2004). *The Global Textile
and Clothing Industry Post the Agreement on
Textiles and Clothing:* www.wto.org.

Nortel: www.nortel.com.

NTT: www.ntt.com.

OECD (2001). *Measuring the Role of Tourism in
OECD Economics*. Paris: OECD.

OECD (2005). *Working Party on the Information
Economy. Digital Broadband Content: The
Online Computer and Video Game Industry.*
Paris: OECD.

OECD (2005). *Working Party on the Information
Economy. Digital Broadband Content: Mobile
Content. New Content for New Platforms.*
Paris: OECD.

OECD (2005). *Working Party on the Information
Economy. Digital Broadband Content: Music.*
Paris: OECD.

OECD (2005). *Working Party on the Information
Economy. Digital Broadband Content: Scientific
Publishing.* Paris: OECD.

OECD (2006). *Working Party on the Information
Economy. Digital Broadband Content: Digital
Content Strategies and Policies.* Paris: OECD.

OECD (2007). *Innovation and Growth in Tourism*. Paris: OECD.

OECD (2007). *Broadband and ICT Access and Use by Households and Individuals*. Paris: OECD.

OECD (2007). *Working Party on the Information Economy. Broadband and ICT Access and Use by Households and Individuals*. Paris: OECD.

OECD (2007). *Working Party on the Information Economy. Participatory Web and User-Created Content: Web 2.0, Wikis and Social Networking*. Paris: OECD.

Office of National Drug Control Policy. *Pulse Check: Trends in Drug Abuse*, January 2004: www.whitehousedrugpolicy.gov.

Omnicom Group: www.omnicomgroup.com.

Omnicom Group (2007-2008). *Annual Reports 2006-2007*.

Online dictionary: www.answers.com.

Opodo: www.opodo.com.

Orbitz: www.orbitz.com.

Ottenbacher, Michael C. (2007). 'Innovation Management in the Hospitality Industry: Different Strategies for Achieving Success'. *Journal of Hospitality & Tourism Research*, vol. 31, 431-454.

Party Poker: www.partypoker.com.

Pascal Blaise (1660). *Pensées*.

Paskaleva-Shapira, Krassima A. (2007). 'New Paradigms in City Tourism Management: Redefining Destination Promotion'. *Journal of Travel Research*, vol. 46, 108-114.

Pearson: www.pearson.com.

Pearson Education. www.pearsoned.com.

Pentagram: www.pentagram.com.

Picard, Robert G. (Ed.)(2002). *Media Firms: Structures, operations, and Performance*. Mahwah, N.J.: Erlbaum.

Pine, B. Joseph & Gilmore, James H. (1999). *The Experience Economy*. Boston, Mass.: Harvard Business School Press.

Pine, B. Joseph II & Gilmore, James H. (2007). *Authenticity. What Consumers Really Want*. Boston, Mass.: Harvard Business School Press.

Politiken: www.politiken.dk.

Politikens Forlag: www.politikens.dk.

Poon, Auliana (1993). *Tourism, Technology and Competitive Strategies*. C.A.B. International: Wallingford, UK.

Pokerstars: www.pokerstars.com.

Pokorny, Michael and Sedgwick, Jon (2004). *An Economic History of Film*. UK: Rotledge.

Portes, A. and Haller, A. (2005). 'The Informal Economy'. Smelser, N. and Swedberg, R (Eds.). *Handbook of Economic Sociology*, 2nd Ed. Princeton: Princeton University Press.

PPR: www.ppr.com.

PPR (2007-2008). *Annual Reports 2006-2007*.

Priceline: www.priceline.com.

PricewaterhouseCoopers (2006). *Global Entertainment and Media Outlook 2006-2010*. New York: PricewaterhouseCoopers.

Professional Travel Guide: www.professionaltravelguide.com.

Publicis: www.publicis.com.

Puma (2007-2008). *Annual Reports 2006-2007*.

Radio One: www.radio-one.com.

Raizman, David (2003). *History of Modern Design*. London: Laurence King.

Ralph Appelbaum: www.raany.com.

Ralph Lauren: www.ralphlauren.com.

RCS Media Group: www.rcsmediagroup.it.

Reader's Digest: www.rd.com.

The Recording Industry Association of America: www.riaa.org.

Redwood Publishing: www.redwood.net.

Reed Exhibitions: www.reedexpo.co.uk.

Reed Elsevier: www.reed-elsevier.com.

ReportSURE (2006). *Industry Survey: Global Media & Entertainment*: www.reportsure.com.

ReportSURE (2006). *Insurance Survey 2006*: www.reportsure.com.

Reuters: www.reuters.com.

REWE: www.rewe.group.com.

Richemont: www.richemont.com.

Ritchie, Brent W. and Adair, Daryl (Ed.)(2004). *Sport Tourism. Interrelationships, Impacts and Issues*. Tonawanda, New York: Channel View Publications.

RKS Design: www.rks.design.com.

RMJM: www.rmjm.com.

Rough Guides: www.roughguides.com.

Royal Caribbean Cruise Lines: www.royalcaribbean.com.

SABRE: www.sabre.com.

SABRE (2008). *Annual Report 2007:* www.sabre.com.

Sage, George H. (2004). 'The Sporting Goods Industry: From Struggling Entrepreneurs to National Businesses to Transnational Corporations', in Slack, *The Commercialisation of Sport*, 29-51.

Saviano, Roberto (2007). *Gomorrah*. New York: Farrar, Straus and Giroux.

Scandlines: www.scandlines.com.

Schement, Jorge Reina (Ed.)(2002). *Encyclopedia of Communication and Information*, vol. 1-3. New York: Macmillan.

Schibsted: www.schibsted.no.

Scientific Games: www.scientificgames.com.

Schoder, Detlef et al. (2006). 'Mass Customization in the Newspaper Industry: Consumers' Attitudes toward Individualized Media Innovations'. *International Journal on Media Management*, 8:1, 9-18.

Scholastic: www.scholastic.com.

Schneider, Friedrich. 'Shadow Economies and Corruption all over the World: What do we Really Know?' IZA DP, no. 1043, 2004, no. 2315, 2006: www.iza.org.

Seatrade (2007). *Cruise Report 2007:* www.seatrade-global.com.

Sex Work and Sexual Exploitation in the European Union: www.ex.ac.uk.

The Shadow Economy: www.shadoweconomy.com.

Sihna, Rajiv K. & Mandel, Naomi (2008). 'Preventing Digital Music Piracy: The Carrot or the Stick?'. *Journal of Marketing*, vol. 72, Issue 1, 1-15.

Sinclair, John (2007). 'Globalisation and Regionalisation of the Advertising Industry in the Asia-Pacific'. *Asian Studies Review*, vol. 31, issue 3, 283-300.

Siwek, Stephen E. (2006). *The True Cost of Motion Picture Piracy to the US Economy*. Institute for Policy Innovation: www.ipi.org,

Siwek, Stephen E. (2006). *The True Cost of Sound Recording Piracy to the US Economy*. Institute for Policy Innovation: www.ipi.org,

Siwek, Stephen E. (2006). *The True Cost of Copyright Industry Piracy to the US Economy*. Institute for Policy Innovation: www.ipi.org,

Slack, Trevor (Ed.)(2004). *The Commercialisation of Sport*. Abingdon, UK: Routledge.

Smart Design: www.smartdesignusa.com.

Smelser, Neil J. and Baltes, Paul B. (Eds.)(2001). *International Encyclopedia of the Social & Behavioral Sciences*, vol. 1-26. Amsterdam: Elesevier.

Smeral, Egon (2006). 'Tourism Satellite Accounts: A Critical Assessment. *Journal of Travel Research*, vol. 45, 92-98.

SNCF: www.sncf.com.

Sony (2007-2008). *Annual Reports 2006-2007.*

Sony BMG: www.sony.com. www.bertelsmann.com.

Sotherby's: www.sothebys.com.

The Special Event Company: www.specialevent.co.uk.

Special Events Magazine: www.specialevents.com.

SportingBet: www.sportingbet.com.

Star Cruises: www.starcruises.com.

Starbucks: www.starbucks.com.

Statistics Denmark. Produktstatistik for arkitektvirksomhed 2005 (Product Statistics of Architect-firms). *Nyt fra Danmarks Statistik nr. 412, 20. september 2006.*

Stenalines: www.stenalines.com.

Steve Kemble: www.stevekemble.com.

Stewart, David O., et al. (2006). *An Analysis of Internet Gambling and its Policy Implications:* www.americangaming.org.

Stonebraker, R. J. 'Economics and Religion'. Bowbaker, *Economics Uncut*, 264-290.

Street & Smith's SportsBusiness Journal, March 25, 2007.

SWECO: www.sweco.se.

Süddeutsche Zeitung: www.sueddeutsche.de.

TabCorp: www.tabcorp.com.

TDC: www.tdc.dk.

Telecommunications Union (2007). *The Information Society.*

Television Bureau of Advertising: www.tvb.org.

Telia: www.telia.se.

Thomas Cook: www.thomascook.com.

Thomson Corporation: www.thomson.com.

Thomson, John B. (2005). *Books in the Digital Age: the Transformation of Academic and Higher Publishing in Britain and the United States.* Oxford: Polite Press.

Thornton, Mark, et al. (2005). 'Economics of Drug Liberalization. Bowmaker, *Economics Uncut*, 68-98.

Time: www.time.com.

Time Warner: www.timewarner.com.

Time Warner (2007-2008). *Annual Reports 2006-2007.*

TNS Media Intelligence: www.tns.mi.com.

Tommy Hilfiger: www.tommy.com.

Torres, Rebecca (2002). 'Cancun's Tourism Development from a Fordist Spectrum of Analysis'. *Tourist Studies*, vol. 2, 87-116.

Toys 'R' US: www.toysrus.com.

TQ3 (2006), *Annual Report 2005:* www.tq3.com.

Travel Industry Association of America (2007). 'US Travel Market Overview': www.tia.org.

Travel Industry Association of America. 'Travel Insights', Aug. 2005.

TripAdvisor: www.tripadvisor.com.

TUI (2007-2008). *Annual Report 2006-2007:* www.tui.group.com.

Turner, Graem (2002). *Film as Social Practice.* UK: Routledge.

UK Design Council (2006). *The Business of Design. Design Industry Research 2005:* www.design-council.org.uk.

UK Gambling Commission (2007). *Annual Report 2006.*

UNESCO: Cultural Heritage: www.unesco.org.

UNESCO (2003). *International Flows of Selected Cultural Goods and Services, 1980-1998.* Paris: UNESCO.

UNESCO (2005). *International Flows of Selected Cultural Goods and Services, 1994-2003.* Unesco: Paris.

United Nations Office on Drugs and Crime (2007). *World Drug Report 2007: www.unodc. org.*

Universal: www.universal.com.

Universal Music Group: www.umusic.com.

US Bureau of the Census (1975). *Historical Statistics of the United States. Colonial Times to 1970. Part 2.*

US Census Bureau (2007). *International Statistics:* www.census.gov.

US Census Bureau (2007). *Statistical Abstract:* www.census.gov.

Vacations To Go: www.vacationstogo.com.

VentureRepublic (2007). *Giorgio Armani – the Ultimate Fashion Brand:* www.venturerepublic.com.

Verganti, Roberto and Del'Era, Claudio (2002). 'Radical design-driven innovation. The secret of Italian design': www.eu-design.net.

Viacom: www.viacom.com.

Viacom (2002-2008). *Annual Reports 2001-2007:* www.viacom.com.

Vivendi: www.vivendi.com.

Vivendi (2002-2008). *Annual Reports 2001-2007:* www.vivendi.com.

VNU Media: www.vnubp.nl.

Vok Dam: www.vok.nl.

VISA: www.visa.com.

VisitDenmark (2006). *Turismen i Danmark 2000-2004* (Tourism in Denmark): www.visitdenmark.org.

Vlachos, Pavlos, Vrechopoulos, Adam, and Pateli, Adamantia (2006). 'Drawing Emerging Business Models for the Mobile music Industry'. *Electronic Markets*, 16:2, 154-168.

Vnunet.com: www.vnunet.com.

Vodafone: www.vodafone.com.

Votolato, Gregory (1998). *American Design in the Twentieth Century.* Manchester: Manchester University Press.

Walt Disney Company: www.waltdisney.com. http://corporate.disney.go.com.

Walt Disney Company (2002-2008). *Annual Reports 2001-2007:* http://disney.go.com.

Walters Klüwer: www.walterskluwer.com.

Warner: www.warner.com.

Warner Music Group: www.warner.com.

Westerbeek, Hans and Smith, Aaron (2003). *Sport Business in the Global Marketplace*. New York: Palgrave Macmillan.

White Architects: www.white.se.

White House. *Pulse Check: Trends in Drug Abuse, January 2004:* www.qhitehousedrugpolicy.gov.

John Wiley & Son: www.wiley.com.

Wikipedia: www.wikipedia.org.

William Hill. www.willhill.com.

William Hill (2008). *Annual Report 2007.*

Wolters Kluwer. www.wolterskluwer.com.

World Access. www.worldaccess.com.

World Association of Newspapers: www.wan-press.org.

World Association of Newspapers (2007). *World Press Trends. The WPT 2007 Report*. www.wan-press.org.

World Health Organization (2007). *The Tobacco Atlas:* www.who.int./tobacco.

World Sex Guide. www.worldsexguide.org.

Worldspan. www.worldspan.com.

World Sports Encyclopedia: www.sportencyclopedia.com.

World Trade Organization (2007). *World Trade Statistics 2007*. Geneva: WTO.

World Tourism Organization (2007). *Facts and Figures*. www.unwto.org.

World Tourism Organization (2007). *Historical Perspective of World Tourism*. www.unwto.org.

World Tourism Organization (2000-2007). *The Tourism Satellite Account*. Madrid: UNTWO.

World Tourism Organization (2008). *Tourism 2020 Vision:* www.untwo.org.

World Travel & Tourism Council (2007). *The 2007 Travel & Tourism Economic Research*. www.wttc.org.

WWP: www.wwp.com.

WWP (2007-2008). *Annual Reports 2006-2007:* www.wwp.com.

XDC: www.xdcinema.com.

Yahoo!: www.yahoo.com.

Yahoo! Travel: www.travelyahoo.com.

YouTube: www.youtube.com.

Young; Sylvester. 'Income from Households' non-SNA production: A Review, 2002: www.ilo.org.

Zara: www.zara.com.

ZIBA: www.ziba.com.

Index

Business information 109, 158, 164-170, 172,
    405
    – financial 70, 164-166, 172, 302
    – industry 58, 63, 68-70, 73, 82, 90-91, 95,
        98, 105-109, 115, 118-120, 133, 156,
        165-167, 169, 229, 258, 261, 264, 269-
        270, 280, 286, 292, 304, 324, 331, 337,
        346, 381, 399, 408
    – market 28, 39, 44, 58, 89-90, 92, 94-95,
        138, 156, 159, 164-170, 179, 229, 240,
        269, 287, 298, 303, 354, 407, 409, 411
    – marketing 106, 109, 122, 132, 134, 141,
        165-166, 169-170, 177-178, 302, 320,
        346, 399, 408
Business model 77, 79, 83, 269, 281, 292
Business travel 72-73, 78, 86, 349
Business Week 158-159

Cable Systems 200, 206, 229, 231, 238, 383
Cable television 123, 197, 205, 208, 214-216,
    218-222, 224-228, 231, 246, 260, 383
Cablevision 213, 229
Caesars Entertainment 311
California 103, 155, 189, 225, 282, 301, 326,
    334, 339, 383-384
Callison 326
Canada 38, 47, 52, 71, 76, 92, 100, 124, 150-
    151, 153, 157, 160, 166-167, 174, 183, 186,
    200-201, 207-208, 211, 218, 221, 224, 227,
    229, 239, 241, 245-246, 248-249, 254, 258,
    260, 265-266, 268, 276, 283, 290, 293, 301,
    305-308, 311, 315, 325, 336, 356, 368, 373,
    385-386, 389, 391-392, 396, 406
Canal + 128, 211, 234-235
Cannabis 392-396
Cannes Film Festival 106
Cap Candy 279
Capcom Entertainment 288, 300
Capital Cities Communications 226
Capitalism 25, 32, 34, 262, 372, 374, 407-408
Capital records 334
Car industry 56, 68-69, 89
Caribbean 54, 57, 87, 99, 221, 225, 227, 248,
    304, 306, 349
Carlsbad 53
Carlson Companies 86, 93
Carlson Wagonlit Travel 73, 86
Carmen Sandiego 288

Carneval Cruise Lines 59, 62, 65-66, 69, 77-78,
    83-84, 86-88, 93, 349
Carrefour 286, 345, 347, 352
Cartier 350
Cartoon Network 231, 280
Cassette tape 263
Casino Royale 248
Casino 248, 304-315
Casino, tribal 307
Casual game 286, 297
Catering 47, 56, 65, 94-95, 108, 261
CBS Corporation 214-215, 220-221
    – CBS Digital Media 214-215, 218
    – CBS Interactive 216
    – CBS Musical Instruments Division 214
    – CBS News 214, 216
    – CBS Radio 214-215, 217, 245
    – CBS Records 214
    – CBS Sports 125, 214-216
    – CBS Television 214-216, 220
Cedar Fair Entertainment 101
Celine 348
Cendant Corporation 77, 89, 93
Central America 85
Central Park 99
CFAO 350
Chack, Moori 334
Champions League 128-130
Chax product line 334
Cheuk, Deanne 334
Chicago Bulls 126
Chicago White Sox 126
Children 37, 54, 60, 101, 105, 134, 158, 209-
    210, 220, 223, 225, 235, 275-279, 281-285,
    347, 351-352, 361-366, 368, 382, 389-390
Chile 33, 246, 306
China 19, 32-33, 35, 38, 46, 51-52, 67, 69, 92,
    97, 101, 103, 109, 116, 123, 150-153, 157,
    160-164, 166-168, 171, 176, 179, 182, 188,
    197-200, 205-208, 212-213, 219, 229, 244,
    248-249, 256-258, 262, 276, 283, 290, 296,
    305, 310-313, 325-326, 329-330, 336, 339,
    343, 352, 356, 368, 378, 388, 390-396, 399-
    402, 406
China National Tobacco Co. (CNTN) 19, 400
Chinatown 99
Chloé 351